The Colonial
Background of
Modern Brazil

Caio Prado, Jr. # The Colonial Background of Modern Brazil

Translated from the Portuguese by SUZETTE MACEDO

University of California Press
Berkeley and Los Angeles 1967

University of California Press
Berkeley and Los Angeles, California
Cambridge University Press
London, England

COPYRIGHT © 1967, BY THE REGENTS OF THE UNIVERSITY OF CALIFORNIA

Library of Congress Catalog Card Number: 67-11849
Original title: *Formação do Brasil*
Contemporâneo, Colônia, published by
Editôra Brasiliense, São Paulo, Seventh Edition, 1963
Published with the assistance of a grant
from the Rockefeller Foundation
Printed in the United States of America

*To my wife
and working companion,
Nena*

Contents

Contents

Introduction

The beginning of the nineteenth century is not distinguished for Brazilians solely by such events as the transfer of the seat of the Portuguese monarchy to Brazil and the acts that paved the way for the country's political emancipation.* It marks a decisive stage in Brazil's development and initiates a new phase in every sphere, social, political, and economic. Beneath these events that took place on the surface, complex processes were at work; the events themselves were only the ferment or, in most cases, only the outward manifestation. For the historian, as well as for anyone who seeks to understand Brazil, present-day Brazil included, the moment is a decisive one. Its interest derives above all from two circumstances: On the one hand, this period shows the final result of three centuries of colonial endeavor and, by eliminating or relegating to a secondary place all that was accidental or incidental, reveals the most charac-

---

* The transference of the monarchical center of gravity from Lisbon to Rio de Janeiro and Brazil's political emancipation took place in 1808 and 1822, respectively. In 1807 when, as a result of Napoleon's Iberian policy, the French general Junot and his army arrived at Lisbon to seize Dom João, Regent of Portugal, he discovered that, on British advice, the Portuguese royal family and court had escaped two days previously and were sailing to Brazil escorted by British warships. The royal refugees arrived in Brazil in January 1808. In 1822, Dom João's son, Pedro, became Constitutional Emperor of an independent Brazil. Political emancipation was thus an act of continuity rather than of revolution.—Translator.

1

teristic and fundamental aspects of colonization. Thus it provides a synthesis. On the other hand, the period constitutes a key to the interpretation of the historical processes that brought about present-day Brazil. There was a moment when the elements that make up Brazilian nationhood—the basic institutions and energies—organized and stored up from the outset of colonization, finally came to flower and reached maturity. It was then that Brazil may be said to have entered its contemporary phase.

Brazil had, at that point in time, reached a stalemate. The colonial regime had accomplished all it had to accomplish; the work of the mother country was felt to be complete. This was due not only to the decadence of the kingdom; however great this decadence may have been, it was only a complementary and accessory factor, which at most simply served to reinforce a tendency that had become inevitable and necessary. There came into question not only the regime of colonial subordination in which she found herself but the whole complex of institutions, the entire *colonial system* with all its economic and social characteristics that had become ripe for changes of a profound order. The potential of the Portuguese colonizing endeavor had been exhausted. The choice that faced Brazil was to change or perish. It was no longer enough simply to break away from the mother country, a preliminary, if necessary, step. More profound changes were called for. And indeed, they took place. Brazil began to renew itself, and the moment that constitutes our point of departure in this work, which the reader may perhaps have the patience to follow, is also the moment of this renewal. But it is only a point of departure, the beginning of a long historical process that has continued up to the present day and is still in progress. With advances and setbacks, this process has unfolded over one hundred and fifty years of vicissitudes.

Contemporary Brazil can be defined as a combination of the colonial past, which balanced its accounts and came to an end with the eighteenth century, and the transformations that have occurred in the course of the last century and a half. In the colonial past, the foundations of nationhood were laid: a semi-desert territory was settled, and a way of life was established there that differed as much from the life of the indigenous population as it did, on a smaller scale, from that of the Portuguese who had undertaken the task of settlement. Something new had been created in the sphere of human achievement. This "something new" is not simply an abstraction; it is embodied in all the elements that go to make up a complete and distinct social organism: a well-differentiated and clearly characterized population, even in ethnic terms, inhabiting a fixed territory; a particular material structure built on the basis of its own characteristic elements; a social organization defined in terms of specific relationships; and finally, an individual consciousness or, more precisely, a collective and particular mental attitude. All this had, of course, been a long time in the making. Symptoms of each of these characteristics had gradually been appearing in the course of colonial evolution, but it was at the end of this long evolution that these characteristics emerged fully and, above all, could be clearly distinguished by the observer.

Brazil entered a new phase. What colonization had achieved, that "complete and distinct social organism" built up during the preceding period, began gradually to change, either through internal compulsion or through the intervention of new external factors. It was then that contemporary Brazil began to take shape. This is why, in order to understand the present, we need to go so far back; in going back into the past, the reader will not merely be indulging in historical reverie, but will be gathering facts, facts which are indispensable for interpreting and understanding the environment in which he lives.

When we analyze the elements of contemporary Brazilian life—"elements" in their widest sense, geographical, economic, social, and political—we find that the past, the colonial past to which I have referred above, is still present and still very noticeable, partly modified, to be sure, but nevertheless present in traces that cannot be denied. When we look at present-day

Brazil, what immediately strikes us is that it is an organism in
the process of open and active change, not yet settled along
any clearly defined lines, an organism that has not yet "taken
shape." It is true that in certain sectors the transformation is
already profound and that we are faced with specifically new
elements. But these are exceptions. In most cases, behind these
transformations that can at times deceive us, we feel the presence of a very old reality which often takes us by surprise and
which is in fact the colonial past.

I refer not only to traditions and to certain glaring anachronisms that exist at any time or in any place, but to fundamental characteristics of the economic and social structure. In
the economic sphere, for instance, it could be said that free
labor has not yet been organized throughout the country. In
many parts of the country there is an active process of adjustment, a more or less successful effort in this direction, but
strong traces of the slave regime are still present. The same
could be said of the fundamental nature of the economy, still
based on the large-scale production of certain commodities for
a foreign market with the corresponding lack of any consolidated and properly organized domestic market—hence the
subordination of the Brazilian economy to foreign economies, a
dependence that is indeed to be found in other sectors as well.
In short, the evolution from a colonial to a national economy is,
even now, not yet complete.

In the social sphere the same holds true. Except in certain
sectors, social relations in Brazil, particularly class attitudes,
have retained a marked colonial flavor. Among other instances,
we could cite the profound differences that divide the rural
population into largely unequal categories, a disparity that de-
pends not only on material living standards, in themselves
wholly disproportionate, but, above all, on the respective moral
status of these categories, which takes us right back into the
past. The descriptions of foreign travelers who visited Brazil at
the beginning of the nineteenth century still have devastating
reality. They apply as accurately to this particular sector as
they do to so many others. Traveling through Brazil today, we

are often surprised by aspects that we had thought existed only
in history books; and if we ponder them a while, we see that
they are manifestations of things deeply rooted in the past and
are not simple anachronistic survivals.

But this is not all. The most fundamental practical problems
of Brazil were defined and posed a hundred and fifty years ago.
And on the solution of many of these long-standing problems,
to which we pay insufficient attention, will depend the solution
of others with which we are now unsuccessfully attempting to
cope. One of the most shocking aspects of the country, and one
which alarms any observer of the Brazilian scene, is the lack of
economic and hence "vital" energy that characterizes most of
its territory. Yet, one and a half centuries ago, in the very areas
today subject to this disease, it had already been diagnosed and
discussed. The authorities had made representations to the
mother country and private individuals had taken an interest in
the problem, referring to it in memoirs and other writings that
have come down to us, whose accuracy and clear-sightedness
have on the whole never been surpassed even by more recent
observers.

There are further examples, such as the rudimentary nature
of agricultural practices—unfortunately still a pressing current problem—had already attracted attention in the eighteenth century; the use of backward techniques had been held
responsible for many of the ills that afflicted the colony then
and still afflict Brazil as a nation now. One such comment
occurs in an anonymous memoir written in the 1770's, *Roteiro
do Maranhão a Goiás* (Log Book of a Journey from Maranhão
to Goiás); some passages of this work read like the report of an
agricultural inspector just returned from a visit to the interior.
Forty years later, St. Hilaire* was to make similar observations,
utilizing his training as a naturalist. At the beginning of the

---

* Auguste de Sainte-Hilaire, nineteenth-century French naturalist, author of several accounts of journeys into the interior of Brazil. A collection
of the separate accounts published appeared in 1852 under the title,
Voyages dans l'intérieur du Brésil, but the author refers to the separately
published narratives. See Bibliography for the complete list.—Translator.

Empire, Brigadier Cunha Matos opens his chapter on agriculture in Goiás, in his "Corografia Histórica"* (published in 1824), with this remark: "Agriculture, if such a term can be applied to the rural labors practiced in the province of Goiás . . ."—a remark that could be repeated today about nearly all Brazil's agricultural activities without fear of undue exaggeration. The problems of internal communication, now just approaching a solution, were posed in almost the same terms at the end of the eighteenth century as they are posed today, despite all the technical progress that has been made since then.[1]

These are merely examples chosen more or less at random. Similar things can be found on all sides. These and other considerations of the same nature led me to seek an interpretation of present-day Brazil in that past which appears distant but which is still all around us. This is also my justification for the plan of the book. I start by summing up the situation of the colony at the beginning of the last century—the period that bestrides the two centuries immediately preceding the present one. Thus we will have a synoptic view of the Brazil that emerged, already formed and shaped, from three centuries of colonial evolution.

---

* The full title is "Corografia histórica da provincia de Goiás" (Historical and descriptive account of the province of Goiás), published in the *Revista do Instituto Histórico, Geográfico e Etnográfico Brasileiro*, 37, I, p. 213 et seq., and 38, I, p. 5 et seq.—Translator.

The Meaning of Colonization

Seen from a distance, the evolution of all peoples has a certain pattern or "meaning." This can be glimpsed not from the details of their history but from the combination of facts and essential events that constitute this history over a broad period. Anyone observing this whole, after clearing away the undergrowth of secondary incidents that always accompany the process and render it often meaningless and confusing, cannot fail to perceive that there is a single, uninterrupted thread of events that succeed each other in strict order, moving always in a specific direction. It is this that must be sought from the outset when embarking upon the analysis of any people's history, regardless of the period or aspect of that history that particularly concerns the analyst, since all periods and all aspects are only parts of the whole and are incomplete in themselves. It is the whole that should always be the historian's final objective, however particular his immediate interests. Such an inquiry is all the more important and essential because it is through a perception of the whole that can be defined, both in time and in space, the individuality of the particular parcel of humanity that interests the researcher: people, country, nation, society—whatever designation fits the case. Only in this way will he find the unity that will allow him to detach this parcel of humanity for separate study.

7

The discovery and colonization of America was simply a chapter in the history of European maritime expansion after the fifteenth century, an expansion which originated in the commercial ventures undertaken by European navigators. It was the result of the development of Europe's continental trade, which, up to the fourteenth century, had been almost entirely carried on by land, the sea trade having been limited to minor coastal shipping. The great European trade route that emerged from the breakup of the Western Empire was the overland route linking the Mediterranean to the North Sea, leading from the Italian republics through the Alps, the Swiss cantons, and the great commercial centers of the Rhine to the estuary where the Flemish cities are situated. In the fourteenth century, thanks to a virtual revolution in the art of navigation and seaborne trade, a new route was established between those two poles of European trade: the sea route that rounded the continent via the Straits of Gibraltar. Subsidiary at first, this new route finally took precedence over the old one. The first effect of this change, imperceptible to start with but which proved to be of a profound order and ended by revolutionizing the entire European balance, was to shift commercial supremacy from the central territories bordering the old route to the territories along the Atlantic seaboard: Holland, England, Normandy, Brittany, and the Iberian peninsula.

This new balance was consolidated at the beginning of the fifteenth century. It created not only a new system of internal relations for the continent, but was also the indirect cause of European expansion overseas. The first step had been taken, and Europe had ceased to be withdrawn into itself and was ready to brave the ocean. In this new phase, due to their more advantageous geographical situation on the very edge of the peninsula that juts into the Atlantic, the Portuguese played a pioneering role. While Dutch, English, Normans, and Bretons concentrated on the recently opened trade route that embraced the entire continent by sea, the Portuguese ventured further out, seeking enterprises where they would not find older and more established competitors and where their geographical advantages would stand them in good stead. They explored the west African coast, trading with the Moors who dominated the indigenous populations. As a result of these exploring expeditions, they discovered the islands of Cape Verde, Madeira, and the Azores and ventured ever further southward along the coast of the Dark Continent. All this took place in the first half of the fifteenth century. Toward the middle of that century, a more ambitious plan began to emerge, the idea of reaching the East by circumnavigating the African continent. This would secure them a direct route to the opulent Indies and the precious spices whose trade had enriched the Italian republics and the Moors who controlled its passage to the Mediterranean. There is no need to recall here the full significance of the circumnavigation of Africa, which was finally achieved after half a century of tenacious and systematic effort.

The Spaniards followed in the wake of the Portuguese. They sought another route, venturing westward instead of to the east. And so they discovered America, closely followed by the Portuguese who also stumbled on the new continent. After the Iberian countries came the French, English, Dutch, and even the Danes and the Swedes. Navigation of the ocean had been opened up and all sought the advantages it offered. The countries that had dominated the old route were left behind and were relegated to a secondary place; badly situated geographically in relation to the new routes and tied to a past that still weighed heavily upon them, they became the laggards of the new order. Germany and Italy fell behind as new stars rose on the horizon: the Iberian countries, England, France, and Holland.

In sum, all the great events of this age, which has rightly been called the Age of Discovery, form part of a pattern that is but a chapter in the history of European commerce. The events that occurred were simply incidents in the immense commercial venture in which the European countries had been engaged since the fifteenth century, and which had opened up new horizons beyond the ocean. This was the true nature of the exploration of the African coast, the discovery and settlement of the Atlantic islands by the Portuguese, the sea route to India, the discovery of America, and the exploration and settle-

ment of its territory. The last is the chapter that concerns us
here, but it is not essentially different from the others. For it
was always as merchants that the various European nations
approached each of the opportunities afforded by their initiative and effort, or by a combination of chance and the circumstances of the moment.

Along the African coast, the Portuguese traded in ivory,
gold, and slaves; from India they brought back spices. To compete with them the Spaniards, closely followed by the English,
French, and others, sought another route to the East; America,
which they stumbled upon in this search, was at first simply an
obstacle to the realization of their plans, a barrier to be circumvented. All their efforts were concentrated upon finding a passage whose existence was taken for granted. The Spaniards,
who had gained a foothold in the Antilles from the time of
Columbus' discovery, began to explore the central part of the
continent and discovered Mexico; Balboa caught sight of the
Pacific; but the much-sought passage remained undiscovered.
They turned their attention southward: Solis' voyage, leading
to the discovery of the river Plate, had no other end in view.
Magellan continued this search and discovered the straits that
bear his name and that proved to be the much sought after
passage; but it was found to be impractical after all and so was
neglected.

Meanwhile, the search continued in the north, in this case on
the initiative of the English who employed the services of foreigners since they did not yet have English pilots with the experience needed for an enterprise of this magnitude. The first
navigators to explore the northern possibilities were the Italian
Giovanni Cabot and his son Sebastian. The Portuguese also figured in these explorations of the far north, through the activities of the Côrte-Real brothers, who discovered Labrador. The
French entrusted the Florentine Verazzano with the same
mission. Others followed suit; but although these activities
served to explore and make known the New World, securing its
possession by the various countries of Europe, the coveted passage continued to elude their search. We know today that it

never existed.[1] At the beginning of the seventeenth century, the discovery of an opening to the Pacific, thought to exist somewhere on the new continent, was still included among the principal aims of the Virginia Company of London.

All this throws a good deal of light upon the spirit in which the European peoples approached America. The idea of peopling the new territory did not initially occur to any of them. It was commerce that interested them and hence their relative contempt for this primitive and empty American territory and, conversely, the attraction of the Orient with its lure of mercantile activity. The idea of occupying the new lands—not in the customary sense of sending out commercial agents, officials and soldiers for the organization and defense of trading stations designed to carry on commerce with the natives and function as links between the sea routes and the territories thus occupied, which had hitherto been the practice—but of occupying by means of effective settlement arose accidentally, as a need imposed by new and unforeseen circumstances. In fact, none of the nations of Western Europe was at that time in a position to support a drain on its population resources, since in the sixteenth century they had not yet recovered from the devastations of the plague epidemics that had ravaged the continent in the two preceding centuries. In the absence of any accurate census, the most likely estimates indicate that in 1500 the population of Western Europe had not surpassed the figure for the previous millennium.

Under these conditions, "colonization" was still taken to mean the activities hitherto practiced; the term implied no more than the establishment of trading stations, which was what the Italians had done over a long period in the Mediterranean, the Hanseatic League in the Baltic, and in a more recent period the English, Dutch, and others in northern Europe and the Levant and the Portuguese in Africa and India. In America, the situation was entirely different. It was a primitive territory, sparsely peopled by an indigenous population and unable to supply anything really worthwhile commercially. For the commercial ends in view, occupation could not be effected in the form of establishing simple trading stations, involving a small number of people who would carry on trade, supervise its administration, and organize its armed defense. It was necessary to broaden this basis, to create a settlement that could supply and support the trading stations established and organize production of the commodities needed for trading. The idea of settling the new lands arose from this need, and from this alone.

As in so many other instances, Portugal was again the pioneer in this field. The first steps in this direction were taken as early as the fifteenth century in the Atlantic islands, where conditions were identical to those of the American continent for the objectives envisaged. The islands had to be settled and production organized. Portugal fulfilled her objectives with brilliant success. In all the problems that arose from the time a new European economic order began to emerge in the fifteenth century, the Portuguese were always pioneers. They worked out all solutions, down to the smallest detail. The Spaniards and later the English, French, and others merely followed in their footsteps for a long time to come, but they learned their lessons so well that they ended by supplanting the initiators and snatching away most, if not all, of their overseas enterprises.

The problems of the new colonization system, involving the occupation of semidesert and primitive territories, varied in each case according to the particular circumstances in which they arose. The first problem was the nature of the profitable commodities that each territory could provide. At first, no one considered anything but the natural products that could easily be extracted. It was still virtually the old system of the purely commercial trading station. In most of the territories, the items considered commercially worthwhile were timbers and dyewoods (such as *pau-Brasil* or Brazil wood); the far north supplied furs and provided important fisheries such as those of New England. The fishing industry became particularly active around the banks of Newfoundland which had attracted the English, Normans, and Basques from the early years of the sixteenth century, possibly even earlier. The Spaniards were the most fortunate; they very early discovered precious metals in the territories they had claimed—the silver and gold of Mexico and Peru. But precious metals, which provided a sufficient incentive and basis for any colonizing enterprise, played a relatively small part in the formation of America. They were the foremost objective in the establishment and occupation of Spanish colonies in Mexico and Peru and later, in the eighteenth century, they were the driving force behind the intensification of Portuguese colonization in South America and impelled the movement toward the interior of the continent. But this was all. Precious metals, which fired the imagination of the early explorers and which were expected to be found in any new territory—a hope fed by the premature Spanish discoveries—proved to be not as widespread as had been imagined. In the greater part of America, the colonies had, at first, to confine themselves to trade in timbers and furs and to fishing; and for a long time, the occupation of new territories, its progress and its setbacks, was dependent on the success or failure of these activities. Later the colonists turned to the land, and the broader and more stable economic base of agriculture replaced the early activities.

It is not my intention here to go into the details and vicissitudes of European colonization in America. But we can—and this is of considerable interest to our subject—distinguish two distinct areas, apart from the areas where precious metals were found, where colonization took two different courses. These correspond to the temperate zone, on the one hand, and the tropical and subtropical zones on the other. The first, which roughly embraces American territory north of Delaware Bay (the other temperate extremes of the continent, comprising what is now Argentina, Uruguay, Paraguay, and Chile, required a long time to take shape and to achieve any significance), did not appear to offer anything worthwhile and was for a long time restricted to the exploitation of natural products: timbers, furs, and fish. During the early years of colonization in New England, any attempts by the few settlers present to turn their attention from the fur stations and fisheries to agriculture were regarded with open disfavor.[2] If this temperate zone was settled at all—and in fact this only occurred after the seventeenth century—it was due to very special circumstances. It was the internal situation of Europe, particularly that of England, with its political and religious struggles, that led certain groups who felt uneasy in their homeland to turn their attention toward America, where they came to seek shelter and freedom for their convictions. This was to continue for a long time; the process can even be compared to a basically identical one that was carried on, with varying intensity, up to the last century. America was to provide a home for Puritans and Quakers from England; Huguenots from France; and Moravians, Schwenkfelders, Inspirationalists, and Mennonites from southern Germany and Switzerland. For more than two centuries the residue of Europe's political and religious struggles poured into America. These groups spread into all the colonies; even Brazil, so distant and hence so much less known, provided refuge for a group of French Huguenots (França Antartica, in Rio de Janeiro). But this type of immigration was almost entirely concentrated in the temperate colonies, where physical conditions were most similar to those of Europe and which were therefore preferred by colonists who had not come to America in search of quick wealth, but for shelter from the political storms that swept across Europe and to try to rebuild their broken or threatened homes.

Another factor contributed to this type of emigration. This was the economic transformation that took place in England during the sixteenth century and profoundly altered the country's internal balance and the distribution of the population. Great numbers of people were forced off the land; as a result of these dislocations, formerly cultivated fields were made available for grazing the sheep whose wool was needed to supply the nascent English textile industry. The displacement of population produced groups of peasants who, having been forced off the land, were willing to turn to opportunities in America, which was beginning to be known. Like political and religious refugees, and for the same reasons, these people also sought the temperate zones. Those who were not in a position to choose their destinations with full knowledge of the circumstances awaiting them and who headed south, to the subtropical colonies in North America, did so in the majority of cases only as a temporary measure. As soon as they were able, most of them moved to the temperate colonies.

Intensive occupation and large-scale settlement of the temperate zone was, therefore, the result of special circumstances and did not derive directly from the ambitions of traders or adventurers. Indeed, these circumstances arose only after the discovery of the New World and are in no way related to the general order of events that initially impelled the European nations across the seas. They led to a new type of colonization— the only one in which the Portuguese were not the pioneers— which assumed entirely different features from that hitherto dominated by the commercial objectives associated with this kind of enterprise. This new category of colonists aimed to build a new world, a society that would provide the guarantees no longer afforded by their homelands. Whether for religious or economic reasons (and indeed the two were intimately linked and virtually inseparable), their survival in Europe had become impossible or extremely difficult. Victims of the agitations and changes in Europe, they were seeking a land protected from these fluctuations, where they could rebuild their threatened lives. The settlement carried out in this spirit, and in physical conditions very like those of Europe, led naturally to the creation of a society which, while having its own distinctive characteristics, nevertheless bore a pronounced resemblance to that of the continent where it originated. It was not much more than a prolongation of that continent.

Very different is the history of the American tropical and subtropical zone. Here, occupation and settlement took quite another course. In the first place, the physical conditions, so different from those of the colonizing nations' original "habitat," repelled colonists who came as simple settlers. The white man's inability to adapt himself to the tropics has been much exaggerated. It is a half-truth that has been disproved by the facts in any number of cases, time and time again. The element of truth is that races originating in and hence more adjusted to colder climates lack the predisposition to tolerate the tropics and to adjust to them. But this lack of predisposition is not in any way absolute, since in subsequent generations at least it has been corrected by a new process of adaptation. However, if the idea, put in absolute terms, is false, it was nevertheless true under the circumstances which prompted the first settlers to come to America. They arrived to find themselves confronted by a harsh and unexplored tropical land, where a hostile nature made man seem reduced and insignificant by comparison, a land full of countless unforeseen obstacles for which they had been unprepared and against which they were more or less defenseless. The difficulties encountered by civilized Europeans in establishing themselves in these American lands, still given to the free play of nature, were also experienced in the temperate zone. In reply to the fashionable theories presented in Turner's famous book, *The Frontier in American History*, the analysis of a recent American writer shows that English colonization of America, although carried out in a temperate zone, progressed only at the cost of a selective process that resulted in the pioneer type of the typical "Yankee," endowed with particular aptitudes and techniques, who marched in the vanguard and blazed the trail for the more recent levies of European colonists.[3] If this was the case in a zone where, apart from the fact that it was unexplored, the physical conditions were very like those of Europe, how much more so must it have been in the tropics.

To establish himself in the tropics, the European colonist was compelled to find different and more powerful motivating forces than those which had led him to the temperate zones. This is precisely what occurred, but only in special circumstances that led to the emergence of a particular type of white colonist in the tropics. The difference in physical conditions between Europe and the tropics proved to be a strong stimulus; the tropics offered European countries the commodities

they lacked—commodities, we might add, that were particularly attractive. Let us imagine ourselves in Europe as it was
before the sixteenth century, cut off from the tropics which
were remote and inaccessible, or could be reached only
through the most indirect means, and let us try to imagine
what this Europe was like, almost entirely deprived of things
so commonplace today as to seem unimportant or minor, but
which were then prized as the ultimate in luxury. Sugar, for instance, although cultivated on a small scale in Sicily, was extremely rare and much sought after, so much so that it figured
in the dowries of queens as a precious and highly prized gift.
Pepper imported from the East was for centuries the chief
branch of commerce of the Italian republics, and the long and
arduous route to India served for a long time merely to supply
Europe with this spice. Tobacco, indigenous to America and
hence unknown before the discovery, assumed a no less important position once it had been introduced into Europe. Similarly, anil, rice, cotton, and many other tropical commodities
later came to occupy important positions in world trade.

This gives us some indication of what the remote tropics sig-
nified for cold Europe and also the reason for their attraction.
America placed immense territories at the disposal of Europe,
vast tracts which only awaited the initiative and energy of
man. It was this that stimulated occupation of the American
tropics. But the European did not bring to this alien and difficult land the disposition to serve his interests by devoting his
physical labor to the land. He came to organize the production
of highly valuable commercial commodities, as the promoter of
a profitable business undertaking, and only under constraint
did he come as an actual worker. Others were to do his work
for him.

The initial selection between settlers who came to the
temperate zone and those who came to the tropics was made
on this basis. Of his own accord, the European settler came to
the tropics only when he could be in a position of command,
when he had the means or aptitude to become a master, when
he could count on others to work on his behalf. Another cir-

cumstance was to reinforce this tendency and this distinction: the character assumed by agricultural exploitation in the tropics. It was organized on a large scale, that is, in large productive units—estates, *engenhos,** or plantations (in the English colonies), each of which brings together a relatively large number of workers. In other words, for each proprietor (estate owner, *senhor de engenho,* or plantation owner), there were many dependent and propertyless workers. I shall have occasion to consider in more detail in a later chapter the causes that determined this type of organization for tropical production.

The great majority of colonists was therefore condemned to a dependent and lowly position—to work for the benefit of others and for their own meager daily subsistence. It was clearly not for this that they had emigrated from Europe to America. Nevertheless, until the enslavement of other races, whether native Amerindians or imported African Negroes, many European settlers were condemned by force of circumstances to subject themselves to this subordinate position. Eager to depart for America, often ignorant of their exact destination or resolved upon any temporary sacrifice, many colonists left Europe to be taken on as simple laborers on the tropical plantations. This happened on a large scale, particularly in the English colonies of Virginia, Maryland, and Carolina. In exchange for their transportation to the New World (which they could not otherwise have afforded) many immigrants sold their services for a given number of years. Others were sent as deportees. Minors, abandoned or sold by their parents or guardians, were also taken to America as indentured servants to work until their coming of age. It was a form of temporary slavery that was entirely replaced around the middle of the seventeenth century by the effective enslavement of imported Negroes.

But most of the colonists simply waited for the right moment to escape from the condition that had been imposed on them,

---

* Literally, sugar mill; by extension, sugar plantation. Hence the *senhor de engenho* is the sugar planter or estate owner (literally, "lord of the mill").—Translator.

and when as in most instances they failed to establish themselves as planters or proprietors, they emigrated as soon as they could to the temperate colonies where they could at least be sure of finding a way of life more suited to their habits and greater opportunities to better themselves. This unstable labor situation on the southern plantations lasted until the definitive and general adoption of African slave labor. The European colonist then came to occupy the only position he felt was his due, that of overseer, manager, or master of the large rural estate.

In the other tropical colonies, including Brazil, white labor was not even attempted. Unlike England, neither Spain nor Portugal, possessors of the majority of the American tropical colonies, could provide workers who were prepared to emigrate at any price. In Portugal, the population was so scanty that even as late as the middle of the sixteenth century, the greater part of its territory was uncultivated and abandoned, and there was a labor shortage in the kingdom which led to the employment of slaves on a growing scale. Initially, the slaves were Moors, both those left behind at the end of Moorish rule and those taken prisoner in the wars Portugal had been conducting in her North African dominions since the beginning of the fifteenth century. Later the Moors were replaced by Africans, who were brought into the kingdom in large numbers from the middle years of this same century. Around 1550, approximately ten percent of the Lisbon population was composed of Negro slaves.[4] There was, therefore, nothing to provoke a population exodus from the kingdom. On the contrary, the drain on the country's population resources caused by the expeditions to the East is well known, and the early decadence of the kingdom dates from this period and is in part attributable to this cause.

Furthermore, the Portuguese and particularly the Spaniards found in their colonies indigenous inhabitants who could be utilized as laborers. And finally, the Portuguese were the precursors in yet another feature of the modern world, the enslavement of African Negroes. Since they dominated the territories that supplied African slaves, slavery was adopted in their colony almost from the outset—possibly even at the very beginning. They preceded the English, always tardy imitators, by almost a century in this respect.[5]

As we can see, the course followed by the tropical colonies was entirely different from that of the sister colonies in the temperate zone. In the latter, colonial settlements were established in the true sense of "settlement" (the term had been consecrated since Leroy-Beaulieu's classic work, *De la colonisation chez les peuples modernes*), and served to filter off the excess population of Europe, which in the New World built up an organization and established a society after European models; in the tropics an entirely original type of society emerged. Although this was not the simple commercial trading station, already seen to be unfeasible in America, it nevertheless retained a pronounced mercantile character: It was a society based on the enterprise of the white colonist who brought to a land that was prodigal in resources labor recruited among the inferior races he dominated, Amerindians or imported African Negroes. The traditional commercial objectives that prompted the beginning of European expansion overseas were adapted to meet new conditions. These objectives, which we saw relegated to a secondary place in the temperate colonies, remained foremost in the tropics and deeply affected the features of colonial life in colonies like Brazil, setting the pattern for their future. Seen as a whole, the colonization of the tropics appears as one vast commercial enterprise, more complex than the old trading stations but retaining the flavor of these, the foremost objective being the exploitation of the natural resources of a virgin land for the benefit of European commerce. This is the true *meaning* of tropical colonization, of which Brazil is one of the results, and this explains the fundamental elements, both economic and social, of the historical formation and evolution of the American tropics.

In most of these tropical territories including Brazil, colonization was founded and carried out on that basis, but ended by achieving something more than the original objective of a mere "fortuitous contact" (to use Gilberto Freyre's apt expression) between Europeans and the new environment. In similar regions European colonization failed to transcend this objective (as in most of the tropical colonies of Africa, Asia and Oceania, the Guianas, and some of the Antilles in America). Brazil did not remain a simple colonial enterprise conducted by distant and haughty white colonists, but moved toward the creation in the tropics of a "society with national characteristics and qualities of permanence." [6]

But this more stable, permanent, and organic character proper to a society that has acquired its own clearly defined features was slow to reveal itself, dominated and stifled as it was by the period which preceded it and which continued to exercise a powerful influence, dictating the essential lines of colonial evolution. If we look for the vital element in Brazil's formation, the element that lies at the very roots of its subsequent growth, we will find it in the fact that the colony was established to provide sugar, tobacco, and certain other commodities; later gold and diamonds; then cotton; and later still coffee for the European market. This was the objective in the establishment of the Brazilian economy, an externally oriented objective, turned away from the country itself and taking account of nothing more than the commercial interests involved. Everything was organized around this central aim; the structure and activities of the country are reflections of it. The white European came to speculate and to trade; he invested the capital and recruited the labor he needed either among the natives or by importing Negroes. The Brazilian colony was made up of these elements, integrated in a purely productive industrial organization. The three centuries preceding the moment from which we approach Brazilian history were dominated by this beginning, which remained deeply and totally engraved on the country's features and way of life. The secondary consequences that flowed from this beginning did tend toward something beyond the mere commercial objectives, but these consequences were still barely noticeable. The path of Brazil's evolution, which is what we have been seeking here, can be found in the initial character of colonization. If we bear this in mind we will understand the essential nature of the situation we find at the beginning of the last century, which I will now proceed to analyze.

PART ONE—POPULATION AND SETTLEMENT

Coastal Settlement

We possess no adequate statistics concerning the population of the colony. No regular and systematic data were collected, and surveys were conducted only for two specific and restricted ends: one ecclesiastical, the other military. Parishes organized the compilation of parochial lists which served to ensure that the parishioners performed their paschal duty, and which also served to establish the divisions between existing parishes and to form new ones. The other source we have is the data collected for purposes of military recruitment. Both types of survey have a serious drawback for the purpose of estimating the population; since their aim was restricted, they took into account only certain categories of the population. The first was limited to persons subject to the performance of the paschal duty, that is, those over seven years of age; the second to men fit for military duty. In both cases there were strong reasons for evasion, and the surveys are consequently marred by the large number of omissions. As far as the parochial lists are concerned, the parishioners' reluctance to perform an onerous duty—performance of the paschal duty involved a monetary payment—coupled with the parish priest's own interest in concealing from the higher authorities the exact numbers in his parish, for fear that it would be split up, account for these omissions. In the case of the recruitment lists, the reason for reluctance to be included is obvious.

25

Added to all this was the general carelessness and negligence of the public administration, both civil and ecclesiastical. It seems that only as late as the last few years of the eighteenth century did the metropolis show any concern for the compilation of general and systematic statistics. This was apparently the purpose of instructions issued in 1797 to the Governor of Paraíba, Fernando Delgado de Castilho, the text of which we possess and which must have served as the model for a circular on the same subject dispatched to all the governors in the colony on the same occasion.[1]

In these circulars, the crown stipulated the annual collection of various data: statistics of demographic movement (births, marriages, and deaths), occupations, trade, and prices. A complete census was carried out at least once. We do not know the results, which are possibly still buried somewhere in the archives of Portugal, but we know that it was undertaken, from Conselheiro Veloso de Oliveira's memoir on the Church of Brazil (*Igreja no Brasil*), published in 1819, in which he refers to a census taken in 1797–1798 which in all likelihood was in consequence of the instructions referred to above. From the same source we learn that the Brazilian population was then estimated to amount to "much more than three million souls." By the time he wrote his memoir in 1819, he estimated that it had grown to about 4,400,000, including nondomesticated Indians, calculated on no real foundation to number 800,000. These, in sum, are the most reliable figures we possess for the colony as a whole at the beginning of the last century. If we exclude the uncivilized Indians—who do not concern us for the moment, since they were not yet incorporated in the body of "colonization" and represented only a future reserve to be gradually absorbed and so contribute to the growth of the colony's effective population—we can estimate that the Brazilian population comprised around three million souls at the end of the eighteenth century.

Their distribution throughout the territory of the colony was, as we can immediately see, extremely irregular. There were scattered population clusters, some fairly dense, sepa-

rated by thinly settled or unoccupied territory. The general
pattern, keeping the numerical differences in due proportion,
of course, is more or less the same as it is today. There is a
striking resemblance between the distribution of settlement at
the beginning of the nineteenth century and the distribution
pattern of our own times. Apart from its subsequent increase,
the general population structure is still more or less the same,
with the exception of the changes that have occurred in the
south and the central-south and the region around the upper
tributaries of the Amazon which today forms the Acre territory
but which at that time was not yet part of Brazil and had not
yet been occupied. But with these exceptions the differences
are slight. The Brazilian population was then already spread
throughout the territory that is now Brazil. In fact, this was already the case a half-century previously, in 1750, when the
Portuguese–Spanish treaty of that year was framed (the Madrid Treaty),[2] in which the divisions between Portuguese and
Spanish territories in the southern hemisphere were clearly
demarcated for the first time along lines that were roughly the
same as those of today. The criterion used for the establishment of this frontier was that of actual occupation. "Each party
will retain its present possessions," reads the preamble to the
agreement setting out the way in which demarcation was to be
effected. This procedure was followed and the boundary line
limiting Brazilian territory, fixed according to this principle of
uti possidetis, has remained practically unaltered up to the
present day.

This proves a priori that the Portuguese had in fact colonized the whole of the immense territory that constitutes
Brazil. The deciding factor in Brazil's favor was occupation.
The famous Tordesillas Treaty, drawn up two and a half centuries before the Madrid agreement, granted the Portuguese
sovereign and his successors a mere fraction of the territory
now occupied and possessed by Brazil. There is no doubt that
the effective occupation and defense of a territory eight and a
half million square kilometers in extent was a considerable
achievement for a handful of settlers who, both before and

after 1750, were more than once called on to defend their possession against the bellicose and insistent claims of powerful rivals. It was an outstanding achievement and a basic factor in the future greatness of Brazil; but at the same time it was a tremendous burden on the colony and subsequently on the nation, leading as it did to this astonishing and unparalleled scattering that separates and isolates individuals, dividing settlement into sparsely populated clusters, with all the attendant difficulties of communication and contact, which sometimes prove insuperable.

Various factors determined this scattered settlement. The first was the extent of the coastline which fell to Portugal under the Tordesillas agreement, obliging the Portuguese to set up various settlements along it in order to establish effective occupation and defense. This was the reason behind the territory's division into captaincies which, despite the failure of the system, ensured the effective possession of the long coastal strip for the Portuguese crown.*

Later, two essential factors contributed to the penetration of the hinterland: first, the *bandeiras* † which, in their search for Indians, precious stones and metals, blazed the trail, explored the bush, and drove back the vanguard of rival Spanish colonization; later came the exploitation of the mines, after the successive discoveries of gold and diamonds in the last years of the seventeenth century, which created stable and permanent nuclei in the areas of concentrated settlement established in the heart of the continent (Minas Gerais, Goiás, Mato Grosso). In the extreme north, in the Amazon basin, another factor of a

---

* In the fifteen thirties, with the object of affirming Portuguese rights, "King John III of Portugal divided the Brazilian coast between the Amazon and São Vicente into twelve captaincies (*capitanias*) which were granted to proprietary landlords known as *donatarios*." C. R. Boxer, *Salvador de Sá and the Struggle for Brazil and Angola, 1602–1686* (London: Athlone Press, 1952), p. 3.—Translator.

† *Bandeiras*—a term originally applied to Portuguese militia companies, but used to describe the exploring, slave-raiding or prospecting parties that roamed the interior. Most of these armed bands, whose members are known as *bandeirantes*, were from the São Paulo region.—Translator.

purely local nature intervened: the establishment of Catholic mission villages for converting and civilizing the natives, principally by Jesuits, closely followed by lay colonization instigated and maintained by an active policy in this respect on the part of the mother country and supported by the exploitation of natural forest products: cacao, sarsaparilla, and other products.

Another factor, also local, operated in the northeast *Sertão,* the hinterland of the colony's largest coastal agricultural settlements, Bahia and Pernambuco, where penetration was effected by the gradual establishment of cattle ranches designed to furnish meat for consumption in the coastal centers.

All these factors were conditioned to a large extent by a negative factor, the inertia of the Spaniards. They had settled principally on the Andean plateau, where the presence of precious metals—the driving force behind their colonization—and of a dense and sedentary native population, providing an abundant and easy source of manpower—circumstances that did not arise on the Atlantic coast occupied by the Portuguese —spared them the necessity of undertaking any exploring expeditions or plunging into the heart of the continent. Physical obstacles, too, were not to be despised: the interior of the South American continent opens onto the Atlantic and not onto the Pacific, from which it is separated by that great accident of nature, the Andes, and by the dense impenetrable forest that covers the eastern fringes of the range.[3] As a result, the only Spaniards encountered by Portuguese colonization were the harmless Jesuits and their native *reduções,* or mission villages. The priests, who were seeking something other than mineral wealth, had gone further afield than their compatriots. They left the colonists to their mines in the Andean highlands, with their dense native populations providing both the raw material and the manpower which the colonists wanted. The priests had established themselves beyond the reach of the conquistadores' greed, where they hoped no one would disturb them in their conquest of souls, prelude to the temporal power they aspired to. They settled along the eastern slopes of the Andes and their underlying valleys, establishing a line of Spanish Jesuit missions during the sixteenth and seventeenth centuries that extended from south to north, from the River Plate to the Amazon, through the interior of the continent: the Uruguay and Paraguay missions, the short-lived Guaíra mission, the Chiquitos and Moxos missions, and the missions of Fr. Samuel Fritz along the Upper Amazon.

The Jesuits had not counted on the other enemy which was to advance on them from the east—the Portuguese. Given little support by their own king, for the most part left to fend for themselves, finding an adversary even in the sovereign of their own land who made common cause with their enemies—when the 1750 Treaty was put into effect, Portuguese forces joined with the Spaniards to wrest from them the area of the "Seven Peoples of Uruguay" *—the missionaries were pushed back, and their grandiose plans collapsed. The interior of the South American continent was not to be theirs, as they had hoped in a beautiful dream that lasted two centuries; but neither was it to be for its legitimate owners, the Spaniards. It fell to the conquerors and effective occupants, the Portuguese and their Brazilian successors, who had the geographical advantage on their side.

Thus, as we have seen, the limits of the territory that was to constitute Brazil had been fixed since the middle of the eighteenth century. We will now proceed to analyze the structure of the settlement established by Portuguese colonization within this territory at the beginning of the last century, at the time when the territorial disputes had already been finally and exclusively

---

* This was the group of mission stations situated in the region between Sacramento and Laguna (the southernmost settlement in Brazil), which, although claimed by both the Portuguese and the Spaniards, was in practice a no-man's land occupied only by these Jesuits and some Indian tribes. Prominent among the Seven Peoples Christianized by the Jesuits were the Tapes, who fought on the side of the Spaniards during the 1735–1737 war against the "Nova Colonia do Sacramento" which the Portuguese had established in the disputed region. The Portuguese managed to repel the Spanish but only by the Madrid Treaty of 1750 did they officially secure the Spanish Jesuit mission area of the Seven Peoples. —Translator.

transferred to the frontier zones. Approximately sixty percent of the population, that is, almost two million inhabitants, was concentrated along a coastal belt which was seldom more than thirty miles wide. This left less than half of the total population to the remaining territory, approximately ninety percent of the total area. This imbalance between the coastal zone and the interior clearly reflects the predominant character of colonization; it was established for the purposes of agricultural production—hence the preference for the fertile, damp, and warm coastal lowlands—and was commercially oriented toward the exterior market. Established from the earliest days of colonization, along this coastal zone, settlement began to penetrate effectively into the interior only in the second century of colonization. The seventeenth century Brazilian chronicler, Frei Vicente do Salvador, had already accused the colonists of being content merely to "scuttle along the seashore like so many crabs." [4] And even in the second century of colonization, penetration of the interior was limited. I am, of course, excluding the *bandeiras,* which had roamed most of the interior in their wide-ranging exploring expeditions. But the *bandeirantes* had traveled as explorers and not as settlers. Permanent settlement of the interior, with the exception of the São Paulo highlands, where a settlement center had been very early established, was confined to the progressive advance of cattle ranches in the backlands of the northeast (the Sertão) and the slow and scanty penetration of the Amazon basin. Intense and rapid penetration of the interior dates from the first half of the eighteenth century, with the successive discoveries of gold in Minas Gerais (in the last decade of the seventeenth century), Cuiaibá (1719), and Goiás (1725), which prompted a flood of immigration, wave after wave of immigrants pouring into the heart of the continent. Some were new colonists who had come directly from Europe, others were slaves brought from Africa. Many, however, came from the agricultural establishments of the coast, which suffered considerably from the constant drain on population and capital. This was a somber period for coastal agriculture, which suffered an eclipse of its former brilliance as

its first cycle of prosperity came to an end. Fields were left untended, *engenhos* were abandoned, plantations went to ruin,
life came almost to a standstill as a new phase was ushered in,
with a vigorous and pulsating life centered on the El Dorado of
the mines.

But the fever was short-lived. By the middle of the century
the mines had already begun to show signs of exhaustion; open
decadence dates from the third quarter of the century. By then
the currents of immigration to the interior had ceased, and in
many cases the tide had turned. The coastal zone was reborn,
and agriculture regained its supremacy.

Despite its violent impact on the colony's economic and population structure, the brief heyday of the mines, lasting little
more than half a century, was not long enough to swing the
balance definitely in favor of the interior. As we have seen, by
the end of the century, when the drift to the interior had already long since ceased, the coast still far outstripped the interior in the number of its inhabitants. Its economic importance had similarly been reestablished, and it once more surpassed that of the interior.

The coastal settlement whose origin and evolution I have
just briefly outlined was extremely unevenly distributed. Settlements were few and far between and were separated by
large tracts of entirely unoccupied territory, some devoid even
of overland communication routes. In this the geographical
features of the Brazilian coastline clearly played a part. On the
whole, the littoral is not very favorable to human settlement; it
extends in a regular and unbroken line almost devoid of curves
and inlets. There is an absence of natural havens, even for
small craft; and the shores are generally fringed either with
marshy tracts—the *mangueirais,* which are flooded with salt
water when the tide rises and the debris of rivers when it ebbs
—or with large deposits of sand that block the openings to the
interior offered by the offshore bars and lagoons. The few
favorable points along the coast were therefore avidly seized,
and settlement was concentrated around them. The most interesting of these, both on account of its extent and by reason of

the curious natural phenomenon that gives it its advantage, is the whole of the country's northeastern tip, stretching from Cape Calcanhar (in Rio Grande do Norte) as far as Maceió.[5] Parallel and close to the coastline is a chain of reefs, on a level with the sea at high tide but which at low tide rises to form a wall whose breadth varies between a few meters and more than a hundred. This happy accident of nature acts as a break-water to subdue the fury of the waves, and counteracts the silting-up caused by sand deposits which, to the north and to the south of this natural barrier, are the chief cause of the lack of practicable havens. Here the ships that ply the coast find a serene sea, calm inlets, and safe anchorage. The large number of small rivers that empty themselves into this part of the coast have unobstructed bars and permit easy access to the interior. To these advantages, nature had added a favorable coastal lo-cation: fertile soil, favorable relief, and an abundance of forest, providing fuel and good building material. Hence this region is one of the ideal points for the establishment of human life on the difficult Brazilian coast, and for this reason it became one of the most concentrated areas of settlement and has remained so up to the present day. A good fifth of the colonial settlers on the coastlands at the beginning of the nineteenth century, ap-proximately 300,000 inhabitants, were concentrated in this region.

Further south lies the *Recôncavo* * district of Bahia. It is sit-uated around a large bay, a veritable "Mediterranean," with an area of more than a thousand square kilometers. Several rivers empty into this bay, whose broad and deep estuaries are navigable for many miles, linking up an extensive area of fertile land. No more was needed for this area to become, from the earliest days of colonization, the most densely populated and wealthiest part of the colony. Professor Luís dos Santos Vil-hena, an intelligent and meticulous contemporary observer of

---

* The Recôncavo is a strip outside the city of Salvador (Bahia) bordering All Saints Bay, some 60 miles long and 30 miles wide. It came to be regarded as the seat of the landowning, slaveholding rural aristocracy.—Translator.

the city and district he lived in, estimated that there were more than 100,000 inhabitants in the Recôncavo. There were 260 sugar mills operating in the district.[6]

To these two principal population centers of coastal Brazil, a third of equal importance must be added: Rio de Janeiro. From the mouth of the Itabapoana River to the south stretches a narrow strip wedged between the mountains and the sea, which narrows progressively as it extends southward to the borders of the captaincy (which became the present state of Rio de Janeiro), and disappears altogether as the mountain plunges sharply into the sea. Within this rough circle, embracing the coastal lowlands known as the "Baixada Fluminense," a plain interrupted only by low rounded hills and isolated hillocks, was concentrated, as early as the middle of the sixteenth century, one of the colony's principal population clusters. In 1789, the population was estimated at 168,709 inhabitants, including that of the city of Rio de Janeiro, the nominal capital of the colony (51,011 inhabitants).[7] By the beginning of the last century it exceeded 200,000. In 1799, according to an almanac published in that year, there were 616 sugar mills (the district's principal source of wealth) and 253 distilleries for rum and sugarcane brandy.

We can divide this part of the coast into two natural regions. The first comprises the highly indented stretch that includes Guanabara Bay and the inland area stretching westward between firm land on the one side, the Marambaia Restinga * and Ilha Grande on the other. In this region, excluding the immense bay with its 131 kilometers of coastline, where, as in the Recôncavo of Bahia, although in fewer numbers, are situated the estuaries of several navigable rivers, there are numerous ports and havens protected by the neighboring land of the Restinga and Ilha Grande (Angra dos Reis, Parati, and Mangaratiba . . .).

The other region comprises the Campos (plains) of Goitacases. These plains are 30 kilometers inland and are separated

* *Restinga*—a long narrow spit of land forming a barrier enclosing a great stretch of water.—Translator.

from the sea by a zone of lagoons and swampy lowlands, which are unusable and which make transit difficult without the execution of preliminary works of some magnitude. They offered, however, such favorable conditions—uniform relief, fertile soil, and a natural vegetation that does not present any obstacle to passage or render occupation difficult—that they began to be intensely settled from the seventeenth century onward, at first for raising cattle—the pioneer economic activity—to supply the nearby market of Rio de Janeiro, then for agriculture, their "fine, white fair clay" [8] soils proving as suitable for cane cultivation as had the *massapê* soils of Bahia and Pernambuco. In the second half of the eighteenth century the progress of the sugar industry was accelerated. There were 55 engenhos in 1769; ten years later there were 168; in 1783 the number had risen to 278; [9] and finally, in 1799, there were 328 engenhos, including four distilleries for rum and sugarcane brandy.[10] The obstacles separating the Campos of Goitacases from the sea are not very formidable: the Paraíba River is easily navigable by small craft over the 42 kilometers that separate their principal center, the town of São Salvador (now the city of Campos) from the coast, and this facilitated contact with the outside world. Some fifty craft transported the eight thousand chests of the exportable sugar produced in the plains to Rio, where it was reexported outside the colony.[11]

In addition to these three large population clusters—Rio de Janeiro, Bahia, and Pernambuco—there were numerous secondary and much smaller clusters scattered along the coast, with a more or less vegetative and restricted existence and of almost no geographic or economic importance. All these clusters, large, medium, and small, were established on account of the particular and local conditions of the coastline, geographical accidents such as natural ports or havens, inlets offering a more or less easy means of access to the land beyond the coastal fringe, or any other feature that might prove favorable for human activity; and all of them, unfortunately very few in relation to the extent of the coastline, became poles of attraction for human settlement. In the midst of each of these clusters arose a small, or even minute, nucleus or center, separated from the others by the thinly occupied territory that surrounded them, exclusively oriented toward the sea, and completely cut off by land from their nearest neighbors. Study of a physical map of the area would enable the careful observer to pinpoint with absolute accuracy the settlement that had been established along the coast. Human endeavor had not yet managed to alter the unfavorable conditions imposed by nature. Where favorable natural conditions are lacking, where man does not find everything at his disposal, human settlement is absent.

We will now proceed to follow this difficult coastline from north to south, simply leaving out the points already analyzed above. The first line extends from the extreme north of the colony, the Oiapoque River to the Araguari River. This is the famous Amapá region, coveted for centuries by the English, Dutch, and finally the French, and only incorporated into Brazilian territory in 1899.[12] Since the marginal coastland is here composed of marshy lowlands where navigation is extremely difficult owing to the dearth of harbors and penetration to the interior is almost impossible, the Amapá had remained practically unoccupied. A few Franciscans and many more Jesuits had extended their missionary activities into the area during the seventeenth century, with little or no result. By the end of the eighteenth century the traces that remained were a few miserable and stagnating villages of semicivilized and degenerate Indians.

Immediately to the south of this inhospitable area lies the immense Amazon Delta. Here, the admirable network of communications provided by the great river and its tributaries facilitated settlement not only locally but in the very heart of the continent. Settlement of the region was initially favored by the fact that sovereignty was still disputed. The Portuguese established themselves at the mouth of the river in 1616, expelling the English and Dutch who, despite the absence of any legal claim to the area, had been its earliest occupants. The disputes that arose were in relation to Spain, but the union of the two crowns postponed the problem. On regaining her independence, Portugal had already succeeded in establishing sovereignty over the area, possessed as she was of the only outlet for this immense Amazonian territory, so difficult to reach from the west and the north where the rival claimant had established settlements. It proved easy for Portugal to establish her dominion over the territory, and indeed no efforts were spared in the attempt, the government joining forces with the religious orders in an active colonization drive. But despite its deep penetration into the continent, settlement continued to be concentrated in the coastal zone around the delta.

This settlement was grouped mainly about the eastern arm of the great river (the Pará River, which was most favorable to navigation), and it was also concentrated in the area bounded by the river, the open sea, and the navigable Guamá River, where settlements were strung along both margins. Along the seashore itself, settlement was sparse and had not penetrated very far inland; it had reached as far as Bragança, situated on the estuary of the Caité River, three leagues above the bar. Here, population was more concentrated by reason of the providential means of ingress afforded by this estuary in a low and swampy coastland, the Caité being navigable as far as the port of Tertugal, which was linked by an overland route to the Guamá River, and the population clusters along its margins. This completes the circuit bounded by the Pará River, the open sea, and the Caité and Guamá Rivers, which contains the principal nucleus of Amazonian settlement. The island of Joanes (the present island of Marajó) was the tributary zone to this cluster and supplied it with meat from the herds in the only local lands suitable for cattle grazing.

Following the coast eastward from Bragança, we cross an almost empty region inhabited only by a few semicivilized Indians. Communications here are effected through the numerous "openings" which abound in this semiaquatic territory. But these were little used and only the Maranhão postal service, established during the last years of the eighteenth century, regularly availed itself of them.[13] The coast continues in this manner as far as the Turiaçu River, which was then the administrative limit of the two captaincies of Grão-Pará and Maranhão, and the small settlement of the same name situated at the end of the estuary and inhabited by a few poor half-breed peasants.

Beyond the Turiaçu River, the coastal strip is no more favorable to settlement than is the preceding tract; but immediately back of the coastal fringe, the plains characteristic of northeast Maranhão, known as the Perizes, begin to appear, plains which are in certain respects well suited to cattle grazing. Flooded during the winter, they are easily navigable by canoes carrying fifty bags of cotton; and on the wet savannas of the swampy areas, cattle pastured "with water up to their necks," as one contemporary writer puts it.[14] They could, however, find shelter in the levees and wooded islands where they were also protected from the summer heat. Since this Perizes zone, stretching across a vast area that extends to the Pindaré River, offered easy access to penetration and occupation, regular settlements were established—regular, that is, by contrast with what we find further north. The Piracumã River and Cumã Bay, where the region's principal center, Guimarães, was established, are both navigable at all seasons of the year and served as local waterways linking the Perizes with the exterior.

We now come to the twin bays of São Marcos and São José, formed by the vast estuary of large rivers navigable far into the heart of the Sertão. The site, therefore, combined a number of exceptionally favorable conditions and so became the most important center in the captaincy of Maranhão, the capital being established here (São Luís do Maranhão). Colonization was solidly established on the island of São Luís where it had been founded, as well as on the mainland and quite far into the interior, principally along the Itapecuru River; and at the beginning of the nineteenth century, the period we are now considering, the area was well on its way to becoming one of the colony's most important centers.

East of São Luís, unfavorable conditions once more predominate and there is nothing to stimulate human settlement. This condition continues as far as the Parnaíba delta, where we find a concentration of some 15,000 inhabitants. The region's progress was due not only to the local conditions, which were favorable to the navigation of the delta (two of its five branches, the Tutoya and Igaraçu, offering a practicable means of ingress), but also to the fact that it was a focus for production from the settlements strung along the navigable course of the Parnaíba, which flows across a regularly settled and well-developed region to the heart of the Sertão. But the real development of the town of Parnaíba, which was the center for the river's trade, dates from 1770, when one of the local traders, João Paulo Diniz, established dried meat factories along the margin of the upper Parnaíba right in the heart of the most important cattle zone. The meat was brought by riverboat to the town, and from there exported to Bahia, Rio de Janeiro, and Pará.[15] By the end of the eighteenth century, the port had become the north's principal supplier of dried meat. Ceará, which had formerly occupied this position, had been visited by calamitous droughts and was out of the market, leaving only its name to connect it with the product known today as "Ceará meat." Every year sixteen or seventeen ships sailed from the south to bring back meat from Parnaíba.[16]

As we come to Ceará, we enter a completely different type of coastal zone. The characteristic local feature is the vast accumulation of sand deposited by the sea currents all along the northern coast of the Brazilian northeast, from Ceará to Cape Calcanhar in Rio Grande do Norte. The effect of this is the singularly unbroken nature of the coastline, where physical accidents disappear under the covering of sand, an effect aggravated by low and irregular rainfall which results in few and irregularly flowing rivers, whose currents are altogether insufficient to arrest or carry out to sea even a small part of the accumulation of sand blocking their mouths. But another characteristic of the Ceará littoral prevented its coastal fringe from remaining completely unoccupied: this is the line of *serras* or mountains that extends in isolated massifs more or less continuously along the coast. Blessed with fairly abundant rainfall, these elevated areas can be likened to oases of fertile and arable soils in the midst of the surrounding aridity. These serras (Ibiapaba, Sobral, Uruburetama, Baturité) attracted settlement which sought an outlet to the nearby sea, giving rise to small ports that managed to establish themselves as best they could along this difficult coastline: Camocim, Acaraú, Fortaleza—which became the capital of the captaincy thanks to its central position, to the somewhat limited protection afforded by the Macuripe Point, and, above all, to the fertility of the Serra de Baturité which forms its immediate hinterland. The last Ceará port to the east, Aracati, is also the most notable. It offers certain advantages; it served as the outlet for the extensive zone of lowlands, watered in the rainy season by the irregularly flowing Jaguaribe River. In 1810, the Jaguaribe Basin supported a population of approximately 60,000 inhabitants, who were engaged in cattle rearing and cotton growing.[17] This then accounts for the presence of a port in such manifestly unfavorable physical conditions.

Apart from these clusters, the coastal zone of Ceará was uninhabited. Consisting of a wide, sandy plain, arid, unprotected, and able to support only a thin covering of useless vegetation, it was not suitable for human settlement. The same conditions prevail in the tract east of this zone, the northern coast of Rio Grande do Norte. Koster traveled through the region in 1808, journeying from Natal to Aracati, and suffered considerably from the arid conditions and lack of drinkable water. He found the region scantily peopled, with only a few miserable dwellings situated at considerable distances from each other.[18] The route followed by Koster was, however, further inland. Along the coastal fringe, the collection of sea salt gave a certain amount of life to the tract, stretching from the mouth of the Moçoró to that of the Açu. The low rainfall and intense rate of evaporation in this dry and overheated atmosphere contribute to the high salinity of the seawater along this stretch, which made it the colony's most important salt-producing region.[19] A little further along, beginning at the Ponta dos Três Irmãos, some protection is afforded to the hitherto exposed coast by a

line of sandbanks, precursors of the *recifes,* or stone reefs, of
the east coast, and scattered settlement reappears over a small
stretch.

We now reach one of the great population clusters of the
Brazilian coastal belt, which begins, although still on a somewhat limited scale, at this point of the eastern coast in the Rio
Grande do Norte. Leaving aside this important settlement area,
which I have already analyzed, we continue southward to
reach its limit at Maceió. South of Maceió there is a break in
the continuous line of reefs, which chiefly accounts for the concentration of settlement in the north. Shipping here no longer
finds the shelter afforded by the reefs from the impetuosity of
the sea. Because of this lack of natural covering, sandy stretches like those of Ceará in Rio Grande do Norte begin to reappear, silting up the natural indentations of the shoreline, and so
creating an unbroken coast to which access is difficult. As we
proceed southward toward Bahia (the Bay of All Saints), the
difficulties increase. The quality of the soils is poorer and
arable land becomes scarcer. In Sergipe, at that time still a
judicial district of Bahia, there are a few rivers offering a practicable means of ingress for small craft: the São Francisco,
Japaratuba, Cotinguiba, Vaza-Barris, and the Real, with its
northern tributary, the Piauí. Of these the most accessible from
the sea is the Cotinguiba, which waters the plains bearing its
name, famous for the sugar they produce.[20] Of the 140 mills
operating in Sergipe, the majority were located here. In spite of
this, settlement decreases considerably in relation to that of the
area to the north forming the Pernambuco nucleus and is virtually nonexistent along the Bahian coastline as far as the Recôncavo.

As previously pointed out, the Recôncavo district was the
principal nucleus of settlement along the colony's coastal belt
as a result of strictly local factors. South of the Recôncavo, we
enter a coastal zone having special and particular characteristics unlike any we have encountered up to this point. The coast
we have hitherto found has been made up of marshy lowlands
with a cover of intricate low-growing vegetation as far as

Maranhão, a somewhat scanty vegetation in the more arid and sandy localities from Maranhão to Paraíba, and a mantle of forest, largely cleared away by man, between Paraíba and Alagoas. The general pattern is one of low vegetation. Its aspect now changes completely. From the Bay of All Saints southward the highlands of the interior move ever closer to the coast, and the flat shoreline strip is sharply terminated a short distance from the shore by a steep mountain covered with dense forest. The beaches begin to appear less frequently and finally disappear altogether, interrupted by the spur of a mountain that juts into the sea to form a promontory. A series of parallel rivers, some fairly large, empty into this part of the coast and their bars offer accommodation for shipping. The slow rate at which they flow across the final level stretch before reaching the sea causes them to break up into canals and lagoons of stagnant water, which make this an unhealthy area. Despite this fact, at the mouth of each of these rivers or canals, a small nucleus of settlement was established: Camamu, Barra do Rio de Contas, Ilhéus, Canavieiras, Belmonte, Pôrto Seguro, and Caravelas being the principal centers. This settlement is characterized by its exclusive concentration on the coastal fringe; it hardly penetrates more than a few miles inland and congregates exclusively around the mouths of the rivers or in their immediate vicinity. The dense forest following the shoreline and forming a broad and uninterrupted belt difficult to penetrate and the irregular relief, particularly south of Pôrto Seguro, where it rises to the great heights of the Serra do Mar, are the factors that isolate the coast completely from the interior.

Settlement developed independently in each of these sectors, forming distinct clusters completely cut off from each other. This can be said both of the former captaincies of Ilhéus and Pôrto Seguro, later incorporated in Bahia (the second only on the eve of independence), and of the captaincy of Espírito Santo. In this part of the Brazilian territory, the first communications between the coast and the interior were opened up only at the beginning of the nineteenth century: the river route along the Rio Doce and the overland route through its valley; the Mucuri road, leading from São José de Pôrto Alegre to Bom-Succeso in Minas Gerais; and the Belmonte and Ilhéus routes also leading to the interior captaincy of Minas Gerais. (I shall return to these lines of travel in a later chapter.) But up to the time when these communications were inaugurated, and even for some time afterward, since they only succeeded in belatedly and partially overcoming the deficiencies of the coast, the clusters of settlement strung along the shoreline vegetated in isolation. Their isolation explains, to a great extent, the lack of progress in the captaincies of Ilhéus, Pôrto Seguro, and Espírito Santo in contrast to those of Rio de Janeiro, Bahía, Pernambuco, and other northern captaincies. This had already been discovered by the astute anonymous author of the *Roteiro do Maranhão a Goiás,* previously cited.

These coastal centers were not only cut off from the interior, but were also isolated from each other on account of the difficulties of overland travel. Luís Tomás de Navarro, a judge commissioned in 1808 to investigate the possibilities of establishing a postal route along the coast from Bahia to Rio de Janeiro, made notes on the obstacles that isolated the towns and settlements from each other: rivers difficult to ford, beaches covered with thick layers of fine sand that render traveling extremely difficult, and steep promontories that advance into the sea from the interior and involve a steep climb.[21] Hence these settlements were left to vegetate, forming small separate pockets whose only outlet was to the sea and supporting a precarious way of life by the production of a handful of commodities—flour, fish, and some coffee—for export to Bahia and Rio de Janeiro.

There was still a further obstacle to development in this unhappy region, the hostility of the natives. The mountain and forest served as a shelter and final refuge for the natives who resisted the advance of the white man and refused to submit to white occupation of this part of the colony. The colonists attacked the Indian tribes in a broad pincer-like movement from two sides, the coast and Minas Gerais. Harassed from both sides, the still numerous survivors were obliged to seek refuge in this intermediate area, which still retained its natural cover of dense forest that colonization had not yet had time to penetrate, and remained there up to the nineteenth century. From their strongholds they descended periodically on the coast, sacking and destroying the settlements.[22] Among these warlike groups the most notable were the ferocious Aimorés, commonly known as "Botocudos" because of the custom which the men had adopted of ornamenting their lower lips with wooden pegs (*botoques*). They were the most formidable of the white man's native opponents and were held in respect by all the neighboring tribes, with whom they were engaged in permanent hostilities. They were also the most frequent "visitors" to the coastal settlements. They had quietened down after the attacks led by Captain João Domingos Monteiro in the third quarter of the eighteenth century, and there was a lull in hostilities which lasted until 1786, when they recommenced with such vigor that many settlements were completely abandoned and others suffered a considerable decline. We learn from the sergeant in command at Caravelas that, "harassed by the barbarians, the settlers had been obliged to abandon the fertile lands of the interior for the barren and swampy areas bordering the sea."[23] Espírito Santo suffered equally. In the early years of the last century the savages were still making forays only a few miles from the capital.[24] This is what led the government in 1808 to declare war on the Aimorés, a matter that will be discussed in a later chapter.

Continuing our survey of coastal settlements, we now come to the part of the coast that falls within the limits of what is now the state of Espírito Santo—the former boundary between the captaincy of that name and that of Pôrto Seguro ran along the Rio Doce. From the Mucuri River southward, and particularly beyond the bar of the São Mateus river, the coast drops considerably as we enter a zone of marshy lowlands with a coastline obstructed by extensive sand deposits. Settlement disappears altogether in this area, and even drinking water is lacking. After São Mateus, where there is a small settlement of Indians and half-breeds, we cross a desert some eighteen to twenty leagues in extent. Judge Navarro, to whom we have already referred above, considered that if the postal route was to pass through this area and transit made possible, the first step would have to be the establishment of a few settlements to provide travelers with halting places and provisions along the way. When Prince Maximilian traveled through the area in 1816, he experienced great tribulations, including thirst.[25] These conditions continue as far as the bar of the Santa Cruz, where the highlands reappear and the Serra do Mar once more approaches the coast.

Here begins the Espírito Santo settlement area proper, in conditions similar to those in Pôrto Seguro and Ilhéus. In 1813 there were approximately 19,000 inhabitants [26] congregated in clusters around the river bars and coastal harbors, all small and insignificant, with the exception of the nucleus centered around the bay of Espírito Santo and its island, which contained most of the captaincy's population and where its capital was located. This settlement had penetrated slightly into the interior, making use of some of the rivers which are navigable by small craft for short distances inland, particularly the Jecu, Santa Maria, Benevente, and Itapemirem. In the Doce area, infested by the Aimorés, there was not much more than the garrison at Linhares, established in the early years of the last century for the defense of the captaincy.

We now reach the captaincy of Rio de Janeiro which is, as we move southward, the third and last of the coast's three largest population clusters. From here onward, that is, from Parati, which forms the southernmost limit of the captaincy, settlement again becomes scarce. The commanding feature of the southern coastline is the closeness of the Serra do Mar, which rises parallel to the coast and forms a steep and continuous barrier with an elevation of over 1,000 meters, dropping slightly to the south but stretching as far as latitude 30° S, almost to the colony's extreme southern limit. It cuts off from their hinterlands the coastal fringes of three captaincies: São Paulo —including the present State of Paraná, which was then the

Paranaguá district of São Paulo—Santa Catarina, and part of Rio Grande do Sul. Wedged between the sea and the mountain, almost isolated from the interior by the obstacle provided by the steep slopes, the colonial settlements strung along this coastal stretch remained virtually at a standstill, despite numerous and well-sheltered ports, such as São Sebastião and Santos in São Paulo and the coastal links around Paraná.

Another drawback to the development of this part of the colony was its remoteness from the primary centers and focus of Brazilian colonization and from the European markets for the chief colonial products. Development of local agriculture was seriously handicapped by this remoteness, and although São Vicente had been the first and for a time an important sugar center, it soon lost its position to its more favorably situated northern competitors; and even before the close of the first century of colonization it had been relegated to a very minor position. Nearly all the colonial establishments along the southern coastal fringe, not exceeding ten in number, were restricted to a purely local and vegetative existence, their communication with the interior being limited. Coastal traffic served as the link with Rio de Janeiro, the principal market for their products: some sugar and cane spirits, flour, and timber. The only two noteworthy centers are Santos and Paranaguá, particularly the former, which was easier to reach from the interior and provided a distribution center for exporting the growing production of the São Paulo highlands.

Around Santa Catarina, settlement becomes more concentrated, particularly on the island of Santa Catarina, the captaincy's principal nucleus and seat of the capital, which was then still Nossa Senhora do Destêrro. In the 540 square kilometers of the island, population density had reached a remarkably high level for the colony—25 inhabitants per square kilometer.[27] This concentration of population was considered by St. Hilaire in 1820 as one of the causes of the island's impoverishment; for as a result of the rudimentary and primitive agricultural techniques employed, it was no longer able, despite its natural fertility, to support such a numerous population.[28] Hence it was necessary to migrate to the mainland. But this migration never took place on the scale needed, since the local inhabitants, extremely sociable by nature, preferred to migrate in large groups, a circumstance which naturally hampered the process somewhat.

This observation, also made by the French naturalist cited, leads us to one of the most interesting although minor aspects of Portuguese colonization in Brazil: this is the sponsored emigration of *married couples* (especially from the Azores islands) who were transplanted in family groups to certain parts of the colony; one of the characteristics that resulted from this special type of colonization was the tendency to remain in large groups. Under this colonization scheme, the government paid the passages of married couples and provided facilities for their establishment—small plots of land, agricultural implements, seed, and so forth—and they sailed for their new homes in large groups to occupy the regions previously set aside and made ready for them. This type of colonization, completely different from that for the rest of the colony, produced interesting results, some of which will be discussed in subsequent chapters. The most notable are the two characteristics pointed out above, the rapid growth of the population and the extremely sociable habits of these immigrants. The system of colonization by family groups was adopted by the mother country as a means of populating frontier regions threatened by external aggression. Santa Catarina, which fell into this category, was one of the favored regions. I shall return to this topic in the appropriate section; for now, it is enough to note the population increase that had occurred in this part of the colony. This was true not only of the island but of certain points on the mainland. Here, referring once more to St. Hilaire's account, we can single out as a particular instance the small area, scarcely more than one league in extent, near the mouth of the Itajubá River, where the French traveler was surprised to find an area that was completely under cultivation, without a single empty plot and with farms set as close to one another as in the immediate outskirts of Rio de Janeiro.[29] This

circumstance was so exceptional in the colony that it indicated
the existence of specific conditions that merit special mention.

From Laguna southward the coastal features change once
more. Gone are the indentations characteristic of the coastline
to the north, with its many inlets and natural havens, facilitating communication and so making it particularly suitable for
human settlement. Here the coastline is accompanied by great
waste stretches of sand, giving way toward the interior to lowlands dotted with lagoons. Settlement disappears in this narrow strip of unusable land. The mountain again approaches the
sea and is only a few miles from the shoreline, leaving this
narrow strip free only to serve as a communication link between Santa Catarina and Rio Grande do Sul. This link was of
some importance; here lay the route traveled by the cattle
raised in Rio Grande do Sul to the markets of Santa Catarina.
This route was also of historical importance, since it had provided passage for the first settlers who arrived in the territory
of Rio Grande and initiated Portuguese occupation of the future captaincy.

At the point where the Serra do Mar—oriented, so far, from
north to south and running parallel with the coastline—bends
sharply westward, almost at right angle, to form the southernmost edge of the Brazilian plateau, we find the famous Campos
do Viamão (Viamão Plains), which lie close to the coast, entirely free from the mountain range which has turned inland.
Bordered to the north by the mountain slopes and to the south
by the Lagoa dos Patos, these plains extend over a wide area
covered with a natural vegetation of grassland, interspersed
with scattered patches of woodland. With their abundant
water supply and ideal climate, they were soon used as grazing
lands by the very first colonists who arrived from Laguna to
settle there in 1719.[30] After a century of rudimentary exploitation, in which nothing was done to improve or even to maintain
the gifts of nature, these natural pastures began to be exhausted by the devastation wreaked by heavy grazing and the
large-scale burning of vegetation (a practice that was, and is
still, common throughout Brazil; it was intended to produce a

renewal of vegetation after a dry period). St. Hilaire, traversing the region in 1820, even then noted the decline of the Viamão grasslands, which were no longer able to support the larger breeds of cattle.[31]

The cattle stations, therefore, began to move westward; in 1820 the old trail leading from Viamão to the upland plains (Vacaria), and thence to São Paulo, once followed by countless convoys of mules and cattle, had been well-nigh abandoned and was reduced to little more than a track.[32] A new trail had taken its place starting from a point closer to the larger and more important cattle stations that had moved westward, the Bôca do Monte-Santa Maria trail, leading across the serra toward São Paulo. In fact, communication between Rio Grande, the north, and the rest of the country became fixed along this route, and a century later the present railroad still follows the line of this old overland trail.

The population shifted away from the abandoned plains of Vacaria. But St. Hilaire still found cattle stations situated close enough together for him to spend successive nights on different ranches during his journey to Pôrto Alegre.

South of the Campos do Viamão stretches the Lagoa dos Patos. Its eastern edge bordering the ocean is formed by a long narrow spit, or *restinga,* completely sandy at its southern tip but covered with scanty low vegetation from the locality of Estreito northward. A number of cattle stations were established along this restinga which, owing to the flatness of the land, lying as it does almost at sea level, suffers flooding during the rainy season, leaving very few patches of dry land. Settlement of the region was therefore scarce and the resources slender. The population was concentrated more toward the interior on the other side of the lagoon, or rather along its two extremes: to the north, along the wide estuary of the Jacuí and the Guaíba rivers, where the capital of the captaincy, Pôrto Alegre, was founded; and to the south, where the lagoon opens toward the sea and where, despite unsuitable conditions to which no alternatives could be found, the captaincy's port, São Pedro do Rio Grande, was established. Not far from São Pedro, along the São Gonçalo River, which provides the link between the Patos and Mirim lagoons, lies a zone which at the beginning of the nineteenth century—in fact, by the end of the eighteenth—was already intensively settled and developed. This was due to the establishment of *charqueadas*, where the beef furnished by the cattle stations was prepared and dried, and where its export to all ports of the colony was initiated on a large scale during this period.* The town of Pelotas was established soon afterward. The local church, which was elevated to a parish in 1811, gives some indication of the region's progress.

We have now reached the colony's southern extreme. Further south, as far as the Chuí arroyo or the Castilhos Grandes, the two points between which the frontier oscillated, fixed settlement was hampered by the instability provoked by the wars, which lasted well into the last quarter of the eighteenth century and broke out again in 1801. Only a few military posts and garrisons were established in the area.

---

* *Charque* or *xarque* is jerked or salted beef. It is still bought by the poorer people throughout the cities of Brazil, and in colonial times it was exported to the West Indies as well as to the northern part of the colony. It is also known as *carne-do-sul*, or "southern meat."—Translator.

Settlement of the Interior

I have already referred to the major factors responsible for the penetration of the colony's vast interior, which, although for the most part situated west of the Tordesillas Line and therefore legally falling within Spanish territory, was allotted to the Portuguese and their Brazilian successors. These factors included mining and the spread of the cattle estates. The particular local factors involved in the conquest of the extreme north of Amazonia will be analyzed last. An immediate difference must be noted between the contributions to settlement made by mining and cattle, respectively. The former impelled settlement in an abrupt drive from the littoral to the heart of the continent; there was no continuity in its expansion. The mines were situated far from the primary sources of the currents of immigration that flowed toward them, and the intervening space remained a wilderness, crossed only by the few lines of communication that had been opened up. These links between the mining centers and the coastal towns, which were their source of life and provided the outlet for their production, did not even follow the routes of the early trails opened up to reach them. Thus, the settlements that sprang up around the mining establishments of central Minas Gerais, which were chronologically the first to be exploited and were destined to remain the most important, were cut off from the original points of departure for the explorers. They were detached from São

51

Paulo, the original center from which the pioneer prospectors
had pushed forward their discoveries and also the point of departure for the first batch of settlers. They were also detached
from Bahia, the second center from which settlement had spread
out to occupy them; and communications converged on Rio de
Janeiro, from which a route had been opened up only in the
early years of the eighteenth century when the mining area
was already well populated. The older trails from São Paulo to
Bahia were relegated to a secondary position.

This illustrates the nature of the dispersion of settlement
provoked by the discovery of the mines. It was so sudden and
so violent that it even lost contact with its original sources. A
very different process characterizes the penetration effected by
the advance of the cattle ranches. From the established centers
along the coast, chiefly Bahia, there had been a slow movement
of cattle and settlements toward the interior. Expansion was
geographically continuous, and the settlers who established
themselves in the Sertão maintained an intimate contact with
the centers from which they had pushed westward. In the case
of Bahia, penetration of the interior had begun as early as the
end of the sixteenth century; the São Francisco River was
reached toward the middle of the following century,[1] and the
settlers moved up its margins along both the left and right
banks, peopling the whole middle course of the river with
estates so numerous that they provoked the wonder of Antonil
in 1711.[*] From here, having crossed the São Francisco Valley
to the north, the estates invaded what is now the state of Piauí,
and descended the Gurgueia River and the river that gave its
name to the captaincy.

It was a rapid expansion, to be sure—the motivating force
that led to this expansion and accounts for its rapidity will be
analyzed in a later chapter—but it cannot compare with the
rapid expansion and area covered provoked by mining. It does,

---

[*] In a classic account of Brazil published in 1711 by André João
Antonil (pseudonym of Giovanni Antonio Andreoni, S.J.) under the title
Cultura e Opulência do Brasil (Culture and wealth of Brazil), the cattle
area described in Book 4, chaps. 1–4.—Translator.

however, surpass this expansion in the territory effectively, if somewhat sparsely, occupied. Another point to be noted is the continuity of its expansion: Unlike the settlement provoked by the discovery of gold and gems, the settlement that followed in the wake of the cattle estates was not made up of isolated clusters scattered throughout the interior and widely separated from each other and from their centers on the coast.

This distinction led to the emergence of a completely different pattern of settlement in the central-southern or mining region and the Sertão of the northeast, once the expansion caused by the successive discovery and exploitation of new mines was over, with the consequent influx of settlers and sudden shifts of population—in short, once the boom came to a close and the population had been fixed and stabilized, which occurred somewhere about the middle of the eighteenth century. The pattern that emerged was one of widely scattered estates, remaining more or less distinct and isolated from one another, spread over an area of not less than 2,000,000 square kilometers, that is, what now constitutes the heartland of the Brazilian territory embracing the states of Minas Gerais, Goiás, part of Mato Grosso, and a small part of Bahia. Approximately 600,000 inhabitants, or slightly less than one-fifth of the colony's total population, occupied this area at the beginning of the nineteenth century.

These scattered mining establishments were grouped into three more concentrated clusters. Each cluster formed an administrative unit, the captaincies of Minas Gerais, Goiás, and Mato Grosso. We will consider them in this order, which is the order of their appearance on the scene.

In Minas Gerais, the "condensation center" (to use a term borrowed from physics, which so aptly fits the pattern of settlement being analyzed) is located along a strip stretching from north to south, from the basin of the Rio Grande to near the headwaters of the Jequtinhonha, more or less between the points where the town of Lavras and the mining camp (*arraial*) of Tejuco (now known as Diamantina) had been established. It follows the Serra do Espinhaço and corresponds geologically to a peculiar formation of the terrain, the Minas and Itacolomi series of mineral-bearing rocks, both part of the Algonkian system where the country's principal gold outcroppings were found to occur. This occurrence sufficiently explains the concentration of settlement in this area, many new settlements being established often quite close to each other. The most important are: the towns of São João and São José del-Rei (Tiradentes), Vila Rica (Ouro Preto); the city of Mariana, Caeté, Sabará, Vila do Príncipe (Serro), and the arraial of Tejuco (Diamantina) where diamonds are exploited.

Around this central nucleus, which constitutes the Minas Gerais (General Mines) properly speaking, the name being applied to the captaincy as a whole, there were secondary areas of settlement: Minas Novas to the northeast opened up in 1726; Minas do Rio Verde, with Campanha as their principal center, opened up in 1720; Minas do Itajubá, where the town of this name was later established, was exploited from 1723 onward; and to the west the Minas do Paracatu, the last to be discovered, in 1744.

Other settlements originated in the activities that arose in response to the demands of the mining communities, and which replaced mining when decadence set in during the latter half of the eighteenth century. The mining regions were not on the whole suited either to agriculture or to cattle raising. The irregular relief and poor quality of the soils were natural handicaps to these activities, and at first the population which rapidly congregated in the mining area depended on the importation of food supplies to meet its needs. Meat, an essential element in the colony's food supply, was provided by the cattle driven from the ranches established along the middle reaches of the São Francisco (Bahia). Stimulated by the proximity of a market, the ranches advanced further up the banks of the river, reaching what is now Minas territory and penetrating as far as the Rio das Velhas. This led to the settlement of a continuous area north of the principal mining centers.

Another pastoral center was established to the south in the Rio Grande basin, which later formed the Rio das Mortes dis-

trict, in the midst of the local mining communities which soon
fell into decay. This pastoral center was the nucleus of what is
now called *Sul de Minas* (Southern Minas). Favored by outstanding physical conditions, the grazing industry made rapid
progress in this region. By 1756 it was sending cattle to São
Paulo and competing with the supply from the southern cat-
tlelands, Curitiba and Rio Grande.[2] Indeed, the Rio das
Mortes district became an agricultural center as well, small
farms being established side by side with the cattle ranches;
and many of Rio de Janeiro's food supplies came from this area,
so that the population increased and the district prospered.

The population of Minas Gerais, estimated at 500,000 inhabitants at the end of the eighteenth century, was distributed as
follows: a central strip, stretching from Lavras to Tejuco,
which was the oldest and most concentrated area of settlement
and remained, despite the decadence of the mines, the most
important part of the captaincy. Grouped around it were four
distinct regions of less concentrated settlement. In order of importance these were, (1) in the south, the district of the Rio
das Mortes (basin of the Rio Grande and its tributaries, the
Mortes, the Sapucaí, and the Verde)—a zone devoted principally to the grazing industry but also to agriculture where the
small-scale mining carried on in the past had completely disappeared. (2) In the northeast, the Minas Novas (the Araçuaí
basin) was a decadent former mining region which had already turned almost exclusively to agriculture, particularly
cotton planting. (3) In the west was the district of Paracatu,
also a decadent mining area which was attempting to make a
recovery through the grazing industry. (4) Finally, in the
north was the Sertão of the São Francisco valley, a thinly settled region of Sertanejo-type * *fazendas,* or estates. (In the
chapter concerning the cattle industry we will consider this
type of estate in more detail.) Life in these thankless natural
surroundings was more or less at a standstill.

---

* *Sertanejo*—of the Sertão; thus, an inhabitant of the Sertão or backlands. In the chapter on races, the author describes the origin of the
Sertanejo type of man.—Translator.

We move now to the second large nucleus of settlement arising from mining, the captaincy of Mato Grosso, second in
chronological order only, since in order of importance it is surpassed by Goiás. Gold was discovered in this area in the region
of the Cuiabá River in 1718. The deposits, however, were shallower than those of Minas Gerais. The influx of new settlers
was therefore smaller and decadence was more rapid and pronounced. Hence, the demographic structure of this nucleus is a
much simpler one. By the beginning of the last century the
captaincy found itself reduced to two small, insignificant centers: Cuiabá, with its 19,731 inhabitants [3] concentrated in the
town of that name and the neighboring mining camps; and
Mato Grosso (Vila Bela) with a mere 7,105 inhabitants in the
whole district. The latter remained a small mining center that
had never shown any appreciable development; despite this, it
became the capital of the captaincy after 1746 when it was elevated to a township, thanks to its strategic position on the
banks of the Guaporé River, dominating the frontier of the
Spanish dominions. Apart from these two centers there was
nothing in the captaincy save the armed forts and military
strongholds with their garrisons and dependencies for protecting the colony's frontiers: the fort of Príncipe da Beira, on the
Guaporé River close to its confluence with the Mamoré;
Coimbra; Miranda; and Albuquerque. In 1800 the garrisons of
these forts consisted of 421 soldiers and more than 230 civilians
dependent on them. In addition we must include in the captaincy's population the 213 tenants on the Camapoã fazenda,
where the town of this name was later built and where was situated the portage between the Pardo and Camapoã rivers, the
canoes used in navigating the rivers between São Paulo and
Cuiabá being conveyed overland at this point.

And so we come to the third and last nucleus of a settlement
owing its origin to mining, Goiás. It is divided into two clusters, one in the south and one in the north. It was in the southern area where the capital of the captaincy, Vila Boa, was situated that the region's gold deposits were discovered in 1725.
This natural division was given administrative recognition in

1809, when the captaincy was divided into two judicial districts, or *comarcas*.[4]

The decadence of Goiás, which dates, like that of the colony's other mining centers, from the third quarter of the eighteenth century if not earlier, was even more perceptible and accentuated than in the other centers. This is because once the placer deposits had been worked out there was almost nothing to take the place of mining. Brigadier Cunha Matos affirmed that, as late as 1824 when he wrote his account of the captaincy, in the whole of the more important southern district, there were still not even as many as a hundred people who believed in anything but mining.[5] Despite all the warning symptoms, any other form of occupation was neglected. Hence, once the mines had been virtually exhausted, the population was considerably reduced. In 1804 only slightly over 50,000 inhabitants were left in the captaincy as a whole, of which 36,000 were concentrated in the southern district.[6] In this district the population was not only more numerous but was also grouped in a more clustered pattern, being concentrated chiefly in the southeast of the captaincy,[7] between the Montes Pireneus which form the watershed between the Tocantins and Paranaíba rivers. To the west, along the trail leading to Cuiabá, the last regular establishment was that of the Claro and Pilões rivers, where gold had been discovered and a small settlement established in the middle of the eighteenth century. When diamonds were found here a little later, the mother country, following the usual policy adopted in these matters, closed off the region, expelled the settlers, and handed over the exploitation of the gems on a contract basis to the well-known Felisberto Caldeira Brant, who later distinguished himself as a contractor in Tejuco.* But exploitation yielded little result and was soon

---

* For a comprehensive account of the crown's policy toward the diamond district of Minas Gerais and the diamond monopoly contract exercised by Felisberto Caldeira Brant (and others), see the chapter entitled "Diamond District" in C. R. Boxer's *Golden Age of Brazil* (Berkeley and Los Angeles: University of California Press, 1962), pp. 204–225.—Translator.

abandoned. In spite of this, the Claro and Pilões rivers remained fenced off and the region abandoned for a long time; not until 1803 was the prohibition lifted. This is one of many examples of the mother country's administrative processes—a subject to which I shall later return.

Apart from these more or less precarious establishments, which attracted settlement only during the rainy season when mining was more profitable, there were only a handful of cattle estates strung along the Cuiabá route.

The settlers in the northern district were much more scattered than those of the south, and occupied only the territory east of the Tocantins. The land to the west of this river was occupied by savage Indian tribes. With the opening up of navigation of the Tocantins at the end of the eighteenth century, settlement moved northward. Indeed, it was mainly to support and stimulate this navigation that the northern county was established. A number of new nuclei were formed along the river and a few cattle ranches appeared, but only to a limited extent and much fewer than had been expected. Part of the Maranhão territory was penetrated by this expansion in Goiás. In 1810 a trader from Goiás, Francisco Pinto de Magalhães, built a settlement on the right bank of the Tocantins between the Farinha and Manuel Alves Grande rivers.[8] The present town of Carolina evolved from this settlement.

The northern district of Goiás suffered severely from the hostility of the Indians, particularly the Acroás and Xicriabás, who completely dominated the western bank of the Tocantins and even part of the other bank where colonization had gained a foothold. Their incursions were periodically repeated, and even as late as the beginning of the nineteenth century the colonists had not succeeded in pacifying or completely repelling them.[9] In 1824, in the neighborhood of the Carmo encampment alone, according to Brigadier Cunha Matos, there were more than ninety estates which had been abandoned largely on account of the hostility of the natives.[10]

These, in sum, are the main nuclei of settlement formed by the exploitation of the mines. There were others of less importance, such as those of Bahia, Jacobina, and Rio de Contas. Gold prospecting was carried on to some extent all over the interior from Maranhão to Paraná. But apart from the points mentioned above, the activities carried on in these mining centers were insignificant, nearly always sporadic and subsidiary to the other and more important occupations. They contributed nothing or almost nothing to the occupation and settlement of new territories, particularly at the time with which we are now concerned. We will turn, therefore, to another part of the Brazilian interior, the backlands settled as a consequence of the expansion of the cattle estates.

I have already stated that it is to the grazing industry that we owe the occupation of a good part of the colony's territory, and that, calculated in terms of the total area effectively colonized, it surpassed that opened up by mining. We have also seen that the cattle estates always spread in a continuous movement from a point that represents the radiation center. This was the characteristic pattern of the settlement that accompanied the cattle ranches and gradually spread to the interior. The radiation centers generally corresponded to an agricultural nucleus or sometimes to a mining center. Whenever such a nucleus was formed, a grazing zone was immediately opened up around it to provide cattle and meat. The principal and oldest of these agricultural centers, those established along the littoral in the northeast sugar zone from Pernambuco to Bahia, also gave rise to the largest and most important grazing zones. Further south the pastoral regions of Minas Gerais are linked to the captaincy's mining centers. Finally, in the extreme south, from Paraná to Rio Grande, is situated the last great cattle-raising district, established to supply the agricultural centers of the colony's southern coastlands, particularly Rio de Janeiro, the most important of these. Other minor cattle areas of more local importance may be mentioned: the Campos dos Goitacases, an important pastoral center in the past which, as already mentioned, was opened up to supply cattle to Rio de Janeiro but which afterward turned to agriculture; and in the far north the island of Joanes (Marajó) which supplied Pará.

The northeast is the most important region as far as settlement is concerned. Throughout the interior of the northeast—the Sertão, the vast region stretching from the middle reaches of the São Francisco to the Parnaíba River on the border between Piauí and Maranhão—certain specific geographical conditions appear with striking uniformity. The particular conditions that concern us here are the nature of the surface configuration and the cover of natural vegetation. The relief consists of broad, flat-topped areas called *chapadões*, the nature of the terrain being more or less flat and continuous; and the vegetation, in contrast to the dense growths of forest or *matas* bordering much of the littoral and covering other areas of the colony's territory, consists of a covering of scrub forest or *caatinga*, which grows sufficiently low and is scanty enough to allow passage and to free man from the necessity of clearing and preparing the land before he can occupy it.

Since there is a water shortage, agriculture here was impossible, but cattle could be permitted to roam freely over wide areas with a minimum of tending, and this was more or less what occurred. The dry vegetation of the Sertão can hardly be said to furnish succulent fodder, but it does supply a minimum subsistence for the hardy and undemanding needs of cattle, particularly when dispersed over wide areas with considerable average areas per head. Natural selection operated to produce a strain adapted to the difficulties of the region: an extremely hardy breed endowed with a remarkable instinct for finding suitable grazing spots in the scrub. The harshness of the climate was also not very favorable to their progress, and cattle died by the thousands during the periodic prolonged droughts. There are, however, certain privileged regions in this respect, such as the margins of the São Francisco, the Parnaíba and its affluents, and other rivers which maintain their flow—rare exceptions in this vast region—and so guarantee at least a dependable water supply, an element indispensable for the local population and the estates established along the river banks.

These unfavorable conditions are partly counterbalanced by the salinity of the soil which provides salt-licks where cattle may find the salt they need. In certain places this mineral occurs in sufficient quantities to give rise to regular commercial exploitation. The region bordering the São Francisco, between its affluent, the Salitre, and the town of Urubu, is one such area.

When all is taken into account, the physical conditions in the Sertão were not really suited to the grazing industry, and this was definitely proved toward the end of the eighteenth century, when it was ousted from its position as a supplier of meat to the northeast by a product derived from a different source, the *charque* from Rio Grande. Up to that time, however, favored by the proximity of a ready market and with no real competitors, the northeast Sertão managed to support itself economically, and even to progress. Colonization and settlement spread right through the backlands.

Penetration of the interior began, as we have seen, at the outset of colonization from two principal points: Bahia and Pernambuco. The expansion originating in these two centers had met and mingled. The two movements, however, can be distinguished and the individual development of each can be traced. Since the movement from Bahia led to the greatest and most characteristic expansion, it had already occupied the whole of the territory comprehended in the present-day state by the beginning of the eighteenth century, including the right bank of the São Francisco, which was then still part of the captaincy of Pernambuco. It had also penetrated Piauí; and in a final westward advance which was still at the pioneering stage during the period with which we are now concerned, it had penetrated as far as Maranhão, occupying a strip of territory that embraces the upper reaches of the Itapecuru and the Rio das Balsas and stretching as far as the Tocantins at the mouth of its affluent, the Manuel Alves Grande—the so-called "território dos Pastos Bons" ("land of Good Pastures"). Regarded as the hinterland of Bahia since it was from Bahia that in the last analysis the settlers and cattle estates had spread and it was on Bahia that communications converged, this whole area constitutes what Capistrano de Abreu has rightly called the

"Inner Sertão," to distinguish it from the other Sertão, the backlands of Pernambuco, which can be regarded as the "Outer Sertão." [11] The latter is closer to the littoral, hence the designation. Pernambucan expansion did not penetrate as far into the interior. It began as a northward movement, following the coastline and occupying the coastal fringe of Paraíba and Rio Grande do Norte, and only gradually occupying the interior. The two movements mingled in Ceará. The movement from Bahia, which on its return from Piauí shifted eastward, crossed the range of mountains separating it from the captaincy of Ceará (the Ibiapaba and Grande Serras), and established settlement in the border region, the basin of the upper Poti River, where Crateús is now situated, an area which at first belonged to Piauí and was annexed to Ceará only in a more recent period (1880).[12]

Apart from this mingling, cattle from Piauí were always used as a source for replenishing the Ceará herds which were periodically decimated by drought. The movement from Bahia also infiltrated into Ceará from the south, in Cariris Novos. Meanwhile, the Pernambucan movement reached Ceará from the east and occupied the valley of the Jaguaribe River.

Occupation of the northeastern Sertão was thus completed. But although the backlands had been opened up since the first decades of the eighteenth century and were more or less settled throughout, occupation was far from being uniformly distributed. On the contrary, it was extremely irregular. On the whole, settlement was scarce and widely scattered. The number of cattle herders employed on the *fazendas,* the only establishments in the Sertão, was not very high. It follows that apart from the cattle marketed on the coast, commerce was not very intensive, and hence the urban clusters which arose were insignificant and widely separated from each other. But within this generally low population density, there were certain more heavily concentrated areas of settlement. Natural factors, particularly a dependable source of water, so precious in this semiarid wilderness, played a major role in this distribution. Settlement was concentrated principally along the banks of the

few rivers that maintained a perennial flow: the São Francisco
and the rivers of Piauí and upper Maranhão (the territory of
the Pastos Bons). The enumeration of settlements in Antonil's
account of 1711 was still applicable in broad outline a hundred
years later.[13] These more favored regions were interspersed
with wide expanses of wilderness, crossed only by communication routes. Despite the local difficulties, a few settlers established themselves along these routes to supply the cattle that
were driven along them, or to collect for themselves at cut
prices a few scrawny beasts, exhausted by their long journey
and so gradually build up ranches of their own. Almost all the
rest of the population was concentrated around the *cacimbas*
(water holes). Thus there was a concentration of settlement
wherever the underlying moisture was permanent and drought
resisting, or could be tapped by the rudimentary techniques
employed by the primitive and poverty-stricken inhabitants of
the Sertão. *Ôlho d'água* (water hole) is a designation frequently to be found in the toponymy of the Sertão. The attraction offered by the presence of water is obvious.

Apart from cattle grazing, there is little activity in the
sertões of the northeast. Agriculture was practiced on a small
scale as a subsidiary activity to provide subsistence for the
ranches. There were, however, a few rare spots of agricultural
settlement. A cluster of farming people was located at the
northern base of the Chapada do Araripe in Ceará, where
springs from the mountainside offered a fairly abundant source
of water to support the crops. This was the Cariris Novos, a
veritable oasis in the harsh desert of the Ceará caatingas. Another agricultural area bordered the banks of the Parnáiba and
its affluents in Piauí, the Poti and Gurgueia rivers, and, on a
smaller scale, the Jaguaribe in Ceará. The way of life in these
regions led to more concentrated settlement, and their commerce increased since they were all fairly important points of
contact and transit. Along the São Francisco River we also find
activities other than grazing.[14] The strip between Juàzeiro and
Urubu was not only a salt-collecting center that supplied a
good proportion of the salt requirements of the backlands of

Bahia, Minas Gerais, and even Goiás, but it was also an important junction of communication routes in the Sertão. Finally, the small-scale mining activities carried out on the Chapada Diamantina, which I have already mentioned, served to reinforce settlement in the backlands of the northeast. The two chief clusters serving these small mining communities were concentrated in Jacobina and Rio das Contas. In the latter district, cotton was also cultivated, which gave a certain importance to the region.

We can briefly summarize the distribution of settlement throughout this vast area, occupying more than 1,500,000 square kilometers, as follows: a scanty basis of pastoral settlement concentrated along the valleys of certain perennially flowing rivers, São Francisco, Itapicuru, and Jacuipe in Bahia and a few others in the remaining northeastern captaincies, notably Piauí; an extremely thin spread of people, settlement being at times almost nonexistent in other regions as in the Sertão north of Bahia and the backlands of upper Pernambuco, along the left bank of the São Francisco from Moxotó to Pontal; and certain extreme regions which had not yet been opened up, such as the upper Parnaíba and Gurgueia in Piauí. On this pastoral basis are grouped together in certain areas clusters of more concentrated settlement, economically more stable and with a greater degree of differentiation: the middle reaches of the São Francisco (salt extraction and commerce), Cariris Novas and the middle reaches of the Parnaíba (agriculture), Chapada Diamantina (mining). This, in sum, is the population pattern of the northeast.

We will now turn to the other extreme of the colony, the south, which was also settled by the establishment of cattle estates. This area stretched from the present state of Paraná, then still simply a judicial district—*comarca*—of São Paulo, to the colony's southernmost limit, and comprehended the plains of Curitiba, the Sertão of Lages (Santa Catarina), and the plains of Vacaria (Rio Grande do Sul). It is a narrow strip of plainland running north to south and is bordered on the east by the edge of the plateau, the Serra do Mar, and on the west by

dense forests not yet penetrated by colonization and still dominated by Indian tribes known locally under the generic name
of "Bugres."* These forests follow the course of the Paraná in a
broad strip. The area forms a characteristic geographical unit:
gentle hills, grassland interspersed with woodland patches, and
isolated forest in which the lovely and precious *Araucária* pine
predominates. It has a pleasant and temperate climate, thanks
to the altitude, which varies between 600 and 900 meters, falling slightly toward the south, where it ends perpendicularly in
the Serra Geral, and there is an abundance of water. It em-
bodies admirable conditions for human settlement, which led
St. Hilaire to describe the region as "Brazil's Paradise on
earth."

Despite these advantages, settlement of the region was still
very sparse at the beginning of the nineteenth century, even
thinner than in the backlands of the northeast, which were so
inferior from the point of view of physical conditions. The explanation is simple. In the northeast the physical difficulties inherent in the character of the land were outweighed by its position as the hinterland of the oldest and most concentrated
area of settlement in the colony, the sugarlands of the northeast. In the south the pastoral grasslands fell within the orbit of
a thinly populated littoral, situated outside the economic axis
of the colony, which was naturally oriented toward Portugal
and Europe. We are in the southernmost limit of the colony
and the period is the close of the eighteenth century. Had it
not been for the steamships that were later to bring this region
into closer contact with the centers of Brazilian life, which
focused on the Old World, the area would certainly have remained in the rearguard of the country's progress; and indeed
this was the situation during the period with which we are now
concerned. But there was a local factor that hampered devel-

---

* The term "bugre" bestowed by the Portuguese upon the Brazilian
natives in general and upon these São Paulo tribes in particular is the
English "bugger" and is explained by the belief of the Portuguese that all
Indians were addicted to sodomy. For an account of the original implica-
tions of "bugger" and its significance in Brazil, see Gilberto Freyre, *The
Masters and the Slaves*, p. 124.—Translator.

opment of the southern prairies: nature had situated these plains on top of a plateau, separated from the coast by a sheer mountain barrier. The interior was isolated from the sea except by way of the steep and difficult ascents which were the only means of passage across the mountains.

Settlement of the Campos Gerais or "General Grasslands" (the generic name for the region) was concentrated along the area's northern border: the Campos of Curitiba. Cattle grazing was combined with some agriculture; and along the forest-clad slopes of the eastern fringe, maté* was collected. These activities encouraged colonization. To the south, in the Campos of Lages, settlement becomes scattered once more; and almost the only sign of man's presence in the area is the trail that constituted the chief connection of the extreme south with the centers of Brazilian life. This was the cattle road, traversed by the droves of cattle and convoys of mules on their way from Rio Grande to Sorocaba (São Paulo), whence they were distributed to the central and northern captaincies. To the west of this trail lay the plains that were called, when they were opened up and occupied at a much later date, the Campos of Palmas and Iraí. But at this period the area was a wilderness in which dwelt only the hostile Indians who frightened off prospective settlers. In the Campos da Vacaria, located in the territory of Rio Grande, the cattle estates begin to reappear and with them a scattering of sparse and exclusively pastoral settlements.

To conclude this survey of settlement in the southern part of the colony, excluding the littoral already described in the previous chapter, we must consider the particular case of São Paulo or, to be more precise, the São Paulo plateau. Geographically this is a zone of transition between the tall chain of mountains in the center (Minas Gerais) and the grasslands of the south, which we have just described. It also forms a table-

---

* Maté is the name of the plant ("yerba maté" in Spanish) and of the infusion made from its dried leaves. It is variously known in English as maté, Paraguayan tea, South Sea tea, and yerba maté. The "tea" is widely consumed in Latin America.—Translator.

land between the central highlands and the littoral. The ascent from the coast to the central uplands is by two immense successive rises: the Serra do Mar and the Serra da Mantiqueira, São Paulo being wedged between the two. It therefore offered greater ease of penetration to the highlands. Another factor must be noted: the great rivers reverse their courses as they enter São Paulo territory and, instead of draining toward the sea, they drain toward the interior and the central depression of the South American continent formed by the basin of the Paraná–Paraguay system.

All these circumstances make São Paulo the center of a vast area, the link between different regions that here come into contact. Hence it became for man a focus of communications. The route through São Paulo was the chief outlet from the interior to the coast, and no route from the coast to the highlands offered greater ease of penetration than this one. The route from the center to the coast had been established from time immemorial by a branch of the Tupi-Guaranis (the Guaranis, to be exact), who, setting out from their original focus and dispersion center, the region between the Paraná and Paraguay rivers, had reached the coast through São Paulo. The trail followed by the Indians, and to some extent utilized by the European colonists, links the littoral through the São Paulo plateau to the Paraguay River.

Once colonization was underway, it was through São Paulo that penetration of the continent was first effected: into the central highlands (Minas Gerais), into the great internal depression of the continent (the Paraguay Basin), and into the country to the south. This early penetration of the interior, carried out initially by groups engaged in exploring and searching for Indians, was later continued by gold prospectors and finally by settlers. Historical and political contingencies were later to deflect these lines of travel into the interior from São Paulo, but the earliest trails followed were engraved on the communication network which, starting from the coast and extending to the borders of the plateau at the point where the Paulista capital was built, radiated in every direction from here into the

interior. This is clearly reflected in the population structure of
São Paulo. This is the case even in our own time but was much
more evident at the time with which we are concerned, before
the economic rise of São Paulo had complicated and confused
the original simplicity and purity of its population pattern.
Colonization of the Paulista territory developed along lines
that followed the routes of travel leading from the coast to the
interior of the continent: to Minas Gerais through the Mantiqueira gorges; to Goiás along the uplands that border the
western edge of the central Brazilian plateau; to Mato Grosso
along the valley of the Tietê, utilizing the course of this river;
and to the south, through the plains that spread as far as the
Plata.

But this very fact, which was the initial reason for the occupation of the territory that was to constitute São Paulo (during
the sixteenth and seventeenth centuries), was also the cause of
the captaincy's stagnation and decadence (during the eighteenth century). As a zone of passage, São Paulo never achieved
a life of its own in the colonial period; the small-time mining
practiced in the region during its first few centuries of colonization and the insignificant and purely local agriculture attempted made little impact. The main sources of Paulista life
were the traffic in native slaves, captured in the heart of the
Sertão and sold in the agricultural centers of the littoral; the
trade in cattle passing through on their way from the southern
grasslands to the coastal centers, especially Rio de Janeiro; and
finally, when gold was discovered in Minas Gerais, São Paulo
was for a long time the sole, or the principal, route of travel to
the mining towns.

All these forms of activity died out in the early years of the
eighteenth century. Traffic in Indian slaves had declined considerably and had already practically disappeared; the source
of Rio's cattle supply had shifted to the Campos dos Goitacases
and later to southern Minas; the route opened up by the
Paulista, Garcia Rodrigues Pais, attaching the mining centers
of Minas Gerais to Rio, had deflected transit away from São
Paulo. Goiás had also established direct links with Rio through

Minas Gerais and had therefore also escaped from the São Paulo orbit; and thus, out of all its great routes to the interior, São Paulo was left with only the Cuiabá River route along the Tietê, which kept its primacy for some time. But by the end of the eighteenth century it was already on the decline and had been almost completely abandoned. Mato Grosso had established a link with Goiás, and hence with Minas and Rio de Janeiro to reach the coast or, as an alternative, had found an outlet to the extreme north through the great affluents of the Amazon, principally the Madeira.

To these factors in the decline of São Paulo was added the drain on its population during the century of *bandeirismo* and later the losses suffered through the migration to the mines. It was only toward the end of the eighteenth century that São Paulo began to recover its strength after the debility induced by two centuries of adventure and initiated, on a more stable basis of agriculture, a period of expansion and prosperity that has lasted up to the present day. At the time we are now considering, therefore, we find this region sparsely settled and hardly exploited, but on the threshold of great advance, a tendency already fairly evident by then.

To complete this survey of Brazilian population distribution we must now turn to the extreme north, the Amazon Basin. This part of the colony has not been left to the last merely for the sake of orderliness or to facilitate exposition. The reason lies in the very nature of the geographical and historical conditions of this great valley. It was formed and remained in isolation from the rest of the country. Despite the enormous distances and the immense gaps in settlement that still remained in the rest of the country at the end of the eighteenth century, there was a certain unity, a general linkage between the various sectors. The northeast, the center, and the south were connected to each other; the links were often loose, but they were effective enough to form a whole.[15]

Amazonia, however, remained outside the system that formed the rest of the colony; its history can be told without recourse to that of the latter. It grew and evolved on its own;

even the links between the two groups of Brazilian captaincies
were still more than tenuous at the beginning of the last century. The prevailing winds and currents were unfavorable and
caused the Amazonian shipping routes to be oriented directly
toward the kingdom of Portugal, bypassing the southern part
of the colony. By land, the intricate equatorial forest that surrounded the territory of the northern captaincies was a considerable barrier to communication. The only routes of travel
were the waterways, and in fact communication was effected in
this manner. Ever then, how great were the obstacles encountered! Over a certain stretch, all the Amazon tributaries are
interrupted by falls and rapids, and passage has to be effected
overland. And what of the difficulties encountered in crossing
hundreds of miles of unhealthy forest—deserted save for the
hostile and belligerent Indians?

If, in spite of all this, the Amazon Basin came within the
sphere of Luso-Brazilian colonization and escaped the domination of Spain—to which most of its territory had been assigned
by the Treaty of Tordesillas—this is because its only practicable and easy means of access lay on the Portuguese side of the
continent. Portuguese occupation and colonization penetrated
inward from the delta and encountered the Spanish advance,
proceeding from the opposite direction after having crossed
the rugged ranges of the Andes. Hence, Portuguese possessions
in America, legally limited to a strip along the Atlantic, spread
almost as far as the Pacific, and Amazonia became Brazilian.

For the purposes of colonization, the great river and its
affluents presented a virtual prolongation of the littoral, a prolongation without the drawbacks of maritime navigation. The
volume of water was deep enough for the largest ships then in
use. There was, therefore, from this angle no obstacle to penetration. But only the margins of the river were accessible in this
way; immediately beyond them the thick forests of the interior
barred any further advance. Hence, settlement spread in linear
fashion in small clusters along the river banks. Apart from this
fixed settlement, there was another form of human occupation
in this region; it was based on the periodic expeditions that

annually traveled along the upper courses of the river in seasonal search for natural forest products. The limit of this form of occupation is marked by the fall line where the river courses leave the Brazilian plateau in the south and the Guiana massif in the north to enter the Amazonian lowlands. It was therefore also the limit of colonial expansion in the valley and roughly establishes the frontiers of the captaincies into which the valley was administratively organized: Pará and São José do Rio Negro. In the south it marked the region's frontiers with the colony's remaining captaincies and, in the northeast, its frontiers with the Spanish dominions. We were more fortunate in the north, since although we had not effected any occupation, we were allotted the territory extending as far as the watershed in the heart of the Guiana massif.[16] Politically, the frontiers were fixed by fortified posts and garrisons, which marked the extreme limit of Portuguese colonization in the valley: São José dos Marabitanas on the Rio Negro, São Joaquim on the Rio Branco.

In the vast area thus delimited, covering approximately three million square kilometers, effective occupation, even taking into account only the river banks, was scanty and, as was only to be expected, extremely irregular. Of the 95,000 inhabitants in Amazonia as a whole, approximately 60,000 were concentrated in the river delta, that is, around its contours and on the islands.[17] The rest were scattered in sparsely populated clusters. These were principally located at the great junctions of the water network that provided the sole means of transport and communication, the confluence of the Amazon with its principal tributaries or the bordering areas. Hence, at the confluence of the Tapajós we find Santarém, together with certain minor agglomerations; at that of the Madeira (and of the Maués River which joins it), we find Vila Nova da Rainha (Parintins), and a great number of small settlements and mission villages or *aldeias* of Indian converts. Finally, at the confluence of the Rio Negro are situated the principal establishments of the captaincy which took its name from this river. Indeed, Barra do Rio Negro, the capital, was located here, its name

being changed to Manaus in 1836. A little further up the
Solimões River we find, at its confluence with the Tefé, the village of Ega, the present-day town of Tefé, which had a certain
importance as the commercial center for the whole of the upper Amazon. On the edge of the Portuguese possessions, along
the Solimões, was the frontier settlement of Tabatinga.

These were the principal nuclei of Amazonian settlement
along the margins of the great river. Occupation also filtered
up the margins of its affluents. The principal of these infiltra-
tions was along the Rio Negro and its largest tributary, the
Branco, both notable for their healthfulness, which was exceptional in the whole of the Amazon valley. Along the Rio Negro,
the chief activity was the gathering of natural forest products.
But fishing had a certain commercial importance, and rudimentary agriculture had been started: cacao, some coffee, anil,
and cotton. Taking advantage of the large clearings that occur
in the forest, the government had established cattle estates
along the Rio Branco at the end of the eighteenth century.
These had already begun to supply meat for the establishments
of the Rio Negro. This region was thus the most densely settled
along the upper Amazon until rubber, almost a century later,
led to the emergence from the wilderness of the establishments
along the upper Purus and Juruá.

Currents of Settlement

Up to now we have seen what can be regarded as a cross-section of settlement in Brazilian territory, its distribution pattern at a given point of time, the turn of the eighteenth century. However, this is only a partial view, since we are not dealing with a static population; at that very moment great changes were taking place. Colonization had not yet settled down. New territories, hitherto deserted, were occupied; others, already opened up, were abandoned; populations flowed from one point to another, becoming denser in some, decreasing in others. Settlement was still far from stable, and its structural pattern at any given moment is no more than provisional, reflecting trends rather than results achieved. It is from this point of view, then, that the pattern of settlement should more profitably be analyzed.

The problem is all the more important since it is from the movements and shifts in the country's population pattern in the period we are considering that emerged the Brazil which prepared itself in the course of the last century to become what it is today. The evolution of settlement may be divided into three main phases, each having its own specific point of departure and deriving its initial impulse from particular and well-defined historical circumstances. The first phase, which began with colonization and continued until the end of the seven-

73

teenth century, represents the period of initial occupation, the
first steps taken by the Portuguese to establish themselves in
the territory of their colony. It includes, above all, the occupation of the extensive littoral from the Amazon (1616) to the
River Plate, where the colony of Sacramento was founded in
1618; the penetration of the backlands of the northeast by the
establishment of cattle estates; and the slight infiltration that
had already made its way up the Amazon. Apart from this
there was only the extremely limited occupation along the
eastern edge of the southern highlands in São Paulo and in
Paraná. I am excluding the penetration effected by the
bandeiras and *entradas,** since, although they opened up an
extensive area of the interior, they did not involve parties of
settlers and were no more than simple expeditions. They do not
directly concern the history of settlement.

The eighteenth century opened with the population revolution provoked by the discovery of gold in the center of the continent, first in Minas Gerais and immediately afterward in
Mato Grosso and Goiás. Within a few decades, settlement in
the colony had been redistributed and presented a different
pattern. The mining communities referred to in the previous
chapter were formed and in them was concentrated one of the
largest clusters of the colonial population. The first half of the
century, with the successive discoveries of new mines and the
attempts to explore and exploit them, witnessed sudden and violent shifts of population which constantly agitated and transformed the colony's population pattern. Toward the end of this
period, these shifts began to ease off and settlement became
more or less stabilized in a precarious balance. This balance
did not last very long, since the alluvial deposits and gold diggings were quickly exhausted and decadence of the mines soon
set in; at the same time various circumstances, which I shall
analyze further on, favored the development of agriculture.
The population began to drift back into agriculture, and since

---

* Expeditions which periodically went up the Amazon and its tributaries to collect forest commodities from the dense forests which lined the
river banks.—Translator.

the areas of the two forms of activity only rarely coincided, this reflux led to important currents of migration that became more pronounced in the second half of the eighteenth century. Secondary circumstances contributed to this, such as the decline of the cattle industry in the backlands of the northeast which were devastated by drought, and the growth of this industry in the extreme south of the colony. In short, a number of factors combined to provoke a new redistribution of settlement.

This redistribution was much slower than that effected in the preceding period by the discovery of the mines. It took place gradually, without any sudden shifts or upheavals, at times in an almost imperceptible fashion that was noticeable more from the results than from the process in progress. Nevertheless, by the end of the century the outline of the principal features of this redistribution could already be clearly distinguished, revealing the country's new population pattern, if not already fully established, at least well on the way to becoming so. It is at this point that we approach Brazil's history. For this reason, it is of paramount importance to analyze the internal currents of migration at work and the transformations that were gradually taking place. Without an analysis of this kind, we would have only a pale idea of the pattern of Brazilian settlement on the eve of her political emancipation.

St. Hilaire, traveling through Brazil at the beginning of the last century, remarked with characteristic insight on the extreme mobility of the Brazilian population. The dominant preoccupation with moving frontiers already existed: people often migrated for no apparent reason, simply with the vague hope of finding better prospects. Everyone imagined that there might be some place where they would be better off than they were. This was a deep-rooted and universal belief that nothing could eradicate, not even actual experience and successive failures. The mobility that so impressed the French traveler, accustomed to a continent in which settlement had been stable for centuries, is a natural feature in any semivirgin territory that has remained comparatively empty of human inhabitants, where most of the area is still unoccupied and where the most

convenient forms of human activity have not yet been discovered—in short a territory in which the individual has not
yet adjusted himself to his environment, understanding and
dominating it. In these regions, the shifts correspond to tentative trials, new attempts and experiments, and the restless
search for the best way of life. In Brazil this is particularly noticeable in the character which colonization assumed: the
ready seizing of the chance offered by a temporarily favorable
combination of events to turn these to momentary advantage,
as we shall see later on from the analysis of her economy.
Sugarcane was cultivated just as gold was extracted or, later,
cotton or coffee planted, that is, simply as the opportunity of
the moment with an eye to external and distant markets, always an unstable and precarious trade. These points shall be
considered further on. What concerns us now is to note that
colonization was not oriented toward the establishment of a
solid and organic economic base, that is, the rational and coherent exploitation of the territory's resources for the satisfaction of the material needs of the people who lived in it. Hence
the instability and its reflection in settlement, creating an even
more shifting pattern of population than is usual even in new
countries, are explained.

In this constantly shifting, often confused pattern, however,
we can distinguish a few relatively simple guidelines which
give coherence to the whole. The most important of these is the
shift from the interior to the coast, an effect of the drift back to
agriculture already noted, the coastal zone having always been
selected for this activity. I am, of course, referring only to the
past. Pernambuco and Bahia, or, rather, the agricultural coastlands of these two captaincies, which had remained at a standstill and had even become decadent in the preceding period,
recovered their strength and even recaptured their former
splendor and the preeminent position they had enjoyed in the
seventeenth century. By the early years of the last century they
had already regained, and even surpassed, the level attained a
hundred years earlier, a level which since then had steadily
declined.

Alongside these traditional centers of Brazilian agricultural wealth, new centers arose. Rio de Janeiro was chief of these. This captaincy had hitherto enjoyed the advantage of providing the chief outlet for the mining centers of the interior. In the second half of the eighteenth century its importance as a great center of production in its own right was established, particularly as a focus for production from the Campos dos Goitacases. Maranhão witnessed a similar evolution. From an almost imponderable unit in the life of the country, it gradually became one of its most important areas; and we witness the same development, to a greater or lesser extent, in all the captaincies bordering the coast.

The rapid increase of the population in these sectors of the country was to a large extent effected by immigration from abroad, but internal migration also contributed a good proportion of this increase. Aside from all other indications, this may be safely inferred from the parallel depopulation that took place in many areas of the interior.[1] Be that as it may, the shift in the economic axis of the colony from mining to agriculture, from the interior to the littoral, corresponds to a great concentration of the population in the coastal area, and this fact must be regarded as the most significant concerning the distribution of people during the period under review.

But along with this population movement, we find parallel and similar events taking place. The first of these affects the sertões of the northeast. Here we find that the long-established movement referred to in the previous chapter, the advance of the cattle estates, is still in progress. The ranches continued to spread, although at a slower rate, and we find them, in the final impulse of an age-old advance, occupying the new lands opened up in the Sertão of the Pastos Bons (the Good Pastures) in Maranhão, and reaching as far as the banks of the Tocantins in their vanguard movement.

On the other hand, in the areas long since occupied, particularly Ceará, the opposite process is taking place: a population drain reflecting the decline of the principal and almost only local activity, cattle raising, which had been hard hit by increasingly prolonged and severe droughts. The "Great Drought" of 1791–1793 had been the most recent and almost fatal blow to the backlands of the northeast in the eighteenth century. I have already mentioned that this was the main reason why the region lost its market in the agricultural sector of the northern coastlands, which turned increasingly to the consumption of *charque* from Rio Grande do Sul. In this region, therefore, we find a concurrent and parallel economic development taking place, which led to a greater concentration of people.

Other notable movements of people were taking place in the colony's central-southern region. One such dislocation is the movement out of the mining areas. Mato Grosso and Goiás are the regions chiefly affected, particularly the latter, where the movement is more noticeable by reason of the greater importance of its centers. Mato Grosso had never become a center of more than secondary importance. In the eyewitness account previously cited, Brigadier Cunha Matos gives reliable and striking information concerning the depopulation of Goiás:

The parish of Crixás once had more than forty thousand communicants; today (1824) it contains less than a thousand souls. Of the three thousand people in the *arraial* of Guarinos, today only one family is left, composed of twenty-eight souls. In the district of Pilar, there were once more than nine thousand slaves; today the entire population, which is still declining, amounts to fewer than three thousand souls, including the slaves. The mining camps of Barra, Anta, Santa Rita, Ferreiro, Ouro Fino, and others are nothing but heaps of ruins; even the capital city (Vila Boa) was once larger and more populous; the countryside is full of tumbledown shacks and houses completely abandoned and in ruins; in short, there is no doubt that the general population of the district of Goiás has declined immensely as regards the number of slaves; it makes little progress as regards the number of free men, and promises to be short-lived unless immigration comes to its aid.[2]

In Minas Gerais the situation is less serious. Here the decadence has not brought mining virtually to an end, as in the

case of Goiás. Some centers, while visibly declining, still retain
a certain vitality. And attempts are even being made, although
the number of instances of it are rare, to rework the old deposits and renew the exploitation of gold in certain districts.
Congonhas do Sabará, the present-day town of Vila Nova de
Lima, is one such instance.[3] On the other hand, this had been a
more concentrated area of settlement and, above all, had been
organized on a more solid social basis.[4] It was therefore possible to restore and replace, at least partially, the vitality lost
through the decadence of mining by finding other bases for existence, cattle grazing and agriculture. But, save in exceptional
cases, this was not possible in the principal mining centers,
where the nature of the soil was unsuited to farming activities.
And as these centers were located in the central part of the
captaincy, we find a centrifugal movement taking place in
Minas Gerais, with people moving out of the center, which had
formerly experienced a concentration of settlement, to the
periphery; the movement had even invaded the territory of
neighboring captaincies at certain points. Parts of this periphery had, as we have seen, already been occupied by small mining clusters; these revived and started a new life on a different
basis; others were still completely deserted and were now occupied for the first time. Only in the northwest of the captaincy, in the backlands of São Francisco, where a primitive
pastoral activity of the Sertanejo-type had long been established, did the renewal of the captaincy's periphery by a new
influx of settlement make no perceptible impact. Its harsh
physical conditions could provide no further accommodation
for people, and offered no opportunities for progress and the
accumulation of wealth.

We must now analyze the centrifugal movement of the
Minas population in more detail. The subject is an interesting
one; it is beyond any doubt the most important historical event
for the future of the country's central-southern region and was
already well under way at this time. The full effects of this
movement were revealed when Minas Gerais was transformed
into a definitely agricultural and pastoral region rather than a

mining area, becoming one of the country's most important stock raising and farming districts. We will now consider separately each of the sectors which received an influx of *generalistas*, as the inhabitants of the captaincy were then known, during these movements of immigration.

To the east the mining cycle had followed the basins of the Araçuaí, Jequitinhonha, and Doce rivers. In the former region, mining had established itself chiefly along the banks of the Araçuaí, since the Jequitinhonha had been closed off after the first discovery of diamonds along its upper reaches.* In this region the "New Mines" were established. In the basin of the Rio Doce, colonization in its mining phase extended as far as the river's upper affluents. From the middle of the eighteenth century small quantities of gold were mined in the Casca, Matipó, Sacramento, Santo Antônio, Grande Suaçuí, Pequeno Suaçuí, Cuité, and Manhuaçu rivers. The center for this region was situated at Peçanha, a camp on the margins of the Pequeno Suaçuí river, established in 1758, and the only establishment where settlement became fixed.

Beyond these extreme points, widely scattered and separated from each other by great distances, the area remained a wilderness, partly because there was no gold to be exploited, partly because the administration, taking advantage of this, had completely closed off the region in order to protect it from possible evasions of payment of the royal fifths and from gold smuggling † by preserving the natural barrier of dense and impenetrable forest that bordered the eastern frontier of the captaincy. In the last quarter of the century, Governor Luís da Cunha Meneses still referred to this part of Minas Gerais in the following picturesque words: "To the east lies the Sertão, known as the Forbidden Areas, the said Sertão being preserved for the purpose of serving as a natural barrier for this Cap-

---

* See C. R. Boxer, *Golden Age of Brazil*, pp. 205–255.—Translator.

† The *quinto real*, or tax of the royal fifths, was imposed on all gold mined or washed in the colony. Constant attempts were made by the colonists to evade payment of this hated tax and to smuggle gold out of the country. For the checkered history of the quinto real, see C. R. Boxer, *The Golden Age of Brazil*, pp. 191–193, 196–200.—Translator.

taincy, to secure it from fraud." [5] This was the main reason why occupation on this side advanced so little, and also because the captaincy's only direct link with the coast was the Rio de Janeiro route, the only line of travel permitted, which passed through a desert.* North of this route, which is roughly followed by the present line of roads and railways which serve to link Minas Gerais to the coast in our own time, that is, along the Paraibuna valley, the forest remained intact and was inhabited only by tribes of savage Indians. [6]

Toward the end of the eighteenth century the situation changed. Mining had almost disappeared in the extreme points of civilization referred to above. In Minas Novas, where it had been of some importance, gold mining was virtually at an end. But agriculture, particularly the cultivation of cotton, had taken over from mining. Minas Novas is one of those regions of the country that prospered from the great cotton expansion that distinguishes the economic history of the colony in the last quarter of the eighteenth century, a subject to which I shall return at greater length in a later chapter. This led to some increase in the population of the region, not on any considerable scale but nevertheless sufficient to maintain its former level and assure its normal development. A similar pattern developed in the other sectors of the captaincy's eastern frontier zone.

The new phase that had thus been initiated did not involve only the maintenance of previous positions reached. Colonization advanced into the *mata*, clearing it and gradually opening up new lands. The administration became less intolerant and even encouraged an advance which would check the aggressions of the indigenous tribes. In the district of Minas Novas this penetration availed itself of the valley of the Jequitinhonha River. In 1817 St. Hilaire visited this pioneer region and traveled as far as its extreme limit, a newly established colony on the margins of the river below the fortress of São Miguel,

---

* The desire of the Portuguese government to maintain its control of gold exports led to the selection of one port of shipment and the prohibition of shipment from any other port. Rio de Janeiro was the port selected.—Translator.

which had already almost reached the frontier of Pôrto Seguro.[7]

In the Rio Doce basin, colonization was also advancing eastward. Martius visited the region in 1818 and described it in his
diary. Occupation in this region was effected chiefly by the
establishment of mission villages for the large numbers of
catechized Indians present in the region who, once subdued,
practised a certain amount of agriculture and were used as
field-hands on the estates being gradually established.[8]

While colonization was thus opening up the eastern part of
the captaincy and occupying new regions hitherto deserted,
the first direct communication between this region and the
coast was established. The main route used was the waterway
of the Rio Doce; overland routes were opened up along the
Jequitinhonha and Mucuri rivers.

Taken as a whole, this eastward advance of colonization in
Minas Gerais, although it had only just started in the period we
are considering, is of great importance; it was here that during
the course of the nineteenth century the province's principal
agricultural zone was established. This is particularly the case
in the southern part of this pioneer area, on the borders of Rio
de Janeiro. Indeed, it was here that expansion from Minas met
and mingled with the expansion coming from Rio in the opposite direction.

We will now turn to the other direction taken by the expansion of the generalistas, the movement southward, toward the
Serra da Mantiqueira, which separates the captaincies of Rio
de Janeiro and São Paulo. In this area, which was later to form
the region known as "Southern Minas," mining had given rise
to a number of population clusters grouped around the "Mines
of Rio Verde" and the "Mines of Itajuba." But by the end of the
century it was only in Campanha, elevated to a township in
1798, that any mining activity was still being carried on. The
region had taken a different course. Agriculture and cattle raising had been successfully established here and it had become
one of the suppliers for the important nearby market of Rio de

Janeiro. In addition it had become a fairly important tobacco-
growing district, tobacco being produced chiefly in Baependi,
Airuoca, and Pouso Alto. In short, this was one of those zones
in the country that, already by the beginning of the nineteenth
century, offered better prospects. I shall have occasion to consider it at greater length in the chapter concerning the economy of the colony. For the moment I am merely pointing out
these aspects of the region's prosperity to explain the population growth that took place in this region from the last quarter
of the eighteenth century onward. This southward-flowing
current of settlement from Minas spread beyond its boundaries
and invaded São Paulo. The lengthy dispute on limits between
the two captaincies, later as provinces and even as states,
which was only resolved in 1936, dates from this period. Local
authorities followed in the wake of the settlers to effect administrative occupation of territories that were still vague and undefined. The newcomers alleged prior rights as justification for
their claims, but only "rights." This was what gave rise to the
majority of the many lawsuits concerning interstate frontiers
that have continued up to the present day.

In the case in question, it is true that the São Paulo back-
landers were the first to establish themselves in the south of
Minas, as, indeed, in the captaincy as a whole, which is the
creation of these early explorers and gold seekers. But the incursions had ceased, and the territory of Minas had become
separate from São Paulo. A few decades later the gold deposits
began to be exhausted in the mining centers, and the excess
population began to drift back to the still unoccupied marginal
zones which were more favorable to other activities. These settlers naturally did not respect administrative frontiers and their
original local authorities considered themselves entitled to accompany their shifting population, hence the conflict. The
actual conflict need not concern us here, but we are concerned
with the events that gave rise to it, unfortunately often forgotten in this dispute and thus contributing to the confusion of the
issue, which becomes the limited province of sterile disserta-

tion on obscure documents fixing theoretical limits on regions still unknown.[9]

Occupation by *Mineiros* (people of Minas Gerais) spread also to areas which, although already effectively occupied by Paulistas, still contained many empty lands. Among these we find the western slopes of the Serra da Mantiqueira and the valley of the Moji-guaçu river, where it spreads out along the strip bordering the old trail leading from São Paulo to Goiás. St. Hilaire, who traveled through the region in 1820, noted the coexistence of two types of population: the original basis, consisting principally of half-breeds and Indians, and the recent immigrants from Minas.[10] He found the original inhabitants coarse and apathetic, and uncouth in their habits; whereas the new colonists appeared to him to be more intelligent, active, polite, and hospitable. This penetration of the captaincy of São Paulo by colonists from Minas, which had recently begun, was later accelerated. People from the mining settlements are responsible for nearly all the population clusters in this region, formed in the first half of the nineteenth century: Franca, Ribeirão Prêto, São Simião, Descalvado, São João da Boa Vista, and others. Caconde, which also owes its origin to the Mineiros, was already in existence in the eighteenth century.[11]

A similar process was taking place in the western part of the captaincy. Along the western border of Minas Gerais lies a chain of mountains (Canastra, Mata da Corda, Pilões), which forms the watershed between the São Francisco to the east and the Paranaíba and Grande rivers to the west. The territory that constitutes the so-called "Triângulo Mineiro," formed as I have already noted, part of Goiás. The route leading from São Paulo to the capital of Goiás passed through this territory, and was almost the only sign of human life in it save for the presence of a few semicivilized and half-breed tribes of Indians and also a few rudiments of mining along the upper reaches of the Rio Velhas (an affluent of the Paranaíba) when, toward the end of the eighteenth century, the generalistas began to establish their cattle estates in the region. This invasion led to the formation of a number of settlements, all of them of Mineiro

origin—Desemboque (now merely a magisterial district of the
nearby city of Sacramento), Araxá, Uberaba, and others—and
was eventually responsible for the official annexation of the
Triângulo to Minas Gerais by the Royal Decree of April 4,
1816. At that time, it was inhabited by approximately four
thousand people.[12]

People from Minas were also responsible for the similar expansion that occurred in the region north of the area we have
just considered, in this case without resulting in any annexation
of territory. Here were situated the mines of Paracatu, with a
brilliant past but entirely decadent and almost extinct at the
period we are now considering. There were no more than two
or three regular gold diggings; and the only other mining activities being conducted by a number of poor *faiscadores*,* who
barely managed to earn their daily bread.[13] Of the twelve
thousand inhabitants that Pizarro had assigned to the district
of Paracatu in 1766, not more than seven thousand were left in
1816. That the depopulation had not been even greater was
due to the development of other forms of activity to replace
mining. Commercial grazing was chief among these. Paracatu
was second only to the Rio das Mortes district as the captaincy's
greatest cattle supplier; cattle were driven across the whole extent of the captaincy's territory on their way to Rio de Janeiro.
Agriculture, with the production of cotton, also figured, though
to a lesser extent, among the region's new activities.

In this way Paracatu slowly recovered from the decline provoked by the exhaustion of the gold deposits. The area was
gradually repopulated, and the migratory currents that moved
into the region overflowed the boundaries of the captaincy of
Minas Gerais and spilled into the neighboring captaincy of
Goiás. I am here excluding the territory that, unlike the Triângulo referred to above, remained within the jurisdiction of
Goiás. This territory at the beginning of the last century received a great number of colonists from Minas Gerais, and the

---

* *Faiscador*—prospector for alluvial gold; from *faisqueira*, the name
given to the alluvial gold deposits because the larger particles glittered in
the sun.—Translator.

only areas that managed to survive the profound decadence that afflicted this territory were the border areas that attracted the new wave of settlers. In these areas, the population increased, particularly so in the Santa Cruz district.[14]

In sum the centrifugal population movement from Minas Gerais, particularly eastward, southward, and westward, was openly under way during the period with which we are now concerned. The importance of this movement is all the greater because it established currents that continued throughout the nineteenth century, forming the basic trend in the evolution of the population pattern for this part of the country. The marginal zones of the province and the border areas of the neighboring territories have continued to be peopled in this way right up to the present day.

Alongside these two major changes in the distribution of peoples throughout the regions we have just considered—that is, the repopulation of the coastal strip and the redistribution of the population in the central south—other changes of some consequence were taking place in the colony. This was the case above all in the São Paulo plateau, a case of particular interest because of the role São Paulo was to play in the nineteenth century.

I have already analyzed the distribution of settlement in São Paulo and the decadence that hit the captaincy in the course of the eighteenth century. But in the last quarter of the century, the crisis in the mining adventure was over, and São Paulo began to rally. As in other regions of the colony, the decadence of the mines favored São Paulo, contrary to what had happened after their discovery, which had paradoxically led to the ruin of their principal promoters. Colonization of São Paulo territory, interrupted for half a century, progressed once more, and settlements developed. We have already seen some instances of this development, for which the generalistas were responsible. The population of São Paulo as a whole grew from 116,975 inhabitants in 1777 to 192,729 in 1805.[15] This growth was particularly evident in the captaincy's central area, between the Moji, Piracicaba and Tietê rivers, roughly forming a quadrilateral bounded by the townships of Moji-Guaçu, Jundiaí, Pôrto Feliz, and Piracicaba (the latter was still only a parish). Sugar-cane gave this region its prosperity; brought from its former production center in the highlands, Itu, the cane had been planted in the *terras roxas* (purple soils), spreading north of Campinas, and was now advancing into these lands.[16]

In the southern part of the captaincy, settlement was spread through the Campos Gerais, where cattle ranches were gradu-ally being established. This was a territory severely afflicted along its western border by the attacks of hostile Indians.[17] The movement that prompted colonization of these campos originated in São Paulo. Most of the ranches established in the region, as St. Hilaire observed, belonged to São Paulo residents who kept an overseer, or sometimes a member of the family, on the estate.[18]

The Paulista expansion also moved in the direction of the Paraíba valley. This region had been occupied since the outset of colonization and was crossed by the route to Minas Gerais. Important nuclei had sprung up along the route, such as Taubaté, where a regional smelting house had been estab-lished in the early days of the gold rush for collecting the royal fifths on the gold leaving Minas Gerais. This region, which had declined with the rest of the captaincy, also made a recovery at the end of the eighteenth century and settlement spread east-ward beyond the point previously reached by colonization, which had come to a halt at Guaratinguetá. Here there was only a little-used trail leading to Rio de Janeiro. Paulista ex-pansion invaded territories that, although unoccupied, be-longed to the captaincy of Rio de Janeiro, and the jurisdiction extended by the São Paulo administrative authorities who accompanied the movement led to the protests of the viceroy who governed Rio. This occurred when the township of Vila Nova de Lorena (the present-day town of the same name) was founded in 1788.[19]

But in spite of these protests, Paulista expansion continued, spreading well beyond this area. This expansion was to be con-solidated when São Paulo secured official possession of the

region. At the time with which we are now concerned, coffee
had begun to be planted in the area, and under the empire it
became one of the country's most important zones of coffee
production.[20]

In Rio de Janeiro settlement also spread. I am not referring
here to the littoral, which is included in my previous observation on the general shift from the interior to the coast, but to
the interior of the captaincy, to the uplands through which the
Paraíba flows before descending to the coastal lowlands. The
central sector of this part of the captaincy was the most
densely populated. The communication routes with Minas [21]
passed through here, and numerous ranches were established
along these routes, chiefly to supply the capital city, but also
for provisioning the travelers and troops moving from one captaincy to another. Some sugarcane was cultivated in the area,
for instance, in Pau-Grande and Ubá, estates visited by St.
Hilaire on his first journey to Minas in 1816.

West of the captaincy there was a stretch of sparsely populated territory, comprehended between three insignificant villages: Pati do Alferes, São João Marcos, and Resende, the latter
created in 1801. The part bordering on Minas Gerais, that is,
the territory between the Paraíba and Prêto rivers, continued
until the last quarter of the eighteenth century to be plagued
by hostile Indian tribes, who were subdued only during the
governorship of Viceroy Luís de Vasconcelos e Sousa, in 1789.
The village subsequently established in the area became
present-day Valença. From the beginning of the last century,
all these territories were actively colonized, and the region
later became one of the country's principal coffee-growing
zones.

The eastern sector was slow to develop. Gold had been exploited above the headwaters of the Macacu river from the
middle of the eighteenth century. This was an irregular and
clandestine exploitation that was only properly organized and
legalized during the governorship of Luís de Vasconcelos e
Sousa in 1786. The small settlement then formed became the
township of Cantagalo, which was elevated to this status in

1814.[22] By the end of the century mining had already been completely abandoned and replaced by agriculture. Settlement originating in the Baixada Fluminense expanded northward and later met the expansion from Minas Gerais along the margins of the Pomba River. The limits between the two provinces were to be fixed along this river.

Summing up, it may be said that the main thing to remember from the analysis of these movements of people in the colony's central-southern region during the period under review is their extreme complexity. We witness crosscurrents of settlement and resettlement, and in contrast with what happened in the rest of the country, particularly the north, colonization of this region shows a singular vitality. Virgin territories are opened up and occupied, new activities are initiated, coffee in particular began a spectacular rise which was to transform the country during the course of the current century. These are all the first signs of the profound changes that were subsequently to take place. Brazil's economic axis shifted unequivocally to this sector. Mining had made it move from the sugarlands of the north to the center of the colony's territory; it now became fixed in this center, which comprised the captaincies of Rio de Janeiro and São Paulo and the bordering region of Minas Gerais. The transformations that took place in this area's population pattern are one of the aspects of the change that was being effected in the economic structure. From all this emerged a new political balance that was to be that of the empire, particularly in its second phase.

Races

Of the three races that went into the composition of Brazil, at least two, the indigenous and the African, give rise to extremely complex ethnic problems. While the whites possessed a degree of homogeneity that may be considered, for historical purposes, complete, the same is not true of the other two races. Among the peoples that the colonizers found on their arrival, and to an even greater extent among those they brought from Africa, there existed great differences that must be taken into account. It is useless to try to simplify the problem and, as has been done especially in the case of the Negroes, to overlook the differences on the pretext that slavery rendered these peoples identical. The diversity is striking; it revealed itself in the very different reactions to colonization of the various African and indigenous peoples who contributed to the composition of the Brazilian population. The different ways in which the Indians reacted to the advance of colonization and the occupation of their territory, the extent to which the several groups were prepared to cooperate with the white colonists, to cohabit and mix with them and so contribute to the country's ethnic characteristics, are circumstances of great historical importance that derive from the ethnic characteristics peculiar to each of these groups or peoples. The same can be said of the African; I need only recall the well-known example of the especial intractability of the Bahian slaves, caused not only by the servile state in which they found themselves but also, and perhaps in greater measure, by the individual characteristics of the African peoples who contributed to this part of the colony's civil population.[1] The ethnic traits of the Negro peoples and indigenous inhabitants of Brazil, and more especially the attitudes taken by each group during the formation of the country, offer ample material for a study which has not yet been systematically attempted. The subject still provides very few elements for the explanation of general historical facts, and in the study of the racial composition of Brazil we must therefore content ourselves with an acceptance of the three races as irreducible elements, considering each in its entirety.[2]

The white component of the racial makeup of Brazil was, up to the beginning of the nineteenth century, almost entirely of Portuguese origin. In the first two centuries of colonization, Portugal's policy regarding the admission of foreigners into Brazil was a liberal one. The Portuguese criterion for selecting colonists was religious rather than national; provided the colonist was a "Christian"—although only Catholics were regarded as such—this was considered sufficient qualification, and nationality was of secondary importance. Unity of religious belief was prized above unity of blood.[3]

During the Spanish domination the situation changed. The more rigid criteria of Spanish colonial policy began to be applied and unrestricted immigration was stopped. Up to her eyes in European politics and involved in constant wars, Spain could not afford to indulge in the same liberal attitude as the Portuguese, who had always kept out of European conflicts and intrigues. The doors of Brazil were thus closed to foreigners after 1580. By way of compensation, there was an influx of Spanish immigrants, who took advantage of Spain's union with Portugal. Spaniards became particularly numerous in the south. The number of Paulistas of Spanish descent is one indication of this, and the minor attempt to revolt against the restoration of the Portuguese in São Paulo, although insignificant in regard to its consequences, is a symptom of the influence exercised in the area by a non-Portuguese spirit.[4]

The Restoration (1640) brought about a return to the old

policy. The colony was once more opened to foreigners. In the treaties that followed, permission was given for foreigners, particularly the English and Dutch—the latter after the Hague Treaty (August 4, 1661)—not only to establish themselves in Brazil, but to carry on trade in the country, subject to a few minor restrictions.⁵ But this did not last very long. After the discovery of gold in the colony a new phase of restricted immigration was initiated. The greed aroused in the mother country by the discovery of gold conditioned its policies from then on. It became narrow and was inspired solely by fiscal interests. This was evident in all branches of administration. In the aspect that concerns us here, the attitude to foreigners, this led to a progressive increase of restrictive measures, until finally all non-Portuguese were completely excluded. Brazil's doors were closed to foreigners for fear that profits would be deflected from the mother country. The sap of the colony had to be tapped to the last drop for the sole benefit of the mother country.

This policy lasted for one century, up to the period with which we are now concerned. In this lapse of time, during which there was a considerable stream of Portuguese immigration into the colony, any elements of foreign blood still left over from the past were completely submerged. On the whole, then, there is practically no non-Lusitanian participation in the Brazil of the early years of the nineteenth century, before the opening of the ports.* It is only with the Portuguese, therefore, that we need concern ourselves here.

We must distinguish two phases in the emigration from Portugal to Brazil. The first lasted until the second half of the seventeenth century, or, more precisely, until the Restoration and the end of the wars with Holland. This is a phase of limited immigration; the colony offered few attractions, and the attention of the mother country was directed mainly to her Oriental possessions. A good proportion of the stream of immigrants en-

---

* A decree providing that Brazilian ports should be opened to foreign vessels was promulgated by the Regent, Dom João, on his arrival in Brazil (Bahia) in January, 1808.—Translator.

tering Brazil in this preliminary phase was made up of deportees. The subject has been very thoroughly discussed, and there is no point in entering into any further discussion here.[6] Jews also played an important role in this phase of colonization; and even without accepting the nationalistic exaggerations of Werner Sombart, who attributes to them the sole credit for the establishment of sugar cultivation in Brazil, it may be said that they made a vital contribution to colonization.

But these influences, for good or ill—and there have been endless and futile arguments on this score—ceased to be of interest and are obliterated in the second phase of settlement, after the Dutch wars, when the current of immigration from Portugal is considerably increased. The situation in Portugal on the restoration of a national dynasty in the kingdom was deplorable. Portugal had been dragged by Spain into the senseless policy of the Hapsburgs, turned toward Europe and completely neglecting the colonial empire, which counted only for the precious metals it supplied to support the continental intrigues and wars. Portugal, who had no interest in European politics, who on the continent had at her disposal only a tiny and out-of-the-way territory, and whose existence depended above all on her colonial possessions, suffered a profound blow. Ousted from her principal colonies in the East and deprived of her fleet, Portugal entered a new phase of her history as an independent nation. Had it not been for the aid of England, who henceforth supported, if not dominated, Portugal, she would perhaps have lost the rest of her colonies and even her existence as a sovereign state.

Repercussions of the Portuguese crisis were felt in Brazil, through the increase in the immigration currents coming from the impoverished mother country. The Eastern trade, which had hitherto absorbed the best of Portugal's energies, had disappeared; these energies were now turned to Brazil, which began to receive the excess population which the impoverished kingdom was no longer able to support. Emigration to the colony increased at such a rate that restrictive measures had to be applied. As early as the seventeenth century we find that four such laws were passed after 1667 in an attempt to restrict emigration to Brazil. But nothing could arrest the movement, and with the discovery of the mines in the last decade of the century it assumed disquieting proportions. In 1732 the *Conselho Ultramarino* (Overseas Council) sounded the alarm: "If things go on in this way, the realm will be depopulated." [7] Up to the middle of the century, we find nine more legal enactments that sought to hinder emigration. [8]

As far as immigration is concerned, therefore, what we find at the beginning of the nineteenth century no longer bears any relation to what had happened in this sphere in the first two centuries of colonization. The sparse settlement of the first phase, which indeed had occupied only a limited area of the colony, is completely overwhelmed by later immigration. It is not possible to define the nature of this later immigration, nor to specify its character; the movement is general and proceeds from all provinces in the kingdom and from all social classes. Immigrants range from *fidalgos*, or aristocrats, and literati, who came mainly to take up administrative posts and in many cases stayed on in the colony with their families, to persons from the more humble walks of life. The wave of new settlers entering Brazil in the eighteenth century can, however, be characterized from the data we possess concerning the lot that awaited them on reaching the country, particularly the functions they were to fulfill. This subject, to which I shall have occasion to return in a later chapter, is of interest here because it gives us an indication of the geographical and social distribution of the white element in the Brazilian population. What we know in this respect is that when a newcomer did not take up an administrative post or go into a liberal profession, or when he lacked funds to set himself up as a proprietor or estate-owner, he generally turned to some form of commercial occupation. There was, indeed, no alternative, since the economic and social conditions of the colony offered no other option. The Marquis of Lavradio, in his report on handing over the vice-regency to his successor in 1779, observed that the newcomers, even those who had been simple peasants in the realm, thought of nothing but commerce.[9]

This preference by the Portuguese immigrant resulted in the concentration of the white element in the urban centers, particularly in the most important of these. This was noted by all the foreign travelers who visited Brazil at the beginning of the last century; the proportion of whites, small in the rural areas, was in the cities in direct ratio to the importance of the agglomeration.

But in addition to this spontaneous immigration, the colony also received an officially sponsored immigration, although fewer settlers were involved. I have already referred to this type of immigration and its objective, which was to people strategic territories which were thinly inhabited, as was particularly the case in Santa Catarina and Rio Grande do Sul and to a much lesser extent in Pará. This type of immigration has individual characteristics that clearly distinguish it from colonization as a whole. It was made up of family groups (hence the name given to this type of colonization, "Colonization by Married Couples"). It was destined solely for agriculture, and all sorts of precautions were taken to ensure the successful establishment and progress of the settlers. The lands to be occupied were chosen before their arrival and laid out in small allotments, sundry supplies and provisions were furnished by the crown free of charge or on a long-term credit basis, and so forth. In short, the plan was similar to those later elaborated and carried out until recently for the establishment of so-called colonial nuclei by the federal and state governments.

Colonists of this type were recruited mainly in the Azores, always a demographic breeding ground which struggled with a population surplus that the limited territory of the islands could not support. Some of this surplus was used to colonize important points in the colony which spontaneous immigration had not hitherto managed to settle in sufficiently large numbers. The first Azoreans arrived in Pará in 1673,[10] and this type of colonization was carried on more or less continuously thereafter. In 1679 a similar scheme was carried out for the mass transfer to Pará of the Portuguese inhabitants of the north African fortress of Mazagão, which had been yielded to the Moors in that year. This settlement in Pará gave rise to the town which took the name of the fortress the settlers had abandoned.[11] At about the same time a similar plan for the establishment of a colony of Swiss emigrants was attempted, which failed.[12]

In the south this type of colonization by Azoreans played a vital role and created the chief basis for the settlement of Santa Catarina (or rather what was then known as Santa Catarina, that is, simply the coastal fringe) and Rio Grande do Sul. Until the onset of colonization of these two captaincies by Azoreans in the mid-eighteenth century, they had harbored a scanty population made up almost entirely of the garrisons established in defense of the colony's frontiers. In 1747, Feliciano Oldenberg was awarded the contract for transporting four thousand peasant families across the Atlantic and establishing them on the island of Santa Catarina.[13]

It was the beginning of an immigration current of this type which for half a century, up to the time with which we are now concerned, reinforced the population of the southern captaincies. In this way, the nucleus of white population formed in the region was proportionately larger than that in any other part of the colony; moreover, this was a rural rather than an exclusively urban population, made up of small farmers, which on any appreciable scale was a unique situation in nineteenth-century Brazil.

The Indian problem was the most complex that colonization had to face. It became such—and this is what distinguishes it from the North American case, so often cited as a parallel to our own—because of the objective in view: to make use of the native in the work of colonization. In what is now the United States, as well as in Canada, the situation was quite different. There it was never the intention to include the Indian on any pretext whatever in the colonizing endeavor of the white man; the attempts to use native labor were never more than tentative experiments, soon abandoned, and, apart from the trade in furs which the natives supplied in exchange for European goods, the colonists made no use of them. Or rather, they did play a part: as allies of one or other party in the struggles which the French and the English kept up between themselves for two centuries in the northern colonies of America. This factor explains the concern for winning the sympathy of the native, the initial friendliness and the methods which both the French and the English laid hold of in their dealings with the Indian. These methods came to attract the attention of the Portuguese administration, which, ignoring the differences in the situation, recommended them as an example for its representatives in Brazil.[14] But relations between colonists and Indians in the North American colonies never went beyond a simple alliance between peoples; there was absolutely no question of incorporating the indigenous population into colonization. So much so that later, when the French had been eliminated from the scene and the English, or their North American successors, had been left in sole possession of the field, the Indian problem was simply reduced to that of their expulsion from the territories needed for the expansion of colonization.[15]

The case of Portuguese colonization was quite different. In Brazil from the very beginning an attempt was made to make full use of the Indians not only as suppliers of native products for trading or as allies, but also as a *participating* element in colonization. In the Indian the colonist saw a *worker* who could be employed to advantage; and the mother country saw a *settler* who could be used to help occupy the immense territory that it had undertaken to settle and that was far beyond its own demographic capacity. A third factor was to come into play and serve to complicate the issue, the religious missions.

The missions (and particularly those of the Jesuits, which, both because of the importance they were to assume and because of the awareness and tenacity of purpose displayed by them in their struggle to achieve their aims, occupy a salient position in this whole issue) did not intervene simply as instruments of colonization, seeking to open up and prepare the

way for settlement in the heart of the native population. They
had aims of their own—whether to propagate the faith and to
further the interests of the Church or those of their own respective orders need not concern us here. But these aims, at
least in the methods shown by the priests, whether forced on
them by circumstances or not, often deviated from and even
opposed the aims of lay colonization. We will not inquire into
the motives that inspired the Society of Jesus to adopt these
modes of action. Such an inquiry would divert us from the central issue and would above all involve us in argument which
would be out of place here. But the fact remains that, in the
activities they promoted among the Indians, in the educational
regime to which the latter were submitted, the Jesuits often
acted in manifest opposition not only to the immediate and
particular interests of the colonists (and there is no room for
argument on this point), but also in opposition to those of the
mother country and her colonial policy. As a nation committed
to colonizing a vast territory for which she lacked the population resources, Portugal could and did aim only at one thing: to
make full use of all available elements; and to attain this end
the Indian element could not be despised. It was thus a question of incorporating the Indian in the Luso-Brazilian community, of leading him out of the jungle and making him an integral part of colonial life, a *colonist,* like any other. This aim
of Portuguese colonization in Brazil—and there could have
been no other—stands out very clearly in the course of colonial
history. More or less accentuated by the laws and other official
enactments, promulgated over three centuries of evolution,
occasionally revealed in terms of resolute and persistent action,
but more often lapsing into hesitancies and uncertainties by
reason of the powerful interests at stake, the Portuguese policy
toward the Indian was nevertheless always directed to this
end.

The activities of the Society of Jesus, seen as a whole and not
simply from the point of view of particular acts, obviously ran
counter to these aims. The regime adopted in the *reduções* (the
name given to the native agglomerations under the superin-

tendence of the priests), and their system of organization, were clearly not the methods indicated for transforming the Indians into active, integrated elements of the colonial order. The segregation in which they lived in the Jesuit mission villages—the missionaries went so far as to keep their charges in ignorance of Portuguese in order to prevent them from making any contact with the white colonists—the almost military discipline to which they were subjected and which turned them into virtual automata impelled by the irresistible and, what is more serious, irreplaceable voices of their masters and leaders, a training which led to their becoming so integrated into the life and routine of the reduções that, outside them, they became incapable of profiting from the elements of civilization they had been taught: all this was hardly calculated to form members of a colonial community, but rather to create encapsulated groups within that community, viscerally dependent on their organizers. If this system was not always fully put into effect by the Jesuits, it was because they were not given enough time and freedom of movement. But where these factors did operate in their favor, the results they achieved were flagrant, as in Amazonia and even more clearly in the famous Uruguay missions. And these are merely instances of their conduct in Brazil, for the problem was similar in the rest of the Americas, and we could cite, among others, the missions of California, Orinoco, the Moxos and Chiquitos missions of Bolivia, and those of Paraguay.

Without entering into discussion here as to whether achievement of their aims would have been more favorable to the Indians—even admitting for the sake of argument that their achievements might perhaps have been superior, morally and materially, to those of Luso-Spanish colonization, or that they might have achieved better results in the sphere of human civilization and culture than the Ibero-American communities that emerged from this colonization—without going so far, the fact remains that, in the more restricted and modest field with which we are here concerned, the work of the Jesuits in its ultimate and essential aims did not contribute to *Portuguese*

colonization in Brazil, or to *Spanish* colonization in the other
colonies. In fact the success of their enterprise would certainly
have resulted in an organization, nation, civilization—or whatever other name one chooses to apply—very different from that
which Portugal or Spain were seeking to achieve, and did in
fact achieve, in their colonial possessions. This explains the
conflict, the inevitable clash, culminating in a series of incidents which need not concern us here, but which had one important consequence that must be borne in mind: the emergence of the native problem as a vital issue, involving endless
and passionate argument and open struggle. Thus it very early
became difficult, if not impossible, to find a satisfactory solution to the problem. Against the colonists' summary enslavement and brutal exploitation of the Indian, the Jesuits opposed
their system of segregation and isolation. And in the struggle
that flared up around these two irreconcilable extremes, both
opposed to the general and higher aims of colonization, extremes increasingly upheld by excesses practiced as a natural
consequence of the passions unleashed, there was no room for
any in-between solution that might possibly have settled the
problem.

The mother country, dragged into the struggle unfolding before her eyes, also proved herself unable to stand aloof from
the quarrel and to take an independent line of action. It became involved in the opposed extremes and oscillated from one
to the other, unable to detach itself altogether from either extreme and to carry on resolutely with the fundamental aims of
its own true policy, of which it had, if not full knowledge, at
least an intuitive grasp that does credit to the common sense of
the Portuguese: a common sense that came to their aid and, in
the general bungling that characterized the Portuguese administration in Brazil on more than one occasion, saved them from
even greater and more fatal disasters.

The struggle continued for two centuries. At last the belated
moment arrived when Portugal was finally prepared to face the
situation and, once disentangled from the conflicting parties, to
impose its own policy, putting the general interests of coloniza-

tion in Brazil before the opposing private interests at stake. This was the achievement of the Marquis of Pombal.*

Pombal's legislation on the Indians is a synthesis of the opposing tendencies referred to above. It accepted the Jesuit thesis of their freedom, of the need to educate and prepare them for civilized life, and of regarding them not merely as instruments of toil in the avid and brutal hands of the colonists, whose activities had already led to the extermination of a good part of the indigenous population. It even adopted the main lines of Jesuit organization—the concentration of the Indians in communities under the superintendence of an administrator entrusted with the care of their education and their interests —and provided for certain measures to be taken to protect the Indians from the colonists. But on the other hand, it did not separate them from the colonial community, and not only imposed the use of Portuguese and permitted the Indians to be used as paid workers (the colonists' thesis), but also allowed and even encouraged the greatest possible interchange between the two categories of the population. It was hoped that in this way the Indian would be prepared for civilized life. These measures were supplemented by others designed to increase the number of mixed marriages. It was a solution through miscegenation, a solution that had, in fact, always come first even without the aid of the law as a way of coping with the great and complex problem of blending the three ethnic strains that went into the composition of the Brazilian people.

The suspension of the priests' temporal power over the Indians, the great apple of discord that was to be one of the mediate causes of the Jesuits' expulsion, was simply a corollary of these measures. It was impossible to maintain this power without compromising the end in view. This would have meant not

---

* Pombal (1699–1782) was born Sebastião José de Carvalho e Mello. After the Lisbon earthquake of November 1, 1755, he became Dom José's most important counsellor and was the author of many sweeping reforms. He was Minister from 1750 to 1777. After Dom José's death, he was dismissed from office and almost impeached.—Translator.

the resolution and harmonizing of the age-old conflict between priest and colonist, but its solution in favor of one of the parties. The least a sovereign power such as the Portuguese crown could demand was to extend its sovereignty over all its subjects in the normal way. The Indians were included among these subjects, or, at any rate, this was the aim envisaged, and the authority and prestige of the priests was a solid wall behind which the royal power was reduced to nought. There was, therefore, no alternative but to demolish this wall. It was impossible to assimilate the priests—above all when they were members of an organization with a semblance of political sovereignty, as in the case of the Jesuits—and treat them as simple administrators who were subject to the royal power. Their functions should not and could not go beyond those exercised in their proper role as priests. Experience had demonstrated that the concession of temporal power to the priests was tantamount to giving them sovereign political power.[16]

The Pombaline legislation put an end to a dispute that had dragged on from the outset of colonization, and it finally regulated the native problem. Its practical results can be variously interpreted, and have been; but I do not propose here to enter into more detailed discussion of the subject, which would call for special treatment. The fact is that, with all its faults and in spite of some lamentable consequences, this legislation paved the way for the solution of the Indian problem, laying the basis for the absorption of the bulk of the indigenous population by colonization within the framework of existing possibilities which, given the ethnic and psychological characteristics of the Indians, were naturally somewhat limited. Enslavement of the Indian disappeared after the promulgation of these laws, although it reappeared in a mitigated form—the effect of years of freedom—at the beginning of the nineteenth century, when the *Dirétorio* of 1757 was repealed (royal charter of May 12, 1798), and when, after the law of 1808 and the later laws to which I shall have occasion to refer, the colonists reverted to the old system of conducting offensive wars against the Indians and enslaving the prisoners captured. The Pombaline laws also put a stop to the *resgates,* or official expeditions into the interior, for ransoming or "delivering" Indians held as prisoners by rival tribes, the barbarous system of *descimentos.** These expeditions were also started up again at the beginning of the nineteenth century, particularly in Amazonia. The growth of the African slave trade, which was encouraged after the Pombaline laws, particularly in the captaincies where Indians had hitherto been the chief source of manpower (Pará and Maranhão), made the colonists less dependent on the supply of Indian labor. The Indians were thus left in comparative peace.[17]

Nevertheless, the Indian's lot under the new regime was still not an easy one. Despite all the measures designed to place them on an equal footing with the other colonists, they remained a "bastard race"; and as such, they were victims of the neglect and oppression of the dominant race. The protection afforded by law, in the persons of their village directors appointed to look after their interests and to guide them, was often ineffective due to the inept and even unscrupulous manner in which these functions were performed. Largely responsible for this—and this was perhaps the greatest failure of the system adopted by the *Dirétorio*—was the method chosen for remunerating the administrators of the Indian villages; it was laid down that they should receive one-sixth of the total output of the village, and the amount should be deducted from this total. This meant that the officials concerned stood to gain directly from the amount of work done by the Indians in their charge; and thus, the method led them to regard their charges not as beings to be guided and cared for, which was the original intention, but as a source of revenue to be exploited.

From the point of view of the material progress of Indians gathered in villages, comparisons have been drawn between the situation that existed before the abolition of the priests' temporal power and the situation that arose afterward. In fact a few decades after this measure, conditions had deteriorated

---

* *Descimento*—literally, "descent," or the bringing to the coast of Indians captured inland.—Translator.

considerably. Most of the villages were openly decadent, very few had made any progress. But to draw any conclusions from this fact, we must consider other aspects of the question. Let us take the case of Amazonia, the case most often cited because we have more or less reliable comparative figures for the area and also because it is the most significant in this respect. In the other captaincies the number of Indians gathered together in villages was relatively small. It so happens that, during the course of the second half of the eighteenth century, various events took place in the region which had nothing to do with the Pombaline laws and which largely contributed to the decadence of the Indian villages. Chief among these was the activity of the commissions appointed to establish the limits of the colony, which worked in the area for many years as a result of the treaties of 1750 and 1777.* Personnel for these demarcation commissions was recruited in the villages, which consequently lost much of their population. In this period, too, large public works were undertaken (fortifications, the residential palace for the Governor of Pará, a military hospital, the building of new towns for the Portuguese colonists transferred from Mazagão, large-scale lumber production for the Royal Arsenal of Lisbon, and so on), and the inmates of the villages provided the labor for these works. To these events must be added the ravages of the smallpox epidemics. River expeditions to Mato Grosso regularly organized during this period also absorbed a large number of village Indians, who were employed as rowers and guides. It is small wonder, then, that the population of the villages decreased.[18]

Another factor was that, since the prohibition of the *resgates* and forced *descimentos,* the villages ceased to receive reinforcements of Indians brought down from the interior. In 1787, writing on the causes of the decadence of Pará, Alexandre Rodrigues Ferreira, who had been officially appointed to investigate the situation, does not mention the possible adverse

---

* Treaty of Madrid (1750) and Treaty of San Ildefonso (1777) both confirming Portugal's extensive territorial gains in Amazonia and demarcating Brazil's new frontiers.—Translator.

effect produced by the abolition of the priests' temporal power. He has nothing to say on the subject, and from his long and minute report, nothing can be inferred.[19] It must be pointed out, however, that Pombal had died in ostracism five years earlier, and that there was a marked reaction against his policies during the reign of the fanatical successor of Dom José, Maria the First.

There is no doubt that the priests, particularly the members of the Society of Jesus, had a capacity for organization and guidance infinitely superior to that of their lay successors. In this case, as in all others, the Portuguese administration was painfully inefficient. But the priests used this capacity to serve their own ends—whether these were good or bad need not concern us here—and not those of colonization, whose aims I shall likewise make no attempt to justify. If lay administration was inefficient in this respect, it was equally inefficient in others. There was no reason to make an exception in the case of the civilization of the Indians on the pretext that ecclesiastical administration had been superior, which would place this branch of public administration in a special position, creating a situation which would in fact have been highly dangerous to the sovereign rights of the crown.

With all its defects, it remains true that the Pombaline legislation made a substantial contribution to the essential aims it had in view and that these aims represented the fundamental interests of colonization, that is, the incorporation of the Indian in the general mass of the population. That this did in fact occur, at least with the Indians already settled in villages—the Pombaline laws take no account of the savages—is proved by developments in Pará and Maranhão, where there were a good many such villages, representing most of the colony's Indian converts.[20] With a population made up mostly of Indians and an extremely small number of white colonists, prominent among them the missionaries, who were the true directors of colonization in the region, these captaincies preserved certain peculiar characteristics up to the time of the Pombaline laws, which not only clearly and profoundly differentiated them from the rest of the colony but also isolated them from it. It was virtually a different country, and the difference became ever more pronounced. Save in the more important centers and within an insignificant radius, the official administration had almost no active voice. When in need of manpower, the few colonists almost always had to ask the priests to supply it; and they obtained the required labor, although not always, only under certain conditions and with many safeguards. The Indians, which is to say almost the entire population of the captaincy, were segregated from the colonists and lived under the exclusive jurisdiction of the missions.

It is obvious that developments in these captaincies were totally unrelated to those in the rest of the country. There were certain clear indications of the differentiation that was taking place in this region. It was apparent, for instance, in the language used: except in official reports and among the small circle of the white colonists, Portuguese was not spoken and was hardly known. The universal language was Tupi. Without the provisions of the Pombaline laws, is it likely that this area of Brazil would have been integrated in the body of the colony? It seems much more probable that it would have evolved in a completely different direction, and would never have become part of the country.

This is what the Pombaline legislation prevented. As a result of this legislation, and the more intimate contacts established between the native mass and the white element, the former was gradually incorporated in the general population and mingled with this general population in spite of the painful crises that arose in the process. We cannot attribute this exclusively to the measures decreed by Pombal, but we must give them their due for the part they played in the absorption of the Indian element into the colony and later into the Brazilian nation.

However, more than any law or system of civilization, miscegenation contributed to the assimilation of the native population that inhabited the Brazilian territory before the arrival of the white man, or, at any rate, the absorption of a not inconsiderable proportion of this population; and likewise, more than any official decree, the physiological impulses of a race with sexual instincts as highly developed as those of the Portuguese contributed to this end, as in the parallel and analogous case of the Negro. The sexual license that always characterized colonial Brazil, observed and deplored in all the accounts that have come down to us, whether written by officials, missionaries, and chroniclers or simply by the occasional local observers or foreign travelers who visited her, at least made one positive contribution to the formation of the Brazilian nation: it was thanks to this loose living that it proved possible to fuse races so profoundly different, both in their ethnic characteristics and in the relative positions they occupied in the social organization of the colony.

Miscegenation, the sign under which the Brazilian nation was born, and undoubtedly its most notable and profound characteristic, was the real solution provided by Portuguese colonization to the native problem. But, leaving this aspect aside for a moment, in conjunction with the analogous case of the Negro, let us turn to the question of the native problem presenting itself at the beginning of the nineteenth century. The Pombaline legislation was, as I have said, rescinded in 1798 (royal decree, May 12). This placed the Indians on an equal footing in all respects with the other subjects of the crown by abolishing the tutelage of the village directors. But although this decree recommended that the authorities keep a watchful eye on the Indians, particularly on their relations with the whites in order to prevent any abuses by the latter, it imposed on the Indians the obligation to work—on condition that they were paid, it is true—for the crown officials or the colonists. They were to be assigned to colonists or officials according to need and at the discretion of the government, when they were found to be "unemployed." The decision as to whether they were in fact employed or otherwise naturally rested with the authorities; the law made no provisions in this respect.

This allocation of the Indians to certain types of work, an

obvious form of disguised slavery, was what the law termed "fining" * the Indians. The term is typical, and I use it here because it is no longer current and in order to indicate the idea of submission involved, which I want to stress. The new laws likewise allowed the *descimentos* to be resumed, ostensibly on the grounds that they were engaged in peacefully "persuading" the Indians to return with them to the vicinity of the white settlements, and permitted the utilization of the Indians so brought down.

Under cover of this license, despite the precautions with which the laws sought to hedge it about, the raids on the Indian villages were resumed. In the captaincy of Rio Negro, where these forays were given the picturesque name of *amarrações* †—doubtless an allusion to the methods employed for rounding up the Indians—the natives so secured were even allowed to be put up for sale.[21] Thus practices which had been abolished for half a century were revived. The main reason for this return to the past is to be found in the colony's economic development and the prospects opened up in the last years of the eighteenth century; in a later chapter I shall analyze the situation, which had an aggravating effect on the manpower problem, the labor force in the northern captaincies being still almost wholly made up of Indian hands. As I have pointed out, the Pombaline laws did not provide effective measures for attracting new native contingents to colonization. On the contrary, it forbade hostile raids and descimentos. At the same time, the expulsion of the Jesuits and the decadence of the other orders brought missionary work almost to a standstill.

There was still a further consequence of the passivity to which the colonists were reduced by law, prohibited as they were from pursuing untamed Indians to their jungle fastnesses. This was a renewed outbreak of attacks by hostile Indians, countered only by a passive defense. This hostility was particu-

---

* The Portuguese is *apenar,* and involves the idea of meting out punishment.—Translator.

† *Amarrações*—from *amarrar,* to bind up or tie together; incidentally, also a tangled-up love affair!—Translator.

larly marked in the second half of the eighteenth century, when the tribes that had taken refuge in the forests covering the border country between the captaincies of Minas Gerais, Pôrto Seguro, and Espírito Santo; particularly the Aimorés (referred to in a previous chapter) launched successive attacks.

All these factors determined the new policy toward the Indians. The reaction grew even more pronounced after the transfer of the Court to Rio de Janeiro. The royal decree of May 13, 1808, declaring offensive war against the Botocudos (Aimorés), permitted the capture of Indians and their unpaid employment in the private service of those in command of the operations. The royal decree of December 2 of the same year extended these provisions and permitted the distribution of Indians among the estate owners, to whom all those over twenty years of age were to be bound for twelve years, and those below that age for twenty years. Similar provisions were written into the royal decrees of November 5, 1808, and April 1, 1809, applicable to the Indians of the Curitiba and Guarapuava campos.

In certain parts of the colony traffic in Indian slaves was organized between the different captaincies. Captain Francisco de Paula Ribeiro, in his account of a tour of inspection to Maranhão in 1815, mentions cases of this nature which he witnessed: Indians captured in Maranhão who were put up for sale in Pará. Things even reached the pitch where Indian captives were branded, thus reducing them to the same level as the African slaves.[22] This revival of barbarous practices against the Indians—particularly in Pará where, as we have seen, the Indians were a principal source of labor and Negroes were rare—contributed much to the agitations and insurrections that devastated the captaincy in the twenty years following independence, known as "cabanagem." *

But apart from the extreme north where there were special

---

* This is the popular designation of the seditious movement which broke out in Pará in 1835. The word probably derives from *cabana,* or cabin, and is analogous to "guerilla" warfare.—Translator.

reasons for its intensity, the anti-Indian reaction of the early
nineteenth century did not produce any more profound effect,
except as a preliminary to the extinction of the more or less
hostile groups of tribes still left in Brazilian territory. The
process of extermination continued throughout the nineteenth
century and has not yet ceased even in our own time. In other
respects the native problem had really been resolved. For good
or ill, whatever one's opinion, the fact is that the problem had
ceased to be a weighty issue in the life of the colony, or at least
in the greater part of it. What remained of the country's original race of inhabitants, with the exception of the jungle tribes,
had mingled with and been absorbed by the rest of the population or otherwise survived in small nuclei whose numbers were
visibly dwindling. They had in fact been incorporated in colonization, and there was no longer any question, except in the extreme north, of exploiting them wholesale as a source of labor
for the whites. Most of the interest in them, therefore, disappeared. Economic progress had permitted the widespread use
of Negro slaves, who provided a more efficient and more easily
secured labor force.

We will start our survey of the geographical distribution
pattern of the Indians and those of their blood at the beginning
of the nineteenth century with the tribes who continued to remain outside colonization and refused, sometimes with weapons in their hands, to be subdued. Most of these were still to be
found in Amazonia, where colonization had hardly penetrated
the interior and was confined to the margins of the great rivers.
The rest of the interior was occupied by savage tribes whose
relations with the colonists varied from open hostility to more
or less cordial contacts, including some interchange of trade. In
exchange for European goods, the Indians supplied natural
products gathered in the forests: cacao, sarsaparilla, and the
other items that make up the bulk of Amazonian production.
They also supplied captives taken in the intertribal wars.
Martius relates that, when he visited the Miranhas along the
upper Japurá, their *tuxaua* (chief) organized an expedition
against enemy tribes and brought back a number of prisoners

because he thought this to be the true purpose of the German naturalist's visit.[23] What he knew of the whites had led him to believe that the visitor could have no other objective.

Bordering and prolonging the Amazon region, and stretching eastward and southward into the territory of the neighboring captaincies, is another region of thick forest which had also not been penetrated by colonization and was still inhabited by primitive Indians who had had no contact with civilized life. The following areas are comprised in this extension of the Amazon region: the northern part of Mato Grosso, as far as the captaincy's mining establishments, which formed the nuclei of Cuiabá and Vila Bela (described in a previous chapter); Goiás, comprising the whole left bank of the Tocantins, and its right bank as far as the northernmost centers of the northern *comarca* (Natividade and São José do Duro are among the principal centers); and the whole of the eastern part of the captaincy of Maranhão, west of the Itapecuru, with the exception of the coastal fringe.

On the borders of the area dominated by the Indians they came into hostile contact with the colonists. This hostility was less active in Mato Grosso, where the mountains bordering the northern edge of the plateau formed a natural barrier between the contenders; but it was more intensive in Goiás, where the colonial nuclei of the northern comarca continued to be targets for periodic incursions by hostile and bellicose tribes, as indeed they had been from the very outset of white settlement.[24] The same applies to Maranhão, where the Indians ranged as far as the flourishing establishments of the Itapecuru river in their raids, Caxias being continually attacked at the beginning of the nineteenth century.[25]

In contrast to this frontier zone, dominated by tribes of savage Indians, the region immediately to the southeast comprising the northeastern Sertão had for a long time been free of their presence. In this open and more accessible region, where colonization had penetrated deeply, the tribes which had not sought refuge in other areas had been eliminated or absorbed by colonization. The only savages left were the remnants of

tribes that had led a nomadic existence in the Pernambucan
backlands between the Moxoto stream and the border zone between Ceará and Paraíba. It would seem that these were ancient tribes who had been catechized in the seventeenth century, but who had subsequently returned to the jungle and
reverted to their savage state. In the first years of the eighteenth century, on the initiative of Dom José Joaquim de
Azevedo Coutinho, Bishop and provisional Governor of
Pernambuco, these Indians were once more converted by the
Italian Franciscan friar, Vital de Frescarolo, and settled in villages in Jacaré and Ôlho Dágua da Gameleira in the vicinity of
the São Francisco.[26]

Stretching from Bahia southward, close to the coast, we find
another continuous area of territories still under the sovereign
sway of savage Indians. I have already referred to these territories in passing. They comprehend the dense forests extending
from the right bank of the Paraguaçu in an unbroken line
southward and covering the slopes and tops of the mountains
that border the littoral from this point to the captaincy of São
Paulo (where the mountain range is the Serra do Mar). These
forests, which afforded a natural protection, served from the
outset of colonization as a refuge for tribes who refused to submit to the white man who dominated the littoral and later,
from the beginning of the eighteenth century, the central territories west of the forests: the mining centers of Minas Gerais.

These tribes therefore remained, up to the beginning of the
nineteenth century, insulated and cut off from civilization, between the establishments of the interior on one side and those
of the coast on the other. Only very gradually did white colonization begin to close the circle around the forests which offered
such a barrier to penetration, not only on account of the
natural difficulties encountered but also by reason of the hostility of the savage tribes who lurked in them.[27] Except for the
settlements that sprang up along the routes to Minas Gerais, it
was only in the second half of the eighteenth century that
penetration of the forest began in earnest; in the east through
the currents of settlement that entered from the coast, and in

the west through the ranches established along the Doce and Jequitinhonha basins. These two movements have already been described in a previous chapter. But up to the end of the century, with the exception of its southernmost extreme—the part occupied by the captaincy of Rio de Janeiro [28]—this forest region continued to be almost completely the absolute domain of the Indians, whose sway extended from the Rio de Contas to south of the Rio Doce.

I have already referred to the warlike nature of these tribes, who launched periodic attacks against the establishments of Pôrto Seguro and Espírito Santo; they also turned their attention in the opposite direction and attacked the mining centers located along the basin of the upper Doce. It was only at the beginning of the nineteenth century that general and systematic action against these Indians was undertaken. In Minas Gerais, Governor Pedro Maria Xavier de Ataíde e Melo (1803) set up military detachments in the five presidios he had constructed for the purpose; Belém, Casca, Guanhães, Peçanha, and the headquarters near the source of the Plata.[29] The royal decree of May 3, 1808 regularized and completed these measures by declaring offensive war against the Botocudos and dividing the infested area in Minas into six military districts.[30] In Espírito Santo, particularly with a view to facilitating navigation of the Rio Doce and establishing communication with Minas Gerais via this waterway, Governor Antônio Pires da Silva Pontes set up military posts at Lorena, the port of Sousa, and Regência Augusta on the bar of the Doce, all intended to keep the savages under control.[31]

Measures for pacifying and civilizing the Indians of Bahia also date from this period. The Camacãs, who occupied the territory between the Contas and Pardo rivers, were subdued by Captain João Gonçalves da Costa in 1806, at the point where he founded the township of Conquista to commemorate his feat. Alongside these violent measures, missionary work was carried on by the Italian Franciscan friar, Ludovico de Liorne, with the approval and support of Baltasar da Silva Lisboa, the *ouvidor* or crown judge of the judicial district of

Ilhéus, who was also a well-known naturalist and chronicler of the *Anais do Rio de Janeiro*.[32]

The third large continuous area of territories inhabited by savage Indians occupies the basin of the Paraná river, extending eastward as far as the Paraguay river and southward as far as the Uruguay. The only part of this southern stretch of the colony effectively occupied by colonization was, as we have seen, the narrow strip bordering the eastern edge of the plateau. In the captaincy of São Paulo, the western limit of settlement was marked by the trail leading to Goiás along the route now followed by the Mojiana railway line; to the south, another trail leading from Sorocaba to the southern grasslands prolonged this limit. Beyond this limit of settlement, with the exception of the few outposts that still formed only occasional isolated nuclei, such as Araquara and Botucatu, the territories occupied by the Indians spread westward, although not in a continuous sweep, into the southern part of Mato Grosso as far as the Paraguay River and the riverside border establishments founded by the Spaniards. Only one line of travel cut through these territories from east to west; this was the river route linking São Paulo to Cuiabá by way of the Tietê, the Paraná and its counteraffluents, and the tributaries of the Paraguay.

Most of the native peoples inhabiting this area lived without making any contact with civilization and harassed the settlers whenever they could. Hence, navigation of the rivers comprising the waterway referred to above was undertaken only in heavily armed convoys. The tribes occupying the Campos de Guarapuava [33] presented a like peril, and devastated the establishments that had begun to form east of the Sorocaba trail at the beginning of the nineteenth century. With a view to protecting these establishments and encouraging colonization of this virtually unpenetrated and unoccupied region, the royal decree of April 1, 1809, ordered the organization of a military expedition that gave rise to the colony of Guarapuava, which grew into the present-day town of that name. The new colony was, at first, a combination of military outpost and mission village.[34]

This sums up the distribution of the savage Indians left in Brazil at the beginning of the last century. Another part of the indigenous population was made up of the so-called "tame" Indians. Pure-blooded or with some admixture of white or Negro blood, these Indians were distributed throughout the colony. The essential features of this geographical distribution will be given below in conjunction with the other races. Part of this domesticated indigenous population had already mingled completely with the mass of the population and lived among the other races and their mestizo derivatives in the same urban centers or rural areas. Another part of this population, racially purer and possibly more numerous, was grouped together in settlements where it formed the majority of the inhabitants. These settlements were former mission villages or those established by the civil authorities (although the latter were few in number) organized into villages (*lugares*), or elevated to townships when they reached certain proportions, by the law promulgated on June 6, 1755. Many of Brazil's northern towns owe their origin to such settlements, as do a few in the south. White colonists gradually settled in these villages after they had been opened up by the Pombaline legislation abolishing the segregation in which they had existed under the authority of the priests.

This fairly numerous Indian contingent [35] can be considered as definitely incorporated in the bulk of the colony's population. This was the most important result of Pombal's laws. The members of this group participated in colonial life, and although they suffered from the uncertainties of their bastardized race and the difficulties of adapting to an alien way of life, they were gradually integrated into the colonial order. This was largely due to miscegenation, which no longer encountered the taboos imposed by the priests.

In addition to the racial intermixture which diluted his blood, the Indian was gradually eliminated as the result of other causes. Great numbers of them died of introduced diseases, particularly smallpox and venereal diseases. There were virtual holocausts among Indian populations not yet resistant to these diseases. They were also decimated by the vices which civilization introduced, chronic alcoholism exacting the heaviest toll. *Aguardente* or the "fiery spirits" of sugarcane brandy had proved the most effective stimulus to make the Indians work, and the colonists took full advantage of its effects.[36] The maltreatment they received at the hands of the colonists, and an alien way of life, all contributed to their extinction. The net result was that the indigenous population that came into contact with the whites was progressively eliminated, repeating once more the pattern that has emerged wherever and whenever races at very different stages of cultural development come into contact: the less developed and dominated race disappears. And had it not been for the miscegenation widely practiced in Brazil, which allowed the indigenous blood to be perpetuated, the Indian strain would have been fatally condemned to total extinction.

The case of the Negro is a simpler one for the historian. The Negro element in the racial composition of Brazil owes its presence purely and simply to the institution of slavery. Whereas the enslavement of Indians was restricted by legislation, there were no such scruples where the African was concerned and enslavement of the Negro was never questioned. It was in the capacity of slave, and in this capacity alone, that Negroes entered Brazil and contributed to the formation of its population. Their relations with the whites presented no problems; in the two and a half centuries that had elapsed between the introduction of the first Africans and the period we are considering, the situation was always the same.

The Negro contribution to the composition of the population was considerable, certainly much greater than that of the Indian. Even before the massive importation of slaves that took place during the nineteenth century, the number of Africans who had already been brought into the country was not less than five or six million [37] and other factors increased the contribution of this initial stock, assuring the perpetuation of a higher proportion of Negro blood. The Negroes' greater resistance to European diseases is one such factor, another is their more intimate contact with the whites, which led to an increase in the mestizo population. There were, however, two circumstances which militated against the perpetuation of Negro blood. In the first place, there was a smaller proportion of women, since the traffic brought in many more men who were, of course, more suited to the principal end in view. The colony never quite managed to attain the perfection of the North Americans who "bred" slaves in order to sell them, and therefore a lower value was set on female slaves in Brazil. In the second place, prejudice against unions with Negroes—legal unions, that is—was much greater than in the case of the Indian. This second factor was not, however, particularly important since in both the Indian and the Negro cases most instances of cross-breeding occurred outside the bonds of matrimony.

Taking all relevant factors into account, the fact is that the Negro element already showed a clear tendency to overtake increasingly the indigenous element. This was already the situation at the beginning of the last century, but the trend was afterward to become even more pronounced. The Indians, even the pure-blooded or quasi-pure-blooded breeds, were still numerous; and we are still in the period immediately preceding the massive importation of Africans that marked the first half of the nineteenth century and lasted until the final abolition of the slave trade in 1850.

The extent of Negro participation in the Brazilian population at the period now being considered is manifest in the magnitude of the figures involved. According to the most reliable figures available for the first years of the nineteenth century, Negro slaves made up one-third of the total population. And what proportion did they contribute to the remaining two-thirds? It is difficult, if not impossible, to give an exact estimate. The number of pure Negroes in the free population must have been very small, since manumission of African slaves seems to have been a rare occurrence. But a considerable proportion of the population of all classes seems already to have had some admixture of Negro blood.

In fact, this is already the most notable feature of Brazil's ethnic formation: the widespread miscegenation that was carried on between the three racial components in this formation. These components were separated in the above analysis for greater ease in tracing the individual evolution of each. But the races should be considered in conjunction, mixing freely and mingling on an unprecedented scale in an orgy of unbridled sexuality that was to make the Brazilian population one of the most varied ethnic mixtures that humanity has ever known.

The population had not yet, however, become quite so mixed at the time we are considering. The three shaping races still continued, in different proportions but in a regular and effective manner, to make contributions to the composition of the population through infusions of pure and fresh blood: the whites through immigration, the blacks through the traffic in slaves, and the Indians through the continuous incorporation of individuals and sometimes of entire tribes who yielded in a body to colonization. Thus, alongside the majority, which was already composed of mixed-bloods, there were smaller but still numerous minority groups composed of pure-blooded elements: the blacks, numerically preponderant to an overwhelming degree, the whites, and the Indians, the last two probably balancing each other in numerical terms. But Brazil had already become a great melting pot of races, and intermixture was proceeding apace; nothing was more unstable or precarious than the survival of these pure elements.

Miscegenation, the sign under which Brazilian ethnogeny was formed, was the result of the exceptional capacity of the Portuguese for breeding with other races. It is to this aptitude that Brazil owes its unity and its very existence, with all the characteristics that have become Brazilian. It was thanks to this quality that the relatively small number of white colonists who came to people the territory were able to absorb the considerable masses of Indians who already inhabited the territory, or the Negroes who were later brought in, and to impose their standards and culture on the colony, so that later, although separated from the mother country, the colony continued to preserve the essential characteristics of the mother country's civilization.

This Portuguese aptitude for miscegenation must have gained much from the centuries of contact between the inhabitants of the Portuguese homeland and peoples of a darker complexion. The Iberian peninsula had been from time immemorial a passageway between Europe and Africa, and it thus became the point of contact between the white races of Europe and the other races whose center of gravity was located in Africa.[38] The Moorish invasion, which kept Lusitanian territory under Arab rule for centuries; the colonial expansion of the fifteenth century, which extended Portuguese contact with the Moors and enabled them to establish contact with the Negro peoples of Africa—all these factors helped to encourage the flexibility of the Portuguese in the presence of exotic races.

It is probable that this predisposition helped to prepare the Portuguese for the new horizons of racial contact that opened up in America. Nevertheless, a much more important factor for the miscegenation carried on in Brazil was the form taken by Portuguese immigration to the colony. As a rule, Portuguese colonists emigrated without their womenfolk. Emigration to Brazil, particularly during the more active phase of colonization which coincided with the lure of the mines, was regarded as an adventure that led men to come alone—as is generally the rule in situations of this nature—hence the lack of white women. Even when the colonists wanted to bring out their families, they generally waited until they had established themselves in the new country on some sort of solid basis before sending for their families, whom they could then offer a measure of security. Faced with the uncertainty of the unknown, the colonists always came, to start with, alone.[39]

The lack of white women was always a problem in European colonization of overseas territories, even those where colonization proceeded along more regular and less adventurous lines than in our own case. In what is now the United States of America, as a result of special circumstances that did not exist in Brazil, large numbers of immigrants came in family groups;

and this was, even at certain times and in certain areas, the general rule. The colonists also relied on the levies of women recruited in England from among orphans and girls without dowries, and even from among criminals and prostitutes who came to the New World colonies by the shipload in answer to the appeal sent out by the colonists. The French in Canada and Louisiana acted in the same way, and more recently, their example was followed in the colonization of Australia and New Zealand.

This provision was lacking in Brazil.[40] Hence, the colonists found themselves without white women. This, together with the ease with which they could cohabit with women of other races, whose social position was inferior and who were therefore submissive, strongly encouraged and even obliged the colonists to seek satisfaction for their sexual needs among these women. Indeed, particularly in the case of India, the ease with which the native women succumbed and the indifference and passivity with which they submitted to the sexual embraces of the white man, is well known. The characteristic impetuosity of the Portuguese, and the total absence of any moral inhibitions, complete the picture: mixed unions became the rule. And although these unions were generally irregular, being effected outside the bonds of matrimony—there was strong prejudice against legal unions with black or Amerindian women, particularly against the former—they became so frequent that they came to be regarded as falling within the category of perfectly acceptable situations and were freely approved by the prevailing moral code. Nor were the illegitimate offspring of these unions handicapped by their irregular origin. I shall have occasion to return to this topic in the section dealing with the colony's social life.

Small wonder, then, that miscegenation assumed the proportions it did in Brazil. It is useless to try and find statistical evidence; even when figures are available, which is the exception, they are by nature completely inadequate and are not worth taking into account. If this is still the case today, how much more so must it have been when prejudice was more rigid and ingrained? The commonplace that "a drop of white blood makes a Brazilian white," whereas "a drop of Negro blood makes an American black" has an element of truth. The ethnic classification of individuals in Brazil is based much more on social status than on racial characteristics and, among the upper classes at least, a man's race is the consequence of his social position rather than of his somatic traits. Koster's anecdote concerning this situation is well known: When he called the attention of one of his mulatto servants to the more than suspect dusky complexion of a certain captain-major,* he was offered the remarkable explanation that: "He used to be a mulatto, but he isn't one any more." And when the Englishman expressed his astonishment at this reply, the servant added: "But, Master, you surely didn't expect a captain-major to be a mulatto?" [41]

It was due to this form of tacit convention that color prejudice—a prejudice paradoxically strong in this country of widespread miscegenation—was reconciled with the ethnically indisputable fact that even the highest officers in the colony had a dash of Negro or Indian blood in their veins.

In the absence of reliable figures, we can nevertheless make a number of general observations that by and large reflect the true position. Of the three possible racial combinations—White-Negro, White-Indian, Negro-Indian—the first was the most frequent. I have already noted that this was due partly to the numerical preponderance of the Negroes and partly to their greater resistance to disease and their more intimate contact with the whites. The third variant, the *cafuzo,* was comparatively rare. This is not difficult to explain. Brazilian miscegenation is first and foremost a result of the sexual problem of the dominant race, and the white colonist is therefore its principal practitioner. In a set-up where, of the three races that came into contact, one is the dominating race and the other two are dominated, it is only natural that things should be arranged to suit the former, in the economic and social spheres to start with and consequently in the sexual sphere as well.

* The Portuguese rank is *capitão-mor*, that is, the captain in charge of a division.—Translator.

Nowhere in the colony, either in the geographical distribution of the races or in the social positions they occupied, was there any common ground upon which the two dominated races could make any intimate and lasting contact. The Negro was relegated to the *senzala* (slave quarters) or was in the domestic service of the whites; the Indian came into contact with colonization almost solely as a worker or to satisfy the white colonist in some other respect; the Negro was concentrated in the economically more prosperous regions from which the Indian was excluded. The net result was that there was very little interbreeding between them, despite the strong attraction, which has often been noted, that the Indian woman felt for the Negro.

Miscegenation between whites and blacks displays a certain characteristic that leads to the formulation of what may be regarded as a fairly general rule. This is the fact that, although spread throughout the population, miscegenation becomes much less frequent as we move up the social scale. At the bottom of the scale, we find the Negro slave and the Indian on a very similar social footing despite the laws favoring the Indian; and as we move upward along the scale, we find a progressive lightening of skin color until among the upper class the white complexion is almost universal. Nevertheless, among the upper layers of the population there was no lack of mixed blood, despite all the precautions taken to disguise this fact and, as Martius observed, although racial purity was much vaunted, "it was difficult for the impartial judgment of a foreigner to accept the claim." [42] The only really pure white component was made up almost exclusively of recent Portuguese immigrants who had not yet had time to mix with the native-born colonials. Among the latter very few indeed could be considered strictly pure, a fact which, particularly among the upper classes, had no social significance since the dash of colored blood was sufficiently small and the social position occupied sufficiently important to make them forget or ignore their origins. They were, to all intents and purposes, pure white, like Koster's captain-major.

This correlation between color and social status made of "whiteness" and racial purity an ideal that performed an important function in Brazil's ethnic evolution; alongside the circumstances already pointed out above, this ideal played a great role in the orientation of interbreeding by reinforcing the preponderant position and prestige of the white man as procreator. Sexual selection thus operated in favor of "whiteness." A symptom of this state of affairs is the widespread preoccupation with "cleaning up or purifying the blood," which was the way then in vogue of alluding to this emphasis on the white strain. Martius relates that many European adventurers were leading the leisurely and carefree lives of well-to-do citizens in Brazil because they had married into families who were seeking to "purify their blood." Even one of his own servants had been approached for this purpose in the backlands of Piauí.[43] Koster makes the same observations and relates similar incidents.[44] Later, Hercules Florence, who wrote an account of the Langsdorff expedition, noted the same tendency in Mato Grosso.[45]

Here we may resume our survey of racial distribution in Brazil at the beginning of the last century. This was as follows: a background of mestizos who made up the bulk of the population, whose "color" varied with the social position occupied and in which the white-black mixture or mulatto was predominant. Against this background are ranged the racially pure groups of the three elements, who received continual reinforcements from the influx of new contingents. The new contingents were small in the case of the Indians, who therefore formed a rapidly dwindling group; but in the case of the Negroes the contingents were made up of large numbers, particularly from the period with which we are concerned onward. The stream of white settlers increased in volume after the opening of the ports in 1808, when immigrants from countries other than Portugal began to enter the country. But right up to the abolition of the slave trade in 1850, the number of white newcomers was always far less than that of the Negroes. The gap was partly compensated for by the higher rate of increase of the whites, whose conditions were more regular from the point of view of family organization, with a proportionately higher number of women among the immigrants.

The new contingents, white, black or Amerindian, did not, however, succeed in basically altering the predominant ethnic pattern. They merely altered the proportions, the tendency being toward an increase in the Negro element, which received the largest contingent of newcomers. The pure elements simply tended to be rapidly eliminated through interbreeding. Similarly, the new contingents did not alter the correlation between color and social position which was the other essential characteristic of Brazil's ethnic pattern. This was because the newcomers were distributed socially according to the existing social situation. Negroes and Indians joined the lower strata, whites moved into the upper layers, if not always on arrival (when they arrived without resources) at least later, when they had succeeded in establishing themselves. There was a general upward mobility of status for the whites, a mobility that did not apply in the case of the Negro or the Indian.

In this way, the ethnic distribution of Brazilian society we have seen above was continually reinforced. Only much later, and in certain restricted areas, did large numbers of white immigrants begin to enter the lower strata of society and to remain there. But this situation arose only well after the period with which we are now concerned.

What we have hitherto described is the situation for Brazil taken as a whole. But regional variations were considerable. We can nevertheless combine these variations into certain basic features. Negroes and mulattoes predominated in regions of intense economic activity, present or past. The reason for this is obvious. The Negro entered the colony as a slave or worker; he went, therefore, wherever manpower was needed and where the highest prices could be paid for this manpower. Thus, the most numerous concentrations of Negroes are found in the large agricultural centers of the coast: in Maranhão, in the far northeast, in the Recôncavo district of Bahia, and in Rio de Janeiro. For the same reason, they are likewise found in

large numbers in the mining centers of the interior: Minas
Gerais, Goiás, and Mato Grosso. The Negro element predominated in all these regions. They can, however, be distinguished
by certain individual characteristics. In the centers where
prosperity had been longest experienced, Bahia, Pernambuco,
and Rio de Janeiro (although in the latter to a lesser degree),
there had been a more widespread diffusion of Negro blood
and hence the tendency for the disappearance of pure whites
and even quasi-whites. Nevertheless, although strictly speaking
this was true only in the larger urban centers, the opposite
tendency operated at the same time. This was due to the
greater influx of white immigrants to these centers. Rio de
Janeiro (the capital), Recife, and Salvador were the cities most
affected by this current of white immigration, and even so,
there were noticeable differences between Rio and the other
two cities, Rio being more favored by the white newcomers,
particularly after the opening of the ports. Martius noted this
difference.[46]

In contrast with these two centers, Maranhão, where prosperity was very recent—dating only from the second half of
the eighteenth century—intermixture of white and Negro elements had clearly not proceeded at the same rate. The blacks
were blacker, the whites whiter.[47] In Maranhão, the Indians
and their mixed-blood derivatives were also plentiful. The
Negro laborer was a newcomer to Maranhão, and up to the
eighteenth century Indians had been the chief source of labor.
They therefore continued to make up an appreciable percentage of the population at the period with which we are now
concerned.

The mining centers also possess individual characteristics. In
the more decadent centers, particularly in Goiás and Mato
Grosso, pure whites had virtually disappeared, not only because the stream of white settlers had dried up but also because
even those who had already established themselves in these
centers were gradually abandoning these impoverished regions.[48] The same situation arose in the mining centers of
Minas Gerais, where, except in the more important centers,

there were no longer any pure whites. St. Hilaire repeatedly comments on this.

In the far north, comprehending the captaincies of Pará and its subordinate, São José do Rio Negro, the Indian strain still predominated; the pure-blooded Indians (Tapuyas) were still very numerous, as were the cross-breeds derived from miscegenation with the whites, the curiboca and the mameluco, the names given to the first and second mixed generations respectively. Negroes were rare, because the low economic standards of the north precluded the acquisition of Negro slaves by settlers generally too poor to pay the high prices demanded. Another factor contributing to the rarity of the Negro element was the fact that the greater part of the region's economic activity was of an extractive nature. For this, the Amerindians, who were completely adapted to the region's conditions, were well suited. They were also far better rowers than the Negroes, another function of considerable local importance.

The other regions where Indian blood predominated were generally those where economic life was not very active or where colonization had not yet taken a firm hold. In such regions, the Indians remained in a fairly pure state. They were generally the remnant of former mission villages. This was particularly the case in Ceará, Rio Grande do Norte (excluding Paraíba), the southern coast of Bahia (district of Ilhéus and captaincy of Pôrto Seguro), and Espírito Santo.

A similar situation, although with certain differences, developed in the backlands of the northeast. In this region the Amerindian was also the predominant strain. Of the many tribes who had inhabited the sertãoes before the advent of the white man (the Cariris being the most numerous and most important of these tribes), a good many had been completely wiped out. Some had sought refuge in Maranhão and Amazonia, where the forest offered greater protection than the *caatinga,* or scrub forest, of their original habitat. The remnant was subdued and settled in villages and gradually interbred with the other races. In this region miscegenation between Indians and Negroes seems to have taken place on a wider scale. The Sertão had always been a refuge for Negroes and mestizos from the littoral: fugitives from a justice that weighed more heavily on these two categories of the population than on the others or men hard pressed by the unfavorable conditions of the more active and regimented life of the coastal centers. The Sertão offered them freedom, a chance to escape from constricting and overburdening authority. In the Sertão it was the law of the survival of the fittest and most able that prevailed and not the law of a privileged class. It represented, therefore, an escape valve for all who were unable or unwilling to adapt themselves to the organized existence of the colony's more populous centers. And the greatest number of malcontents was naturally to be found among those who were forced to bear the brunt of this organization, those who were branded by the color of their skin, stigma of an oppressed and bastard race, the Negroes and their duskier offspring. In the Sertão, they could mingle with the indigenous population on the equal footing imposed by the physical conditions of the environment, and they interbred with the natives on a wide scale, giving rise to the Sertanejo type, with all its singular psychological and ethnic characteristics, so distinct from those of any other type. The dose of white blood contributed to this complex is so negligible as to be almost nonexistent.

In the São Paulo region there was also a large contingent of persons of Amerindian stock. Pure-blooded Indians, however, were very few. The captaincy's mission villages, once so populous, were by the end of the eighteenth century almost deserted,[49] and the captaincy's formerly numerous indigenous population had either disappeared or been dispersed throughout the centers occupied by the white settlers, interbreeding with them on a wide scale. Before the period of rapid economic development that characterizes the history of São Paulo in the nineteenth century, causing an influx of large numbers of Negro slaves and bringing in considerable contingents of European immigrants, it can be said that ethnically the captaincy's population consisted of white-Indian half-breeds, the proportions of white and Indian blood varying from almost pure Indian in the lower classes to almost pure white in the upper layers of the population.

In the south, in Santa Catarina and Rio Grande do Sul, the situation was completely different. Miscegenation was not widespread and the majority of the population consisted of pure whites. This was due to the system by which settlement of the region had been effected, a system which was based on the emigration of family groups from the Azores, thus assuring the maintenance of a racial purity that conditions in the other captaincies had rendered difficult to preserve. On the other hand, the low economic level of the southern captaincies at the period we are considering prevented the influx of Negroes on any scale. Indians were not very numerous, either in the littoral or in the interior where, although still present, they kept away from civilization and buried themselves in the western forests from which they put up a determined resistance to the advance of colonization.

In Rio Grande the indigenous population who had been catechized and converted by the Jesuits had settled in their famous *reduções* of the "Seven Peoples," * and remained in a semicivilized and racially pure state under the authority of the priests up to 1767, when the Jesuits were expelled from the Spanish dominions. The Seven Peoples then came under civil administration and their territory was conquered by the Luso-Brazilians and included in the Portuguese dominions in 1801. At that time, of the Seven Peoples only twenty-one or twenty-two thousand were left.[50] Many had become nomads as a result of the wars and frequent changes of authority that had taken place since 1750 and roved the interior of the captaincy. They were used as cattlemen for the cattle stations that had begun to spread through the region during the last quarter of the eighteenth century and as soldiers in the external and internal wars that characterized the political history of Rio Grande in the last century.[51] Azoreans and their descendants

* A group of mission stations situated near the left bank of the Rio Uruguay.—Translator.

predominated in the coastal zone. Negroes began to arrive only after the *charque* establishments, set up at the end of the eighteen century, gained impetus at the beginning of the nineteenth and began to develop. Negroes were brought in to supply manpower for these establishments.

PART TWO—MATERIAL LIFE

Economy   In the chapter in which I attempted to point out the meaning of Brazilian colonization, it was pointed out that this "meaning" is to be found in the desire to establish a plantation colony that would supply highly valuable tropical or mineral commodities, such as sugar, cotton, and gold, for the European market. We will consider them all in detail further on. The colony's economy was entirely subordinate to this end and was to be organized and to function solely for the production and export of these commodities. Anything else—which did not really amount to very much—was to be subsidiary and destined only to support and make possible the attainment of this essential end. Thus the first thing to consider is the way in which the production of the commodities that provided the basis of the colony's wealth and activities was organized.

In agriculture the basic element was to be the large one-crop plantation worked by slaves. This type of agrarian organization, which arose from large-scale agricultural exploitation as distinct from the small-scale peasant type of exploitation, did not result from an arbitrary choice of one alternative selected from among the others that presented themselves to colonization. In order to appreciate fully the depth to which the roots of this type of organization penetrated, it is of the utmost importance to inquire into the causes that determined its choice. By choosing this solution for the organization of the colony's

133

economy, Portuguese colonization was to proceed along lines strictly determined by the circumstances of its development and to experience the inevitable contingencies that arose from the combination of internal and external events that accompanied all that colonization accomplished in Brazil. The regime of large-scale agrarian exploitation—the sugar plantation (*engenho*) and large estate (*fazenda*)—was a natural and necessary consequence of this combination of circumstances. It was determined by all the factors that had contributed to the initial occupation and exploitation of the territory that was to become Brazil: the tropical nature of the land, the objectives that inspired the colonists, and the general conditions of the new economic order which had come into being as a result of the great maritime discoveries and in which temperate Europe was to figure as the center of a vast system extending to the tropics in order to bring back the commodities so badly needed by this center, commodities that only the tropics could supply. In the final analysis, these were the factors that determined the agrarian structure of colonial Brazil. The three characteristics —the large estate, the one-crop system, and slavery—are forms which combine with and complement one another and derive directly from these factors as their necessary consequence. Indeed, this is not specific to Brazil, but is common to all the colonies where these factors have occurred.

In Part One we saw the type of European colonist who came to the tropics and stayed on. He was not the worker or the simple settler, but the entrepreneur seeking a profitable business undertaking. He came originally to command, and if he was obliged to turn toward the land it was only the large-scale enterprise, the exploitation of a commercial crop on a large estate in which he could figure as the master, that held any interest for him. Hence we see that from the very beginning large areas of land were conceded to the colonists in Brazil. Except in the case of the Azorean colonization scheme for Santa Catarina and Rio Grande do Sul (and this was only as late as the eighteenth century) and in a few other instances which represented only a negligible fraction of the total, the *sesmarias*—the term applied to the land grants—extended over huge areas of land. None of these colonists who had emigrated to better themselves and had no intention of leading the humble life of a small peasant-proprietor in Brazil would have accepted anything less. The mother country's policy in this respect was inspired by courtiers or individuals close to the throne—we know that many of the colonists, particularly those in the early levies, were *fidalgos* (noblemen) or of aristocratic origin—and since they constituted the contingent most readily available to the crown for carrying out the tasks of colonization, they naturally influenced the shaping of this policy which from the outset was clearly and deliberately oriented toward the establishment in the colony of an agrarian latifundiary regime. Save for the exceptional and belated instance of the Azorean immigration cited above, it never occurred to the crown, as it likewise was not to occur to any of the *donatários* or lords-proprietor who at one time shared its sovereign powers, to even attempt some other regime, such as a system of landholding based on the small peasant-proprietor.*

This orientation may have been influenced by Portugal's previous experience in colonizing the tropics and the knowledge she had gained of the processes to be adopted in tropical lands. But whether this experience did indeed have some effect or whether some other motive prompted her policy, the fact remains that the colony's natural conditions lent themselves to the policy adopted. As we have now learned from the long experience of the history of the tropics, this was bound to happen. The large estate, worked by dependent laborers, whether slaves or paid workers or else some intermediate form of labor, is a system of agrarian organization that has always come to predominate in the tropics even when other systems have been initially attempted. The difficulties presented by the physical environment for any effective exploitation by isolated individuals, particularly in lands which have not yet been cleared,

---

* The *donatários* were the proprietary landlords appointed to settle and defend the captaincies into which the coastal belt of Brazil had been divided in the 1530's.—Translator.

combined with the technical demands of tropical exploitation (the equipment needed and the organization of activities), have led to the predominance of the large-estate system.

The English North American colonies, because of the juxtaposition of different zones within them and the variety of experiments tried out, as well as the fact that they all had the same national origin, provide a striking example of this norm. In the English-settled temperate colonies (New England, New York, Pennsylvania, New Jersey, and Delaware), the small peasant-type system of landholding was established; and although we sometimes find the large estate, as in New York, it is generally subdivided into lots to be leased out on a sharecropping basis. In any case, small-scale exploitation (the small holding that could be tilled by a man and his family or, at the most, with the help of a few hired hands), was the system established.

South of Delaware Bay, however, in the hot and humid coastal plains where the physical environment is already subtropical in nature, we find that the system established is that of the large estate worked by slaves, the Southern plantation. In the same latitude, but further inland, in the high valleys of the Appalachian range where the altitude corrects the excesses of the climate, colonization by small landowners reappears. The influence of the physical factor on the distinction between the two agrarian systems is so pronounced that it eventually prevails even when the initial and deliberate aims of the founders of the agrarian colony are quite different. Thus, in Carolina and Georgia, where we find ourselves in a distinctly subtropical zone, the original intention of the colonial planners (in this case, as in most of the English-settled colonies, these were companies or individual concessionaires) was to establish a regime of small holding, each colonist to have no more land than he could properly cultivate; and colonization was initially organized along these lines, with land grants distributed according to this criterion. But this aim was frustrated, and the original plan failed; it was soon replaced by the usual type of organization found in tropical colonies.[1]

A similar development took place on the island of Barbados. Here the first type of organization established was the evenly divided estate, and slave labor was not employed on any appreciable scale. But shortly afterward, sugarcane, an eminently tropical crop, was introduced into the island: the estates began to merge and soon they had become immense plantations, the number of slaves rising from less than 6,000 in 1643 to more than 50,000 twenty-three years later.[2]

Monoculture is a necessary accompaniment of the big tropical estate; the two things are correlative and derive from the same causes. The sole aim of tropical agriculture is the production of certain commercially valuable, and hence highly lucrative, commodities.[3] It was established with no other end in view; and had there been no opportunity for speculative profit, it would never have been attempted or would soon have been abandoned. It was therefore inevitable that all efforts should be channeled into this production, particularly since the system of the large estate worked by inferior manpower, as is generally the rule in the tropics, cannot be used for diversified farming calling for a high level of technical knowledge.

With the large estate and the one-crop system came the establishment of slave labor in Brazil. This was not only because Portugal did not have enough people to provide her colony with the manpower needed, but also because the Portuguese, like all the other European colonists, had not emigrated to the tropics, in principle at least, simply to take on a job as paid fieldhands. Slavery, therefore, became a necessity; the problem and the solution found for it proved to be identical in all the tropical and even subtropical colonies of America. In the English colonies of this type in North America, where other forms of labor had been initially tried, including a form of semienslavement of white workers, the "indentured servant" system, it was not long before Negro slaves replaced white workers. In fact, it was this demand for labor in the tropical colonies of the Americas that led to a rebirth of slavery in Western civilization, an institution which had been on the de-

cline since the end of the Roman Empire and had already
become almost completely extinct by the end of the sixteenth
century when colonization of the tropics began.

At first the colonists employed the natives. Where there was
a sufficient density of population and where the natives were
accustomed to stable and sedentary work, as in Mexico and the
Andean highlands, the native slave, or semislave, made up the
bulk of the labor force. In Brazil, the native element was
scarcer and above all was not suited to the system of organized
work which colonial agriculture called for. The Indian was
employed for want of any better solution, particularly in regions
where the economic level was lower and the colonists could not
afford the high prices paid for African slaves. But whenever
possible, he was replaced by Africans, and as we have seen, we
find the Negro slave in all large-scale agricultural enterprises
and in mining. By the end of the colonial era approximately
one-third of the colony's population consisted of Negro slaves.

The three elements constituting the agrarian organization of
colonial Brazil were thus complete: the large estate, monoculture, and slave labor. These three elements combined to form a
distinctive system: the large-scale rural enterprise, that is, a
large number of individuals brought together to form *a single
unit of production,* which became the basic cell of the Brazilian agrarian economy, as it was likewise to become the principal base on which the whole economic and social structure of
the country was founded. It should be noted at this point, although this is probably implicit in what has already been said,
that the system we are dealing with here did not involve simply the ownership of the estate, which could at the same time
be associated with exploitation on a shareholding basis—an
exploitation which would then be carried out through the various forms of renting and leasing parts of the estate—as is the
case to greater or lesser extent in all the European countries. It
involved ownership of the large estate plus large-scale exploitation of the estate, which not only is not the same thing but also
creates all kinds of consequences of a completely different
order.

Mutatis mutandis mining, which after the eighteenth century was together with agriculture among the colony's principal activities, adopted an organization which, apart from the technical distinctions involved, was identical to that of agriculture. The same general factors, combined perhaps with the influence of the general character which the Brazilian economy had already assumed when mining began, contributed to this type of organization. It was thus exploitation on a large scale that prevailed: large units worked by slaves. The activities of the *faiscadores,* or itinerant prospectors, corresponded in mining to the work of the individual independent smallholder in agriculture. These activities reached considerable proportions in Brazil and were the result of the decadence of the economic and social system of the mines. They were a symptom of the decline and gradual breakup of the mining economy and were never the result of an organic and stable form of mining. Itinerant prospecting was thus the transition toward complete decadence.

The third sector of the Brazilian economy's principal activities was the *extractive sector.* Extractive activity was concentrated almost exclusively in the Amazon valley. This sector of the economy was organized along completely different lines since it was not based on ownership of land. Collection of cacao, sarsaparilla, edible nuts, and other forest produce was not fixed to a limited area owned exclusively by the individuals concerned; the gatherers were free to wander where they pleased in the forest, which provided enough for all and was considered common property. Besides, extraction was not a permanent activity, each undertaking being organized periodically during the due seasons for collecting the various forest products and dissolved at the end of each season. In short, it was a primitive and rudimentary form of exploitation, a sketchy effort at economic organization which was not superseded until the end of the colonial era. But apart from this, the extractive sector was not distinguished from the other sectors of colonial activity in its system of labor organization and its economic structure. As in the other sectors, we find here the entrepreneur who, although not a landowning proprietor like the planter and miner, was nevertheless still the organizer and exploiter of a làrge labor force who worked for him and under his orders.

Besides these fundamental activities—fundamental because they represent the base on which colonial life was founded and even constitute the very reason for its existence—we could add others, such as cattle raising, certain types of agricultural production, and in short all the activities which were not directly concerned with production for a foreign market, unlike the three fundamental activities specified above. But these activities cannot be placed on the same plane, since they belong to another and secondary category; they were all subsidiary activities, destined to support and make possible the attainment of a purely commercial end. They had no independent life of their own but were simply an accompaniment to, and entirely dependent on the central activities. In other words, they do not characterize the Brazilian colonial economy but are mere accessories of that economy. We shall, therefore, disregard them for the time being.

I shall not attempt to stress here any points that will subsequently be clarified by the text. I shall merely attempt to indicate the fundamental and characteristic elements of the colony's economic organization. As we have seen from the foregoing account, in all sectors whether agricultural, mining, or extractive, organization was based on the large unit of production. In the extractive sector, this unit was not fixed in time or in space; it was set up separately for each collecting expedition and dissolved at the end of it. Nevertheless—and this is the important point—it was still a large productive unit insofar as it brought together a relatively large number of workers under the orders and on the behalf of a single entrepreneur. It is this fact that we should chiefly consider, since it is in this system of organizing labor and property that lies the origin of the extreme concentration of wealth that characterizes the colonial economy. The fact that thirty percent of the population was made up of slaves, and that an unknown but surely high percentage was made up of individuals who possessed no worldly goods whatsoever and vegetated in obscure poverty with the lowest type of material living standards, is both the immediate consequence and sure symptom of this concentration of wealth which was a result of the country's economic organization.[4]

These in sum are the basic characteristics of the Brazilian economy: on the one hand, this organization of production and labor and the concentration of wealth which resulted from this organization; on the other, its orientation, which was that of an externally oriented economy based on the production of certain commodities for international trade. Brazilian colonization had been founded on this basis, and on this basis it continued right up to the time with which we are now dealing. In fact, there were no substantial changes in the system during the first three centuries of colonial history. Throughout this period, nothing was done beyond the extension of this system and its application in the new areas opened up by colonization.

It naturally became more complicated in certain aspects, and new elements, or at least new tendencies, emerged which altered the original simplicity of the pattern which we have outlined—that of a colony established to produce certain commodities for the mother country's trade. The elementary fact of the growth of the colonial population was in itself a factor for the transformation of the original pattern, since it determined the establishment and development of the domestic market and, with this, of an economic sector which was truly national, that is, no longer oriented exclusively toward the export market but toward the country's own needs. This sector gradually gained in importance and tended to change from a subsidiary and unimportant element of the Brazilian economy as a whole to a highly important aspect of this economy, amounting to something in its own right and with a life of its own that was not dependent on the impulse provided by the other sectors. It is true that the growth of the population was quantitative rather than qualitative. At the beginning of the last century the

bulk of the Brazilian population was made up of slaves or
former slaves, or of essentially unstable individuals who
formed a shifting group whose economic and social position
had not yet been fixed or defined. I shall have occasion to
analyze this aspect of Brazilian society in a later chapter. For
the time being I will confine myself to the economic significance of the situation.

The social distribution of the population meant that its
growth made far less impact on the domestic market than
would otherwise have been the case. Essentially, then, the general outline and basic characteristics of Brazil's economic
organization continued to be the same: three centuries after
the beginning of colonization, Brazil was still the same colony,
viscerally linked economically (not to mention the political
and administrative subordination) to the European economy, a
mere supplier of goods for the European trade. It was still the
business enterprise of the white colonist, powered by the arms
of the alien races, dominated but not yet fused with the colonial
society.

Such is the essential feature of the Brazilian economy, and it
is interesting to note that this was not only affirmed in the economic theories of the period but was also even elevated to the
category of a postulate, an absolute and irreplaceable necessity. Among other writings on the subject, we have one valuable document, written probably in the last quarter of the eighteenth century, which in my opinion contains the most lucid
synthesis of the Brazilian economy at the end of that century.[5]
What the author seeks to expound and demonstrate is, in brief,
that the colonies existed and were established for the exclusive
benefit of the mother country; that this benefit derives from the
production and export to the mother country of the commodities she needs, not only to meet her own requirements but also
in order to use the surplus for trading with other countries.
Finally, the settlement and organization of the colonies should
be subordinated to these aims, and that it was not their business
to engage in activities that were not in the interests of the

mother country's trade. At most, and only as an exception, the author allows that the colony may produce certain commodities strictly needed for the subsistence of the population which it would be impracticable to bring in from the outside.

The outstanding interest of this document lies in the fact that its author, in stating what he regarded as a norm of political economy, is doing no more than recognize an existing state of affairs. In effect, the essential nature of the Brazilian economy was precisely as he described it. Later in the work he considers the few deviations from the rule and attributes to them the ills that beset the colony, warning the mother country against them. The deviations were in fact very few and none of them was in any way serious.

The author was preaching to the converted: never had the crown or its policy shown the slightest intention of using the colony in any way other than that which he indicated. Brazil existed to supply the kingdom with gold and diamonds, sugar, tobacco, and cotton. This was taken for granted by the crown and was reflected in all that it did. All the acts of the Portuguese administration in relation to the colony were aimed at favoring activities that would enrich the mother country's trade and, conversely, at hindering any others. As soon as the colonists attempted to engage in any such activities, the mother country immediately and violently intervened to put them in their place. The abortive attempts to start up manufacturing industries, steelworks or salt production, as well as many other enterprises, are well known.

The result of this policy, which reduced Brazil to the status of a producer of certain commodities destined for the international trade, was that the attitude it created finally became so closely identified with Brazilian life that it was no longer based solely on her colonial subjection, no longer due simply to the administrative policy of the crown. By the end of the colonial era, the responsibility of the mother country had become simply that of contributing, by her sovereign action, toward the maintenance of a situation which had become effective even in spite of such action, which had in fact become stronger than her purpose, even had this now been the very opposite, which was, of course, not the case.

The proof that it was not simply the colonial regime that artificially maintained the situation is that, once this regime was abolished by the proclamation of independence, the situation continued to be perpetuated. Even as a sovereign nation, Brazil would not readily emerge from her colonial status in other respects, which the "7th of September" was to leave untouched.*

The actual situation that existed under the colonial regime corresponded effectively to the legal situation; this is easy to understand. The population at the end of Brazil's colonial history was still made up of that same heterogeneous aggregate: On the one hand, there was a small minority of white, or quasi-white, colonists; they were true promoters, in collusion with the mother country, of colonization and owners of the land and all its wealth. And on the other hand, there was the great mass of the population, slaves, or little better than slaves, who were simply the working machines with no other role in the system. Thus, by the very nature of such a structure, Brazil could not have been other than it had been hitherto—a factory for Europe, a mere supplier of tropical products for her trade.

From all this was to result the final and perhaps the most serious consequence: the pattern assumed by the colony's economic history. This has been characterized by a cyclical evolution both in time and in space, with successive periods of strictly regional and always short-lived prosperity, followed sooner or later by total decline, a process that was already taking shape in the period that we are now considering and that was to continue along the same lines in the future. The first phase of prosperity which affected the colony's oldest established sugar-producing centers, particularly Bahia and Pernambuco, lasted up to the end of the seventeenth century and was followed by the decadence that set in soon after the beginning of the eighteenth. The sugar regions were then replaced by the

* The date of the Declaration of Independence in 1822.—Translator.

mining centers, which rose to prosperity just as the sugar industry had passed its zenith, a prosperity which really was not to last beyond the middle of the eighteenth century; by the third quarter of that century we witness the progressive decline of these centers. Prosperity then returned to the original agricultural centers of the coast, other centers being added to these; and sugar was to be subsidized by cotton. During the period of Brazilian history at which we take up the story, the latter cycle was reaching its zenith. And although the subsequent period falls outside the scope of this work, we know that this phase, like those that preceded it, was to be short-lived. By the middle of the last century the situation had already been completely reversed. The downfall of the regions which had hitherto been paramount had already begun, and new regions had come to take their place, this time with the rise of a new product, coffee.

The origin of this fitful cyclical evolution, which led to the successive development and decline of one after another of all the country's areas of concentrated settlement, is found in the very nature of the Brazilian economy. The economy was based on very precarious foundations. It did not create the foundation needed to support and maintain a population dependent on such a structure: *an organized system of production and distribution of resources for the material subsistence of the population.* Instead, it created a "mechanism" for which the population was nothing but the element of propulsion, designed to function solely for the benefit of completely extraneous objectives. The economy was therefore entirely subordinate to these objectives, and had no strength of its own and no autonomous existence. It functioned in terms of the combination of international circumstances that favored whatever product it could supply and hence gave an illusory impression of wealth and prosperity. As soon as the particular combination of circumstances changed or the available natural resources were exhausted, production declined and withered away, making it impossible to maintain the life it had sustained. The organization of production of each of Brazil's major staples has

been the result of the purely momentary advantage to be
gained. To seize the opportunity of the moment, all the necessary elements were mobilized; whatever area of the territory
happened to be most convenient was settled by white promoters and organizers and slave laborers—a veritable labor
gang. The land was cleared, the soil tilled, the necessary material equipment installed, and production was immediately
organized. There was no escaping this system of organization,
nor did the conditions which had given rise to it allow of any
change. It was to continue until the available natural resources
had been finally exhausted or until the international situation
had ceased to be economically favorable. Then all was abandoned for some new enterprise, new frontiers, new opportunities. What remained behind were the leftovers, the scraps of a
parcel of humanity in decay.

This is how the Brazilian economy was formed and how it
has always operated: a succession of small and short-lived enterprises, neatly set off in time and space, each proving initially
successful to a greater or lesser extent. Some of these enterprises rose to spectacular heights, but little or nothing has
remained. On the whole, the economy never had any economic
organization deserving of the name, and the colonial period
came to an end without having managed to achieve a stable
balance in its economic life. It alternated violently between extremes, each time sowing a little more destruction and misery
in this vast territory in which it operated. The results, the final
balance of three centuries of ups and downs, could only be
meager and grievously lacking in dynamism. And so they were;
but we shall leave this to the analysis of the situation which I
will undertake further on.

In short, what we learn of the Brazilian economy from the
foregoing, what stands out and characterizes it, is, firstly, its
structure, as an organ of production set up solely as such and
with a few entrepreneurs and administrators who ran everything, and the great mass of the population who served as the
labor force; secondly, its *function* as the supplier to international trade of the commodities needed; and finally, its *evolu-*

tion, a consequence of the two foregoing features, as an extensive and purely speculative exploitation, unstable in time and space, of the country's natural resources. This is the Brazilian economy as we find it at the point at which we will now take up its history.

Large-Scale Agriculture

Agriculture is the economic nerve of civilization. It was agriculture that led to colonization—if we exclude the insignificant extractive cycle based on Brazil wood—and it was agriculture that provided the chief source of the country's wealth. In short, occupation and exploration of the greater part of Brazilian territory and of its best lands was intrinsically based on agriculture. Mining was little more than an interlude, and a brief interlude at that. And, particularly during the period which concerns us here, it had already been clearly relegated to a secondary plane. Cultivation of the land had regained the dominant position it had occupied in the first two centuries of colonization.

I have already pointed out the chief factor that led to this reversal of positions. The gold deposits, which had proved rich only on the surface of the soil, had been exhausted, and their exploitation was no longer profitable. But besides this negative factor there were a number of other factors which caused the colony's activities to flow back into agriculture. The markets for its products were expanding rapidly. This was due chiefly to the notable growth of the European population in the course of the eighteenth century; at the same time there was an increase of economic activity and commercial contact throughout the world, foreshadowing the new age that began with the second half of the eighteenth century, the age of the Industrial Revolution. This was intensely reflected in the colonial world.

148

Its markets expanded and the value of its products increased. The importance of colonial trade for the European countries manifests itself in the struggles which were kindled around it during this period. The colonial problem was always the *ultima ratio* of all the European conflicts from the War of the Spanish Succession onward, including the Napoleonic Wars.

Since the main theatre of all these European wars was almost always the great sea routes, the sea battles were to contribute to the rising value of colonial products by hampering their regular supply so that they became scarce and much sought after commodities. Portugal now found itself fortunately situated. In the second rank of European colonial powers and sheltered by its powerful English ally, Portugal was the European country least involved in the conflicts. From this position of dubious neutrality, which was to end in disaster, Portugal went on for as long as she could taking the considerable advantages it offered. For a time she even dominated the colonial trade and so recovered a position she had enjoyed two centuries before and which seemed to have been irretrievably lost.

But if Lisbon became toward the end of that century the great center of the colonial trade, its American colony was no less favored by the mother country's position. All the other producers of tropical commodities had been hard hit by the struggles in which their respective mother countries were involved. Portuguese neutrality was extended to Brazil and its trade. Brazil was thus left in peace to develop its wealth of resources and to sell its products freely. But this was not all. In the last years of the century, its chief competitors suffered even more serious blows than those they had been dealt by the wars. These were the political and social agitations which transformed the English and French colonies in the Antilles, particularly the collapse of Santo Domingo in 1792. Brazil thus came to occupy a unique position in the tropical trade.

There was yet another factor that stimulated Brazilian agriculture in the second half of the eighteenth century. Hitherto, the great tropical commodity had been sugar. Another product

now came to vie with it in importance and soon to outstrip
it, cotton. Although cotton had been known from time immemorial, it had never played a prominent role, particularly in
Europe, where there was nothing to give it the advantage over
the locally produced fibers hitherto used for the same purposes, that is, linen or wool. The technical progress of the
eighteenth century enabled cotton to be used to an almost unlimited extent, and it became the most important industrial
raw material of the time, entering international trade in proportions hitherto unheard of in any of its branches. Arkwright
constructed his spinning jenny in 1769, the year that Watt pat-
ented the steam engine that was to make it possible for this
form of power to be used on a large scale. In 1787 Cartwright
invented his mechanical loom. These are precious dates for
Brazil. Consumption of cotton in England, the great center of
the modern textile industry, rose accordingly. In the five-year
period, 1771–1775, the total amount consumed did not exceed
4.76 million pounds; by the last years of the century, following
the introduction of the mechanical loom, it had risen to 26 million pounds.

The traditional Oriental suppliers could not meet a demand
of this magnitude and America, taking advantage of its immense reserves of virgin land, stepped in to fill the gap and become the leading modern producer of cotton. Brazil had its
share, which at first was by no means a small one, in this unparalleled expansion of the cotton trade.

All these factors combined to make the last years of the
eighteenth century a period of great progress for Brazilian
agriculture. The old established agricultural regions, such as
Bahia and Pernambuco, which had been decadent from the beginning of the century, revived and recovered the brilliance of
the first two centuries of colonization. New sugar lands were
opened up, as in the Campos dos Goitacases [1] and in São
Paulo, where cane planting spread to the northern part of the
captaincy in the fertile soils of the *terra roxa* lands of Campinas. In the São Paulo coastal zone, São Sebastião and Ubatuba
also began to emerge as sugar producers.[2] In Maranhão a simi-

lar expansion was taking place, in this case with cotton planting. Up to the third quarter of the eighteenth century, this captaincy was still of negligible importance in the colony as a
whole; from then on it rapidly prospered and was soon one of
the leading captaincies. Similarly, in Pará, where the only form
of activity had hitherto been the gathering of forest products,
agriculture began to assume some importance. The first cacao
plantations, the chief Amazonian product, were established at
this time.

All these transformations were in striking contrast to what
was taking place in the mining regions, where decadence was
becoming more and more pronounced. These regions were in
fact turning wherever possible to rural activities. The contrast
is reflected in the economic discussions of the time, in which
the prestige of agriculture and the growing loss of faith in mining is clearly evident. The two were balanced against each
other, and the alternative between them was the great topic of
the day, opinion being almost unanimously in favor of agriculture. Only it was seriously expected to yield promising results.
The country had at last awakened from its dream of precious
metals and precious stones.

I have already indicated the most important consequences of
this agricultural revival for the general features of the colony.
This was the shift in its axis from the inland captaincies to
those of the seaboard (the distinction between the two types of
captaincy was already made at the time, and they were already
given these designations). The zone naturally selected as the
most suitable agricultural area was the strip stretching from
north to south along the northeastern coast. Agriculture had
been initially and exclusively established along this strip during the first two centuries of colonization. For the production
of the tropical commodities then in demand, particularly sugar,
there were no better lands than those of the warm, humid,
coastal lowland where the exceptional quality of certain of its
soils complemented the excellence of its climatic conditions.
There was still another factor that favored this location. Since
production was exclusively export oriented, access to the ports

of shipment and exportation would naturally determine the priority of location for the colony's economic activities. In Part One we saw the important role played in determining settlement by accidents of the coastline favorable to maritime navigation, the ports of export being located wherever such accidents occurred. The anonymous author of the *Roteiro do Maranhão* previously cited, who was such an astute analyst of the colony's economy, did not overlook this fact: "The settler, whether he is an agriculturalist or a merchant, will in no way extend settlement, cultivation, and trade to the interior of the country, by establishing himself in those parts where the produce that has to be transported to the ports [of shipment] will not give a sufficient return for the work involved in acquisition [i.e., production], and the expense involved in transportation. Hence it follows that the returns the settler receives from his produce in the ports . . . will be the rule for determining the limits of expansion for settlement, cultivation, and trade in the interior of the country." [3]

The disadvantage of the inland captaincies in this respect is therefore obvious. In an essentially export-oriented economy such as that of the colony, the location of these captaincies was unfavorable. Agriculture alone would not have led to the penetration of the interior, and this is why, up to the seventeenth century, the Portuguese continued to "scuttle along the seashore like so many crabs." It was mining and cattle raising that gave the impetus to penetration of the interior. The first for obvious reasons; the considerable value of gold and diamonds and the fact that they weighed little and could be made up into small packages obviated the transport problem. The second activity also offered no transport problems since, to quote the picturesque description of the author already cited, "cattle do not need anyone to carry them. They are the only ones who feel the full weight of their bodies on the long marches." [4]

It was this fact that determined the priority given to cattle raising when the central captaincies which had been settled because of the now decadent mines were forced to find another basis for existence in some form of rural activity, and this, as we have seen, was what happened in Minas Gerais. But whether they turned to pastoralism or to subsidiary agriculture —the activities chosen to replace mining—these were always activities of secondary importance. Large-scale agriculture, that is, agriculture producing crops for export, which was the only form of activity that afforded ample opportunities, was established in the interior only in exceptional circumstances.

In the period when production was boosted by the fever of speculative profit aroused by the abnormally high price it commanded, cotton provided one such exception. Finding in the interior both highly favorable physical conditions and relatively abundant labor made available by the dislocations provoked by the decadence of the mines, cotton planting began to spread to unexpected sectors. Cotton regions of some importance were formed high in the heart of the interior, in the upper sertões of Minas Gerais and the hinterland of Bahia. These areas were in fact not the only ones affected, as we shall see later. But the situation was always to be a precarious one and destined not to last very long; and production in these interior centers never managed to counterbalance the production of the strip of territories closer to the sea, even in the special case of cotton.

The situation of São Paulo in this respect seems a paradoxical one. Here we find a reversal of the general rule. Up to the end of the eighteenth century, the seaboard continued to prevail over the highlands of the interior; and it was in the coastal zone—still according to the rule—that São Paulo's first agricultural cycle occurred. But when, following the general trend for the colony as a whole, agriculture in São Paulo gained real momentum and for the first time began to be of some significance in the colony's economic structure, it was not the littoral that was chosen but the plateau, the former being relegated to a secondary plane. It was on the plateau that the captaincy's chief sugar region was to be located, and it was with sugar production that São Paulo began its recovery and progress.

This exception to the rule is accounted for by the unfavorable conditions of the São Paulo coastal plain, which were in contrast to the great advantages of the plateau and its magnificent soils, undoubtedly the best in the country. Also, although the plateau is separated from its ports by the steep barrier of the Serra do Mar, it is not situated very far inland.*

We must also bear in mind that coffee growing, although still only in the initial stages of its spectacular expansion, had already found a niche for itself among the colony's principal agricultural activities. The coffee tree does not thrive in the coastal lowlands, which are not well adapted to its requirements; it does best on the higher terraces of the mountain slopes overlooking the lowland fringe. Nevertheless, it did not advance very far inland until much later and for a long time remained concentrated along the eastern edge of the plateau bordering the sea.

Thus, by and large it was the strip of territories closest to the sea that benefited from the colony's agricultural revival. Another factor was to reinforce the general trend toward the coast. This was the decadence of the northeastern sertões, afflicted by droughts, which caused them to lose their position as the colony's chief suppliers of meat to the *campos* of Rio Grande do Sul. I shall analyze this at greater length in another chapter. I mention it here only in order to complete the picture of the reversal in the colonizing movement from the interior— the trend in the seventeenth and above all in the eighteenth centuries—back to the coastlands—the trend from the eighteenth century onward.

Agricultural development in the period we are now dealing with, although fairly considerable, was quantitative rather than qualitative, which explains its instability and, save in exceptional cases, its short duration. Technical progress in Brazilian agriculture at this period was practically nil. At the beginning of the nineteenth century and for a considerable time thereafter, agricultural practices continued to be more or less confined to the same processes employed at the beginning of colonization. These wasteful and primitive methods were explicable and even unavoidable in the first phase of occupa-

---

* Less than 35 miles.—Translator.

tion, but the disastrous effects of their continued practice were beginning to make themselves felt.

Nothing had replaced the primitive burn-and-slash method of clearing the land for cultivation, copied from the natives; no solution had been found for the problem of soil exhaustion other than that of simply abandoning the locality for a number of years before attempting to rework the land, the intervals lengthening as the gradual impoverishment of the soil began to spread, until finally exhaustion was complete. The forests which had once covered most of the areas occupied by colonization, chosen for the natural fertility of their residual soils, rapidly disappeared in the destructive wake of the fires that devoured them. Thus, to cite only one of many instances, in the northeastern coastlands, of the dense and uninterrupted forest which had extended from Paraíba to Alagoas, only a few patches remained at the area's two extremes. An attempt was made to preserve these remaining patches from a final assault in the last years of the eighteenth century, not, however, in the interests of agriculture or out of any concern to maintain a reserve for the country's future development, but to supply timber for the dockyards of the Portuguese Royal Navy. This was the usual narrow criterion, and one which was to be partly responsible for the inefficiency and uselessness of the conservation method adopted. Destructive exploitation of forest resources was to continue as before.

Indiscriminate and uncontrolled consumption of wood for fuel contributed particularly to this destruction. Chiefly responsible were the sugar mills, which used up enormous quantities of firewood.[5] The use of bagasse as fuel, which had become common practice in the English, French, and Dutch colonies, had not yet occurred to the Brazilian planters.[6]

Wholesale destruction of the forests gradually created a trail of barren wilderness in the wake of the colonist as he pushed forward in his search for fresh soils that would require little effort on his part. It was only on account of the exceptional and providential fertility of the massapê soils of Bahia and Pernambuco that it proved possible to continue to grow sugarcane in the district for so long. But the gradual gaps that were formed in the forest around the sugar mills by the continual devastation created other, equally serious problems. Firewood had to be brought from considerable distances; it frequently became inaccessible, and the sugar mills were brought to a standstill. We learn from the testimonies of the period that lack of fuel was one of the most common causes for the abandonment of engenhos.[7]

Care of the land was also neglected, and no attention was paid to the better utilization, restoration, or even simple conservation of the natural properties of the soil. The one-crop system and the spirit which animated the colonial planter were the chief factors responsible. All efforts and attentions converged toward a single end: maximum exploitation of a temporary advantage. The result was a veritable "bombardment" of the soil's natural resources—"extractive agriculture," as it has been called. The fatal separation of agriculture and grazing, which was a corollary of this system and formed one of the most characteristic features of the colony's rural economy, was also disastrous in its effects on the soil, by depriving it of animal manure, the only fertilizing element of which it could readily avail itself. And no attempt was made to obviate, as far as possible, the manifest disadvantages of this situation, by turning to account the large numbers of oxen used for working the rural establishments. No planter appears to have acted in this way.[8] Even the bagasse, which was needlessly wasted, was never used as a fertilizer. When it had accumulated to the point of becoming a nuisance, it was burnt.[9]

Naturally, more complex methods of soil improvement were never for a moment considered: Irrigation, so badly needed in many places and sometimes fairly easy to undertake; drainage and other projects for regulating the supply of water necessary to support or preserve the crops; and all the measures which are so highly important in a climate particularly subject to erratic and violent precipitation and rapid run-off were practically unheard of in the colony. Only the Jesuits, in their Fazenda de Santa Cruz in Rio de Janeiro, made some use of these techniques. Indeed, the Jesuit estates, as well as those of the Benedictines, and to a much lesser extent those of the Carmelites, are the only examples to be found in the colony of less primitive forms of rural economy. Unfortunately, their impact on the economy as a whole was insignificant.

The methods used for preparing the land for cultivation were equally backward and inefficient. Apart from the *queimada*, or burning over of the land and clearing away the indispensable minimum of brushwood—and this in a most summary fashion that was no improvement on the well-known *coivara* system of the Indians *—the only thing done was to dibble the soil or to make furrows for planting the seed. Agricultural equipment was of the crudest type and confined to the hoe or digging stick. Nothing could be more primitive.

The problem of choosing the right varieties of products to be cultivated can be regarded as unknown. Up to the beginning of the nineteenth century only one variety of sugarcane was known, the same variety that had been cultivated since the beginning of colonization and therefore came to be called "Creole cane," when the Brazilian cultivators found that it was not the only one in existence. Only in the early years of the nineteenth century did they begin to plant a more resistant variety of cane, the Cayenne or *Otaiti* (Tahiti) variety.[10] As far as cotton is concerned, the rudiments of selection appeared much earlier. From the last decade of the eighteenth century it was noted that the particular variety known as "Maranhão cotton" —although it had nothing to do with that captaincy—gave greater yields; and it began to be adopted after 1796. But it appears to have made slow progress.[11] If this happened with the

---

* The *coivara*, properly speaking, is the burning of the heaped brushwood, branches, half-burnt tree-trunks, etc., after the land has been cleared by felling with an axe all but the largest trees, which are girdled, or by setting fire to the woods, which was known as a "queimada." Gilberto Freyre makes a comparison between this system in Brazil and the similar process practiced in the American South: ". . . a region that has suffered and preserved the scars . . . of the same devastating regime of agrarian exploitation: fire and ax, the felling of the forests and the burning over of the land, the 'parasitic husbandry of Nature.'" *The Masters and the Slaves*, p. xix.—Translator.

colony's most important commercial crops, we can imagine what went on with the others.

The same backwardness characterized the industries related to agriculture. The cane establishments had never been modernized, and the description of them written by Antonil at the beginning of the eighteenth century still applied in every detail to the engenhos of a century later. In support of this statement we may compare Vilhena's equally revealing description, written at the beginning of the nineteenth century.[12] I have already referred to the nonuse of bagasse as fuel in Brazil, although elsewhere it had already been used as such for more than fifty years. The cane-grinding processes were all antiquated, and output from the outdated devices in use was small —and this in spite of all the technical progress in this respect long since applied in the other sugar-producing countries.[13]

The use of running water as the motive power for the sugar mills (the mills driven by waterpower being known as *engenhos d'água*), which almost doubles the output achieved in mills operated by oxen, was also not very common. From the detailed statistical description of the captaincy of Pernambuco which was made during the governorship of José César de Meneses (1777), we learn that out of the 369 sugar mills operating in the captaincy only 18 were *engenhos d'água*.[14] Indeed, the use of waterpower in any sector was an exception. The foreign travelers who visited Brazil at the beginning of the last century and left us such exhaustive accounts of the colony, even those observers of the caliber of a St. Hilaire with his scrupulous accuracy and attention to detail, rarely found occasion to note the existence of any water wheels. Apart from the *monjolo*, that ancient and primitive mechanical pounding device probably brought back from the East by the Portuguese, the use of waterpower was not at all widespread in the colony. Of the various sources of energy then known, only the most rudimentary were used on any appreciable scale in Brazil, where the very first forms of energy which man had thought of using—animal power and manpower—were relied on.

The same backwardness was evident in the methods used for

processing cotton. In spite of the fact that Whitney had invented his saw gin in 1792 and that it had immediately been put into widespread use in the United States cotton region, Brazil continued to employ the ancient principle of the Oriental hand driven *churcka,* a device developed countless centuries ago for removing the seeds from cotton.[15] An invention which had revolutionized cotton production in America and given it the impetus which completely altered the course of its development was thus completely ignored in Brazil. Seven years after Whitney's invention, one of the most cultured and well-informed men in the colony, Manuel de Arruda Câmara, botanist and planter—the man who can be regarded as the father of Brazilian agronomy—wrote his *Memoria* on the cultivation of the cotton plant, in which is revealed his complete ignorance of the most important event of his time for the field in which he worked. In 1813, *O Patriota,** moved by the praiseworthy desire to help foster Brazilian agriculture and bring the planters up to date, published Arruda Câmara's *Memoria,* the only manual on the subject written in Portuguese, without a single addendum or even a note about subsequent developments—and this in spite of the fact that an entire chapter of the manual was devoted to the question of the possible improvements that could be made to the cotton gin then in use. Brazil, for whom cotton represented a major source of wealth, continued in total ignorance of the technique which had given cotton cultivation in the United States its greatest impetus. And even twenty-five years after Whitney's invention, Martius in 1817 and St. Hilaire two years later, found the same antiquated methods still in use in the major cotton-producing areas they visited.

The most common method used for baling cotton at the time that Arruda Câmara wrote his memoir was still "hand-operated."[16] The lint-baling press which he had introduced had made little impact; Arruda Câmara himself deplores this

---

* A journal devoted to politics, literature, trade, commerce, etc., published monthly in Rio de Janeiro in 1813 and bimonthly in 1814. Three volumes appeared. See also note 5 in the last chapter.—Translator.

fact. But it is only fair to add that Martius states that the cotton press was everywhere in use. However, two years after the German botanist's visit, St. Hilaire found that baling presses were not used in the regions he visited, and although these were not the same areas that Martius refers to and were also not as important, they were nevertheless still fairly prominent. Progress in this respect had therefore not yet become general.

These aspects of Brazilian agriculture, which I have deliberately dwelt upon both because they are of considerable interest in their own right and because they have consequences of the utmost importance, leave no room for doubt as to the extremely low standard of agricultural practices. They reveal the rut into which the planters had fallen and the general ignorance and backwardness that prevailed. The chief factor responsible for this state of affairs is, of course, the general system of colonization based on the inefficient and generally semi-barbarous use of the African slave. It would have been difficult to achieve anything better with workers of this type. In one of his admirable letters, Vilhena described the activities on a cane establishment in Bahia, the largest and most important of the colony's sugar centers. The ignorance, inefficiency, and negligence with which the production of sugar was managed are simply astounding. There is nothing to redeem the blackness of this dismal picture.[17]

But it was not only slave labor that was responsible. In other tropical colonies where slave labor was also a feature, the standards of agriculture and its related industries were considerably higher. The real reason for the difference—and there can have been no other—lies in the very nature of the Portuguese colonist, and, above all, in the political and administrative system imposed on the colony by the mother country. This system meant, at least in the last century, that Brazil was cut off from the rest of the world and deliberately kept in isolation, which prevented all but a reflection of the already low intellectual level of the kingdom from reaching the colony.

On the other hand, no attempt was made to make up for the isolation in which the colony was compelled to exist by providing even an elementary system of education. The meager instruction given in the few official schools that existed in some of the colony's largest centers did not go much beyond the teaching of reading, writing, and arithmetic, with a little Latin and Greek, and this can hardly be said to constitute an educational system. Created only after 1776, these schools were generally neglected and understaffed, the teachers badly paid, the pupils unruly, and the classes unorganized.[18] The cultural level of the colony was extremely low and the crassest ignorance prevailed. The few scholars who distinguished themselves were in a world apart, ignored by a country utterly unable to understand them. All was weighed down by a petty administration, zealous only in its preoccupation with tax revenue and its concern for the individual profit of the mob of inefficient and unscrupulous bureaucrats dispatched across the Atlantic by the mother country.

We shall see, in the appropriate section, that I do not exaggerate; what has already been said in this respect provides ample evidence to explain the backwardness and primitive level of the colony's chief economic activities. But there is a still further consideration of a more general nature to be made concerning colonial agriculture. European colonization of the tropics gave rise to a new type of agriculture, the large-scale production of tropical cash crops. For some centuries, indeed, up to a very recent period, it was only in the tropics that this form of agrarian production was to be found. Today we find large-scale commercial agriculture in temperate zones too, particularly cereal production, as in the United States, the Soviet Union, and Argentina. But in these countries it is the result of notable technical and mechanical progress, and took place only after this progress had succeeded, at least partially, in counterbalancing the disadvantages of the cash crop system. The drawbacks of such a system are by no means slight, the soil exhaustion provoked by the very heavy demands made on it being the most serious.

In tropical agriculture, on the other hand, there are hardly any rational processes for extensive cultivation even today, let alone in the past. Besides, any system of large-scale agricultural production requires considerable initial capital investment, and the costs of the preliminary works needed after this initial investment are equally high. In the tropics, all this was lacking or proved impossible to realize at the time when they began to be exploited. The only sources at their disposal for initiating large-scale production were the abundance of natural resources, the exuberance of the vegetation, and the reserves accumulated over the centuries in the rich virgin soil. But all this was doomed to exhaustion. In the first centuries of colonization no account was taken of the fact that a capital was being squandered, and that it was not simply a question of gathering the fruits. This was either never grasped or else no immediate danger was perceived; there was, it seemed, enough and to spare.

Only gradually did realization dawn of the extent of the damage done. In Brazil, toward the end of the eighteenth century and the beginning of the next, the colonists began to realize what was amiss and to become aware of the implications. The authors I have cited above, as well as others I will mention later, all refer to the problem and wrote from first-hand knowledge of the situation. It is only natural that they should sometimes have been led astray by current misconceptions and we must not forget that they were facing an unprecedented situation, completely different from any that had arisen in the past, at a time when exploitation of the tropics was almost in its infancy. They lacked the scientific knowledge that was to become generalized only much later. They therefore did not really understand the evil that was sapping the energies of the colony. They discerned its effects and knew instinctively that something must be done, but were not quite sure of the answer. The solutions they proposed were generally taken from the storehouse of European experience, as in the case of the anonymous author of the *Roteiro do Maranhão*, who suggested that the soil could be properly tilled only if the land in which the crops were to be planted were completely cleared of tree stumps, as if, in the vast areas covered by the colonial plantations and with no other aid than that of the human arm or animal power, it were possible to achieve what even today has almost invariably proved to be unfeasible.

The low productivity of Brazilian agriculture, which culminated in the almost total barrenness of large areas of land—except, for a time, in the special and restricted case of coffee, in which the last of the accessible and available lands were opened up—is in the final analysis simply a consequence of the factors indicated above. And in the period which concerns us here the decline in production was already very marked.

What must be concluded from the foregoing, however, is that the technical backwardness of our agrarian activities and the resultant consequences should not be blamed entirely on the incapacity of the colonist. In many cases, perhaps even in the most important, the colonist could not have acted otherwise. He could of course have kept up with his competitors in the other colonies and have made some attempt to attain the superior level of their agricultural practices. But this would not have been enough. The evil went deeper: it was the system itself, the destructive form of large-scale exploitation that squandered with prodigal disregard for consequences the wealth of land resources which could not be replaced. And if on the one hand this consideration partly exonerates colonization, on the other it also increases its responsibility. The problem then becomes a much more difficult one. If educating the colonists and the population as a whole to improve their agricultural practices and adopt more up-to-date techniques would have been no easy matter, it would have been even more difficult to change the system, which would have called for far-reaching economic and perhaps even social reforms.

However that may be, it was in a precarious condition, despite the providential protection of a favorable combination of international circumstances, that the Brazilian economy entered the nineteenth century, a century in which freedom and free enterprise were to bring it into the open market to compete with rivals who were infinitely better equipped. Defeat was inevitable; and since the economy continued to be based

solely on foreign commerce, dependent on markets over which
it had not the slightest control, complete collapse would not
have been long delayed if Providence had not come to the colony's aid. And this is precisely what did occur. Although this
takes us much further afield from our subject, we must point out
that the economy did reach the very verge of collapse and that
Providence, in the nick of time, intervened to save it. It came
in the guise of a commodity which nature had admirably
equipped us to produce, coffee. With coffee, yet another large
portion of the gifts with which nature had endowed us was to
be squandered. But in the areas where these gifts were lacking
or where they had been exploited beyond redemption, Providence failed us and the inevitable collapse ensued.

At the beginning of the last century, however, the prospects
for colonial agriculture were not yet quite so gloomy. On the
contrary, we have seen that the international and domestic
economic situation was highly favorable to agriculture. The
colony's products were increasing in value and selling on a
rapidly expanding market; possible competitors were in a
weaker position; domestically, the decadence of mining had
placed at the disposal of agriculture energies which otherwise
would have found no outlet after the cessation of mining. Fortune smiled on agriculture, and it seemed to be making a triumphant advance. Let us now take a closer look at the structure and organization of this source of strength, which had
once more became the mainstay on an apparently solid basis of
colonial life.

In Brazilian colonial agriculture we must distinguish two
sectors which differ completely in character. I touched on this
subject in the previous chapter, but did not go into detail about
the specific case of agriculture, the case which concerns us
here. On the one hand there was *large-scale* commercial agriculture: cultivation of sugar, cotton, and certain other less
important commodities destined for the foreign market. On the
other, there was *subsistence agriculture:* production of commodities for the maintenance of the country's population and
hence destined for local consumption.

There is no need to stress the basis of this distinction, since this has already been indicated previously. It is, in fact, a distinction that must be made even if we do not take into account observations of a more general nature and confine ourselves to the sphere of agriculture, rather than to the colony's economy as a whole. In the first place, the difference is evident in the importance and economic significance of one of these sectors and the insignificance of the other. Large-scale production represents the very nerve of colonial agriculture; the growing of crops for local consumption—manioc, maize, and beans being the chief of these—was a mere appendage of commercial agriculture of purely subsidiary significance. This subsidiary role can be seen from the actual structure of agrarian production. In most cases, subsistence crops were grown in the rural establishments devoted to commercial agriculture. They were destined to supply the people engaged in the latter and were grown solely to meet this demand. I note this merely as an example at this point, and will analyze this interdependence in more detail later.

Another basic distinguishing feature between subsistence agriculture and commercial agriculture is the way in which production was organized. For the moment I shall concern myself with commercial agriculture, leaving the organization of subsistence agriculture to the next chapter.

The essential feature of commercial agriculture is large-scale exploitation. Each unit of production, bringing together a great number of workers and covering a vast area, is integrated into a *usina* (factory unit), with a collective and even specialized organization of labor. This occurred particularly in the production of the colony's most typical agricultural product, sugar, where the engenho with its complex of machinery and equipment forms a veritable factory organization. But it is not only in the industries connected with agriculture that we find such characteristics. In a less accentuated form we find them even in the organization of cultivation of the land. Preparation of the soil, planting, care of the crop, and harvesting, as well as other connected activities, are all organized on the basis of collective labor.

This is an important point, because it is precisely the features pointed out above that characterize large-scale agricultural exploitation and distinguish it from other forms of rural exploitation. And this is of great economic and social significance. It was from the technique of production and organization adopted by Brazilian agriculture that was derived the entire structure of the country: the arrangement of classes and categories of the population, and the particular status of each and that of the individuals who composed them. In other words, the whole complex of social relations at their deepest and most essential level derived from this basis.

Such, then, together with slave labor, are the basic and common elements of large-scale commercial agriculture in Brazil. More accentuated in certain of its sectors, as in that of sugarcane, and less so in others, particularly in that of tobacco, these elements nevertheless appear in all sectors and form the most distinguishing feature of agricultural production for export as a whole.

We will consider each of the staples of the export trade in turn. The first, both chronologically and in order of importance since it made the greatest contribution to colonization, is sugarcane. Sugarcane served as the material base for the establishment of the European in the territory that was to constitute Brazil and brought him, even in comparison with mining, his greatest share of prosperity. We can even say that Brazil, to parody Herodotus, is "the gift of sugar," and at the end of the colonial period sugar was still the economic mainstay of the country.

Sugarcane was widely distributed throughout the colony. We find it all along the coastal fringe from the extreme north, in Pará, to the south, in Santa Catarina. In the interior, except in the semiarid regions of the northeastern Sertão, it appeared to a greater or lesser extent in all the inhabited zones of the colonial territory. Like manioc, it was almost a necessary accompaniment of man.

The great sugar-producing centers, however, were restricted to a few limited areas along the coast. It was here that large-scale commercial sugar production, properly speaking, was located. In the other areas there was merely small-scale local production, where the cane was used less for the production of sugar than for the production of cane spirits, molasses, and *rapadura*.* This production was of little significance in the sugar economy as a whole. The northeastern coastlands, from Paraíba to Sergipe, and the contours of the Recôncavo in Bahia were the two most important and also the oldest established sugar areas. In the first of these areas the sugarcane plantations and sugar mills were concentrated along the lower courses of the small rivers that run parallel to each other from north to south, from the Mamanguape in Paraíba, increasing considerably in number in Pernambuco, as far as the Real in Sergipe. These waterways served as lines of penetration and communication; they also served to transport the product and to water the massapê soils which were so eminently suitable for cane.[19] In the Recôncavo of Bahia, sugarcane cultivation was similarly concentrated along the estuaries of the numerous rivers, inlets, and indentations that punctuate its contours. These all provided an easy means of access and communication.[20]

Next in importance was the captaincy of Rio de Janeiro. Here the distribution of the sugarcane plantations was more varied than in the northern areas described above; there are different sectors to take into account. Two of these sectors were similar to those of the northern captaincies. In the Guanabara sector the cane was planted around the bay and along the lower courses of the rivers which empty into Guanabara Bay. In the southern part of the coastland along the highly indented arc of the circle extending from Ilha Grande to Joatinga Point, the limit of the captaincy, a sector that includes the districts of the island, Angra dos Reis, and Parati, the sugar plantations were also fixed along the seaboard. North of Guanabara Bay the situation was different. Here the coastline is accompanied by large sandy deposits dotted with lagoons, and the soil is unsuited to cane cultivation. Sugarcane was therefore planted

---

* *Rapadura* is a kind of sugar cake, a hard square of raw brown sugar eaten as food or candy.—Translator.

further inland, in the captaincy's southeastern sector, behind the series of lagoons stretching from the Maricá to the Araruama lagoons, and also in the last and most important of the captaincy's sugar sectors, the Campos dos Goitacases, which are formed by the lowlands extending between the Feia lagoon and the Paraíba river and its affluent, the Muriaé.[21]

In São Paulo, sugarcane cultivation was at this period ushering in a phase of great prosperity. Apart from the lower areas along the coast, Ubatuba and São Sebastião, which were less important centers, cane planting was advancing on the plateau, particularly along the strip linking the Tietê and Moji-guaçu rivers between Itu and Moji.[22]

Organization of the sugarcane industry was more or less the same in its general features throughout the country. It was centered on the engenho, a term that was extended from its original designation of the actual "factory" or processing plant —that is, the installations for grinding the sugarcane, extracting the juice, and crystallizing the sugar—to embrace the entire plantation with its lands and crops. The engenho covered a large area, from one to four leagues of land and even more in Bahia.[23] It was partly exploited and controlled directly by the owner and partly cultivated by *lavradores* (copyholders), who were obliged to send their cane to the owner's mill for processing. These were the "contract fazendas," in which the tenant received half the sugar produced from his cane and was obliged to pay for the hire of the land he worked a certain percentage which varied from place to place and was deducted from his half-share.[24] There were also free copyholders who owned the land they worked and could send their cane to be ground at the engenho of their choice. These received half the sugar produced, with no further deductions. It would be interesting to compare the relative production of the *senhores de engenho* and the *lavradores*, but I have come across only one reference in this respect, the figures for the Campos dos Goitacases in 1779. In this year, the engenhos in the district produced 1,761 chests of sugar for the mill owners and approximately 400 for the copyholders.[25] If we take into account the system of division described above—assuming that none of the smallholders was under contract for the hire of his lands, which was certainly not the case for the majority of these, since in the campos land ownership was particularly concentrated in the hands of a few proprietors—the actual figures would be 1,361 chests for the owners and 800 for the tenants and copyholders. As we can see, the contribution made by the smallholders is large. We should add, however, that the copyholders were not really tenants in the same category as peasants; they were slaveholders, and their canelands, whether hired or independently owned, formed large units like those of the engenhos themselves. Vilhena places them in the same category and ascribes to them the same social status as the *senhores de engenho*.

The engenho was a complex and costly organization. Although not as valuable as the comparable installations of the Antilles, according to Koster the total value of the engenho with all its equipment, lands, crops, and processing plant amounted to seven or eight thousand pounds sterling in the coastal area, and £3,000–5,000 in the interior,[26] a considerable sum despite the deficiencies of the equipment which I have indicated above. The engenho integrated a number of buildings and installations into a single unit: the mill, the boiler vats, the purgery,* etc., as well as the big house occupied by the planter, the slave quarters, and the auxiliary installations or luxury additions such as workshops, stables, etc.[27] (The term *casa grande*, "big house," was used only in the north; in the south the owner's house was the *morada*, "house," or more recently, the *sede*, "headquarters.") The lands not devoted to cane were used for a number of other purposes: for pasturing, since the engenho required a large number of mules and oxen for operating the mills; for the growing of food crops to feed the large numbers of people living on the plantation; and for a reserve of woodland (in cases where it had not already been laid waste) to be used as fuel or building mate-

---

* That part of the sugar house where molasses is drained from the sugar.—Translator.

rial. The engenho was a miniature world in which the entire life of a small parcel of humanity was concentrated and epitomized.*

All the work was done by slaves. There were a few paid workers to perform specialized tasks or to undertake management: technicians, *purgadores* (purgery workers), overseers, packers (who made up the sugar chests), and so forth.[28] These persons were usually former slaves who had been given their freedom. The number of slaves employed on a major plantation, according to Koster (for Pernambuco), was at least eighty; Vilhena (for Bahia) tells us that any plantation owner who employed fewer than eighty slaves was deemed a "very poor 'senhor de engenho.'" [29] But this number, at least in Rio de Janeiro, for which we have specific figures,[30] was not often reached. In this captaincy there were extreme cases, such as that of the engenho taken over from the Jesuits, with its 1,400 slaves; the engenho run by the friars of the Order of St. Benedict, with 432; and the one owned by the Viscounts of Asseca, the great "feudal barons" of the Campos dos Goitacases, with 200. But on the whole the number of workers was much less.

Besides the raw sugar extracted from the cane, the juice was also used for making cane spirits. This was an important by-product, consumed on a large scale in the country itself and exported to the African coast, where the rum and sugarcane brandy was used for barter in the slave trade with west Africa.[31] Along with the distilleries connected with the engenhos there were establishments set up exclusively for making rum and sugarcane brandy. These were the plantations known as *engenhocas* (small engenhos) or *molinetes* (little mills), which were usually smaller than the conventional plantation, since the technical equipment required was much simpler and installation was thus less costly. It was, therefore, easier to establish a distillery, and the production of cane spirits was more democratic than that of aristocratic sugar. Nevertheless, there were

---

* Freyre describes the big house as "fortress, chapel, school, workshop, house of charity, harem, convent of young women, hospital . . . and bank." *The Masters and the Slaves*, p. xxxi.—Translator.

some distilleries that employed a large number of slaves.[32] The engenhocas generally made use of the "molasses" (the thick residual syrup formed by the cane juice that cannot be crystallized), which they acquired from the engenhos.

Another sugarcane product is *rapadura* (sugar cake), which took the place of sugar and was eaten in large quantities in certain regions, particularly in the Sertão of the northeast. Nearly all the sugarcane grown in this region, or rather in the few agricultural oases found in the wetter spots, was used by the small, local *banguês* * to make rapadura. I have referred to these secondary cane products simply to complete the picture; but these do not fall within the category of large-scale agriculture. At most, they constitute a marginal sector of commercial agriculture.

Production of cotton was a much simpler and less costly enterprise than that of sugar. St. Hilaire observes that in São Paulo, whereas sugar was a product of the wealthy landowners, cotton was produced by the modest smallholders.[33] It was this that made possible the rapid expansion and development of cotton planting. As we have seen, the initial impulse for this expansion came from the growing demand for cotton fiber in the European textile industry, particularly in England. The crop had long been grown in small quantities in the colony, probably from the outset of colonization. We know that it is native to America, although there is no indication that it was used by the indigenous inhabitants of Brazil. But colonization brought about a spread of cotton planting, and it was grown in many small scattered areas throughout the colony. The chief of these was Maranhão, where the cotton skeins and cloth woven from cotton fiber were once used as currency,[34] a habit which became so deeply rooted that even as late as the beginning of the nineteenth century, according to the testimony of Gayozo, the local value of money was expressed in terms of cotton merchandise, one cotton skein or one roll of cloth being the equiva-

---

* *Banguês*—a Brazilian regional term for sugar plantation, *engenho de bangué* being the correct term; it is derived from the brick-paved trough, or *bangué*, through which the sugar foam is drained.—Translator.

lent of 10 Reis.[35] But up to the third quarter of the eighteenth century, when it began to be exported, cotton represented no more than an insignificant crop of purely local importance and very little commercial value. Spun and woven into rough cloth, it served to clothe the slaves and the poorer classes.[36]

It was only when world demand created an expanding market that cotton planting really began to spread and even became one of the colony's chief sources of wealth. Once more we see the effects of export orientation on the Brazilian economy: the export market was the sole factor responsible for economic activity of any magnitude. This was again proved in the sector of cotton production after the period with which we are dealing now, when the tide turned and the output of the Brazilian product, ousted from the world market by its competitors, began to fall off. The cotton regions that could count on no substitute for their chief product collapsed, as was the case of Maranhão in particular, and their brief and brilliant period of prosperity came to an end.[37]

The first consignment of Brazilian cotton to the exterior seems to have been made in 1760. It was shipped from Maranhão, which in that year exported 651 *arrobas* * of cotton.[38] Cotton began to be exported from Pernambuco after 1778, but up to 1781 the quantities exported were insignificant.[39] Bahia and Rio de Janeiro followed suit. But it was in Maranhão that the phenomenon of cotton expansion was most interesting, since here it began from scratch in a poor region of little economic significance in the colony as a whole. Cotton brought life to Maranhão and transformed it within a few decades, making it one of the colony's wealthiest and most important captaincies. This was due chiefly to the activities of the Companhia Geral do Comércio do Grão-Pará e do Maranhão (The Grão-Pará and Maranhão General Trading Company), which had been granted a monopoly contract by the crown for

---

* An *arroba* varied from 25–32 *arráteis*, which was the Portuguese pound, weighing 12–16 ounces according to region. The arroba is thus a Portuguese quarter, equivalent nowadays to 15 kilograms or 28 pounds. —Translator.

exploiting cotton in 1756. The company provided credit, slaves, and agricultural equipment for the cotton growers and stimulated the expansion of cotton planting, since the growth of the demand for this product was already noticeable. The company was destined never to gather the finest fruits of its efforts: it was wound up in 1777, when its concession failed to be renewed. But the impetus had been given, and Maranhão production continued to rise. It was later outstripped by the production of Pernambuco and Bahia, which could count on ampler resources for launching this new enterprise. But for a brief period, Maranhão played a part in the Brazilian economic scene.[40]

In the peak period of the early years of the nineteenth century, when Brazil took its place among the world's great cotton producers,[41] cotton planting was widely spread throughout Brazilian territory. According to St. Hilaire, the cotton area extended from the extreme north [42] to the highlands of Campos Gerais (Paraná) and was advancing southward as far as latitude 30.2° S., in the vicinity of Pôrto Alegre.[43] In the interior, even Goiás was producing and exporting cotton.[44] The whole country was affected by the boom. But it proved to be no more than a short-lived fever. When prices began to drop at the beginning of the nineteenth century, chiefly as a result of the considerable increase in North American production boosted by the application of new techniques that Brazil had failed to adopt, the colony's cotton area began to recede and eventually became limited to one or two points, where yields were very low.

The cotton crop was not planted in the old established centers of the traditional Brazilian tropical crops, sugar and tobacco. The crop dislikes too much moisture and particularly irregularities in precipitation, since rain damages the fiber if it occurs in the season when the boll begins to open. Hence, the regions away from the coast, where rainfall is less frequent and more regular in its occurrence, are better suited to its requirements than those selected for the growing of cane and tobacco. In Maranhão the crop spread well inland, advanced along the margins of the Itapecuru, and became concentrated principally around Caxias. More than half the total production of Maranhão came from this district.[45] In Ceará, cotton planting spread to the Jaguaribe basin, and the chief center was located in the upper Sertão around Icó. Aracati, the natural outlet for this region, became an important port of shipment and in 1794 was already exporting 16,000–18,000 arrobas of cotton.[46]

The northeast witnessed a similar development. Sugarcane was grown in the lower areas along the coast and cotton in the intermediate strip between the coastal lowlands and the *caatinga* of the inland Sertão, the *agreste*.* Koster, who lived in Pernambuco for many years, described the gradual shift of cotton planting in this captaincy from the coastlands to the interior as the planters absorbed the lessons of experience. He refers to the significant fact that the owners of cotton gins gradually transferred their equipment and installed themselves in the new centers inland, first in Goiana and then in Limoeiro and Bom-Jardim, whereas before they had been concentrated only two leagues inland from Recife.[47] In Paraíba similar developments occurred; and since in this region cotton became the chief product, ousting sugar from its supremacy, the economic axis of this captaincy slowly shifted from the coastal zone to the new regions opened up inland, far from the traditional centers of Paraíba's wealth.

The remote interior also benefited from the preference of the cotton plant for a drier climate. In the sertões on the borders of Bahia and Minas Gerais, a fairly important cotton region was established. In the southern part of Bahia it embraced the area extending east of the São Francisco River, including the Serra de Monte Alto, Rio de Contas, Gavião, and Conquista, its chief center being in Caitité. In Minas Gerais, the cotton region ex-

---

* *Agreste* literally means "wilderness." It is "sub-xerophytic vegetation which occurs on the eastern margins of the Northeastern region, in the form of woodland carrying tall trees with a vigorous undergrowth. This woodland, known as "agreste," forms the transition zone between the coastal forest and the xerophytic caatinga." H. Robinson, *Latin America* (McDonald & Evans, 1961), p. 355.—Translator.

tended southward from the comarca of Minas Novas (Fanado, the present-day town of Minas Novas, Água-Suja, São Domingos, and Chapada), as far as Peçanha in the Rio Doce valley.[48] Most of the cotton shipped from Bahia came from this region, which also exported part of its product through Rio de Janeiro.[49] In Minas Gerais, the region west of the São Francisco also supplied cotton. We have already considered production in Goiás.[50]

It is obvious from the foregoing account that cotton had opened up new agricultural possibilities in areas which had hitherto been restricted to pastoral or mining activities. But cotton production in these areas was always on a precarious footing. Distance from the ports of shipment and difficulties in transportation were obstacles that finally led to the decline of cotton cultivation in these areas. International competition and falling prices eliminated these less favored areas; and the only cotton regions that survived, although their position on the international market was a very minor one, were those of Maranhão and the northeast.

The expansion of cotton planting was faciliated by the relative simplicity of cotton production. Unlike sugar, it required little effort beyond the care of the crop. Processing was confined to the separation of lint from seed and subsequent baling of the lint, simple operations calling for only the few basic installations. Even so there was a certain separation between the actual planting and care of the crop and the processing, as we can infer from Koster's account of the transfer of equipment owned by independent operators, so that the cotton planters were spared the need to process their crops and thus avoided any further investment.

Despite this separation, cotton planting was organized along the same lines as sugarcane cultivation. In both cases it was large-scale exploitation that prevailed. Although cotton processing is less complex than sugar planting, cotton is more suited to large-scale exploitation. The crop requires a large labor supply, particularly during harvesting, and this in itself favors large-scale cultivation.[51] Thus we find cotton cultivation, particularly in the chief production areas of Maranhão and Goiás, concentrated on the large estate. Gayozo, who wrote the most comprehensive account of Maranhão at the beginning of the nineteenth century, gives the following figures for a typical cotton plantation: 50 slaves, producing 2,000 arrobas of unseparated cotton in one year—that is, 600 arrobas of lint, not taking into account the tithe paid to the crown.[52] The influx of slaves into Maranhão provoked by expansion of cotton cultivation is a clear indication of its nature.[53]

The third of the colony's major cash crops was tobacco. It had been cultivated in Brazil since the seventeenth century, and by the beginning of the eighteenth it had already begun to figure in appreciable quantities in the export trade.[54] The level of production reached at this period was maintained throughout the eighteenth century. There was, however, no marked increase and it remained stationary until the beginning of the nineteenth century, when it began to drop.[55] Be that as it may, tobacco only lost its place to cotton as the colony's most important export staple after sugar in the last years of the eighteenth century.

The bulk of the tobacco exported was destined for Africa, where it was used for the purchase of slaves. It was particularly important in the Bahian slave trade. When, under the 1815 Treaty between Portugal and England, slave traffic north of the Equator was prohibited, thus excluding Guinea, Bahia's chief source of supply—the vigilance of the English ships had undertaken to see that this prohibition was respected which assured its effectiveness—the Bahian tobacco production suffered a severe blow. Its decline dates from this period, and only much later did tobacco growing in Bahia make a comeback.

As in the case of sugarcane and cotton, although on a smaller scale, tobacco planting spread to all parts of the colony. It was, however, more concentrated, since the important tobacco-growing areas were smaller in extent than those devoted to sugarcane and cotton. I am, of course, excluding the areas where it was grown only in small quantities and where cultivation was therefore not widespread. The most important tobacco center was Cachoeiro in Bahia; it had already become so in Antonil's day and has in fact continued to be the chief tobacco region down to the present day. Next in importance was Inhambupe, also in Bahia, in the Campinhos de Santo Amaro da Purificação, followed by Sergipe, then still a comarca of Bahia.[56] Some tobacco was grown in the Rio de Janeiro area, on the islands in the bay, on Ilha Grande, and along the coastal fringe, as in Parati.[57] It was also grown in Espírito Santo. In São Paulo it was planted along the coastal lowlands (the snuff produced in the island of São Sebastião was highly prized) and in the Paraíba valley, where tobacco growing was the chief activity of the inhabitants of Guaratinguetá and Lorena.[58] More important than either of the two foregoing districts, indeed a region of some importance, was that of Southern Minas—Aiuruoca, Carrancas, and particularly Baependi and Pouso Alto. In this region, the wealth of the tobacco growers can be gauged from the number of plants raised on their lands, and in some estates there were as many as 60,000 plants.[59]

Of all the crops raised in Brazil, tobacco was the one to which most care was devoted. It provides an honorable exception to the general carelessness of agricultural practices, and the attention given to tobacco raising is a slightly redeeming feature of colonial agriculture. The nature of the plant is responsible for this fact, since if not treated with due care it withers and dies; it therefore demands a degree of attention not strictly necessary for the cane and cotton crops.[60] It was the only crop for which fertilizers were used in the preparation of the soil. The plant was treated with special care while it grew. It was properly transplanted, protected from the excessive heat of the sun, and regularly pruned and caterpillars and insect pests were carefully removed. Vilhena recommends that the latter be achieved by allowing a flock of turkeys to wander among the plants, "for these creatures appear to be inordinately fond of such pests." The care required considerably reduced the advantages of large-scale cultivation, and this, together with the absence of any need to establish elaborate installations for processing and preparing the crop—the only thing needed being a curing shed in which the leaf was hung up to dry and subsequently twisted into rolls—made tobacco growing accessible to the poorer planters. Besides the large-scale planters who produced as many as 200 rolls, there were those who produced no more than the modest contribution of 20 rolls.[61] But, although the figures we have for tobacco production are not as precise as those for sugar and cotton, we can judge from the testimony of those who concerned themselves with the matter that the nature of tobacco cultivation was, on the whole, no different from that of the colony's other great agricultural products. The predominance of slave labor on the tobacco plantation is an indication of this.[62]

The three crops we have considered in the foregoing account were the mainstay of colonial agriculture. In terms both of the amount of production involved and the number of people engaged in this production, they represent almost the entire agrarian economy of the country. I do not propose to give here any account of coffee production. It had been introduced into Pará at the beginning of the eighteenth century, from whence it had spread to Maranhão and later to Rio de Janeiro, and was beginning to penetrate important sectors of the latter captaincy, spreading thence along the Paraíba valley into the border zones of Minas Gerais and São Paulo. Although coffee had begun to be produced before the period we are now considering, it belongs not to this period but to the one following, when it was given the tremendous impetus that led to its development. At the period with which we are now concerned, however, coffee production was still too insignificant to warrant consideration; it later became so great that it no longer fitted the limited role it had hitherto played. I shall therefore confine myself to a brief consideration of the colony's other large-scale agricultural activities, "large-scale" in the sense to which I have limited the application of this term and in the economic character of the production involved, in the objectives that inspired it and the structure adopted.

Cacao cultivation is the chief agricultural activity of the northern captaincies, Pará and Rio Negro. Cacao is a spontaneous product of the Amazon forest and was exported from the time that penetration of the region was first effected. In the second half of the eighteenth century it began to be regularly cultivated. Soon afterward it was introduced into Maranhão and was also planted in Ilhéus in the captaincy of Bahia, which later became the country's most important cacao center and still occupies this position.

Rice, which was also regularly consumed in the colony itself, was a major export commodity in Maranhão and occupied second place in this captaincy's export trade, although its position in relation to cotton was a modest one. Rice was also cultivated on a smaller scale in Pará and Rio de Janeiro.

Anil, or indigo, was a commercial crop that never fulfilled its promise. In the eighteenth century, America became the world's greatest producer of indigo, outstripping India which had hitherto occupied this position. It was cultivated chiefly in Carolina, Georgia, and Santo Domingo. In Brazil, an attempt was made to introduce the cultivation of indigo on the initiative of the Marquis of Lavradio in 1769. The indigo plantations prospered in Rio de Janeiro, particularly around Cabo Frio where, at the end of the eighteenth century, there were 206 establishments for processing the indigo produced on the plantations in the area, and exports reached a level of 1,500 arrobas.[63] The captaincy's total output in 1796 was 5,000 arrobas.[64] But at about this time decadence set in as a result of renewed competition from India, where England, having lost her American colonies, had invested large sums in order to reinstate the country's indigo industry. This competition in fact affected all the American producers; but Brazil was particularly hard hit since its product, badly prepared and often adulterated, had a very bad reputation on the international market. The indigo plantations were thus abandoned and soon the cultivation of indigo practically disappeared.[65]

Subsistence Agriculture

I have already indicated my reasons for making a distinction—a basic one for an economy such as Brazil's —between large-scale, export-oriented agriculture and the type of agriculture which I termed "subsistence agriculture"; the latter was concerned with the growing of crops for the colony's own needs. Apart from this basic distinguishing feature, there was also a difference in the system of organization adopted in these two sectors of colonial agriculture. Whereas in commercial agriculture we find exploitation organized in large units of production (plantations and estates), employing a large labor force and collective organization of labor, in subsistence agriculture, on the contrary, other types of agrarian organization predominate which vary according to the specific conditions involved.

The two sectors do, of course, share a common ground. All the products of commercial agriculture—sugar, cotton, tobacco, and other commodities—were also consumed in the country itself, and in this sense they were therefore also "subsistence" crops. In the same way, certain products falling into the latter category were also exported, although only in small quantities and generally only occasionally. But the amounts produced were to such an extent favorable on the one hand to export and on the other to local consumption that there could be no possible confusion. Apart from this quantitative criterion, however, we must take into account the intrinsic economic nature of the two categories of agricultural production: the basis, the foremost objective, and the raison d'être of each.

Let us pick out a few branches of agricultural production in which the characteristics of the different types particularly overlap. Sugarcane spirits is the first of these. The position of this commodity is in any case a special one: it is a by-product of the sugar industry, and most of its flourishing production was due to this fact. Had it not been for sugar, the amount of cane spirits produced would certainly have been very much smaller. On the other hand, it falls into the special category of commodities used for barter in the slave trade.[1]

Similarly, cotton and rice, although produced for export, were also fairly widely consumed locally. In the case of the former, production had long preceded the period in which it began to be exported. But the situation was then completely reversed, and cotton began to be cultivated chiefly for export. Its consumption in the colony, where it continued to be used for manufacturing the rough cloth for the slaves, occupied a secondary and insignificant position.

As for rice, although widely consumed in the country, the bulk of its production was destined for export. We can even distinguish a sector of commercial rice cultivation, as in Maranhão and to a lesser extent in Pará and Rio de Janeiro, where the stimulus was clearly provided by the export trade and another, much smaller sector, spread over a number of regions, in which the cultivation of rice had the same character as that of the other crops destined solely for local consumption, such as manioc and maize.

Even in these extreme cases, then, a closer analysis reveals that the two sectors into which I have divided colonial production can be clearly distinguished. And having made these preliminary remarks, let us now see how subsistence agriculture was organized and distributed in the colony. In the first place, we find it in the very domain of large-scale agriculture, on the sugar plantations (engenhos) or the estates (fazendas). These were generally self-sufficient as regards the food requirements of their inhabitants and workers. The food crops needed were

grown either on the same lands as the main crop—as in the
case of maize, which was grown between the cotton plants, or
manioc, which was planted between the sugar cane [2]—or in
areas especially set aside for their production. Cultivation of
these subsistence crops was carried on partly on behalf of the
plantation owner, who employed for this purpose the same
slaves who tended the cash crops during the periods when they
would otherwise have been idle, and partly by the slaves themselves, who were given one day a week, generally Sunday, to
tend their own small allotments. In the case of particularly
benevolent planters, this concession was sometimes even extended to two days.

The cattle estates of the northeastern Sertão, which will be
considered in greater detail in a later chapter, were also self-
sufficient as regards the production of foodstuffs for their
workers. Along the alluvial plains bordering the rivers (the
only localities where agriculture was possible in this semiarid
region), the settlers attached to each estate raised agricultural
produce for the consumption of the *vaqueiros* (cattleherders).
A similar arrangement existed in the southern cattle estates of
Minas Gerais, Campos Gerais, and Rio Grande. Thus, by and
large it can be said that the food requirements of the rural population engaged in the production of commercial crops and
stock raising, who constituted the bulk of the total colonial
population, were sufficiently provided for by the local cultivation of subsistence crops as a subsidiary activity, and that there
was no need to resort to an outside supply.

The urban population was in a different position. Its needs
had to be met from sources outside the urban areas. Foodstuffs
were supplied partly from the surplus production of the large
estates. This surplus was generally small and frequently nonexistent; there were periods when the rise in prices for the export crops stimulated production to such an extent that the
food crops were completely abandoned, and even the large
estates were forced to resort to outside sources for their requirements. Hence specialized cultivation concerned solely
with the growing of crops for local needs began to emerge, and

we find the development of a different type of agricultural exploitation, separate from large-scale agriculture and with an organization which varied from establishment to establishment. These ranged from the large estate, organized along lines outwardly similar to those of the commercial plantations—and these were in a minority—to the modest *roça, chácara,* or *sítio,** where there were no slaves or paid workers and where the smallholder or tenant farmer did his own work.

We must distinguish between the independent smallholder and the tenant farmer, since the latter was frequently attached to the large estate as a sharecropper (*agregado*). The agregado is a rural worker to whom the owner has conceded, generally on a freehold basis or in exchange for a form of vassalage and the performance of small tasks on the estate, the right to establish himself on and exploit some unused part of the estate. I shall analyze the social status of the agregado in the chapter on the social organization of the colony. For the moment I wish merely to point out that in the economic sphere he occupied the position of a small independent producer. Although attached and subordinate to an estate owner, he was not really geared to the usual organization of large-scale agriculture.

Thus, whatever the degree of independence of the smallholder and whatever the size of his holding, side by side with the commercial estate there developed an individual and specialized type of farming which was concerned solely with the production of food crops for domestic consumption. It was a subsidiary sector of the colonial economy and depended entirely on the other sector, which gave it life and strength, hence its low economic level and the generally stagnant and precarious nature of its existence. Productivity was low and showed little vitality. Only in rare instances did subsistence agriculture rise above this level. In general, the labor in this

---

* All these are types of smallholding. The *roça* is a small patch of cleared land for the shifting cultivation of food crops; the *chácara* is a more permanent rural establishment, usually a smallholding on the outskirts of a town, with fruit trees, chickens, etc.; the *sítio* is simply a small farm.—Translator.

sector was not furnished by slaves; the humble small-time
farmer worked his own land. He sometimes had the help of a
Negro or two or, more commonly, the semislave labor of an Indian or half-breed. The exceptions in this sector were the
estates, which we shall consider in greater detail further on.

By preference subsistence agriculture would naturally be located close to the great urban centers whose needs it especially
catered to. Thus in Bahia it was carried on around the fringes
of the Recôncavo, where the lands devoted to food crops were
dotted between the sugar and tobacco plantations. Since food
crops could be grown in inferior or impoverished soil, no
longer able to support sugarcane or intensive plantation agriculture, in this region the subsistence farmers took over a few
leftover lands that were advantageous because of their proximity to the great markets for their products. In Pernambuco
the city was not well placed from this point of view. Its nearest
suppliers were situated at a considerable distance. Among
these the most notable were Tejucopapo and the island of
Itamaracá. Rio de Janeiro, like Bahia, is surrounded by a wide
bay and the lands bordering it are not all suitable for plantation agriculture. Therefore, there was ample land for the cultivation of food crops in the area, and they could also be grown
on the nearby islands. Thus, on the whole, the colony's capital
was well supplied, since the plots given over to the production
of food were situated on the outskirts of the city and spread
over a radius of more than one league inland.[3] The same pattern was repeated, although on a much smaller scale, in the
colony's other agglomerations.

Apart from these concentrations around the urban centers,
others were formed which, although distant from the centers,
were nevertheless their tributaries. The regions in which the
major cities were situated were always centers of large-scale
agricultural production; indeed, they had developed in consequence of such production since it was the only activity in the
colony capable of stimulating the growth of any sizable urban
agglomerations. (The case of the mining towns will be considered below.) Consequently, the lands near the cities were

nearly all given over to large-scale agriculture with its estates and plantations; there was not enough land left over for the cultivation of food crops, the "paltry" cultivation referred to by Judge João Rodrigues de Brito, who later became a Deputy to the Côrtes * in Lisbon, when asked to comment on the agricultural situation in the colony.[4] The disastrous consequences of this contemptuous dismissal will be considered below.

In consequence, food crops generally had to be grown far from the cities, although these were their only markets. Nevertheless, the most accessible sites were chosen for this purpose, particularly those along the coastal belt, since coastal shipping offered the cheapest means of transport for their produce. Thus any points along the coast not sufficiently favorable for commercial agriculture but acceptable for agricultural activity of a secondary order became the most concentrated areas of subsistence farming. The coastal belt extending from the Recôncavo of Bahia to Rio de Janeiro and thence southward was one such area. North of Bahia, beyond the strip taken up by large-scale plantations which extended as far as Paraíba, the coastal fringe was composed of sandy stretches unsuited to agriculture and was never used for this purpose. South of Bahia, however, a number of small agricultural centers were formed, all strictly geared to the production of foodstuffs for the colony's major centers. They succeeded each other along a continuous strip comprising the comarca of Ilhéus and the captaincies of Pôrto Seguro and Espírito Santo. Similar developments took place south of Rio de Janeiro along the coastal belt of the captaincy of São Paulo, including the coastland of what is now Paraná, on the island of Santa Catarina and the adjoining mainland, and finally in Rio Grande do Sul. These areas were all, and almost exclusively, given over to the production of agricultural commodities for consumption in Rio de Janeiro, Bahia, and Pernambuco.

With the exception of Espírito Santo and São Paulo—and then only to a very limited extent—large-scale agriculture had

* The Côrtes was the parliament of the three estates (clergy, nobility, and commonalty).—Translator.

either never been established or else had been a failure in these areas. For one reason or another they were not suited to this type of exploitation, and the people who had settled in them, for the most part leading economically marginal existences with a low standard of living, had only done so because they had failed to find a place in better favored areas where prospects were brighter—that is, those devoted to commercial agriculture. The mediocrity of the paltry subsistence agriculture carried on in these less favored southern areas which, given the economic conditions prevailing in the colony, could have played only the minor role it did, with its extremely low economic level, meant that spontaneous economic and moral social selection would operate to bring them only the inferior categories of colonization. Hence, as a rule we find in these only a residual human element, mainly Indian half-breeds who had preserved the indolence and negative qualities of the Indian, qualities ill-adapted to a higher pattern of material and moral existence. Others were degenerate and decadent white men.[5] Martius, Prince Maximilian, and St. Hilaire, who traveled through these regions, have left us distressing accounts of the conditions they witnessed. They usually make an exception only of the inhabitants of the extreme south, Santa Catarina, and Rio Grande, where there had been the intervention of a special factor in the formation of the population: the sponsored colonization of Azoreans, which gave this area of settlement its distinguishing feature. In spite of this, however, it was also occupied by poor settlers with a mediocre standard of living.[6]

This type of autonomous subsistence agriculture, that is, separated from the domains of commercial agriculture and specializing in its own particular field, was also found on a considerable scale in Minas Gerais. The majority of the population in the mining districts—and this was still the case at the beginning of the nineteenth century in spite of the decadence of the mines—was engaged in the extraction of gold and diamonds which, unlike export agriculture, did not permit the overlapping of activities we find in the latter; thus, it was possible for the people engaged in it to devote part of their attention to growing subsistence crops. Mining is a more continuous form of activity, and the labor force employed is fully occupied. In this respect, the mining population was in the same position as that of the urban centers. In Minas Gerais, which was more densely populated than the other gold mining centers, this fact stimulated the in some ways appreciable development of an agriculture entirely geared to the production of food crops for local consumption. This development was so marked that at one time it alarmed the mother country and her administrative officials who, magnetized by the precious metal and gems whose supply was beginning to dwindle, saw in this agricultural activity one of the causes of the decline in mining and the consequent fall in the revenue of the sacrosanct Royal Treasury.[7]

The proximity of a coastal nucleus of settlement as important as Rio de Janeiro reinforced the tendency to turn to agriculture. And thanks to these exceptional circumstances, agriculture in Minas, although almost exclusively of a subsistence type—the only exceptions being the cotton plantations of Minas Novas and the tobacco plantations of Southern Minas—managed to reach a much higher level than in the other regions of the colony in the same position. And it is in Minas Gerais that we find one of the few instances of the exception mentioned above in the organization of subsistence agriculture: the large estate devoted solely to the production of commodities for domestic consumption.

Other special areas where subsistence agriculture found favorable conditions for development were those along the great communication routes over which traveled large numbers of mule convoys, the sole means of transporting goods overland, and cattle droves on their way to the coastal markets from the fazendas of the interior. The mule convoys are the most important for the aspect that concerns us here, since muleteers and animals had to be supplied with provisions along the road. The volume of this traffic was considerable, and in the chapter on communications and transport I shall attempt to give some indication of its importance. For the moment it need only be pointed out that it was sufficient to amply compensate the establishments that sprang up along the major routes, notably those linking Minas Gerais, Goiás, São Paulo, and Rio de Janeiro, and to provoke a rural activity that was by no means insignificant. The amount of maize consumed by the mules was sufficiently large for it to become a profitable enough business for the suppliers to offer not only accommodation on the *ranchos* * established as resting places along the way, but also, as an incentive to the travelers, free food for the muleteers and fodder for their horses.[8] The cattle droves also contributed, although to a lesser extent, to the establishment of settlement and agricultural activity in areas that would otherwise have been neglected. The anonymous author of the *Roteiro do Maranhão* refers to this agricultural activity.

The secondary role to which the country's economic system, centered around export agriculture, consigned subsistence agriculture created a problem which grew to be one of the most serious facing the colonial population. This was the supply of food to the more densely populated urban nuclei, where shortage of staple commodities became the invariable rule. Rio de Janeiro is the only exception, by reason of the circumstances noted above, and seems to be the only center that did not suffer from the permanent shortage of foodstuffs that afflicted the colony's other major cities. In these, particularly in Bahia and Pernambuco, there was a chronic dearth of food which frequently amounted to open and widespread famine. This happened particularly when there was a rise in prices for the agricultural products of the large plantations, when all activities and energies were immediately switched completely to export agriculture and subsistence crops were neglected and abandoned. This was a paradoxical situation, since misery and hunger lurked under the shade of the prosperity brought about by these high prices.

Colonial legislation had long concerned itself with this difficult problem and had attempted to remedy the situation.[9] The

---

* Rancho—a rude hut where herdsmen or travelers may find shelter.— Translator.

royal decree of February 25, 1688, had stipulated that the sugar planters were to plant at least 500 mounds of manioc for each slave employed in the cultivation of the land; and the decree of February 27, 1701, stipulated that the owners of ships engaged in the African slave trade should possess lands given over to the cultivation of sufficient manioc for their crews and the slaves they transported. Both laws were reinforced by the royal provision of April 28, 1767.[10] Later, a clause was inserted in the title deeds of land grants (*sesmarias*) requiring the grantee to plant a certain number of mounds of manioc from the first year of taking possession of his land.[11] Another legal enactment stipulated that no one was entitled to set up as a sugar planter unless he owned more than seven slaves.

It seems, however, that the emphasis on such precautions and the various measures adopted did not have any appreciable effect. The planters all attempted to evade compliance with these requirements, and one can imagine how ineffectual they would prove when the planters saw a chance to profit from rising sugar prices and the prospect of a substantial business deal. Vilhena, who was living in Bahia during one such propitious period in the last years of the eighteenth century, could find no words with which to deplore the widespread disobedience to these decrees and warned against the dangers that loomed ahead and were already perceptible in the inferior quality and exorbitant prices of foodstuffs.[12] The precaution taken at this period was to ban the export of foodstuffs from the captaincy. The greatest sufferer from this ban was Pernambuco, which depended on Bahia for its supplies.

There is no need to enlarge on the bitterness provoked by these legal measures. All sorts of ills were attributed to the stipulations made in them and although these were seldom observed, they were held responsible for most of the difficulties that beset the planters. In the inquiry conducted in Bahia in 1807 on the orders of Governor Count da Ponte, the persons consulted, all occupying important positions in administration, agriculture, and commerce, fulminated against the measures that deprived or sought to deprive them of the fat profits which they directly or indirectly reaped from cane cultivation. They found these measures so absurd that one of them, the notorious owner of the Engenho da Ponte, Manuel Ferreira da Câmara, did not hesitate to utter his formal defiance of the law: "I will not plant a single root of manhiot, so as not to fall into the absurd situation of renouncing the best crop in the country for the worst one in it. . . ." [13] But none of them considered discussing the true problem, the famine that periodically afflicted the Recôncavo. Why should they have recalled this fact when the huge profits they reaped from sugar gave them more than enough to pay the prices, which for them were not high, of the foodstuffs they needed?

Pernambuco seems to have been the captaincy most seriously affected by the shortage of food. Apart from the fact that local production was extremely restricted—it was far less than that of Bahia—the situation was aggravated by the droughts which plagued the Sertão at frequent intervals, when the starving populace of the interior poured into the coastland in search of some relief for their misery. Thus, during the Great Drought of 1793, which took a terrible toll of lives, Bahia had to come to the aid of the afflicted peoples, sending large consignments of provisions. [14] Although less populous than Bahia, Pernambuco depended much more on its external supplies; in the tables of commodities shipped from Rio de Janeiro cited previously, Pernambuco's quota is approximately twice that of Bahia's. [15]

Maranhão was in a like situation. Famine was frequent, since the cultivation of foodstuffs was sacrificed to the growing of cotton. This neglect occurred not only in the capital but throughout Itapecuru, the great cotton region. [16] Martius observed that in São Luis there was sometimes "such an extraordinary lack of foodstuffs" that the inhabitants were forced to rely on rice to ward off hunger. [17] Fortunately for the captaincy, there was at least an abundant supply of rice, thanks to the fact that this was an exportable crop. As we can see from the foregoing account, even the feeding of its population was in colonial Brazil dependent on the export trade.

In conclusion, let us now consider the distribution of the

different food crops in the country. There is no need to recall that both in the area devoted to it and in the quantity produced, manioc—"the bread of the land"—occupied an undisputed position. In Brazil manioc was the necessary accompaniment to man. As a result of its nutritive value, the adaptability of its cultivation to any soil, and its exceptional hardiness, manioc, introduced through its traditional use by the native, was universally adopted by the colonists as the basic item of diet, and cassava flour has remained the staple foodstuff of Brazilians down to the present day.[18] This is undoubtedly the greatest contribution to Brazilian life by the indigenous culture.

Nevertheless, despite its universal distribution, certain variations in the degree to which it was cultivated may be observed in the different regions of the country. Thus, in the south, maize predominates. Capistrano de Abreu, commenting on the greater dominance of maize in the diet of the south, considers the use of this cereal to be a cultural trait, indicating the predominance of Paulista influence. And, linking the use of maize as a staple foodstuff to the *monjolo* used for pounding the grain, he associates the cultivation of maize with the prevalence of running water, used for operating this device. In the sertões of the north, where water is scarce, *munguzá*, which corresponds to the Paulista *canjica*,* was only served in the big houses, where there were slaves to pound the corn.[19] This association of Capistrano's is extremely interesting; but we must take into account other factors that contributed to the greater diffusion of maize in the south: natural conditions other than the occurrence of running water, possibly ethnic traits, or the greater use of mules as pack animals in the mountainous regions of the south, the mules' basic feeding stuff being corn.[20] The fact remains that, whereas in the north,

---

* *Munguzá* is a gruel prepared from corn and coconut milk (or sometimes cow's milk) not unlike rice pudding. *Canjica* is one of Brazil's great national dishes. It is a dessert made from grated green corn, pounded to a paste, with various ingredients added: sugar, cinnamon, and coconut milk, or simply sugar and butter.—Translator.

manioc reigns supreme, maize occupying a much less prominent position, in the south the situation is reversed. Referring
to São Paulo, Martius even avers with some exaggeration that
manioc is hardly cultivated "because it is considered unwhole-
some" and adds that in the northern captaincies the same opinion was held concerning *fubá* (corn meal).[21]

We can trace the dividing line between the areas dominated
by manioc and maize, respectively, roughly along the frontiers
of Bahia and Minas Gerais. In the latter, maize took pride of
place. Listing the foodstuffs consumed in Minas Gerais, the
anonymous author of *Considerações sôbre as Duas Classes de
Povoadores de Minas Gerais* (Notes on the two types of settler
in Minas Gerais), attributed to Vieira Couto, refers only to
maize, beans, and "certain products of the cane-mills." On his
long journeys through this captaincy, which he thoroughly explored, St. Hilaire also noted the much greater frequency of
maize.

In the north, on the contrary, this cereal was little cultivated.
The report on the products of Pernambuco and the captaincies
attached to it previously cited, *Idéia da População da Capitania da Pernambuco e das suas Anexas,* written during the
governorship of José César de Meneses, refers to the presence
of maize in only one district, the parish of São Lourenço da
Mata. In Pará, the staple diet consisted of fish, rice, dried meat,
and manioc, the latter in its most indigestible form, *farinha
d'água.*[22] It is interesting to note that in the north, maize
seemed to be associated with cotton planting and, together
with beans, formed the staple diet of the slaves employed on
the cotton estates of Pernambuco.[23] Martius makes the same
observation about Maranhão.[24] In fact, these two crops do
well together, and the same type of land can be used for both,
maize and cotton being planted in alternate rows. And similarly, manioc was planted together with sugarcane—associa-
tions which may not be without significance.

Along the coastal belt, the limit of manioc was further south
than in the interior. It would seem, therefore, that climate is an
important factor. In the southern coastlands of Bahia, maize

was so scarce that Judge Luis Tomás de Navarro, who traveled through the region in 1808, found it extremely difficult to feed his mules as far as Canavieiras.[25] From this point southward —in Espírito Santo, Rio de Janeiro, São Paulo, and even Santa Catarina—maize was much more common, but manioc still predominated.[26] In São Paulo, maize abounded on the uplands, whereas manioc outstripped it on the coastlands.[27] In Santa Catarina, a captaincy which was then confined to the coastal belt—the interior plateau had not yet been incorporated in the captaincy and formed a separate district—the production, consumption, and export of manioc was much greater than that of maize.[28] Further south, manioc disappeared, even along the coast. In Rio Grande do Sul it was not grown at all.

After manioc and maize, the foodstuffs most consumed in the colony, and hence those most grown, were beans and rice. Beans were grown throughout the colony with almost no differences in the quantities produced, although the crop appears to have been more important in the central-south: Minas Gerais, Rio de Janeiro, São Paulo, and Espírito Santo. Rice, a major export item for Maranhão and also exported but to a much lesser extent from Rio de Janeiro and Pará, was widely cultivated for domestic consumption on the coastal lowlands from the extreme north to São Paulo. The climatic factors of heat and humidity are obviously the most important. Hence, further south, in Santa Catarina and Rio Grande, rice was not cultivated.[29] Wheat was cultivated in the south from São Paulo, particularly in the Campos Gerais (the present-day state of Paraná) to Rio Grande. In the latter captaincy, wheat was the staple foodstuff, apart from meat, and a fair amount of the cereal was consigned to the other captaincies.[30] The same applied to Santa Catarina.[31] Wheat in small quantities was also grown in Minas Gerais—Guanhães, Serro, and Peçanha on the Serra da Piedade close to Sabará [32]—and in Bahia, which sent wheat flour to the capital.[33]

The other food crops were not sufficiently important to merit attention. Very few green vegetables were grown. Even in the major cities fresh vegetables were rare, and only the wealthy could afford such luxuries. Fruit was in more or less the same category. Orchards and, less frequently, vegetable gardens were sometimes attached to the large estates, in the engenhos of the northeast and the fazendas of the south, where they were regarded as luxuries for the masters' tables. In the southern captaincies, particularly in Rio Grande do Sul and Santa Catarina, vegetable gardens were more frequent. Onions were widely grown in these regions, and fair amounts were sent to the other captaincies. This was no doubt due to the influence of the Islanders.*

---

* The Azoreans were known as the Islanders.—Translator.

Mining

In order to facilitate exposition the two types of agriculture were considered in succession, but I should properly have dealt with mining immediately after commercial agriculture, since the economic character of mining was the same as that of large-scale agricultural exploitation and it therefore belongs in the same category. Both were concerned with the exploitation of products destined solely for export, and in both cases organization was directed toward this end, their development being extraneous to the actual needs of Brazilian society. This fact explains their precarious nature insofar as the fundamental interests of this society were concerned and their inability to provide a solid economic basis and a stable way of life for the human community that they supported. We have already seen this in relation to large-scale, market-oriented agriculture which, among its other consequences, even prevented agriculture from resolving the Brazilian population's most basic problem, its food supply. We shall find a similar situation in mining.

At the beginning of the nineteenth century the mining industry in Brazil, which had begun under such brilliant auspices and claimed the lion's share of the country's attention and absorbed most of its activity for a hundred years, had almost reached utter ruin. Warning symptoms of this had long since revealed themselves to observers not completely blinded by greed. From the middle years of the eighteenth century on-

195

ward mining had steadily declined. In those years the zenith
had been reached; productivity was at its peak before the successive discoveries, which kept the flame of hope flickering in
some areas even as it was being snuffed out in others, came to
an end. Mining activity was spread over the widest area it was
to encompass.

The causes of the decadence that followed this peak of prosperity are not difficult to determine. In this decadence the
peculiar characteristics of the gold deposits found in Brazilian
territory were allied to other, more profound factors of an economic and social order. Gold exploited in Brazil was nearly all
derived from recent placer deposits; the auriferous rocks were
few in number and their ore content was poor.[1] At first only the
placer deposits were worked.[2] Later, as each became exhausted, the following were successively worked: the more recent
and superficial "veins" of alluvial gold found in the river beds,
where the deposits beneath the layers of sand and gravel were
at times so rich that the *bateia* (pan) could be dispensed with
and the gold particles picked out by hand; the older and
deeper deposits of the river banks and their immediate vicinity
(*tabuleiros*); and finally the deposits in the rifts and clefts of
the neighboring hills (*grupiaras*).

In all these workings the problems were more or less easy to
solve. With the rudimentary techniques and implements at
their disposal, whatever the degree of effort involved, the
miners managed to uncover rich deposits of alluvial gold beneath the fairly shallow layers of sand, earth, or clay covering
the easily washed *cascalho,* or subsoil of gravel mixed with
quartz, which contained the gold particles. But once these accessible deposits were exhausted and the gold-bearing rocks
had to be tackled, the situation changed completely. On the
more accessible outcrops, or where the veins were found in the
more friable rock (these semidecomposed rocks were termed
"rotten rocks" by the miners), methods of extraction were still
comparatively simple. But where the rocks were hard—
generally quartz, pyrites, itabarites, and other extremely com-
pacted igneous rocks—the lack of expert knowledge and the

rudimentary techniques of the miners proved insuperable obstacles,[3] which mounted as the deposits became scarcer and deeper.[4] The lack of suitable techniques and equipment, therefore, made it difficult, and finally impossible, to exploit deposits in depth. The implements employed, and the routine nature of the methods used, the almost total ignorance of mining techniques of the miners, whose knowledge extended no further than the few practices learned from experience and which they never varied, made it impossible in each case to continue exploitation beyond a certain point. It was only because Brazilian gold was spread over a wide area that it was possible to continue to exploit it—initially with extraordinary success, thanks to the high touch * of the alluvial gold found in certain districts—for the best part of a century. And thus, by moving continually from place to place, although the surface was virtually only scratched, the miners found enough gold to occupy them over a long period.[5]

The truth is that the mining industry in Brazil never went beyond a fleeting adventure. It had hardly touched one point before it was ready to abandon it for another, moving ever onward. And this is the main reason why, in spite of the wealth produced by mining—most of which, incidentally, was drained out of the country—it has left so few traces, other than the wholesale destruction of natural resources wreaked throughout the mining districts, leaving them with a bleak aspect which even today still offends the eye of the beholder, that general aspect of ruin that provoked the consternation of St. Hilaire at the beginning of the last century and that has gone unremedied even in our own day.

Thus, at the dawn of the nineteenth century, throughout the whole of the vast area in which they had occurred, practically all the gold-bearing gravels and surface deposits had been exhausted. Mining had reached the point of final collapse. Nothing had been stored up during the period of prosperity to meet

---

* C. R. Boxer tells us that the touch of the gold found in Minas Gerais oscillated between 21.5 and 22.5 carats. *The Golden Age of Brazil*, p. 39.—Translator.

such an eventuality. The resources needed to restore mining on the new basis that the situation demanded had, under the onerous system of taxation then in force, evaporated in the vain sumptuousness of the court of Dom João V and the costly and inefficient Portuguese administration. The few crumbs that remained from this financial orgy were soon to be squandered by the improvident dissipation of the miners themselves. Ignorance, backward techniques, and the inability to organize the chaotic society which had evolved from the mining communities combined to complete the disaster—the only criteria governing organization being the collection of the royal fifths for the spendthrift king and his court of parasites and, with what remained, satisfaction of the immoderate appetites of the horde of adventurers who swarmed into the region. It would have been impossible with purely local resources to resurrect the mining industry in Brazil.

Foreigners, particularly the English, who were given permission to establish themselves in the mines in 1824, were to gather the sorry spoils of this adventure of the past and to instill some life—a fresh albeit light breeze—into the Brazilian mining industry. Before their coming, the true picture of the period is given in the odyssey of a man like Eschwege,* who attempted to impart basic scientific information and to teach concepts known in Europe for centuries and to appeal to the intelligence and common sense of the miners, and who desperately knocked on the doors of a stubborn and inept administration that was unable to grasp the need for efficient legal measures—only to see all the efforts of a tireless activity that lasted eleven years (1810–1821) finally frustrated.

Let us now rapidly survey what remained of mining. In the final throes of its death agony, gold was still being exploited in the four central captaincies, Minas Gerais (still first and foremost), Goiás, Mato Grosso, and to a very limited extent in Bahia.[6] The mining activities carried on elsewhere were neg-

---

* This is not M. C. von Eschwege, the German explorer previously cited on p. 6, but W. L. von Eschwege, author of *Pluto Brasiliensis*, a mining expert appointed as consultant by the government. Later in this chapter the author discusses his work in greater detail.—Translator.

ligible: In São Paulo what could be considered as mining had disappeared a century before; in Espírito Santo nothing remained of the mines of Castelo in Itapemirim; [7] the same applied, more or less, to the mines of the sertões of Macacu in Rio de Janeiro; [8] and the unprofitable mines of Caríris Novas (Ceará) had long since been abandoned. [9] There is no need to expatiate on the new attempts made at the beginning of the nineteenth century, as in Rio Grande do Sul, since they were of minimal significance. [10]

In Mato Grosso, although mining continued to be the captaincy's prime source of production and wealth, it was nothing compared to the past. Some gold was still extracted from the old workings in the vicinity of Cuiabá and Vila Bela, as well as along the upper Paraná, where the gravels of the rivers closed off after the discovery of diamonds in the region in 1746 remained unworked, in spite of urgent and oft-renewed requests by the captaincy's inhabitants, until 1805 when the region was finally opened up and mining allotments (*datas*) were distributed by Governor Abreu e Meneses. [11] The mines of the upper Paraguay, a reserve which had by chance been retained by reason of the administration's narrow policy on diamonds up to the nineteenth century, for a time reanimated the decadent mining activity of this captaincy; in 1828—we have no earlier figures—there were still 3,000 slaves working in these mines, according to an estimate made by D'Alincourt. [12] In Vila Bela at that time there were no more than 400 and in Cuiabá there remained only a few itinerant prospectors.

In Goiás the situation was no better. The state of profound economic and social disintegration which afflicted this captaincy, whose sole source of income had been gold, has already been described. [13] Exploitation of gold in this captaincy was distributed between the two regions into which it was divided, south and north. In the southern region the diggings were concentrated along the headwaters of the Tocantins and Araguaia on the one side, and the affluents flowing into the right bank of the Paranaíba on the other side of this watershed, which runs across the captaincy from east to west and along which the greater part of the captaincy's population was, and is still, con-

centrated. New workings were also opened up at the beginning
of the nineteenth century in this part of Goiás, causing a renewed outburst of mining activity which proved to be yet another flash in the pan. These new diggings were the mines of
Anicuns, discovered in 1809,[14] and those along the Claro and
Pilões rivers, which had been closed off during the governorship of Gomes Freire de Andrade,* when Goiás was still attached to Minas Gerais, after diamonds had been found in the
region, the crown enforcing its customary policy in this respect.[15]

In the northern region, where mining had never really
amounted to much, it had now become altogether insignificant.
Cunha Matos affirmed that in this district "the business of mining nowadays is of such little account that it can rightly be said
that the land is no longer properly worked for gold, but merely
scratched a bit here and there." São José, Santa Rita, Cachoeira, and Conceição were the only districts in which some
activity survived.

Only in Minas Gerais was gold production still of some
importance, compared, that is, with the other captaincies since
decadence in Minas was also profound. For this district we
possess the detailed statistical records compiled by Eschwege
in 1814. According to the tables published in his *Pluto Brasiliensis*, the number of diggings in Minas Gerais was 555; the
number of people working them was 6,662, of whom 6,493
were slaves; and the number of *faiscadores,* that is, miners
working on their own, was more than 5,749, of whom 1,871
were slaves. Gold production for that year was 228,449 *oita-
vas* † (approximately 800 kilograms).[16] Distribution of the
gold diggings still roughly corresponded to the former pattern
of settlement analyzed in the chapter on the settlement of the
interior. Although very much reduced in importance, particularly in the marginal zones of Minas Novas, Sul de Minas, and

---

* Gomes Freire de Andrade was Governor of the captaincy of Minas
Gerais from 1735 to 1752.—Translator.

† An *oitava* is one-eighth of an *onça* (28.69 grams or 1/16 pound).—
Translator.

Paracatu, there were still diggings in all, or nearly all, of the districts opened up in the eighteenth century.

In contrast to agriculture and the colony's other activities, mining was from the very beginning subject to a special regime which strictly controlled its every detail. The first definite news that gold strikes had been made in Brazil reached the mother country in the last years of the sixteenth century; this was a report of the insignificant finds in the stream gravels of São Paulo, which never really came to anything. And by 1603, the first legislation on gold had been drafted, the royal charter of August 15 of that year. This legislation established the basic principles which, despite later modifications, were to be retained in all subsequent enactments: the diggings could be freely exploited and the crown reserved the right to exact one-fifth of all gold extracted. When at the end of the seventeenth century the first really rich strikes in the territory were reported—the discoveries in the region that was to become the captaincy of Minas Gerais—the earlier law was replaced by the Mining Code of April 19, 1702, the "Regimento dos Superintendentes, Guardas-Mores e Oficiais Deputados para as Minas de Ouro" (Regulations for the Superintendents, Crown Representatives and other Crown Officials appointed to look after the Gold Mines).[17] This code, with certain subsequent amendments that did not alter its basic features, remained in force up to the empire period.[18]

This is not the proper place to expand on the mining legislation passed in colonial Brazil. An admirable critical study based both on the authority of his scientific knowledge as an expert on the subject, and on his authority as the government's officially appointed investigator, was made by Eschwege in his *Pluto Brasiliensis*. An excellent modern summary, although written from a point of view of indirect concern to the historian, is given in Calógeras's great work, *As Minas do Brasil*. I shall therefore confine myself to a general outline of this legislation in order to give some idea of the system of exploitation in force throughout the colonial period.

Discovery of any gold strike had to be reported to the proper authorities.[19] These authorities then proceeded to the site of the discovery, demarcated the gold field and the *datas*—the name given to the mining allotments—and distributed them to the miners present. Anyone was free to attend the distribution of datas, but miners were forbidden to appoint representatives to attend on their behalf. The man who had first discovered the new gold deposit was given the right to choose the site of his data. An allotment was then chosen for the crown and put up for public sale, the proceeds being credited to the Royal Exchequer. All the other datas were distributed by drawing lots, each prospective miner being allowed an area in proportion to the number of slaves he owned, on the basis of two and a half fathoms (*braças*) for each slave, up to a maximum of thirty fathoms.[20] If any gold fields remained unallotted, a supplementary distribution was made; if, on the other hand, the number of applicants was too great, the area of each data was proportionately reduced.

Once the datas had been distributed the miners were required to begin working them within a period of forty days on penalty of dispossession. Dealing in datas was not permitted, and their sale was authorized only if the owner could prove that he had lost all his slaves. In this case the miner was entitled to receive another data when he could prove that he had acquired new workers. But this concession could only be made to the same person once, his right to a new allotment being forfeited if he sold it a second time.

In order to implement the provisions of the mining code, collect the royal fifths, supervise the mining work, and settle any disputes that might arise between the miners or between miners and third parties on any matters pertaining to mining,[21] a special administrative body was set up, the Intendência de Minas. In each captaincy where gold was extracted an intendancy was established that was empowered to act completely independently of the other colonial authorities and directly responsible to the crown. The intendancy consisted of a superintendent (commonly known as the intendant), who supervised the administration and organization of his department, and a *guarda-mor*, or chief officer, responsible for the distribution of datas and inspection of the gold diggings to see that the provisions of the code were observed. The guarda-mor could be replaced by another crown official in the "remoter areas"—a stipulation made in the code—although in practice this provision led to a number of abuses, which will be considered later. The deputies of the guardas-mores were known as *guardas-menores* (minor officers) and could be nominated for the purpose by the guarda-mor himself. Clerks and other petty officials were next in rank.

Attached to the intendancy was the *casa de fundição* (smelting house), where all gold extracted was by law to be brought for smelting and where, after a fifth of its value (the *quinto real*) had been deducted for the crown, the gold was cast into bars and returned to the owner with a certificate of origin to prove that he had fulfilled the legal obligations laid down. This certificate was to be produced when the gold bars were circulated. Not until this had been complied with was the gold allowed to circulate freely and be consigned outside the captaincy.[22]

It is obvious from the foregoing enumeration of the duties and responsibilities of the intendancy that its functions were of a hybrid nature, and it is easy to see the disadvantages inherent in the system. It was a body that was at one and the same time administrative, in charge of the supervision of mining; judicial, functioning as a court of first and last resort for the actions that came within its purview; and fiscal, entrusted with collection of the royal fifths. It was also, or at least should have been, a technical body for the planning and development of production. Without taking into account the conflicts over its jurisdiction and legal competence as against other authorities, conflicts in which the intendancy would constantly find itself involved, the great number of its functions and its lack of specialization inevitably resulted in the neglect of some of these functions to the benefit of others.[23] The intendancies regularly and effectively exercised only their fiscal function, that of collecting the royal fifths and of attempting to control gold smuggling and evasions of payments, or "defrauding the royal fifths." For this they were well equipped and always acted with the utmost

severity. But this was all; the rest went by the board. The officials (generally bachelors of law or bureaucrats knowing nothing of mining) never took any step to promote improvements
in mining techniques or to help even in a small way the industry entrusted to their care or the persons engaged in it. Not
even in controlling the ownership of the gold diggings did the
intendancy show itself able to act with any degree of efficiency;
in this respect utter chaos was the general rule. And while the
interminable plaints and disputes dragged on through the
lengthy and bureaucratic stages of the legal actions that arose,
it was not uncommon for diggings to be abandoned while their
owners awaited a decision. The guarda-mor, whose functions
were so important and so delicate, as a rule did nothing to prevent abuses and settle disputes; and in the end it became virtually an honorific, and in many cases even an hereditary title,
accompanied always by the handsome rake-off received for the
sale of nominations to the position of guarda-menor.

In practice all that mattered was the payment of the royal
fifth, whether voluntarily or under compulsion; nothing else
was held to be of any importance. The miners were left to manage as best they could; if they failed to meet their obligations
there was always distraint for debt, confiscation of property,
the dungeons of the Limoeiro,* or deportation to the Portuguese African colonies. But distraint notwithstanding, the yield
from the royal fifths began to decline; and in the half-century
during which it dropped in Minas Gerais [24] from 118 arrobas
in 1754—the maximum collected—to only 35 arrobas exactly
fifty years later, it had not once occurred to the administration
to attribute this decline to anything but fraud. This explains
the outbreaks of violence which are only too well known.†

Finally, when the colony's mining industry had fallen into
utter decay and among the ruins was revealed a groaning and
impoverished populace, whose flagrant misery could no longer
escape the notice even of the myopic administration and the
greedy exchequer, reforms were at last put in hand. In 1803 an
attempt was made to introduce a minimum of efficiency into

---

* The Limoeiro is a notorious prison in Lisbon.—Translator.

† The author is alluding to the seizure of the slaves, goods, and be-

the administration of mining, the more scandalous abuses were stopped, and even the royal fifth was reduced to a royal tithe (*dízimo real*). But things had reached such a pitch of deterioration that these measures were to no avail. It was either no longer possible to remedy the abuses, because the people capable of introducing reforms could not be found, or else the passive resistance of a bureaucracy lolling back in the midst of privilege, affecting not to understand any project that might threaten its comfortable position, was impenetrable. Only five years after its promulgation, when no attempt had yet been made to put it into effect, the charter of 1803 was repealed, and all continued as before.[25]

This was what happened in the higher circles of mining administration. We must now consider a more modest aspect of this administration, the way in which exploitation of the gold deposits was organized and functioned. Here we find two types of organization; the first is that of mining in the more important placer mines. These were fixed establishments where some equipment was used and where, under the direction of one man and working as a group, a number of workers were gathered together, varying from a few to several dozen.[26] Placer mining was carried out during the golden age of mining when there were still large resources and production was abundant, making it possible for large-scale enterprises and more ambitious works to be undertaken.

To this system was opposed the small-time extraction carried on by individual prospectors using only the *bateia* (pan), the *carumbé* (bucket), and other makeshift equipment on their workings. As a rule they did not stay in one place, as in the placer mines; they were footloose nomads, moving indifferently from place to place, hunting around for gold in any site not already taken. Sometimes they banded together in large numbers in certain districts which were open to all comers, as in parts of Vila Rica; but each man worked for, and usually by, himself.

---

longings of defaulters (the distraint he refers to previously), imprisonment, banishment, etc., and to the demonstrations, riots, and disturbances that broke out from time to time in Minas Gerais in protest against these measures.—Translator.

Some of them were free, prospecting on their own account, others were slaves whose owners had fixed the amount of gold they were obliged to hand over but who were allowed to keep the rest for themselves for their own maintenance or for buying their freedom, if they were lucky in their strikes.[27]

To greater or lesser extent the *faiscador* (itinerant prospector) always existed in the colony's gold industry. Under certain conditions the individual prospectors found that their work was as productive as in the more elaborate diggings, costly equipment for this type of extraction being uneconomical. These conditions included where the gold was concentrated in the layers of sand, or even in the *cascalho*,[28] and the river was not too full, in which case it was unnecessary either to bring the water used in the washing operations from a considerable distance or to divert its flow by damming; and where the touch of gold was too low to pay for elaborate installations and large numbers of workers. The number of itinerant prospectors, therefore, tended to grow as the deeper alluvial deposits were exhausted. The same occurred when resources for purchasing the equipment needed or for engaging a large number of slaves to establish a large-scale digging began to run out. In these cases the faiscador appeared on the scene. Thus, an increase in the number of faiscadores present was a sure indication that mining was on the decline. Large numbers of people began to appear engaged exclusively in this precarious activity, prospecting and digging for their daily bread in sites unsuited to large-scale digging or abandoned because their former owners no longer had means to work them. The miners who still owned slaves sent them out to dig on their behalf and awaited comfortably at home the arrival of their gains.

I have already cited figures for the total production of gold in Minas Gerais in the early nineteenth century. We also have the corresponding figures for its production by the two categories of miners: the site miners and the faiscadores. These were 113,127 drams and 115,321 drams, respectively. This proportion, favoring the faiscadores, is one of the characteristic symptoms of the state of the mining industry at that time—and this in Minas Gerais, the only one of the gold captaincies which maintained a higher level of production. In Goiás and Mato Grosso there were hardly any organized diggings left, almost all extraction of gold being in the hands of poor faiscadores.

Faced with the lack of individual resources that handicapped the impoverished miners and the need for more ambitious works if mining was to continue, in a few rare cases the miners considered pooling their efforts and forming companies. But this solution, which seems an obvious one and should have been adopted from the outset,[29] was resorted to only tardily and on an insignificant scale. The attempts to organize companies date only from the last quarter of the eighteenth century and even then were merely timid. We know from the correspondence of the Governor of Goiás, Luís de Cunha Meneses, that he had attempted to form a company whose subscribers would contribute a total of 400–450 slaves for undertaking the diversion of the Maranhão river at its confluence with the Tocantins, which was reputed to have extremely rich alluvial deposits.[30] But the actual formation of a working company was put into effect only many years later. This was formed for the exploitation of the Anicuns Mines, also in Goiás, which had been discovered in 1809. The governor at that time, Don Francisco de Assis Mascarenhas, later Count of Palma, was the promoter of this company. The shareholders were to contribute twelve slaves apiece, and the director and managing director were to be superintendent of mines and guarda-mor, respectively. These appointments were made by the Governor himself, which reveals the official nature of the enterprise and the lack of any private initiative.[31] An interesting detail is that the company's articles of association explicitly allowed for the engagement of free paid workers. This company, although it actually started to operate, was not very successful; after 1812 it could no longer support itself and was wound up by the new Governor, Fernando Delgado de Castilho.[32]

I have left diamond mining to the last, since the special regulations governing the extraction of diamonds and its subordination to gold in the economic and social life of the colony call for separate analysis. It is in fact much more interesting not as an economic activity, since its position in the economic field despite the aura of prestige with which it was surrounded was a secondary one, but as one of the pages, probably the most illustrative, of the sorry history of Portuguese colonial administration in Brazil.

I shall not expand on the various systems successively adopted by the mother country for regulating the exploitation of diamonds. From the earliest discoveries, which took place around 1729, these were: free exploitation, subject to payment of the royal fifth, up to 1740; exploitation on a monopoly-contract basis, from 1740–1771; and finally, a crown monopoly or *real extração*, by which the diamond mines were operated directly on behalf of the crown, from 1771 onward. This monopoly was established by the decree of July 12, 1771, and the *Regimento* (Standing Orders) promulgated on August 2 of that same year, contained in the notorious "Green Book" (*Livro da Capa Verde*)—an allusion to the color of the binding of the copy kept in Brazil—which came to symbolize the Regimento. The Regimento was the epitome of tyranny, the terror of all who were directly or indirectly affected by it for over half a century.* Only this last system of regulating the extraction and disposal of diamonds, which lasted up to the empire period, although considerably attenuated after the Proclamation of Independence, need concern us here.

First of all we should note that, like the previous systems in force, the Regimento applied only to a small district of Minas Gerais, the so-called Diamond District (*Distrito Diamantino*). This area had been carefully demarcated and was therefore also known as the *Demarcação Diamantina*, an area centered on the present-day town of Diamantina, which was the only part of the colony where exploitation of diamonds was legally authorized. Extraction was strictly prohibited in any other part of the colony, a measure adopted in order to restrict the output of diamonds and so maintain prices, as well as to facilitate the

---

* The last vestiges of the *real extração* were only abolished in 1835.— Translator.

levying of the crown duties and to prevent smuggling. I have already referred in passing to some of the districts closed off when diamonds were found in the vicinity: the mines of the upper Paraguay in Mato Grosso and the Claro and Pilões rivers in Goiás. No one was allowed to enter these districts on any pretext whatsoever, and severe penalties were imposed on anyone found infringing the ban. In Bahia, where diamonds were found in 1732, the establishment of dwellings, shops, taverns, etc., was prohibited anywhere within a radius of ten leagues of any point where diamonds were found.[33] A like ban was placed on the Jequitinhonha River, where diamonds were discovered in 1734, and a series of military posts and detachments were established along the river banks to police the area and prevent any attempt to start illicit diggings. The soldiers remained in this district up to the Proclamation of Independence.

The district which had been officially fixed for the exploitation of diamonds was the area encircling the mining camp (*arraial*) of Tejuco, the present-day town of Diamantina. Its limits had been strictly demarcated after the creation of the Intendência dos Diamantes in 1734, a body organized along the lines of the intendancies established for the administration of the gold mines. This district, whose boundaries were enlarged five years later to include neighboring areas where diamonds were found, is described in J. Felício dos Santos's *Memórias do Distrito Diamantino*.[34]

In this district no one was allowed to establish himself, or even just to enter it, without the express permission of the intendant. The lives of the district's 6,000 inhabitants—the total population at the beginning of the nineteenth century—were completely in the hands of this "kinglet," who could dispose of them as he thought fit. There were no judges or courts, nor any other higher or even equal authority, to whom the inhabitants could appeal. The intendant's powers included confiscation of all property and infliction of the "civil death penalty," without any form of trial or appeal.[35] All this was designed solely to control extraction and prevent the smuggling of precious stones. "The only example in history," comments Martius, "of an attempt to isolate a territory in which all the conditions of the civil lives of its inhabitants were subject to the exploitation of a crown property." [36]

Extraction of diamonds was, as we have seen, operated directly by the crown on its own behalf. This involved the organizing of a special administrative body composed of a large number of people, all completely under its authority. This was the *Junta da Administração Geral dos Diamantes* (Council for the General Administration of Diamonds), presided over by the intendant of the diamond district.

This administrative council was completely independent of any other colonial authority and was directly responsible to the crown. A veritable foreign body encapsulated in the colony, the diamond district was cut off from the rest of the country and lived in isolation under a sui generis organization in which there was neither governor, municipal council, judge, fiscal department, nor any other authority or administrative body. There were only the intendant and the body of officials subordinate to him, who were supposed to be all of the foregoing rolled into one guided solely by the Regimento that gave them the most far-reaching and unlimited powers. I shall refrain from comment.

Vieira Couto, commissioned by the government in 1798 to study mining in Brazil, describes the outcome of this system, the ultimate in tyranny and clearly the work of madmen blinded by greed:

The land is being abandoned, trade is trickling to a standstill. Some dare not spend their money because they know not the hour at which it will be lost to them or those who buy their fazendas. The merchants of Rio de Janeiro, who give bountiful credit to any other comarca, will not even hear spoken the name of Serro Frio; [37] those few people who linger on, malcontent and as if half-stupefied, have lost all spirit, and dare not venture on any new thing, while they cast about their gaze to find a place of refuge. In short, the specter of despotism— chilling, gaunt and haggard—has revealed its hideous visage to this people, and today Tejuco, formerly the most beautiful settlement of Minas, is just the image of one of Constantinople's poorer quarters.[38]

As for the actual exploitation of diamonds, without going into the technical aspects of the matter, which need not concern us here—the destructive, haphazard, and incompetent way in which it was managed are described in Vieira Couto's "Memoir"—we need only add a word on the methods used by the administrative council for operating the crown monopoly. The mining was carried on by slaves hired from their owners (the council having no slaves of its own) or by a much smaller number of free paid workers. The amount paid for these workers, whether bond or free, was 675 reis per week at the end of the eighteenth century.[39] The administrative officials were entitled to hire out their own slaves, a fixed number being determined for each official according to his category in the administration.

The crown monopoly for exploiting the diamond mines led to the appearance of a figure who has become semilegendary: the *garimpeiro*.* Loathed and persecuted by the administration, admired by the populace, feared by all, the garimpeiro was an outlaw, living always one step ahead of the forces of the crown or just out of range of a bullet, entering the forbidden areas to carry on his clandestine mining activities, and defying the authorities, whom he had often to resist by force of arms. The garimpeiros usually went about in bands, in which an iron discipline reigned under the command of the boldest and most intelligent member. Rebels and enemies of the law, they naturally drew closer to the humble and the oppressed, whom they protected and defended. All this tended to surround the garimpeiro with a halo of sympathy, respect, and even glory. Their deeds, handed down from generation to generation, are still commemorated.[40]

From the beginning of the nineteenth century, although extraction of diamonds continued to be a privilege of the crown,

---

* *Garimpo* was the name given to illicit diamond mining, and persons who followed this calling, whether whole or part-time, were called *garimpeiros*.—Translator.

the diamond areas began to be opened up, but only for exploitation of the gold found within them. We have already indicated a few districts where the ban was lifted: the upper Paraguay in Mato Grosso and the Claro and Pilões rivers in Goiás. This was done in order to reanimate the moribund gold-mining activities in these areas, and it was hoped that exploitation of virgin mines would prove highly profitable and so bring about a revival of the industry. The long closure of these areas had led people to imagine that great wealth was stored up in them. But reality fell far short of the expectations woven around the new mines, and they yielded very meager results. The opening up of the diamond regions did, however, deal the first blow to the crown monopoly and the senseless fiscal system that had been established to exploit them. The gold miners could clearly not be forced to ignore any precious stones they might find, as had been envisaged, or to hand them over in dutiful submission to the authorities, who would pay for them at prices not only far below their real value but also never in cash but only in the shape of promises or credits. The contraband trade in diamonds could, therefore, no longer be controlled, and the administration was obliged to turn a blind eye to the activities of the smugglers. St. Hilaire observes that diamond mining was openly carried on along the Pilões river, and that the most expected of the illicit miners was that they exercise a certain amount of discretion.[41] The official diggings had in fact been practically abandoned through progressive exhaustion of the diamond deposits; only a negligible quantity of diamonds remained, which was insufficient for anything but a miserable prospecting activity.

Finally, as a reflection of the agitations affecting the kingdom and its colony, even the Diamond District—the last bulwark of the fiscal policy on diamonds hitherto pursued—was opened up. The crown monopoly was doomed and from then on gradually crumbled away and dissolved, until the law of October 25, 1882, at last officially recognized the situation and abolished it altogether. And thus what was perhaps the blackest chapter of Portuguese colonial administration came to an end.

Stock Rearing

Meat played an important role in the colony's diet, all the more so since the general dearth of other foodstuffs, particularly in the larger agglomerations, made it indispensable. The problems of its supply, therefore, became of vital importance for the life of the colony and were constantly discussed in the public documents and private writings of the time. They were, however, never satisfactorily solved, except of course in the actual stock-rearing regions themselves. Elsewhere, no attempt was made to tackle the problems involved. Vilhena's outspoken attack on the conduct of the meat trade in the last years of the eighteenth century, in a center as large and important as Bahia, provides a salutary lesson for even the most tolerant of historians. And his is not the only criticism. The first and most elementary step toward improving the meat supply—the provision of proper slaughterhouse facilities—had not yet been taken, and the meat markets were very far from being adequately provided for. There was a general outcry against the lack of abattoirs, which were found only in the largest cities and towns. Major Francisco de Paula Ribeiro protested against this lack in Maranhão,[1] and the anonymous author of *Roteiro do Maranhão* made the same complaint about Minas Gerais.[2]

The extent of the meat trade can be gauged from the ceaseless march of cattle convoys across the colony, which were encountered at every step by the early nineteenth century travel-

213

ers, who commented on this in their diaries. In the city of
Bahia alone, more than 20,000 oxen, driven down from the
remote sertões, were consumed annually.[3] In São Luís do
Maranhão, 6,000 head of cattle, also brought from hundreds of
miles away, were slaughtered annually at the beginning of the
last century.[4] Belem do Pará, with only 13,000 inhabitants,
consumed 11,000 head of cattle in 1828.[5]

The constant demand for fresh meat and the relatively large
meat trade formed the impulse behind one of the colony's chief
activities, cattle raising, the only occupation apart from those
connected with the export products which managed to achieve
major importance. It has been unjustly relegated to a secondary plane in Brazilian history. Admittedly its impact was outwardly less spectacular than that of the political feats, and it
never ranked in the forefront of the country's great events.
Buried in the heart of the Sertão, it was hidden from sight by
the intense life of the coast, with its engenhos and canefields
and other cash crops. And it did not offer the natural attractions of gold and diamonds. Nevertheless, quite apart from its
role in the colony's subsistence, the contribution of cattle raising to the opening up and conquest of the Brazilian interior
would be enough to place it among the most important chapters of its history. If we exclude the narrow strip bordering the
sea taken up by agriculture, the vast area which today forms
Brazilian territory can be divided, according to the factors determining its penetration and occupation, between the gathering of forest products, which was mainly responsible for the
settlement of the extreme north; mining, which impelled settlement to the central-south; and cattle raising, which opened up
the rest of the country. Of the three, it would be difficult to
award first place in this singular competition to any particular
one.

But if cattle raising was not the most grandiose and dramatic
of the three, it was to modern eyes at least the most evocative:
In this sphere the past has remained unchanged; the cattle
droves are with us today; now, as in the past, they tramp across
the country, driven along the roads and covering with their

slow, plodding steps the vast distances that divide Brazil, achieving what only the airplane in our own time has been able to emulate, the conquest of space. Over the centuries the hooves of countless animals have cut paths across the wilderness, the same unending scene has been enacted throughout the country, unchanged by time. The same droves, so colorfully described by their first chronicler (Antonil), could reappear today, blocking the roads to the despair of the modern motorist, and none could tell the difference.

But this intimate link with the past is not merely a picturesque scene witnessed by successive generations of Brazilians; it also recalls one of the most significant facts of our economic life, and one which was to have the most far-reaching consequences. I am referring to the complete and drastic separation between cattle raising and the culture of the land which it reveals. I have already referred to this fact and have indicated its most important consequence, which was to rob the cultivated land of its only readily available fertilizer, that is, the dung of grazing animals. I also pointed out the ultimate reason for this state of affairs—the general system governing the economy and agriculture of Brazil, a system which concentrated on the all-absorbing production of a few commodities for the export trade, with monoculture as its necessary consequence. The lands that could most readily be utilized, both because of their extent and because they were within easy reach of the ports, were avidly occupied by the planters, leaving no room for any other industry; and consequently the attention of the people concentrated in these privileged areas was monopolized by large-scale agriculture with its far greater attractions and greater opportunities for profit.

In considering the colony's food crops we have already seen the detrimental effects of the exacting role played by large-scale agriculture on other occupations. Its effect on cattle raising was even more serious, since this activity by its very nature calls for much more space, particularly as extensive grazing was then the only viable way of raising livestock, in the absence of adequate stabling, ensilage, and the other requirements of intensive rearing. Such measures were, of course, beyond the means of the colonists; even the simplest preparation or improvement of pastures, apart from the crude system of burning over the land—the *queimada*—was unthinkable.[6] The lack of resources, together with the generally backward technical level of the colonial economy, which we have already seen in its most important sectors, was bound to give rise to a primitive and undemanding form of cattle raising, really little more than a rudimentary extractive industry. There was little in the way of systematic animal husbandry. Cattle were left to roam the ranges freely, with the minimum of attention, the most that was done being to see that they did not stray and to herd them when required.

Such a system, particularly in view of the low-grade natural pastures, called for extensive areas in which to operate. Thus, cattle raising was relegated to the distant backlands which were not suited to agriculture. In the coastal region there was not even enough land which could be spared for grazing to support the cattle used as draft animals on the plantations. In Pernambuco, when the mills were not in operation, the draft animals—oxen and horses—were taken to other regions for pasturing. Bom Jardim, situated in the hinterland of the most important agricultural centers, found one of its principal sources of activity in this transhumance; every year, animals from the engenhos, exhausted by the intensive labor of the harvest period, were brought to its pastures to recover.[7] Even the law excluded cattle raising from the ten maritime leagues which had been laid down as the area reserved for agriculture.[8]

The displacement of grazing lands to zones distant from this agricultural preserve occurred from the outset of colonization. It can be clearly observed in the colony's first two agricultural nuclei, in the north (Bahia and Pernambuco) and São Vicente. In the first case, as we have seen, the cattle ranches moved into the sertões, including remote Piauí; in the second, they occupied the southern Campos Gerais. The only exceptions to this

practice of confining the grazing regions to the distant backlands are the Campos dos Goitacases in Rio de Janeiro and the
island of Joanes in Pará. In these cases, special circumstances
intervened to which I shall return later.

Bypassing the evolution of cattle raising in the first three
centuries of colonization, I will confine myself here to the period with which we are now concerned. At the beginning of the
last century, then, stock rearing was carried on in three key
regions: the northern sertões, the southern part of Minas Gerais,
and the plains of the south, including the Campos Gerais of
Paraná but more particularly those of the extreme south in Rio
Grande. Distinctive conditions in each of these zones, arising
not only from their geographic location but also, more particularly, from the cattle-raising systems adopted in each, make
them quite different in character. Apart from these three major
regions there were other minor grazing areas of purely local
significance, which will be considered last.

We will begin with the northern sertões, which formed the
oldest established pastoral zone in the colony. This was still the
most extensive and most important cattle region, although at
the beginning of the last century it was clearly beginning to
lose ground to its southern competitors. I have already deline-
ated the limits of this area in the chapter on population distribution. It embraced the entire territory of the northeast, with
the exception of the narrow coastal fringe,[9] and extended from
the Parnaíba River to the northern border of Minas Gerais. The
Minas Gerais section is included because of the similar physical conditions and because the form of cattle raising practiced
was more or less identical to that of the sertões. To the north,
the area extended beyond the Parnaíba River and included a
small part of upper Maranhão, the territory of the Pastos Bons
described in the above-mentioned chapter. In Itapecuru, the
cattle ranches which had pioneered the opening up of the
region had been replaced by cotton plantations. To the west,
the limit of the Sertão zone was fixed along the left bank of the
São Francisco; beyond this limit, in the border area of Goiás,

colonization had not yet penetrated, and the area served only
as a link between the routes connecting the captaincy of Goiás
with Bahia and Minas Gerais.

The whole of this vast area, covering more than a million
square kilometers, was devoted almost exclusively to raising
cattle for consumption by the dense population of the agricultural zone, extending from Paraíba to Bahia. It also supplied
Maranhão, and, although only in modest proportions during the
period with which we are dealing as compared to the past, it
still sent meat on the hoof to the mining centers of Minas
Gerais.[10]

I have indicated in a previous chapter the factors which enabled the pioneers to utilize the immense Sertão region for cattle raising. Indeed, ranches had very early been established in
the region, and by the end of the seventeenth century the
whole area was devoted to stock rearing. Recapitulating, these
factors were: the nature of the natural vegetation, the *caatinga*
being sparse enough to offer immediate possibilities for man's
establishment since it required no preliminary effort for clearing; the uniform relief, with its extensive *chapadas* (broad, flat
uplands); and the frequent occurrence of saline outcroppings
which provided the salt licks essential for cattle. In the central
part of the region, easily accessible through the waterway
offered by the São Francisco, there were even commercially
exploitable salt deposits. Martius gives a detailed description
of these,[11] which occur along the São Francisco from the
Salitre River to the township of Urubu, in a strip almost 60
leagues long and 25–30 leagues in width. The deposits were
more concentrated on the right bank; along the left bank they
were less frequent and not regularly exploited. The salt produced supplied all the requirements of the upper Sertão from
Piauí to Minas Gerais, as well as Goiás and Mato Grosso.
Annual production was over 35,000 bags (*surrões*), weighing
30–40 pounds each. This explains why the São Francisco, if we
discount the fact that, unlike nearly all the other rivers of the
Sertão, it is perennial, became such an important focus for the
cattle ranches. According to Antonil, by the beginning of the

eighteenth century there were already more than a million head of cattle in this area.

With all the advantages offered by the Sertão, there were serious drawbacks: the poverty of its natural pastures, the shortage of water, and so forth. But on the whole and in view of the lack of any more favorable regions, the Sertão of the northeast offered some scope for the pastoral industry. This enabled human occupation and regular settlement to spread over an area which would otherwise have been deserted. The rapid advance of the cattle estates is explained, on the one hand, by the growing demand for cattle in the coastal and mining regions, coupled with the low economic density and productivity of the industry, and on the other, by the incredible ease with which a ranch could be established in the backlands. The would-be rancher need only put up a simple dwelling covered with a palm-thatch roof—the leaves of the carnauba palm were used for this purpose—and throw together a few makeshift corrals, bring in the cattle (the term used for the acquisition of the herd was "rounding up the hooves"), and his three leagues of land had been transformed into a ranch.[12] Only ten or twelve men were needed to run the ranch. There was a ready supply of labor; and in the absence of slaves, the Indian half-breeds, mulattoes, and Negroes that abounded in the backlands were only too ready to work on the ranches, since being by temperament lazy and averse to work in principle, they had a special inclination for the adventurous and not too demanding life of the ranch, which called for only intermittent effort on their part.[13]

Another factor contributing to the rapid increase of the ranches was the system adopted for paying the herdsmen (*vaqueiros*). The vaqueiro received one out of every four calves born on the ranch; a payment that accumulated to be handed over only at the end of his first five years of work. In this way, the vaqueiro received a large number of beasts at one time and could, therefore, set up on his own. This he did on lands which he had managed to acquire, or more commonly, on a piece of land rented from the *grandes senhores,* or great landowners, of the Sertão who had been allotted lands through the system of *sesmarias*. In this way, fazendas were formed which were owned by more humble proprietors, who usually lived on the ranch and took part in its management, completely integrated in the work and life of the Sertão. In these cases the vaqueiros and even the auxiliary workers (*fábricas*) attached to the ranch were often sons of the owner.[14] But this type of owner was far from being the only, or even the predominant, type. The most common type was the absentee landowner, often owning vast territories and dozens of ranches, who lived in the coastal towns and whose only contact with his estates was the receipt of the profits it yielded.[15]

A ranch usually occupied three leagues in length by one in width and was situated along a watercourse, extending half a league on either bank.[16] This standard area for a fazenda was derived from the royal decree of December 27, 1695, which laid down the new measurements for all sesmarias granted from then on, dimensions confirmed by subsequent decrees.[17] As a result of these decrees, the standard area eventually came to prevail. A further provision was that there was to be a distance of one league between sesmarias or fazendas, a space which was to be left unoccupied. None of the ranchers on the boundaries of this area was allowed to put up any buildings or undertake any works whatsoever; it was to serve merely as the dividing line between fazendas, a necessary precaution where there were no fences or any other form of enclosure to prevent cattle from straying into neighboring territory and so confusing the herds.

The installations of a fazenda were, as I have pointed out, of the most summary type; makeshift corrals and rude dwellings were the only structures put up. Only a few workers were required, the vaqueiro and a number of auxiliary workers known as *fábricas*. The vaqueiro was responsible for running the ranch and was, as we have seen, paid out of the ranch's product: he received one-fourth of the herd increase every year. On the larger ranches there were sometimes two or even three vaqueiros, who shared this fourth between them.[18] The num-

ber of fábricas varied between two and four according to the
size of the ranch; they worked under the vaqueiro's orders and
helped him in all his tasks. These auxiliaries were sometimes
slaves but more often paid workers who received monthly or
annual monetary payment. The auxiliaries were entrusted with
the care of the plots of land given over to the production of
food crops. The plots were generally laid out in the *vazantes*,
that is, the dry beds of the intermittently flowing rivers and
streams of the Sertão where the last drops of moisture lingered
during the dry periods. If such plots were not provided the
ranch owner was required to supply the food for his workers.
Their diet was supplemented by slaughtering one of the animals for meat once a month. On the larger ranches the
vaqueiro was required to contribute one-fourth of the meat
provided; that is, for every four cows slaughtered the vaqueiro
forfeited one head of cattle from his final payment of a fourth
share of the herd increase. This compulsory deduction was
known as "paying the dead cow." [19]

The number of cattle on a ranch varied considerably. The
importance of a ranch was not in fact judged from the head of
cattle it contained, a figure which was generally either not
known or not taken into account, but from the number of
calves annually raised, or "broken in,"as it was called. The better estates raised from one thousand to as many as two thousand calves; but on most ranches the number of calves raised
was much smaller than these maximum figures.[20]

In addition to raising cattle the estates went in for horse
breeding; there were even fazendas devoted entirely to this
end. Three of the crown fazendas of Piauí were of this type,
and four others were mixed cattle and horse ranches. In the
north the horse performed the same role as the mule in the
central-south and was used as pack animal and mount. Horses
were even used sometimes in place of oxen as draught animals
for operating the mills. On the cattle ranches the horse was indispensable; in the enormous areas covered by the fazendas,
this animal alone made it possible to prevent the cattle from
straying. A ranch, however small (the small ones being com-

monly known as *chiqueiros* *), had to have not less than 25 or
30 horses; but no fazenda could be properly managed with
fewer than 50 or 60.[21]

The stock-rearing techniques employed in the sertões of the
northeast were, as I have already indicated, of the most backward and primitive type. Cattle roamed the ranges freely, grazing the scanty grasses and leathery foliage of the strange vegetation found in the caatinga region. The Sertão offered only a
miserable subsistence for cattle, hardy enough to survive; and
it was impossible to avoid producing the scrawny and muscular
bullocks that furnished the unappetizing meat eaten in the
colony. Animal husbandry was restricted to the minimum of
care; the cattle were cured of the sores caused by the botflies
that burrowed into their skins and protected against the attacks of the wild beasts and bats which abounded in all the
sertões. The pastures (a term which seems hardly apt) were
completely unimproved, save for the annual burning over of
the land before the rainy season to ensure more succulent
forage when the vegetation sprouted afresh. Salt rations were
not regularly distributed, since the salt was provided by the
cattle licks.

Milk was not utilized commercially; it was used only to meet
the requirements of the ranch and was eaten in the form of
curd or made into coarse and inferior cheese. Butter, on the
other hand, was not made by the ranchers at all.

Apart from these minor activities the main work on the
fazenda was the supervision of the range animals to ensure that
they did not stray, an arduous task that took up almost all the
vaqueiro's time and that of his assistants, since vigilance was
particularly difficult in such vast areas where hedges, fences,
and other forms of enclosure were unknown. There was the
constant risk of losing some of the herd, for once an animal
strayed off into the brush it would be lost forever in the
scantily peopled Sertão which offered no obstacle to its path
and where the landscape never varied for hundreds of leagues,
the natural vegetation being indistinguishable from its home

_____
* Literally, a "pigsty" or "filthy hovel."—Translator.

pastures. But there was another and perhaps more serious risk, that the animals might go wild and flee from man's approach. These fugitives became, in their wild state, completely unmanageable, and there was no alternative but to destroy them so that they could not lead the tame beasts astray.

To avoid all this, apart from the practice of branding the cattle with initials or fanciful designs which distinguished the herds of individual ranches within a radius of hundreds of leagues where their brands were always recognized, the ranchers took great care in domesticating the animals. Up to the age of three months calves were confined to the corral; once they were fully grown, care was taken to see that they were herded together every evening after sunset to spend the night in fixed cattle pens until they became accustomed to the locality. Especial attention was given to cows about to calve to prevent them from wandering off, as they frequently did, to give birth in some inaccessible and hidden spot, where there was a danger that the calf would succumb to botflies or never be found and brought back to the corral for breaking in.

These tasks kept the vaqueiro busy. On horseback, from dawn to dusk, his days were spent tending the herds scattered over many leagues of land. Under these open-range conditions and in the harsh natural environment of the backlands, the fazendas were bound to show a depressed economic level. From the figures I have cited we can judge their low productivity in relation to the area occupied: a few hundred calves for every three square leagues, that is, amost 11,000 hectares. Most of these calves were killed by bats, wild beasts, botflies, or died from lack of pasturage and water, to mention only the most frequent hazards. Thus, even the most important fazendas could furnish an annual drove of only 250–300 head of cattle.[22] This figure excludes the heavy losses incurred on the long and exhausting journey across the arid caatinga to the markets of the coast. Martius estimated that 50 percent of the animals died en route,[23] which appears to be no exaggeration considering the enormous distances they had to cover, the poor nature of the vegetation, and the lack of water.[24]

On top of all these unfavorable conditions, the condition in which the cattle finally arrived at the market was deplorable. Already scrawny from the poverty of their normal subsistence and emaciated by their long and arduous journey, they were slaughtered immediately on arrival before they could be rested or fattened in pastures near the city.[25] These factors, in sum, explain the apparent paradox that it took a territory of nearly a million square kilometers to supply meat—in insufficient quantities, moreover—to a few hundred thousand inhabitants. We must, of course, take into account that only a fraction of this territory was utilized, since most of it was too arid to be used for grazing. At the end of the eighteenth century, in the four captaincies that extend from Ceará to Pernambuco—including Alagoas, part of Pernambuco, and the entire left bank of the São Francisco, which today forms part of Bahian territory but was then still included in Pernambuco—there were only 2,366 fazendas.[26]

Apart from meat supplied on the hoof, the Sertão also provided dried meat. The fact that meat prepared in this manner could be kept almost indefinitely, and that its weight was reduced by about 50 percent, obviated the problems of transport involved in sending it, with the precarious means of conveyance available, across the vast tracts of the Sertão. The arid climate was highly favorable to this particular activity, and the preparation of dried meat therefore early became an important local industry. At first Ceará was the chief supplier of dried meat, and in the north the product is still called *carne-do-Ceará* (Ceará meat). But it lost its favored position in the last quarter of the eighteenth century, being replaced initially by Piauí. I have already referred to the particular circumstances that led to this replacement; the fact is that Piauí, with the largest and best herds in the north and with the convenient means of transportation offered by the Parnaíba River, managed to supplant all its competitors and dominated the colonial market for dried meat until, as we shall see below, it was ousted from its supremacy in the last years of the nineteenth century by the *charque* produced in Rio Grande do Sul.

The by-products of the grazing industry must also be re-called, particularly hides, which gave rise to a fairly important trade. In all the northern ports, from Maranhão to Bahia, hides and skins accounted for a large percentage of exports. Salt-cured hides, tanned hides, sole leather, and leather used for lin-ing purposes figured prominently among the exports shipped from these ports.

The ascendancy of cattle raising in the northeast lasted until the beginning of the eighteenth century, when Antonil de-scribed it in such graphic and glowing terms. It still main-tained its prosperity at the end of that century, as we can see from the growth of the population, the formation of new cap-taincies, and the establishment of parishes and towns. All this was due almost entirely to cattle raising, which was the sole lo-cal occupation. Piauí was made an independent captaincy in 1758; and it was in the course of the same century that Ceará witnessed its greatest colonizing expansion and settlement, the formation of most of its population clusters dating from this period.

Decline set in toward the end of the eighteenth century. Local production in Minas Gerais deprived the northeastern sertões of their markets in the mining centers. Recurrent droughts which succeeded each other at more or less lengthy intervals but with dramatic regularity in the eighteenth cen-tury gradually destroyed the sources of this unhappy region's economic life.[27] The final blow was dealt by the prolonged drought lasting from 1791 to 1793, which assumed such pro-portions that it became known as the "Great Drought" and was still remembered with horror many decades later. The Sertão never recovered from this blow. Henceforth it was to stagnate in a state of chronic and inherent debility which has lasted down to the present day. Its role as chief supplier of meat to the agricultural centers of the northeastern coastlands was taken over by Rio Grande do Sul; and despite this captaincy's distance from the coastal centers, the Sertão never again man-aged to compete.

We will now take a look at the colony's second cattle region,

Minas Gerais. As already indicated, the northern part of this captaincy was included in the Sertão area we have just considered, although it does not display the extreme characteristics found in the latter region. The droughts which afflict the northeastern sertões, for instance, are attenuated in northern Minas Gerais, although the area is still one of low rainfall. But its vegetation and topography are similar to those of the Sertão. The chief resemblance between the two regions, however, was the way of life established in them, which was identical in both.[28] Actually, the region is both geographically and historically an extension of Bahia. It was settled as a result of the penetration effected by the cattle ranches that advanced up the banks of the São Francisco in the eighteenth century, already reaching as far as the Rio das Velhas by this period. And long before the opening up of the territory that was to become Minas Gerais, whose biggest and most characteristic contingent of settlers were to enter it from the south, the northern part had been occupied by people from Bahia.[29]

I shall therefore not concern myself with this particular area but with the southern part of the captaincy, which was included in the Rio Grande basin, at that time a district of the Rio das Mortes. What characterizes this region, as compared to that of the northeastern sertões, is in the first place its abundant supply of water. Large rivers, such as the Rio Grande and its principal affluents, the Mortes, Sapucaí, and Verde, form a wide network of waterways; and all these rivers are perennial, unlike those of the northeast. In addition, regular and evenly distributed rainfall makes this region, in contrast to the northern one, an area of fertile lands well suited by nature to rural activities. Although the surface relief is uneven, the region consisting mainly of hilly uplands with many steep mountains difficult to cross, there are more than enough broad rolling lands for man to establish himself comfortably. The vegetation is also favorable, particularly for stock rearing. The dense forest, which extends inland from the coast and covers the mountain to the east and the south, is interrupted in this region, where the altitude is around 1,000 meters, and gives way to the scattered thickets of forest which shelter in the humid valleys, leaving the upper slopes bare save for a covering of grassy vegetation which furnishes good natural pastures.[30]

As we can see, then, the southern part of Minas Gerais offered a combination of circumstances which made it well suited to cattle raising; and as soon as the region began to be opened up by the gold prospectors, a parallel rural activity was initiated, stock rearing being its most prominent branch. Gradually it began to take over the nearby markets offered by the flourishing mining centers. Supplied at first by the northern Sertão and the southern Campos Gerais, the miners soon turned to the local source, which was more accessible and above all better equipped than its competitors. Southern Minas next began to overtake and finally to replace the Rio de Janeiro suppliers: the Campos dos Goitacases and the more distant Campos Gerais. The first-mentioned campos turned from stock raising to cane cultivation, and its pastures were converted into canefields. In 1765 the new cattle region sent its first droves to Rio de Janeiro.[31] Although closer to the southern campos, even São Paulo began to use the Minas region to meet its cattle requirements. In fact, the Mineiro ranchers began to advance southward in the eighteenth century, moving down the Serra da Mantiqueira to establish their ranches in São Paulo, in the region bordering the serra to the east from Franca to Moji-Mirim. It was this movement that led to the establishment in São Paulo, where good natural pastures also predominated, of a cattle region which was to adopt the models of its founders and organizers.[32]

Since the prevailing natural conditions were so different, and so much better suited to cattle raising than those of the northeastern Sertão, in Minas Gerais the industry was organized along quite different lines.[33] The most striking difference, even at first glance, is the manifest superiority of the techniques employed in the Minas region. To start with, the installations were much more sophisticated and more care was taken in their construction. The ranch house was not the primitive makeshift dwelling covered with carnauba palm thatch that we found in the north; on the contrary, it was a carefully constructed house, which St. Hilaire even compared to the *fermes* of his native land. Similarly, there were well-built corrals and —a feature not found in the sertões—there were separate dairy establishments, since milk was utilized commercially.

But the major difference, which led to a completely different type of stock breeding, lay in a small detail: the use of fencing, both outside the fazenda, to divide it from its neighbors, and within its bounds, to form separate enclosures for its different parts. The fences were made of wattle (*pau a pique*), of which the forest provided an abundant supply, in contrast to the northeast where the natural vegetation was too poor to furnish materials which could be used for fencing purposes. Earthwork enclosures were also made, and occasionally stone walls were put up where stone was plentiful, as was frequently the case in these hilly uplands.[34] Unfeasible in the north, this measure had an important effect on the way the ranches were managed. Since the fazendas and pastures were enclosed, the need to keep constant watch on the herd to see that the animals did not stray was considerably reduced, and the herders were released for other duties. The herds could be kept within bounds without much effort and could, therefore, be more easily defended against natural enemies and pests. In this region, as a result of this systematic care, the semiwild cattle of the Sertão were unknown—that particular indomitable breed which made cattle raising in the Sertão such a difficult and hazardous undertaking, and lent it the epic character, admirable in the dramatic effects so graphically depicted by Euclides da Cunha,* but deplorable in the more mundane sphere of the economy.

The tasks performed on the Minas fazendas, revealing a level of technical accomplishment far superior to that of their counterparts in the Sertão, were also more numerous and more complex. Greater attention was paid to pasturage. This does not signify that the Mineiros planted any selected feed, a measure

---

* In *Os Sertões*, the Brazilian masterpiece translated and annotated by Samuel Putnam as *Rebellion in the Backlands*. (Univ. of Chicago Press, 1944).—Translator.

which was at that time still unknown in Brazil; nor that they had given up or replaced the primitive queimada process, which was universally practiced in the colony; but simply that they took certain special precautions. The pastures were divided into four fields, known in Minas as the "green pastures," each field being burned over in rotation every three months, to ensure a constant supply of fresh and succulent fodder. There were special separate pastures for the bulls and the cows. The cows were segregated until they had grown sufficiently to be served at the proper time to ensure that the calves were born vigorous and healthy. They were also herded into the corrals every evening.

Diet was more carefully regulated. Salt rations were provided regularly; indeed, this provision was essential since the soil was not impregnated with salt, as in the northeast. This was fortunate for the cattle, since they were thus provided with pure salt and did not have to ingest with it the large quantities of earth so harmful to their health, which was what occurred with the salt licks of the Sertão. The distribution of salt rations offered another advantage; it was an important factor in the domestication of the animals, since it helped them to become accustomed to the corrals where it was distributed, and to the men who performed this task.

The Minas region was also suited to agriculture; and the cattle could, therefore, be provided with supplementary rations, a feed of bran mash being the chief addition to their diet. In short, these and other measures adopted indicate a care which, although not particularly noteworthy in another context, nevertheless places stock raising in southern Minas on a level unparalleled in the rest of the colony. As a result, the cattle from Minas were superior in condition and quality, being noted for their strength and size.[35] The cattle population was, however, relatively sparse. St. Hilaire notes that there were between 600–700 head of cattle in an area of two leagues. This can be explained in part by the system of pasture rotation and the segregation of the cows.

The dairying industry, practically unknown in the north,

played an important role in Minas. Better treated and better
fed, the cows yielded milk which St. Hilaire compared in quality to that of the mountains of Auvergne.[36] The milk was used
to make the already famous Minas cheese, which was sent in
large quantities to Rio de Janeiro and other parts of the colony.[37] As in the north, butter was unknown and curd was not
used.

Another characteristic of cattle raising in Minas was the
technique of labor adopted and the type of social organization
deriving from it. In this region slave labor was employed, and
the only free people on the fazenda were the proprietor and his
family. This was probably a consequence of the more sedentary nature of the work on the "fazenda Mineira," as compared
to those of the northeast, the tasks involved being more compatible with the African laborer's capabilities. The use of slave labor was a consequence also of a higher economic level of stock
rearing in southern Minas, which allowed more capital to be invested.

The rancher and his family took an active part in the management of the fazenda, and absentee landlords were unknown.
The presence of slaves, however, did not signify that the ranchers of southern Minas led aristocratic lives, since cattle raising,
unlike commercial agriculture and mining, brought the landowners into more intimate contact with the workers, the two
classes coming together in the labors they shared. The ranchers
did not avoid work which in other regions would have been
considered degrading and undignified. St. Hilaire noted this,
giving the fact some prominence since it had impressed him as
being such a unique exception in Brazil. He cites, among other
instances, the case of a modest drover whom he met leading a
mule convoy along the Rio de Janeiro trail, and to whom he
was later introduced as the son of a wealthy rancher in Minas,
owner of all the merchandise the mules had been transporting.

This more democratic way of life and easier social relations
were widespread in southern Minas, not only in cattle raising
but also in local agriculture which, as we have seen in a previous chapter, was of some importance. A number of factors

must have contributed to this, but one in particular seems to stand out. The grazing area was situated in a mining region, where gold extraction had always absorbed most of the attention. This was the captaincy's all-important industry. The more modest elements were, therefore, relegated to activities of a secondary order, a situation paralleled in fact in regions devoted to commercial agriculture. What happened in Minas, however, and what startled the travelers who visited it, was that, as a result of special circumstances (the excellent natural conditions and the nearby markets of the mining centers and Rio de Janeiro), these secondary activities grew and acquired an importance that the parallel activities developed in other regions had never managed to attain. And hence we find big landowners, legitimate ranchers who owned a large number of slaves, descending from the pedestal on which the other privileged members of colonial society, the senhores d'engenho and the miners, continued to place themselves.

As a natural and inevitable consequence of the greater intercourse between master and worker which occurred in southern Minas and the greater part taken in productive activities by the former, there was also a greater uncouthness of habits and manners among the upper classes as compared to those of the mining districts, where the role of proprietor never went beyond aloof supervision of the slaves. St. Hilaire, an aristocrat by birth, breeding, and instinct, could not disguise the slight uneasiness he experienced in his contacts with the uncouth *fazendeiros* of the south, infinitely preferring the finesse and polish to be found in other parts of the captaincy.[38]

In addition to cattle, a large number of pigs were raised in this region, particularly in the eastern districts, where the most important pig-breeding center was Formiga. Most of the colony's pigs were concentrated in this center, which was also the leading pig market. The concentration of pig breeding in the eastern districts is explained by the fact that the natural pastures were poorer in this area; and hence pigs, which could be fattened on maize, had the advantage over cattle, whose requirements are more exacting since they cannot do without herbage. The pigs played an important role in the colonial economy, particularly in the captaincies of the central-south, including Rio de Janeiro and São Paulo. In this part of the colony, pork was a major item in the diet of its inhabitants.[39] But its chief use was in salted form, *toucinho,* or fat bacon, which was used to add flavor to many dishes, particularly beans. Pork fat is still the universal cooking fat in the Brazilian cuisine.[40]

Sheep were also fairly widespread in this region. They were raised mainly for their wool, which was woven into rough cloth for clothing the slaves, and also used to make the broad-brimmed, small-crowned felt hats so characteristic of the Mineiros.[41]

We will now turn to the third and last of the colony's chief cattle raising regions, the southern "Campos." I have already referred to these campos. They extend southward from Parana-panema, enclosed on one side by the Serra do Mar and its dense forest covering and on the other by the forests bordering the Paraná River and its large affluents. This strip of plain widens as we proceed southward, and in the southern extreme of the colony we find the limitless grasslands of the frontier zone, the pampas, which are really part of the vast grassy plains of the Plata basin.

These southern plains, or Campos Gerais, as their northern and longest-occupied part was known (Paraná),[42] offered admirable physical conditions for settlement, and I have already had occasion to cite St. Hilaire's observation that this region was "Brazil's Paradise on earth." Its topography is ideal: gently rolling country which can be opened up without effort, and well-balanced vegetation. The forest-grassland distribution is divided between grassy plains, which provide the country's best natural pastures, and forest patches which carpet the valleys with a predominance of the Araucaria pine, whose kernels can be used for food and whose wood provides the most valuable building timber in Brazil. Water is also plentiful, and crystal-clear streams flow along the rocky beds—another notable feature which is exceptional in Brazil.

Cattle were early introduced into this region, in the northern

part—the Campos Gerais properly speaking—by settlers entering from São Vicente; and in the southern part, Rio Grande, a
little later on (perhaps in the early years of the seventeenth
century) by the Jesuits of the Uruguay missions or by Spanish
settlers entering from Paraguay.[43] The cattle thus introduced
had literally spawned all over the pampas, and animals from
the Campos Gerais and Curitiba were being sent to the markets of São Paulo and Rio de Janeiro in quantities sufficient to
meet the demand. Cattle in the far south, however, came
within the Spanish orbit, as this region remained almost completely cut off from the rest of the country until the middle of
the eighteenth century. Paulista expansion had, however, penetrated the region by this time, and the first Luso-Brazilian settlers, moving down the coast from Laguna, had already established themselves on cattle ranches that were to supply the
nascent settlements of Santa Catarina. Apart from these minor
attempts, however, the present territory of Rio Grande do Sul
remained empty of Portuguese colonization. In contrast, the
Spanish Jesuit missions were opening up the region's far west,
subduing the local tribes and forming the mission stations of
the "Seven Peoples of Uruguay," which were to become the
great apple of discord in future disputes.

It was only in 1737 that regular, official, and intensive colonization of this territory was undertaken, a territory that was
finally to become Brazilian only after the longest and bitterest
struggles in its history. Up to 1777, this territory was involved
in constant conflict: Portuguese versus Spaniards; Portuguese
and Spaniards versus Jesuits and their rebellious mission Indians, who refused to hand over to the Portuguese the territory
they had been awarded by the 1750 treaty. These struggles are
of great interest to the topic with which we are now concerned.
The wild and unclaimed cattle which roamed this area—completely unruly and administratively disorganized as a result of
the constant hostilities—supplied meat for the embattled armies. The final settlement was reached at San Ildefonso in
1777, and although this treaty was revoked shortly afterward,
it did succeed in establishing peace between the two contend-

ers and gave the territory a long respite from hostilities, which
only broke out again in the early years of the nineteenth century.[44]

During this lull, the cattle herds, which had been decimated
by the wars, began to increase rapidly. Peace brought about an
expansion of settlement, and the first cattle ranches were established in the territory, particularly along the frontier, where, as
a consequence of the wars, the population tended to become
more concentrated, being at first made up exclusively of soldiers and guerrillas. Hundreds of land grants were given, since
the authorities were keen to consolidate Portuguese possession,
which had hitherto been guaranteed only by force of arms. The
legal decrees limiting the areas of land grants to three leagues
did not succeed in curbing the abuses that arose, and vast *estancias* (cattle estates) were soon formed. Sesmarias were applied for not only in the prospective grantee's own name, but in
the name of wives, sons, daughters, babies still in the cradle,
and infants not yet born.[45] The pattern which had proved so
harmful in the northeastern Sertão in the previous century was
here repeated, and the captaincy's land wealth was thus concentrated in the hands of a few powerful territorial magnates.

But although cattle raising was from the outset tainted by
these abuses, it managed to take a firm hold and was organized
on a solid basis, prospering rapidly. At the end of the eighteenth century there were 539 cattle raisers in the southern part
of the captaincy.[46]

At first the chief product was hides, large quantities of
which were exported. Meat production was neglected, since
there was little demand; the scanty local population and the
small size of the Santa Catarina market were not enough to absorb the huge herds. Cattle on the hoof sent to Santa Catarina
and Curitiba accounted for only 10,000–20,000 head annually
at the beginning of the nineteenth century.[47] Cattle were
killed only for their hides, and the carcasses were left rotting
on the plains. There was not even any systematic grazing, and
the herds of semiwild cattle that roamed the ranges freely were
"hunted" rather than raised. They were "owned" by whatever

proprietor found them on his land. Right up to the end of the century, hides formed the captaincy's staple export product.

This chaos was gradually organized. This was chiefly due to the growth of an industry that was to free Rio Grande from its handicap as a distant outpost in relation to the markets for meat, the *charque* industry. Its appearance in the colony's trade coincided with the decadence of cattle raising in the northeastern sertões, which were no longer able to meet the demands of the market. Rio Grande thus found the doors wide open for its product, and production expanded rapidly as a consequence of the considerable advantages it enjoyed, with the vast herds simply waiting to be exploited. The opportunity was not wasted. In 1793 the captaincy was exporting 13,000 arrobas of charque; by the beginning of the nineteenth century exports had already reached the figure of nearly 600,000 arrobas. If we exclude the gold rush, the colony had never witnessed such a fantastic increase of activity.[48]

The charque industry set up in the *charqueadas* (meat drying works) was located in an ideal spot, the area between the Pelotas and São Gonçalo rivers. It was close to the great cattle raising region of the frontier and to the port (Rio Grande) from which the charque was shipped to the rest of the colony, which although very deficient was the only one possible. This location of the industry gave rise to Pelotas, an urban nucleus which was to become the captaincy's most important center after the capital and indisputably foremost in wealth and social prestige.[49]

The technical level of cattle raising in Rio Grande at the beginning of the nineteenth century was no higher than that of the northeastern sertões. It was still too close to the unruly origins described above. What may sometimes obscure the comparison is the manifest superiority of Rio Grande's physical condition, the abundance of its natural pastures as compared to the miserable conditions of the north. This superiority lends a pleasant gloss to life on the southern cattle ranches which is totally lacking in their northeastern counterparts. Besides, in Rio Grande the industry was on the rise, whereas in the north it

had passed its zenith and was now openly decadent. These factors must be taken into account because, in actual fact, the role
played by man was identical in both regions: cattle roamed the
ranges freely in both in a semiwild and almost untended state.
The herds had been incorporated into the *estancias* (the southern counterpart of the fazenda) in the same condition in which
they had been found wandering about unclaimed. With the industrialization and commercial exploitation of meat, which began around 1780 when the first charqueadas were established,
greater care began to be taken. Nevertheless, in 1810 a contemporary observer who, being a cattle trader, was well qualified
to comment, noted that even on the better estancias only one-
fourth of the cattle were domesticated, the rest being left to
roam the area in a wild state with no attempt to tend them.[50]

The estancias covered vast areas of land as a result of the
abuses which it had proved impossible to curb. There were
thus estates 100 leagues in extent.[51] Each league was capable
of supporting between 1,500–2,000 head,[52] a carrying capacity far higher than that of the northern region or Minas, which
indicates the superior quality of the southern pastures. The estancias were managed by an overseer and a number of ranch-
hands (*peões*), who were slaves only in rare instances, being
for the most part Indians or half-breeds who were paid a wage.
These formed the bulk of the prairie population.[53] Luccock
ascribed six attendants to each lot of 4,000–5,000 head of cattle.[54] There was not sufficient permanent work for a larger
number of hands to be employed, and during the busy period
extra cowboys were recruited from among the large roving
population of the prairies, offering their services, living on
maté and barbecued meat, constantly on the move, and never
settling in one fixed place. They had acquired these adventurous and nomadic habits largely on account of the constant
wars. These socially unstable people flocked to the rodeo—a
red letter day on the estancia—which took place twice a year
when the cattle were rounded up, inspected, marked, and cas-
trated, all this amidst boisterous scenes with displays of skilled
horsemanship, which was the great sport of the pampas.

Apart from this roundup, the regular tasks did not amount to much. Pastures were burned over yearly; the herds could be tended with relative ease in these open treeless prairies, which offered no concealment for cattle as did the thickets of the northeast, and where natural enemies were far less dangerous. Salt was not regularly distributed. According to Dreys, the animals' need for salt was met partly by the salt content of the natural pastures, which were exposed to the sea breezes that blew across the unprotected prairies.[55] In short, there was little attempt at systematic animal husbandry in Rio Grande. The propitious nature of the land was responsible for the successful establishment of cattle raising, and man relied more on the natural advantages than on his own efforts. For this reason, production was not particularly outstanding; we have already seen that the cattle of the region were much inferior to those of the Plata region and yielded fifty percent less meat in spite of similar physical conditions. This percentage is confirmed by the budgetary estimate made by Governor Silva Gama in 1803, who estimated that the region's bulls yielded an individual average of nine arrobas of meat, only one arroba more than those of the northeast.[56]

The dairying industry was not very well developed, and fell far short of that of Minas Gerais. Cheese figured among the captaincy's exports at the end of the eighteenth century, but disappeared from the tables of exports for the following century, and figured instead among its imports, although only in limited quantities. We must bear in mind that in this region, unlike the rest of the country, butter was produced and consumed, a difference undoubtedly attributable to the climate, the cooler climatic conditions of Rio Grande being better suited to a commodity so easily deteriorated by heat.

As for the other by-products of the grazing industry, we find in this region, as in the others, hides, horns, and hooves; but we also find among Rio Grande's exports one commodity of which it was the colony's sole exporter: tallow, used in the colonial manufacture of ropes and ship's tackle and also for manufacturing crude soap. This production of tallow was undoubtedly due to the quality of the cattle, and indicates that they were not quite the scrawny, muscular animals of the northeastern Sertão.

In addition to cattle, horses and above all mules were bred. In the captaincy itself only horses were used, mules being neglected to a point where it was even considered degrading to mount them. It is interesting to compare the different regions of the country from the point of view of the pack animals used. The horse was the most important means of transportation in the north, and the mule in the center. In the south, the horse once more predominates. Topography is certainly the decisive factor in this difference; the plains of the broad flat-topped uplands of the north, and the southern pampas, contrast with the mountainous region of the central-south, where the hardy mule, slower, stronger, surer-footed, gives better service. But the colony's supply of mules came from Rio Grande and, through this captaincy, from the Plata region. We will consider this topic at greater length in the chapter on communications and transport. Rio Grande exported 12,000–15,000 mules on the hoof per annum at the beginning of the last century. In comparison, it exported only 4,000–5,000 horses.[57] There were also fairly large numbers of sheep, raised as in Minas Gerais for wool rather than for meat, the wool being used to make the famous *ponchos* worn by cowboys and lower classes of the population.[58]

Hitherto we have considered only the southernmost part of the colony's southern grasslands. We must now turn to the other part, which, although very similar in its physical environment to the region we have just considered, developed without establishing any contact with its neighbor. Cattle raising in the second region was described in detail by St. Hilaire.[59] Although not as important as in the previous region, the livestock industry was far better organized and seems to have been more stable.[60] We do not find cattle in the semiwild state of the more southern region; herds were formed in quite a different manner, a much more orderly and peaceful process. A factor which contributed to the greater domestication of cattle in this area was the regular distribution of salt rations, a necessity imposed by circumstance but one which helped to domesticate the animals in the manner I described for Minas Gerais. In this region, however, salt was not distributed as bounteously as in the latter captaincy.[61]

The fazendas of the Campos Gerais—fazendas, not estancias, since it was only in the far south that the Spanish name was adopted—were large, but not as huge as the vast estates of Rio Grande. St. Hilaire, who had not yet visited the latter captaincy, was surprised by the size of Colonel Luciano Cordeiro's estate in Jaguariaíva, which contained 2,000 cows apart from bulls and calves. In Rio Grande this fazenda would have caused little surprise. In fact, the Campos Gerais region was not as important as the southern one. The charque industry was nonexistent, and the only regular markets for cattle on the hoof were the coastal settlements of Paraná (Paranaguá), which were of little significance, and São Paulo, likewise of minor importance. And production was not even sufficient for these minor markets, since as we have seen, Rio Grande contributed several thousand head per annum. The Campos Gerais had long since ceased to be the chief supplier of all the country's southern captaincies, including Rio de Janeiro.

Some sheep were raised but no mules, since the breeding of mules was prohibited north of the Iguaçu river in order to protect the industry in Rio Grande, where, with the idea of establishing a firmer grip on the southern border, the government had decided to encourage settlement.[62] The Campos Gerais served simply as the winter pasture for mules on their way to the annual livestock fair held at Sorocaba, the most important market town and distribution center for the mule trade.

The country's other cattle raising regions are of secondary importance. In the far north there was a grazing zone on the island of Joanes.[63] The island supplied the colonial establishments situated at the mouth of the great river, where the greater part of the Amazon valley's population was centered. The choice of Joanes for this activity was dictated by the lack of any alternative in this heavily forested and semiaquatic re-

gion of the Amazon Basin; no other area was suitable. Cattle
were introduced into the island in the seventeenth century, and
the first proper fazenda was established in 1692.[64]

In 1750 there were 480,000 head of cattle on the island; in
1783 the number of fazendas was 153, and by 1803 this figure
had risen to 226 with a total of 500,000 head.[65] As we can see,
the herds had not made much progress, which was only to be
expected. The conditions in which cattle were raised in this region were precarious. Although the part of the island chosen
for the grazing of cattle consisted of higher lands that stood
above flood level (whereas other parts were completely inundated), the low altitude and gentle slope of these raised levees
meant that the water was never properly drained, and this, together with the abundant local rainfall, transformed them in
the rainy season into vast swamps, where only a few patches of
dry land stood out above the stagnant waters. These bits of
firm land were known as the *tezos*,* and it was here that the
cattle took shelter in the rainy season, when they were obliged
to pasture with their heads literally thrust into the water![66]
Calves born in this season nearly always died of drowning. The
pastures were of poor quality and, as if this were not enough,
cattle were victims of two ferocious enemies, the piranha and
the alligator.

Under such conditions, cattle raising could hardly be expected to flourish, nor could production increase sufficiently to
meet the growing local demand. This growth in the demand for
meat occurred in fact only long after settlement had been established. In the early days, the colonists in the region adopted
native habits, and their diet consisted principally of fish and
game, both of which abounded in the area. The first slaughterhouse in Pará was only opened in 1726.[67] With the growth of
the demand for meat, the captaincy had to augment its supply
by importing large quantities of dried meat from Ceará and
later charque from Rio Grande.[68]

A small grazing center was formed in upper Amazonas, the

* Literally, a stiff, rigid object; by extension, the top of a hill or elevated bit of land not inundated during a flood.—Translator.

plains of the Rio Branco being utilized for this purpose. Governor Lobo de Almada organized crown fazendas and introduced cattle into the area, and his example was followed by private individuals.[69] Having only been recently established (in 1793), this region was insignificant in the period with which we are dealing, but had already developed sufficiently to supply the establishments along the Rio Negro, particularly the capital of the captaincy, Barra. Cattle were shipped downriver to this center in *ajoujos* (canoes lashed together).

Finally, we must mention a few remaining areas which to complete the picture should not be omitted. These areas include the campos of northeastern Maranhão, known as the "Perizes," where there was a sparse cattle population; certain parts of Goiás, which managed to send a number of droves each year to Bahia; and Mato Grosso, where cattle were raised for local consumption in areas near the mining establishments but where this activity was not very significant. The phase of prosperity for the livestock industry of Mato Grosso, which was to unfold in these endless southern plains, had not yet started and belongs entirely to the nineteenth century.

Extractive Products[1]

The extractive industry's chief importance is not its commercial value as one of the colony's sources of income, for as such it played a minor role. Its importance lies rather in the fact that it was almost the only basis for existence in the country's largest region, determining a way of life whose characteristics were so specific to this region that it cannot be compared with anything that happened in other parts of the country. I am referring to the Amazon Valley, the colonization of which cannot be understood without analyzing the chief and almost only activity practiced in it, the collection of natural forest and river products.

In the lower part of the basin near the mouth of the river, that is, the territory occupied by Pará proper, we find an economic and social organization which can be put on the same footing as that of the other coastal captaincies. The same crops—sugar, tobacco, and the other commercial commodities —were grown, although in small quantities, and the same structure of large-scale agricultural exploitation prevailed. There were even black slaves, and African blood, completely absent in the interior, was evident in Pará.

Further inland, along the innumerable watercourses that intermingle to form the most complex and vast network of waterways in the world and where colonization and settlement of the

242

valley became fixed, the local economy is based solely on extractive activities organized in an individual and distinctive system.

The colonists found in the Amazon Valley an enormous variety of commercially utilizable natural commodities: clove bark, cinnamon, Brazil nuts, sarsaparilla, and above all cacao, not to mention timber and the abundant products of the animal kingdom. Of the latter, the turtle and its eggs and the *manacaru* * (known as the "bull-fish"), were particularly useful on a commercial scale. Without these sources of wealth it would have been impossible to occupy the great valley. The colonists would never have attempted to settle it, and the missionaries would not have found the material basis for subsistence while they carried out their work of catechizing the native.

It is true that an attempt was made to establish agriculture, and that the administration and the more enlightened colonists, who realized the need for a more solid basis than that provided by the precarious extractive industry, did not spare their efforts in this direction. But goodwill by itself was not enough. In the ever-shifting rearrangement of a land still far from physical consolidation, man becomes insignificant, and his efforts are annihilated. For the thick and semiaquatic forest area bordering the basin of the great river is subject to a rainfall whose irregularity, with the enormous volume of waters brought down, assumes catastrophic proportions as the currents inundate vast areas of *igapós* † and tear away large masses of soil from the river banks. The struggle calls for almost limitless effort if man is to come to terms with this land and go beyond the stage of docile submission to the natural conditions. Such efforts were beyond the capacity of early colonization. It lacked the essential element, a sufficient number of people. The few white men and the relatively large numbers of Indians—the latter un-

---

* The *manacaru* is the manatee, popularly known in English as the sea cow.—Translator.

† *Igapó:* "A forest bordering a river which is subject to such fluctuations of water-level that for months the trees are partly inundated." Webster's New International Dictionary (under "Gapo").—Translator.

suited to the work demanded of them—could not cope with such a task. Amazonia was to remain what it had been from the outset, a land untamed.

Agriculture, which calls for a certain degree of control over nature, could only have been a fitful activity at best. In the lower areas around the delta, the most accessible part of the valley, where conditions were more favorable, agriculture was attempted. Similarly, along the Rio Negro, which was also a better-favored area, there was some agricultural activity. In these areas, in addition to the colony's classic commodities, the settlers cultivated native crops, such as cacao, sarsaparilla, cinnamon, vanilla, and *ipadu* (the coca plant). A few other crops were introduced, such as coffee and indigo. But nothing was produced in any significant proportion.

By and large, the region continued to depend almost entirely on the gathering of indigenous forest commodities. This activity could not have been adapted to the systems of organization determined by other ways of life. This fact explains the distinctiveness of Amazonian life, which was to produce in the region a system without parallel in the rest of the colony, another Brazil. This radical difference can immediately be seen in Amazonia's ethnic formation. It was possible here to utilize the Indian, which could only be done on a small scale in the other captaincies. The activities carried on in the Amazon Valley can be practically reduced to two: penetration of the forest to collect forest products or to catch fish, and navigation of the rivers in the boats or canoes which were the universal means of transportation and the sole means of travel. For both of these activities the native was admirably equipped. Gathering, hunting, and fishing are the Amerindian's natural activities. As fishermen they were unsurpassed, and the colonists learned much from their methods. Their superiority in the handling of canoes was also unchallenged; none could match their endurance on the long voyages upriver, when they rowed from sunrise to sunset without a break; none had their ability to observe and understand the vagaries of the current and to turn them to advantage; none shared their amazing skill in negotiating the intricacies of the *igarapés.**

Used, therefore, to perform tasks with which they were familiar, in contrast to the work expected from them in agriculture and mining (although no attempt was in fact made to use them for the latter), the Indians here adapted themselves more easily to colonization and the domination of the white man. Colonization in the Amazon region was, thus, permeated by the Amerindian contingent, which more or less blended into colonial life, ended by dominating it and giving it its tone. In no other part was the native to have such a profound influence on the way of life and even the psychological attitudes of the white man.

I have already mentioned the type of settlement effected in the region. This was likewise adapted to the requirements of forest gathering. Collection from wild stands naturally meant that the gatherers had to roam about in search of these stands, wherever chance had happened to place the plants they sought. And, since these wild stands were as a rule scattered irregularly over wide areas, Amazonian settlement became widely dispersed. The population, which at the beginning of the last century did not yet amount to more than 100,000 inhabitants, was already spread thinly along thousands of miles of watercourses.

Another consequence of this way of life was the attraction of the rivers. Riverside locations were preferred not for the sake of the water itself, but because of the means of travel it offered. With a form of activity in which the sources of production are irregularly scattered and in which there are no points where production is appreciably concentrated, it is not the sources of production which lead to the fixation of settlement, as in the

---

* *Igarapé:* "a waterway in a forest passable by canoe" (Webster), or "a narrow natural channel between two islands, or between an island and a mainland; a canoe passage" ("Glossary of Brazilian Amazonian Terms," compiled by D. Farquhar, H. MacMillan, and B. Siegel, from the *Strategic Index of the Americas*). Washington, Office of the Co-ordinator of Inter-American Affairs, Research Division, 1943.—Translator.

case of agriculture and mining, but the communication
routes. In this case, therefore, the communication routes did
not follow settlement; it was the other way round. However, it
was not only the difficulties in the way of access and occupation that led the colonists to prefer riverside locations for settlement. These difficulties could, if necessary, have been overcome as they had been in other parts of the colony. But why
should the colonists have chosen to settle away from the splendid routes offered by these "liquid highways," when any other
spot was equally remote, or otherwise only slightly better situated in relation to the sources of the products exploited? The
area which the humble gatherer of indigenous products had to
cover was inevitably vast and, furthermore, extremely variable,
since the sources were soon used up in this primitive form of exploitation. Natural and easy communication routes provided by
the watercourses were, therefore, the only strong and permanent magnets for settlement.

The element most sensitive to the requirements of a collecting economy was, of course, organization of labor. Labor was
sporadic, coinciding with the due collecting seasons, and thus
carried on in brief spurts in the form of expeditions which periodically set out upriver to search for forest products, followed
by the long inactivity of the "dead season." The first step in this
organization was for the promoter of an expedition to recruit
the necessary gatherers. These were Indians, engaged under
the supervision of the authorities, after the passing of the protective Pombaline laws, at an officially stipulated wage.[2] The
Indians could not refuse to serve, particularly after the royal
decree of May 12, 1798, which categorically imposed on them
the obligation to work in the service of the colonists. But in
spite of this, recruitment of Indian workers was not a straightforward operation. Apart from the reluctance of the workers,
which was manifest in their frequent desertions and escapes,
the entrepreneurs had to contend with competition from others
interested in this insufficient labor supply. The administration
also tapped this source to secure the labor it needed to carry
out public works, and the crown officials were, of course, given

priority over the colonists. In a previous chapter I indicated the extent of this intervention on the labor market by the authorities, which deprived the native villages of their residents and robbed the colonists of their workers.

These disputes over native workers—which unfortunately helped them but little, since they were unable to grasp the situation and profit by the advantages it offered—resulted in frequent outbursts of violence; in many instances special authorities had to be appointed to try to settle the disagreements. Thus in Ega, a "judge" was chosen from among the settlers and posted to the most concentrated area of "tame" Indian settlements, at the mouth of the Içá, where he adjudicated upon the disposal of the available Indian hands.[3]

Once organized, the expedition proceeded upriver, heavily armed because of the constant risk of attack by hostile tribes. Of these savage tribes, the Muras proved particularly troublesome, and large numbers of them were still resisting colonization with arms during the period we are considering. Regular troops sometimes accompanied the expeditions, having been specially assigned the task by the authorities. Thus prepared, the convoy of canoes, *igaras*, *igarités*, and *ubás* * set out navigating upriver in search of favorable stands, which were sometimes situated at great distances from the points of departure. To cite one particular instance, Ega was the starting point for expeditions which went up the Jupurá, Içá, Juruá, Jutaí, and Javari rivers, covering a radius of hundreds of kilometers.[4]

Once the cargo had been stowed, which took weeks and sometimes even months, the expeditions returned downriver and the gatherers were dismissed, being generally paid in kind in spite of the regulations concerning their proper payment, which stipulated that they were to receive a fixed cash sum. The promoter of the expedition then sold his produce to the lo-

---

* An *igara* is a dugout canoe; an *igarité* is a "large canoe with a span of two to three metres amidship, propelled by a trapezoidal sail or paddles, and usually decked over in the stem, forming a cabin. . . ." An *ubá* is a primitive canoe hollowed out of tree trunks. "Glossary of Brazilian Amazonian Terms."—Translator.

cal traders, who in turn shipped it downriver to be exported by the traders of Pará.

Other extractive activities, such as the collection of turtle eggs, used for preparing turtle butter, a highly valuable commodity from which cooking fat and oil for lighting purposes were made, were organized in more or less the same way. The egg-laying season lasts from October to November, when thousands of turtles head for certain chosen beaches to bury their eggs in the sand, to be hatched out by the heat of the sun. Once the gatherers had discovered the beaches used by the turtles, they merely had to wait for them to retire before moving in to uncover the eggs. The "butter" was prepared immediately in the same canoes used to transport the collectors.[5]

Fishing was a much more sedentary occupation and involved a more continuous activity. Hand-to-mouth fishing was, of course, widespread; most of the rural population practiced this type of subsistence fishing, and since communities were situated on the banks of well-stocked rivers, the inhabitants made use of their natural skill as fishermen. Fish was the basic item in the Amazonian diet.

But apart from this type of fishing, there was a considerable output of fish caught on commercially organized lines. This fishing industry centered on the *pesqueiros* (fishing grounds), where the fish caught was commercially processed for shipment to other parts of Brazil. Some of these installations were temporary, being set up at the appropriate time of year and in the most convenient place for catching a particular species. But more common and more important were the fixed pesqueiros, which were often of considerable size, the largest of all being that of Lago Grande de Vila Franca in the present-day town of this name, where in a period of two years the catch of turtles and manatees alone amounted to 8,500 specimens.[6] Some fishermen worked on their own account, but there were also crown fishermen whose catch was sold on behalf of the State Treasury. The labor force for exploiting these fishery resources was, of course, Amerindian. The catch was either salted or, in more substantial proportions, dried, fish processed in this way being one of the captaincy of Rio Negro's major exports.[7]

Such, in sum, were the chief and most characteristic features of this way of life supported by the collection of natural forest products, which formed the principal and almost sole basis for the colonization of the Amazon Valley. By and large, this colonization achieved meager results. The instability and uncertainty of a life based on these activities, the complex problem which it indirectly created of assimilating large masses of the indigenous peoples, made of Amazonian colonization more a speculative venture than the establishment of a stable and organized society. The general characteristics of Brazilian colonization—this enterprise for exploiting the tropics—were here revealed in all their crudeness and brutality. Here they were not offset, as they were in other parts of the colony, by the emergence of parallel and counterbalancing elements which matured with time to produce superior and more organic social forms. Here Brazil's evolution from tropical colony to nation, so difficult and so painful, a process not yet completed even today, was very much retarded. In this sense Amazonia lagged far behind the other occupied and colonized regions of Brazilian territory.

As for the material results of this colonization, these too were lacking in achievement. There is a striking contrast between what was actually achieved and what the burning imagination of the European colonists misled them to dream of achieving in their contact with the tropics. Exploitation of the natural resources of this vast forest, which the white man's fancy had filled with hidden treasures, yielded nothing but a pitifully small output of a few miserable products whose commercial value was insignificant. And it proved impossible to broaden the basis of this production and to give it more stability by cultivating these commodities. Amazonia's economy continued to be based solely on the collecting industry, and thus it was condemned to stand back, impotent, while its chief natural sources of wealth were ousted from the market by the products cultivated by its better-equipped competitors. This happened in the case of cacao. Once an Amazonian monopoly, cacao was planted in Bahia in the middle of the eighteenth century and the Amazonian product was soon out of the Brazilian market. The same happened a century later in a more dramatic form and on an international scale with rubber. Thus colonization of the Amazon Valley is still an unknown quantity.

A few other extractive products must be mentioned. Although these still played a certain role in the colonial economy at the beginning of the last century, their special characteristics and small output offered no possibilities for further development. These were timber, whale products, salt, saltpeter, and maté.

At the end of the eighteenth century the authorities began to turn their attention to the colony's wood resources; I am, of course, referring to *timber*, since dyewood, the symbolic but extinct *pau-brasil*, was no longer of any significance in the colony's activities. Hitherto neglected, in spite of the restrictive clauses in the title deeds of land holdings which in many cases forbade the cutting or burning of hardwoods, timber began to figure increasingly in the mother country's administrative provisions, particularly since she was attempting to rebuild her decadent and half-dead navy. This was part of Pombal's great program for reconstructing the kingdom—only partially and badly carried out after his downfall—which sought to profit by Portugal's unique position on the seas as the only neutral country among the maritime powers. The plan was that Portugal's American colony should contribute the timber to the restoration of the kingdom's navy.

The richest and most important sources of timber—apart from the Amazon forests which, from a commercial point of view, were more illusory than real and never contributed any appreciable quantity—were the surviving patches of the originally dense forest covering of the northeastern coastlands. These were the *matas* of Paraíba and Alagoas (a detailed description of the latter region is given in *Relação das Matas das Alagoas*, 1809). The comarca of Ilhéus in Bahia possessed wide areas of forest which, as we have seen, had hardly been touched by colonization. The history of these forests was recorded by Accioli in his *Dissertação Histórica, Etnográfica e Política.* These forests had always yielded a certain amount of timber, and there had been a minor lumber trade which included exploitation on behalf of the crown, known as the *cortes reais* (royal lumbering centers, literally, royal cuttings).

After a succession of orders, decrees, edicts and instructions on the subject—such as the *Regimentos* of September 12, 1652 (Clause 12), and October 13, 1751 (Clause 29), which like the clauses in the sesmarias forbade the cutting or burning of hardwoods—came the royal letter of March 13, 1797, which attempted to regulate the matter once and for all. The crown reserved the right to exploit all the forests and woodlands along the coastal fringe, and along the rivers that emptied straight into the sea, down which the logs could be rafted in *jangadas* * for shipment from the ports. No sesmarias could be granted in these areas, and existing grants were canceled. An attempt was made to put these measures into effect, but it did not produce the desired result. The next step was the creation of the *Conservadoria das Matas* (Forest Conservation Commission) to supervise lumbering activities in the cortes reais and to prevent further devastations of the forest. The office of *conservador* (conservator) in Ilhéus was for a long time held by the well-known naturalist, Baltasar da Silva Lisboa, chronicler of the *Anais do Rio de Janeiro* and *Ouvidor* † of the comarca.

But in spite of these endeavors, timber continued to be inadequately exploited and the lumber trade never came to much. Apart from this extractive activity, brief mention must be made of the shipbuilding industry, intimately related to lumbering, which developed in some of the colony's ports, particularly

---

* The *jangada* is a raft of Amerindian origin, consisting of a hull platform made of five or six lightweight logs lashed together and fitted with a steering oar and a single mast.—Translator.

† *Ouvidor*—a crown or royal judge. Also the senior judicial authority in a comarca.—Translator.

Bahia, where a royal shipyard was established. But no really large ships were built, and the industry never developed beyond the construction of small ships for the coastal trade.

Whalefishing in Brazil had its heyday in colonial times. The whaling installations in Bahia (at the harbor bar, between the sea and the chapel of St. Benedict, and at Itaparica), were the oldest in the colony and had been established in the first half of the eighteenth century. Further south, there were establishments at São Domingos, in Praia Grande (the present-day town of Niteroi), set up in 1782; and at Bertioga in Santos, which already existed in 1789. There were the six establishments of Santa Catarina: Piedade, on the island's northern inlet (1746); Lagoinha, on the eastern coast of the island (1772); Itapocoróia (1777 or 1778); Garopaba (1795); Embituba (1796); and finally, the establishment on Graça island, situated at the entrance of the São Francisco canal, in 1807.

Whaling was a royal monopoly, operated on a contract basis by concessionaires. It was an important activity; during the 12-year contract operated from 1765–1777, the contractors made a profit of four million *cruzados*.* On one expedition alone, 523 whales were caught. But Brazilian whaling declined after English and North American whalers began to operate off the Falkland Islands at the end of the eighteenth century, preventing the whales from reaching the Brazilian coast in their winter migrations, as they had done in the past. The whale population was, in fact, much reduced as a result of the widespread devastation wrought by improved whaling techniques. In 1801, the crown could find no one to tender for the monopoly, which thereupon lapsed, and whaling was thrown open to general exploitation. It continued to be carried on although manifestly on the decline, until it disappeared altogether in the third decade of the last century.

The whaling industry is documented in the following works: José Bonifácio de Andrada e Silva, *Memória sôbre a pesca da baleia* . . . (Memoir on Whale Fishing); Pizarro, *Memórias históricas* IX, p. 289; St. Hilaire, *Voyages aux Provinces de St.*

---

* Cruzado—a coin equivalent to 480 reis.—Translator.

Paul, II, p. 308 (which gives a detailed description of whaling at the beginning of the nineteenth century); Martius, *Viagem*, II, p. 275 (describing the installations at Bahia); Almeida e Sá, *Armações da pesca da baleia* (Whaling Installations); Lúcio de Azevedo, *Novas Epanáforas*, p. 43; and an interesting document in the collection of letters written by various authorities, *Correspondência de várias autoridades*, p. 109.

As far as the production of *salt* was concerned, I have already referred to the exploitation of the salt pans along the middle São Francisco in the chapter on cattle raising. Rock salt was also extracted along the Jauru River in Mato Grosso. These saltworks had been exploited from the founding of this captaincy and were still productive in 1797, according to Almeida Serra's *Descrição geográfica de Mato Grosso* (p. 164). Production of sea salt was, however, more important, and there were saltworks at various points along the coast: Tapuitapera in Maranhão; Moçó, Cocó, and Mandau in Ceará; Açu and Moçoró in Rio Grande do Norte (the largest in the colony and to this day the most important in the country); Itamaracá and Pau Amarelo in Pernambuco; Cotinguiba in Sergipe; Lagoa de Araruama (Cabo Frio) in Rio de Janeiro.

The salt trade was a crown monopoly, one of the most burdensome the colony had to bear, since it affected a staple commodity and pushed up its price. This monopoly was only effectively abolished in Brazil in 1803, after many broken promises and ineffective measures. It was rendered even more onerous by the protection which the government always afforded to the Portuguese salt industry, one of the kingdom's chief branches of production. In pursuance of this, colonial salt production was systematically hampered. It was never openly permitted and was carried on in face of enormous handicaps and unrelenting persecution. If it managed to survive in spite of all restrictions, this was because the shortage of salt and the high prices paid, as well as the derelictions and abuses practiced by the contractors, made it difficult to control smuggling and impossible to repress it altogether. Documentation of the subject can be found in the following: an anonymous work written at the beginning of the nineteenth century, *Notas sôbre tôdas as marinhas em que se faz sal na costa do Brasil* (Notes on the Saltbeds of the Brazilian Seaboard), which deals particularly with the saltworks of Rio Grande do Norte. For the Lagoa of Araruama, cf. *Memória histórica da cidade de Cabo Frio* (Historical Account of the Town of Cabo Frio) (1797). Other works are cited in my article, "Indústria salineira no Estado do Rio de Janeiro," published in the periodical, *Geografia,* vol. 1, no. 3, p. 290.

Saltpeter was also exploited in the colony. Official attempts at this exploitation, which date from 1755, were made with no appreciable result in the Serras of Montes Altos and Rio Verde in Bahia (cf. Lúcio de Azevedo, *Novas Epanáforas,* p. 44, and Vilhena, *Recopilação,* p. 597). Later, saltpeter was extracted by private enterprise from the river which took its name from the mineral, the Salitre, a small affluent of the São Francisco near the town of Juàzeiro (Martius, *Viagem,* II, p. 405); and also in the northern Sertão of Minas Gerais, particularly in Formigas (Montes Claros) (St. Hilaire, *Voyage aux provinces de Rio de Janeiro,* II, p. 312). Production, particularly in the latter district, reached fairly considerable proportions and supplied the royal gunpowder factories at Vila Rica and Rio de Janeiro. At first saltpeter was also exported; but this was forbidden by the decree of November 23, 1810, a ban which dealt a crippling blow to the industry. When St. Hilaire visited the region in 1817, it was, however, already becoming decadent as a result of the exhaustion of the deposits.

The plant yielding *maté* grows wild in the forests of the Paraná basin and was also widespread in the southern Campos Gerais. In Brazil it was first exploited in the Campos de Curitiba, particularly in the forests along the eastern edge of this region, bordering the Serra do Mar. In the seventeenth century the Jesuits established their fazenda of Borda do Campo in the area, where they exploited this commodity. They were possibly the first to do so commercially. Be that as it may, collection of maté leaves gained in importance and became one of Curitiba's chief occupations. It is interesting to note that consumption of maté was much more widespread in the Spanish American colonies of the Plata; Buenos Aires and Montevideo became the principal markets for the product, which was exported through Paranaguá. In Brazil, it was little known outside the southern producing centers. Even today, it is consumed on a relatively small scale. St. Hilaire, who classified the plant and gave it its botanical name, *Ilex paraguayensis,* gives us a detailed account of its harvesting and processing in his diary, *Voyage aux provinces de St. Paul,* II, p. 155 *et seq.*

Crafts and Industries

To complete this survey of the sectors of colonial production we must reserve a place—albeit only a small one, commensurate with their insignificance—for crafts and industries, that is, activities not dependent on agriculture and mining, concerned with the processing of raw materials. Not that in themselves these activities played any significant role in the economy; on the contrary, they had only a tiny part to play, and only a very detailed analysis reveals their presence. But not only because they did play a particular role with individual characteristics but also because they comprise a separate and distinctive category of colonial society, no survey would be complete if they were passed over in silence.

We must begin by distinguishing between the urban centers and the rural zone, since the "mechanical trades" were practiced differently in each. Outside the large cities—which will be considered further on—the mechanical arts and industries were merely accessories of the agricultural or mining establishment. To enable these establishments to run smoothly or to meet the needs of the large numbers of people concentrated in them, the owner and his family, slaves, and tenants, it became necessary, as a result of the enormous distances separating the various populated centers or for other practical or economic reasons, to set up an entire small industry of carpenters, blacksmiths, and other craftsmen and frequently even household

256

manufacturing of cloth and the making of clothes. In certain regions, such as Minas Gerais, which contained deposits of iron ores, there were even a few small foundries for manufacturing implements and tools for the use of the parent establishment.

This small domestic industry employed the more skilled slaves [1] or the womenfolk of the household for spinning and weaving cloth and making clothes. Although carried on behind the scenes and thus hardly noticeable at first sight, this industry played its role in colonial life, since it completed the self-sufficiency of the great rural establishments already noted in other sectors, which was such an important and characteristic feature of the colony's social and economic life. Apart from this, it also constituted the beginnings of a larger-scale and more important industry, which was unfortunately nipped in the bud by the mother country's policy and certain other factors, which will be indicated later.

As independent activities, the mechanical trades were practiced outside the urban areas by itinerant artisans who went about the colony offering their services from door to door. The most common journeymen were blacksmiths, who acted as farriers to the mules used by the dragoons who patrolled the interior; Luccock, among others, notes their presence in Minas Gerais.[2] But it was, of course, in the larger urban centers that the mechanical professions were most numerous—professions, that is, in the sense that they were unconnected with any other activities and carried on independently, which was the exception in the rural areas.[3]

These trades were generally plied by mulattoes who, according to Martius, were the colony's most skilled workers.[4] As was the universal rule at this period, the trades were organized in craft guilds or corporations. There is nothing distinctive about this type of organization that need be mentioned: the corporations were administered by "judges" and clerks elected from among the members and functioned in principle in the same way as their European counterparts.[5] In Brazil, however, the craftsmen were not as closely bound to their corporations as in Europe, the regulations were slacker, and control was not as strict. In short, there was greater professional freedom or liberty of labor to a degree not yet enjoyed in Europe. Martius deplored this fact, attributing the want of organized labor and the poorness of the services supplied to the lack of proper regulation. Martius's premise was true, but his conclusion false. It was not the lack of regulations and the freedom enjoyed by labor that were to blame for the shortcomings of the colony's mechanical trades; there were other, deeper causes, which will be considered later.

Colonial artisans generally relied on slave help. There can be no doubt that this resource, made possible by the prevailing system of servitude, had a very harmful effect on the colony's standards of craftsmanship since it contributed toward the growing tendency for the colonists to abandon the apprenticing of children and adolescents. As we know, apprenticeship everywhere played, and still plays, an important role in maintaining these standards, by training new generations of craftsmen and helping them to develop their professional skills.

Another category of artisans—although more commonly found on unskilled work requiring purely physical effort—was made up of hired slaves, the *escravos de serviço,* hired out by owners who made this a source of additional income, a "business" particularly widespread in the colony's big cities. Many of the escravos de serviço had even been specifically trained for this purpose.[6]

Small essential industries and others that can be regarded as specialized local handicrafts were scattered throughout the colony. Among these domestic manufacturing establishments were tileyards and limeworks. The tileyards manufactured building tiles. As we know, baked bricks were not used in colonial construction, the housing elements being either simple stud and mud or wattle and daub in the most rustic dwellings or, in the more sophisticated houses, lath and plaster or adobe (an unburnt brick dried in the sun).[7] In the coastal settlements the raw material used for preparing lime was provided by the shellmounds or *sambaquis* found abundantly along some parts of the Brazilian coast and still plentiful today. Production of lime became fairly important in certain areas; Santa Catarina, for example, produced enough to be able to export lime to the other captaincies.[8] Lime from Piriquiaçu, near Aldeia Velha in Espírito Santo, was also shipped to other parts of the colony.[9] Rio de Janeiro was supplied by the limeworks established on the island of Paqueta, which manufactured shell lime from the material provided by the sambaquis found along its bay.[10]

Pottery was a widespread craft industry. The art of ceramics was practiced by the Indians and although in many cases they had lost their spontaneity and native skill on contact with the whites, they were nevertheless employed on a wide scale by colonization to manufacture clay goods. Thus in the southern coastlands of Bahia, the comarca of Ilhéus, and the captaincy of Pôrto Seguro in the former Indian villages founded by the Jesuits in the seventeenth century and raised to the status of townships by the Pombaline laws, pottery was the principal local occupation, and the utensils produced supplied Bahia and Pernambuco and particularly their hinterlands. In Olivença almost all the inhabitants were engaged in the manufacture of pottery ware, and exports of these wares accounted for more than 1,000 cruzados yearly, a considerable sum for these poor Indians and half-breeds.[11] The island of Santa Catarina was famous for its pottery, particularly the *moringas* (water jugs), which were exported to all parts of the colony. St. Hilaire gives details of this handicraft.[12] We should also recall the large Carmelite potteries in Maranhão, where ninety slaves worked on the order's *Fazenda do Carmo*, or the "Carmo Pottery," as it was also known, producing roof tiles, floor and wall tiles, clay pots, and crockery.[13]

Tanneries were, of course, located in the chief cattle regions or main cattle trading centers: Rio Grande do Sul, Bahia, Pernambuco, and Rio de Janeiro. In Maranhão there was a ranch specializing in the production of fine calf leather processed in milk.[14] Soap-making—the soap being of a crude type—was a local industry in certain places. On the engenho of Jacuacari, near Belém do Pará, soap was made from cacao pod ash, tallow, and andiroba oil;[15] and in Rio Grande do Sul, in one of the islands located in the bar of the harbor, the soap was made of ordinary wood ash and the tallow so plentiful in the region.[16] Felt hats using the wool yielded by the region's sheep were, as we have seen, made in Minas Gerais, particularly in São João del-Rei; hats were also made in São Paulo.[17]

Besides these more widespread domestic industries, there were specialized local craft industries, whose products figured to a certain extent in interregional trade. Thus the *esteiras* (mats woven of straw) of Taubaté (São Paulo) were sold in Rio de Janeiro; *coxonilhos* (horse blankets) were made in Curitiba; [18] Olivença, in Southern Bahia, which specialized in pottery, also produced rosaries made from *piaçaba* (piassava) palm nuts, more than 40,000 of which were dispatched to Bahia, bringing in an annual income of 1,000 cruzados.[19] The Indians and half-breeds of the Bahian coast were skilled in making vessels from gourds, which were produced on a commercial scale in the Ilha das Flores in the Bay of Camamu.[20] Finally, rope was made along the upper Rio Negro, using piassava fiber, which Martius considered stronger than hemp. Ropes and cables produced in this region were used in the naval yards of Belém (Portugal) and exported to the Azores and Cape Verde Islands. They were also the source of a minor trade with the Spaniards of San Carlos, an establishment in the frontier zone of the upper Rio Negro.[21]

The list of craft manufactures could be extended, but those already indicated serve to give some idea of the character of colonial industry at the beginning of the nineteenth century. Two more important sectors must, however, be mentioned: textiles and iron manufactures. For both of these the colony possessed an abundant supply of raw materials and a relatively large domestic market. I have already mentioned the existence of textile manufacturing and iron production in the larger self-sufficient establishments, where these activities were part and parcel of the organization and the output sufficed to meet the establishments' needs. But having originated in this way, these industries tended to free themselves of domestic restrictions as they developed and to become independent—proper manufacturing enterprises, commercially organized. This trend was more pronounced in the textile industry, particularly in Minas Gerais but also in Rio de Janeiro, where relatively large, independent textile factories appeared in the eighteenth century. The Marquis of Lavradio, Viceroy of Rio de Janeiro, mentions their existence in his report on handing over the viceregency to his successor in 1799.[22] He warns against the danger of such activities, which not only created competition for the mother country's textiles but also made the colonists too independent. He mentions instances in which he had been forced to intervene to curb the expansion of manufacturing, by closing down factories which had become too well known, such as that of Pamplona in Minas Gerais, and others.

The viceroy's warning did not fall on deaf ears. A few years later, the royal decree of January 5, 1785, ordered the cessation of all textile manufacturing in the colony, except for the manufacture of rough cotton cloth used for clothing the slaves and for sack-making.[23] This was the deathblow to the colony's industry, in spite of the exception provided for by the law, which enabled it to maintain a precarious and unstable level of production, hanging by a thread under the protection thus afforded. When the court was removed to Rio de Janeiro, it seemed that better days lay ahead for the Brazilian textile industry: the royal decree of April 1, 1808, revoked the prohibition of 1785. But by then it had to contend with serious handicaps, not the least of which was the competition of the far better-equipped, industrially and commercially, English textile industry, favored by the opening of the colony's ports to international trade and shortly afterward by the considerable advantages conceded to the English by the 1810 Treaty.* Luccock, himself a merchant and therefore directly affected by

---

* The Anglo-Portuguese Commercial Treaty of 1810, by which João VI obtained British support by further strengthening British interests in Brazil, giving priority to British-made goods.—Translator.

these measures, noted this circumstance when he came to consider the reopening of the textile mill of Registro Velho in Minas Gerais, on the Barbacena–Rio de Janeiro route.[24]

The iron industry was no less affected by the persecution of the colonial administration. Iron production was favored in certain regions of Minas Gerais not only by the abundance and easy access of extremely rich iron ores, but also by the high price of tools and implements which were subject to burdensome import duties on entering the country and to heavy tolls and taxes before they arrived in the captaincy. Another circumstance favoring local production was the difficulty of transporting these goods from the ports of entry.[25]

All these circumstances stimulated the growth of the industry, opening up attractive prospects for further development. Mining offered a steady market for iron goods. Had it not been for the stubborn opposition of the authorities, the industry would undoubtedly have expanded at a rapid pace. But official resistance was gigantic; anyone who knew how to cast iron was automatically suspected of harboring extreme and subversive opinions and became the victim of every kind of persecution.[26] The Portuguese authorities feared competition for their own merchandise which, although not produced by the kingdom, was a great source of trading profit. They also feared anything that might lead to the colony's greater economic independence, a prelude to political emancipation.

The metal industry was, however, more fortunate than textile manufacturing and benefited from the breeze of liberalism and greater foresight in colonial matters that began to waft through the mother country in the last years of the eighteenth century. By 1795, the government frankly permitted the establishment of iron foundries.[27] But after the earlier persecutions, it was difficult for the industry to get back on to its feet, and no great progress could be expected. Nevertheless, foundries using native ore and also some imported ore began to multiply in Minas Gerais, producing implements, tools, and horseshoes, the ironware most in demand at the time. St. Hilaire visited these forges during his first journey to Minas Gerais, and singled out the establishment run by Captain Manuel José Alves Pereira in Bonfim as the finest in the captaincy.[28]

The Government's change of heart was to be even more pronounced after the regent's arrival in Brazil. The revival of Ipanema in São Paulo, under the direction of Varnhagen, and the large-scale enterprise established in Gaspar Soares (Minas Gerais) by Manuel de Arruda Câmara date from this period. It was also after Dom João's arrival that the crown created its own royal gun foundry in São Paulo, under the direction of German master gunsmiths and staffed by German craftsmen,[29] and gave official support to the private firm of gunsmiths established in Itabira (Minas Gerais).[30]

Finally, we must recall the restrictive measures against goldsmiths, who were also the target of systematic persecution, because it was suspected that they encouraged gold smuggling, helping their customers to evade payment of the royal fifths. They were initially forbidden to exercise their craft in the captaincy of Minas Gerais by the proclamation of Governor Gomes Freire de Andrade of July 31, 1751, which ordered their expulsion from the captaincy. The royal letter of July 30, 1766, extended this ban to apply to the captaincies of Bahia, Pernambucco, and Rio de Janeiro.[31]

To sum up, then, Brazilian industry at the beginning of the nineteenth century was still only in the earliest stages of development. And only with some effort can the rudimentary manufacturing activities I have described be compared with what is commonly understood by industry. We saw the mother country's share of responsibility for this, a share by no means insignificant. But it would be wrong to put the blame entirely on the laws and official enactments, which are only one aspect—one of the least important at that—of the general system that guided the colonization of Brazil. If the country's political and administrative situation, as a mere colonial appendage of a shortsighted mother country that was jealous of its privileges, was a serious handicap to its industrial development, the economic regime was even more to blame; and to go into this aspect would be merely to repeat what has already been said in earlier chapters to show the narrow horizons permitted to a colony established to supply a few tropical commodities. For even when freed from the domination of Portugal and its oppressive legislation but with its original economic foundation still unreformed, Brazil continued to mark time in this sphere. Such progress as there was was so localized and so insignificant that it is lost to sight in the national life of the country as a whole, still entirely dominated by other activities—or rather, semiactivities. At a time when the world's industrial progress was making giant strides and science was daily placing at its disposal new inventions, new techniques, and new possibilities, progress in Brazil is dwarfed to insignificance. And put into its proper perspective, Brazil's tiny colonial industry in the nineteenth century was for its time no more than a semblance of manufacturing activity.

Commerce   The analysis of a country's commercial structure always reveals, more clearly than any individual analysis of particular sectors of production, the essential character and organization of an economy. It provides a synthesis which both summarizes and explains this economy. Our study of colonial trade at the beginning of the last century will, therefore, put the finishing touches to the foregoing account of the colonial economy.

No exceptional insight is needed to predict the most distinguishing characteristic of the colonial commercial system. It was, of course, directly derived from the very nature of colonization, regulated as this had always been on the basis of the production of tropical commodities and precious metals to supply the international market. Other activities were subsidiary to this fundamental aim and existed merely to support it and make possible its achievement. The nature of these two categories of activity and their geographical distribution throughout Brazilian territory provide the supplementary information needed to chart the currents of colonial trade and analyze its structure.

Colonial trade can be divided into two sectors, foreign and domestic. The first sector for obvious reasons is much better known. It naturally attracted the lion's share of attention from contemporary observers, who understood the nature of its role and were uninterested in that of domestic trade. This sector is therefore well documented. It can be said that Brazil's foreign trade was entirely seaborne. Her frontiers all ran through thinly occupied areas with a low economic level or territories which had not yet been opened up. The vanguard of Portuguese colonization, advancing inland from the Atlantic, had barely encountered that of the Spaniards, moving inward from the Pacific, and there were still vast unoccupied territories between the two. Commercial relations could therefore not be established overland. Besides, from Brazil's point of view, the neighboring colonies did not offer favorable conditions for intercolonial trade; their economies were too much like its own, their products in the same category. In any case, the colony had always been divided from the Spanish colonies by the state of latent hostility that reflected the rivalry between the two crowns, a hostility that, particularly in the second half of the eighteenth century, frequently broke out into the open, leading to a chronic state of war.

A few reservations to this general statement must, however, be made. Thus, a more or less flourishing contraband trade was carried on along the southern frontiers; livestock from the Rio de la Plata, particularly mules, reached Rio Grande do Sul in this way. Because mules bred in the Plata region were superior to those of Rio Grande, which supplied the rest of Brazil, they offered strong competition to the locally bred animals and even affected the breeding of horses.[1] Horses were imported into Mato Grosso from the former Jesuit missions of Moxos (Bolivia), a trade which started in 1771.[2] Other intercolonial commercial relations, more common and more regular, were maintained along the upper Amazon with the Peruvian provinces of Mainas, Quichas, and Macas. The supply stations for this trade were provided by the frontier towns of Tabatinga on the Brazilian side and Loreto on the Peruvian border. Through this route the Spaniards of the eastern slopes of the Andes secured supplies of European manufactured goods, which reached them more easily along the great river than along the regular Spanish trade routes. Through this route also they exported their own local products, which were in fact the same as those of the Brazilian part of the Amazon Valley.[3] Portuguese and Spaniards also traded occasionally along the upper Rio Negro; we have seen that ropes manufactured in the Brazilian captaincy of Rio Negro were consigned to the Spanish riverside establishment of San Carlos, the most advanced Spanish post in this area.

But all this foreign commerce by land amounted to very little. Maritime trade was what really mattered. This circumstance, dictated by geographical and economic conditions, had great political and administrative significance, since it facilitated—not to say made possible in the first place—the establishment of the mother country's monopoly in the colony's trade, a monopoly she sought to preserve. For this it was enough to close Brazilian ports to foreign ships, a measure which was much simpler than patrolling the frontiers, a task made difficult, if not impossible, by the length of the country's borders. This ban was maintained up to 1808, when the royal decree of January 28 of that year opened the colony's ports to international shipping. But until that date, the mercantile privileges of ships flying the Portuguese flag assured Portugal an exclusive hold on Brazil's foreign trade.

Apart from this restriction, none of the restraints of the past were still maintained. The privileged companies had finally disappeared after the chartered companies created by Pombal ceased to operate in 1778.[4] The convoy system, which had been introduced in 1649 and which obliged the Brazil fleets to sail at set times from Lisbon and from Brazil, escorted by three or four warships had also been abolished by the royal decree of September 10, 1765. The colony's maritime trade thus enjoyed within the limits imposed for Portuguese advantage; a relative freedom of movement. This freedom was, of course, not unhampered by the numerous petty and irritating measures for regulating trade, impossible to summarize here, proper to an age in which true freedom of trade—which was to come only with the nineteenth century—was still unknown.

Portugal's legal privilege in the Brazil trade did not prevent the existence of a flourishing contraband trade, which attained such proportions that it cannot be ignored. The English, the great friends, allies, and protectors of Portugal, were the worst offenders, in spite of the long-standing concession which they had been granted by the treaty of 1654 * and which permitted them to send ships to Brazil provided they called in at Portuguese ports on their outward and return voyages. The English were not interested in this concession, at least in the period with which we are now concerned. We find no references to this indirect but legitimate foreign trade with Brazil, and it had most probably fallen into disuse.[5]

Smuggling was easier and more profitable. We have valuable documents concerning its proportions. In 1794, the *Juiz-de-Fora* † for Rio de Janeiro, Baltasar da Silva Lisboa, whom we have met in another context performing different functions, denounced the scandalous contraband trade which, according to him, was shamelessly carried on under the noses of the authorities, who either grossly neglected their duties or were guilty of actually conniving at the smuggling. The figures he cites are most revealing; in the 15 months preceding his denunciation, no fewer than 39 foreign ships, mostly English and all heavily laden with merchandise, had docked at Rio de Janeiro![6] Another denunciation penned in the same year to the governor by a certain Amador Patrício da Maia, whose official status I have been unable to determine, makes similar accusations, giving colorful details about the way in which the goods were smuggled ashore: how the illicit ships anchored in the more or less hidden recesses of the bay, how they made contact with the local smugglers and merchants who bought the "fraudulent" merchandise—all with the scandalous connivance of the authorities, who made no attempt to disguise their participation in these illicit activities.[7]

Another interesting document in this respect is the report of

---

* An Anglo-Portuguese treaty devised by Cromwell, when the Puritan government became involved in war with Spain. English aid for Portugal's own war with Spain was given in exchange for a number of commercial privileges.—Translator.

† Crown judge or magistrate appointed from a region other than that in which he administered justice.—Translator.

a Portuguese merchant who traveled on business to England and Ireland in 1798 and was so outraged by what he witnessed in these countries relating to the contraband trade with the colony that he decided, with the agreement of the Portuguese consul and the largest Portuguese business concern in London, the firm of Dias Santos, to communicate his findings to the Portuguese government to warn them of what was afoot. He reported that from London, Liverpool, and other English ports, ships were regularly putting out on the pretext that they were sailing to harass the French, then at war with Great Britain, or on whaling expeditions, whereas in reality they were carrying cargoes of merchandise destined for Brazil and bringing back large consignments of the colony's products. There were many ship owners whose ships were solely engaged in this traffic, such as a certain John Bamess and others. Even Portuguese merchants voyaged in these ships, and came from Brazil to England on business connected with the contraband trade.[8]

Legally monopolized by the Portuguese and largely controlled by the English through the contraband trade, such were the general characteristics of the colony's foreign trade on the eve of the opening of the ports. Let us now consider the content of this trade. I need hardly repeat that exports consisted of the colony's chief products, which have been analyzed in the chapter on the economy, and represented the economic lifeblood of the colony. Hence, among other consequences, this explains the fact that the outports coincided with the colony's major cities. Their importance derived from their nature as supply stations for the export trade, and the growth of centers such as Rio de Janeiro, Bahia, Recife, São Luís, and Belém was due to this fact. It was within reach of these cities that the colony's major activities were concentrated, all of them destined first and foremost to the production of exportable commodities.

The import trade also became concentrated in these ports, which, as centers of the economically most prosperous regions, provided the chief consumer markets. Imports consisted of luxury items such as wine, olive oil, and other provisions; salt, a staple commodity which was, as we have seen, a crown monopoly; and a great variety of manufactured articles and metals, particularly iron.

The most important branch of the import trade was, however, the traffic in slaves brought to Brazil from the African coast. The value in money of this trade has never yet been calculated. According to Gayozo, who made a careful analysis of the slave trade during the period we are considering, the cost of a slave intended for sale in Maranhão, including the price paid in Africa and the duties levied at the ports on both sides of the Atlantic, was 85,500 reis.[9] To this amount must be added the transport costs, which Gayozo did not take into account, although he considered that the price at which slaves were sold in Maranhão was excessive: 250–300 mil-reis a head. Since what interests us for purposes of comparison with other items of the import trade is the cost of the slave on arrival in Brazil, not including any profits made by intermediaries, we must make a rough estimate of the transport costs involved. These must have been high, for the mortality rate on the long and difficult Atlantic crossing was very high.[10] We would therefore not be too wide of the mark if we estimated that the cost of a slave on arrival in Brazil was somewhere in the region of 100,000 reis at a conservative estimate.[11] Since the total number of slaves imported annually into Brazil was in the region of 40,000, the total value of this trade must have amounted to more than ten million cruzados per annum. The rest of the colony's imports for the decade 1796–1806 amounted to an average of 28 million cruzados per annum.[12] Slaves, therefore, made up more than a quarter of the colony's imports. This figure confirms what has been said about the nature of the Brazilian economy: the Negro slave means sugar, cotton, gold—export commodities.

Let us now turn to the domestic trade, which will shed more light on the essential character of colonial organization. There is a paucity of data on this subject. As a subsidiary commerce it aroused little interest, and contemporary accounts do not provide much information. We can, however, safely say that the bulk of the domestic commerce of the colony consisted either of merchandise destined in the final analysis for export or of merchandise which had been imported (or smuggled) into the country. The flow of commodities from one part of the country to another was from the source of production and the hands of the producer to the outports and export merchants; and from the ports, which acted as distribution centers for the foreign goods which made up the bulk of imports, to the rest of the country.

Reliable statistics on the movement of internal trade are few and, unfortunately, likely to remain incomplete. But from what we already know, and from the incomplete records we do possess—although uncorroborated by figures—the conclusion reached is inescapable.[18] The remainder of the domestic commerce was limited to the supply of foodstuffs for the large urban centers, since the rural communities and establishments were generally self-sufficient in this respect, and to the supply of merchandise for small rural trading posts where people from outlying villages and hamlets could buy it at the markets held on Sundays and holidays, a subject which I shall deal with in a later chapter. The commodities which these rural people did not produce themselves and, therefore, had to buy were, of course, always goods imported from abroad: iron, salt, and manufactured articles.

Thus, with the exception of the sector dependent on foreign trade considered above, domestic commerce only attained appreciable proportions in the convergence of food supplies on the large urban centers. We have already seen in this respect the role played by certain regions. We must also note that the supply of foodstuffs even gave rise to a fairly important coastal trade between the cities and ports of the seaboard, foodstuffs being shipped all along the Brazilian coast. I have already noted the insufficiency of this supply and the consequent chronic dearth and high prices of food in these cities.

The most noteworthy aspect of the domestic commerce, however, was the livestock trade. This played a significant part in the colony's internal commercial activities. Cattle raising has already been considered in some detail, and the different regions supplying cattle for various markets have already been indicated. In the next chapter we will see the routes followed by the cattle droves from the backlands to the markets, forming the immense network of overland connections extending over the populated parts of Brazilian territory from north to south and from east to west, linking up communities which would otherwise have remained cut off from each other in isolated clusters, and so playing a major role in the unity of the country and its formation and evolution.

Alongside the cattle trade, but completely separate from it, there developed the substitute trade in the dried meat of the north and the *charque* of Rio Grande do Sul, the latter, as we have seen, having already almost completely replaced the former. The charque trade, although considerable, was much more straightforward than the cattle trade and had no notable features, since it was conducted by sea, originating in one specific region and distributed almost exclusively to markets along the seaboard. Charque was not eaten in the interior, where there was a steady local supply of fresh meat.

By summarizing these essential features of the colonial trade, we can now trace a diagram of its major circulation currents. For this purpose, however, we must first distinguish the three sectors involved: the *seaboard*, which includes the colony's most populous and economically active areas, producing agricultural commodities for export and containing the large centers of foreign trade and the ports of shipment; the *Sertão*, which includes all the cattle raising regions of the backlands; and finally, the *mines*. This classification and these designations had already been applied in the period we are considering and can be found in the oft-cited work of that notable economist, the anonymous author of the *Roteiro do Maranhão*. With this sanction from an able contemporary observer, we can proceed to apply these designations, which could scarcely be bettered and deserve to be generally adopted.

The colony's pattern of trade, then, can be represented by the following diagram:

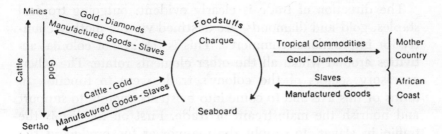

It must be understood that, while portraying the essential
features of the economy, this is no more than a diagrammatic
representation, the basic outline we are left with after eliminating all of negligible importance in the detailed analysis of the
various sectors of the colonial economy undertaken above.

We can now return with greater authority to the general
considerations I thought it appropriate to make before embarking on that analysis. We saw at the outset the nature of the colonial economy—a mercantile enterprise for exploiting the
tropics, entirely geared to international trade in which, although
an essential part, it functioned only as a source of supply for
specialized commodities. In the different aspects and sectors of
the Brazilian economy discussed, we not only saw this fact repeatedly corroborated, but also saw the role it played in the
colony's formation and evolution, conditioning its very existence. It conditioned the character of settlement, which was
made up of a small minority of white entrepreneurs and a preponderant majority of the other races they dominated and enslaved, whose function was to work and to produce the sugar,
tobacco, and cotton required by the European market. It conditioned the distribution of settlement, which concentrated exclusively in areas where it was possible to produce the desired
commodities and where it would be easiest to deliver them to
international commerce. It conditioned the structure of the
economy, its organization, land system, technique of production, and labor. And finally, it conditioned colonial trade; and
in the diagram delineating the pattern of colonial commerce
and with it the nature of our economy, it is the same fact which
stands out.

The direction of trade is clearly evident: outgoing tropical staples, gold and diamonds, are destined via the mother country for international commerce. This is the axis of colonial activities around which all the other elements rotate. The other, accessory sectors of the colony's trade were to function in terms of this axis and to come into existence merely to support and nourish the mainstream of trade. First on the list is the traffic in slaves, to supply the manpower for producing the commodities of which the mainstream was composed; next comes the supply of products needed to support the population directly or indirectly engaged in producing these essential commodities. In minute proportions, we find those products which made life a little more pleasant for the promoters of the enterprise. And this, in aim and essence, is the colony's circle of trade.

Placed at the midpoint of this great current of tropical products, gold, and diamonds, Portugal was the compulsory intermediary between the colonial sources of supply and the markets. And for as long as she could maintain her privileged position as mother country—a position she was on the eve of losing in the period we are here considering—she took full advantage of her privileges. It was thanks to this alone that she was to count as a power to be reckoned with in the Concert of Europe. Portugal's trade statistics for this period make this only too plain. Approximately two-thirds of the kingdom's exports to other countries was made up of the colony's products; and the figures we possess do not include the production of gold and diamonds which, although very much reduced, still continued to contribute to the mother country's wealth. Portugal was to realize the full magnitude of her colony's contribution when the bonds began to slacken. This was one of the main causes of the 1820 constitutional crisis.* When Portugal realized that Brazil was breaking free, the watchword of the period was

---

* That is, the revolution which broke out in Portugal in 1820 and which aimed to make the kingdom a constitutional monarchy. Dom João VI was recalled to Portugal by the Constituent Assembly, leaving his son Pedro as Regent of Brazil.—Translator.

"Recolonize Brazil!" And the final break, which came soon after this crisis, brought about the kingdom's collapse. Portugal, once a great power, passed from the middling power she had become to the mediocrity of one of Europe's most insignificant countries.[14]

Communications
and Transport

Whatever the truth of the statement that "roads create the social type," it is certainly true that in Brazil communications and transport exerted a powerful influence on the formation of the country. The vast distances and obstacles to travel in a territory such as this—its rugged terrain, its dense forests presenting barriers to penetration at strategic points, the unbroken nature of its coastline, and its rivers which with few exceptions are interrupted by falls and rapids and follow courses adverse to the directions taken by colonization—meant that communications were difficult to establish and slow to develop. This left its imprint on internal colonial relations, imposing on them that slow and retarding tempo which should indubitably bear a large share of the blame for the generally slack tone that characterizes the life of the colony.

To understand the colony's system of communications, we must make a brief survey of its origins and evolution. Its development clearly accompanied the progress of settlement. First established along the seaboard, settlement penetrated inland from the coast, either in a steady progression or in a scattering of isolated nuclei, more or less distant from the sea. Communication routes originally took the same direction. Later there was a movement in the opposite direction, as clusters of settlement established in the interior sought an easier or more direct outlet to the coast, and new routes were opened up, linking the interior to the seaboard. This was what happened in the case of the mining centers of Minas Gerais; having originally been reached from São Paulo, and later from Bahia, they now sought different outlets to the coast, at first through Rio de Janeiro, and much later through Espírito Santo, Pôrto Seguro and Ilhéus.

These lines of penetration linking the coast to the interior, all of them detached from each other, led to a fragmentary arrangement of communications in which each axis developed an isolated and self-sufficient system, establishing no interconnections with the other lines of travel. Each system consisted of the two extreme points—coastal centers and interior—linked only along the route established between them and leading a more or less separate existence. These distinct systems succeeded each other from north to south along the Brazilian coastline, from the northernmost system established in the Amazon basin to the southernmost one in Rio Grande do Sul. At first the only connection between systems was by sea, coastal communication being what maintained the unity of the whole. But as penetration of the interior pushed forward, the communication lines which accompanied settlement began to multiply and finally, although starting out from different points along the coast often great distances apart, began to converge on the interior. This was due to two particular geographical circumstances. The first of these is the general configuration of Brazilian territory, limited as it is by a coastline which, in the neighborhood of latitude 5° S., abruptly changes direction from northwest to northeast. The second factor leading to this convergence of routes on the interior was the trend of the relief, followed by the courses of the rivers which guided the advance of settlement and which exhibit the peculiar feature of draining inland and coming together at the headwaters of their respective basins.

The influence of the first geographical factor can be seen in the northeast, from Maranhão to Bahia, where the different lines of travel, starting from the east and north coasts respectively and running almost parallel to the coastline, all came together in the interior, thus completing a series of circuits which extended, by way of the interior, between the two coasts. The influence of the curious drainage pattern of Brazilian rivers on this convergence of routes on the interior was particularly evident in the case of the roads leading to the central captaincies of Goiás and Mato Grosso. The two sets of routes starting from the south coast and the north, respectively—the northern routes ascending the Amazon and gaining the uplands by way of its major tributaries, the Tocantins, Tapajós and Madeira—converged along the upper courses of these rivers.[1]

The major overland connections focusing on the interior of the colony were thus completed, interlacing it from north to south and matching the coastwise connections by sea which had hitherto been the colony's only means of maintaining communication. This process, which had started at the outset of colonization and had been completing itself by successive stages, had reached its last stage by the second half of the eighteenth century. By then—and only then—the full extent of the colony's territory had been officially recognized, and the land routes had all been opened up, so that it was now a question of making use of the practical and commercial advantages offered by these routes. Some of the oldest established routes had long been fully utilized, but the newer routes had simply been opened up and were little frequented. The authorities and private individuals pooled their efforts to stimulate development of the new routes, and the individuals who wished to utilize them for commerce were given every encouragement. This was particularly evident in the case of the utilization of the Amazon's southern tributaries, the last major internal communications to be established, and which had only been fully opened up to navigation in the phase immediately preceding the period we are dealing with here. The efforts to utilize them commercially will be considered below.

Before embarking on these general considerations we must make a rapid survey of Brazilian communications at the turn of the century. We will start with the oldest and most important of these, the sea route along the coast and the land routes which formed the small, independent systems referred to above which, although connected to each other through coastal communication and also by the numerous feeder trails which had later been established in the interior, still retained a relative independence and individual local importance as communication routes. All these systems, large or small, shared one thing in common: they were turned, with the cluster of settlement they served, toward the sea. The pattern of trade analyzed in the previous chapter accounts for this fact. They were, however, distinguished by their size and particularly by the extent to which they had penetrated the interior. Some of these systems, indeed most of them, were concentrated near the sea. It must be noted that I am referring here to penetration as continuity of settlement and not merely as the establishment of links with the interior. Such links will be analyzed later, since they are not really part of the internal local systems of communication of the maritime population clusters they served, which is what immediately concerns us.

In this restricted sense, penetration had not advanced very far inland. Thus, in the northeast, from Paraíba to Sergipe, settlement was concentrated along the lower courses of the small rivers that succeed each other down the coast from north to south and served as the local means of transportation, constituting the essential element of each small system. The same was true in the Recôncavo of Bahia and Guanabara, where the bays acted as the focus of local communications. In another part of the captaincy of Rio de Janeiro, however—the Campos dos Goitacases—the local line of travel by way of the Paraíba river had penetrated further inland. And in other nuclei along the seaboard, effective penetration had advanced even further. The first and most sizable of the self contained communication systems from this point of view was that of the extreme north, in Pará, where it was no longer confined to the seaboard but had effectively penetrated into the heart of its hinterland. This was an exceptional case, possibly due to the wonderful system of inland waterways afforded by the Amazonian network, and it really should be considered in the context of internal circula-

tion proper, which will be discussed below, rather than in this
survey of small independent systems.

The next system, from north to south, was that serving the
cluster of settlements concentrated in Maranhão, where colonization had penetrated as far inland as the point where Caxias
was formed, and where the artery of communication was provided by the navigable waters of the Itapecuru. This was followed by the Piauí system, with the great highway of the
Parnaíba, which afforded a route as far as its confluence with
the Gurgueia, branching off by way of the Poti and the
Canindé rivers. The last local communication system which
had expanded far inland was that of Rio Grande do Sul, penetrated by way of the Lagoa dos Patos, the Guaibá River, and
still further inland by way of the Jacuí.

I shall not go into detail about each of these systems. The
essential feature of each is that the principal line of penetration
was afforded by water, whether bays, estuaries, or rivers. The
land routes integrated in these systems were all subsidiary and
acted merely as feeders. The waterway was the main axis of
penetration and acted as the general outlet for the system. Indeed, it was the ease with which communications could be
maintained by water that provided one of the principal stimuli
for the fixation of settlement in these areas.

As for the major connection between all these areas of concentrated settlement which served to integrate the various systems into a whole, this too was chiefly and almost solely by
water, effected by means of the coastal links all along the
Brazilian seaboard. The corresponding overland routes
presented obstacles which often proved insuperable and were
always less convenient and less economical than the sea route.
The colony's seaboard being by nature divided into distinct
geographical compartments required that the few direct overland links between these compartments should generally follow a very circuitous route, running in great loops to circum-
vent the obstacles of the coast. This was particularly evident in
the south, where the coastal nuclei from Rio de Janeiro southward were linked by means of an overland route running along

the plateau.[2] Hence the importance of coastal communications, which formed the real backbone of the country's transportation system. We will see below the exceptions to this general rule.

We will now turn to internal communications. Four different sectors are to be distinguished which although more or less interconnected were nevertheless distinct and maintained an independence derived not only from their historical origin but also from the geographical peculiarities they exhibit.

The first is the Amazonian network of waterways, which, although possessing an uninterrupted link with the coast and thus comparable to the coastal systems referred to above, was of such magnitude and covered such a vast area that it must be included in the discussion of internal circulation. There is, however, no need to elaborate on its features, since these are very simple and have already been essentially described in the consideration of settlement.

This is followed to the south by the colony's northeastern sector, the area comprehended between Bahia, its capital, and Maranhão. The hub of internal communications in the north was in the central part of the captaincy of Piauí, where its capital, Oeiras, is located. This region was intimately linked to Maranhão, since it adjoined this captaincy's principal zone, extending along the Itapecuru River. It was also linked by way of the Parnaíba to the Piauí seaboard. In the opposite direction, three major lines of communication started from this center, striking east, southeast, and south, either as single routes or sending off several branches from which, in turn, there was a secondary ramification of feeders. All three lines were used as transit routes for cattle, Piauí being the northeast's principal source of supply.

The eastern line led to Ceará, passing through Arneirós and Icó, whence it continued to Paraíba, which it crossed along the axis of the region, reaching the Paraíba River by way of Pombal and Patos, then following the course of the river as far as the present-day town of Itabaiana. Here it bifurcated, one branch continuing along the Paraíba as far as the capital of the captaincy and the other continuing southward to Pernambuco.

The second line, striking southeast to the São Francisco, was from its point of departure in Piauí divided into three branches. The easternmost branch reached the São Francisco between Cabrobó and the confluence with the Pontal River; the westernmost, known as the "old route," ran by way of the Piauí River; the last and most frequented branch, the "new route," ran between the first two, following the upper margins of the Canindé and continuing by way of the Pontal River. This was the route chosen for the modern railway line built from the São Francisco to Piauí. The three branches joined up along the São Francisco and converged on Juàzeiro, where there was a registo, or dry customs, post. Having crossed the river, the single route then proceeded to Bahia, following the line of the modern Eastern Railway (*Viação Férrea Leste Brasileiro*), traversing a region severely afflicted by shortage of water.

This communication line, the most important in the northeast Sertão, played an important role in colonial history. It was along here that the pioneers and their cattle ranches, advancing into the hinterland from Bahia and the São Francisco, had penetrated into Piauí in the seventeenth century and had colonized the region. It soom became a major route for the cattle driven down to the Recôncavo of Bahia. At the beginning of the last century approximately 20,000 head of cattle traveled along this trail and were registered at the Juàzeiro Registo.[3] It finally established a direct connection between the coasts of the two most important areas of concentrated settlement along the seaboard, Bahia and Maranhão. This connection was all the more important since the differences in the prevailing winds and currents in these two coastal regions made sea communication between them extremely difficult, and Maranhão had tended to remain cut off from the more southern captaincies. After 1815, when the slave trade north of the Equator was abolished, Maranhão, awkwardly placed in relation to the African ports that continued to supply slaves, began to receive them overland from Bahia. The route we have just described was utilized for this purpose.[4]

The third major line of communication starting from Piauí led southward, following the Gurgueia River as far as the Paranaguá, crossed the uplands which separate Piauí from the territory that is now part of Bahia but which then belonged to Pernambuco, and reached the Rio Prêto, an affluent of the Grande, crossing it at Vaus, where it joined the route coming directly from the Bahian capital. It continued along the eastern São Francisco, turned west and bifurcated, reaching Goiás by way of two passages cut across the tabular uplands which form the Tocantins-São Francisco watershed: the passage of Duro, which linked up with the northern comarca of Goiás and that of Tabatinga, which linked up with the captaincy's southern nuclei, including the capital.[5]

Apart from these three major communications centered on Piauí, we must mention two important lines of travel in the northeast. The first was the line linking Ceará directly to Bahia, which, starting from Fortaleza, crossed Ceará from north to south, following the Jaguaribe as far as Icó and then accompanying the Salgado to the oasis of the Ceará Sertão, the Chapada do Araripe, after which it traversed 30 leagues of arid caatinga in upper Pernambuco to reach Ibó on the São Francisco; from here, by way of Geremoabo, the road led to Bahia. This route was the course later followed by the postal services from Fortaleza to the capital of Bahia (1821); the total distance covered is 289 leagues, and the postman took forty days to travel this distance.[6] The road followed the old trail used by the cattlemen who, from Bahia, penetrated and occupied the hinterland of Ceará in the eighteenth century.

The other line of travel—a much less important one—was the route following the coastline, although more or less well inland, from Maranhão to Pernambuco. This was, in fact, the only fairly extensive route along the Brazilian seaboard which was at all frequented, although even then only to a limited extent. The English traveler, Koster, has left us a description of part of this route, from Pernambuco to Fortaleza, which he traveled in 1810. The same road was later followed by the postal route between these two points.[7]

All these routes were used principally by the droves of cattle traveling from the various parts of the Sertão to the coastal markets. But apart from this function, they also served another of outstanding importance in the history of Brazil's formation. They linked up the different parts of the Sertão and established connections between the people who had settled there; they made possible the dislocations of population and mass migrations which occurred so frequently during the periodic droughts, enabling the Sertanejos to move to less afflicted areas and return to their homes when the rains came. They served to bring together and integrate all the disparate elements that went into the making of the population of the backlands, which, having come from many different and distant parts of the colony, gradually established communication and came into contact. The routes described above mark the great lines along which the process of fusion took place, making of the Sertão a vast melting pot which produced a distinctive ethnic type. Although derived from such different races, and varying considerably from individual to individual, this type nevertheless displays on the whole an unmistakeable unity, remarkable even in Brazilian terms.

We must now turn to the second sector of the colony's internal communications, the central-south, which occupies the largest area of the colony and played the leading role in Brazilian history. This sector includes the routes linking the central captaincies, Minas, Goiás, and Mato Grosso, to the seaboard. We will consider them in this order.

Communications with Minas were established, in chronological order, from the following three points: São Paulo, Bahia, and Rio de Janeiro. The São Paulo route ascended to the plateau of Minas Gerais by two successive and clearly marked stages: the Serra do Mar and the Serra da Mantiqueira. The first ascent was made through a number of passes, occurring in succession between Rio de Janeiro and Santos. The points of departure for these trails across the mountain were, of course, located along this part of the seaboard: Rio de Janeiro, which by way of São João Marcos, Bananal, São José do Barreiro, and

Areias, reached the Paraíba Valley at Cachoeira; Angra dos Reis and Parati, both in the captaincy of Rio de Janeiro; Ubatuba, Caraguatatuba, São Sebastião, and finally Santos, through which the capital of Minas was reached along the *Caminho do Mar* (The Coast Road), so prominent in the annals of São Paulo.

The second stage, the Serra da Mantiqueira, was reached through the passes afforded by the various ravines that cut across the mountain,[8] the most important and most frequented of which was the Embaú pass, or the "Ravine of the Registo," as it came to be known after a toll was established at the head of this pass. The present motor road leading from the Paraíba Valley to southern Minas follows the course of this old mountain trail which at the top of the mountain opens out to the valley of the Rio Verde. Antonil, at the beginning of the eighteenth century, had already described this trail and noted the course it followed to the mines of the central part of the captaincy, which had begun to be opened up in his time.[9]

The Bahian link with Minas also figures in Antonil's account. This was the route used to enter the General Mines by the *Emboabas* * who clashed with the Paulistas entering along the São Paulo route described above. Starting from the Recôncavo, this route followed the Paraguaçu River to its upper reaches, then accompanied the Contas River southward, and having crossed this river, bifurcated to the São Francisco and Rio Verde. The first branch ran by way of the São Francisco River and its tributary, the Velhas, to the mines in the central part of the captaincy; the second followed a shorter route along the banks of the Verde Grande. After Antonil's time more direct

---

* *Emboaba*—a scornful nickname applied by the Paulistas to newly arrived Portuguese who came in search of gold and precious stones. The Paulistas and Emboabas came to blows in the so-called *Guerra dos Emboabas*, which plunged Minas Gerais into civil strife at the end of 1708. The word is of obscure etymology, probably Amerindian in origin, and various meanings have been ascribed to it, among them, "chicken in trousers"—a derisive reference to the fact that the newcomers from Europe wore breeches and shoes, while the Paulistas went barefoot and barelegged in the bush.—Translator.

routes were opened up. One new road left the Paraguaçu a little above São Félix, its point of departure in the Recôncavo,
and turned southward to follow the Gavião River to the camp
of Rio Pardo, the modern town of that name, in the captaincy
of Minas Gerais. Another and even shorter road was opened up
in the first years of the nineteenth century, after João Gonçalves
da Costa had subdued the warlike Camacã Indians of the upper Cachoeira River, and founded the town of Conquista; the
new road passed through Conquista and led to the Rio Pardo.

The last road to Minas led directly from Rio de Janeiro and
had been opened up at the beginning of the eighteenth century, immediately after the gold strikes made by the *Sertanista,**
Garcia Rodrigues Pais, son of the famous Fernão Dias. At the
beginning of the nineteenth century, this road started from
Pôrto da Estrela, which travelers from Rio reached by ship
from Guanabara Bay, gained the top of the great escarpment
by way of a pass where the present-day town of Petropolis is
situated, and descended along the Piabanha Valley, crossing
the Paraíba to continue by way of the Paraibuna into Minas
Gerais. A variant of this route, known as the "land route" because it dispensed with the voyage from Rio de Janeiro to
Pôrto da Estrela, passed through Iguaçu to the base of the
Great Escarpment, climbed the mountain, and at the crest
joined the first route at a site still called "The Junction"
(*Encruzilhada*). A variant to this combined route was opened
up in the early years of the nineteenth century: the Paraibuna
River route, which passed the registo of Matias Barbosa—the
present-day town of this name—and branched off to follow an
overland trail to Pau Grande, and entered Minas further to the
west by way of Valença and Rio Prêto. This was a shorter route
to the comarca of the Rio das Mortes in southern Minas, and
its opening up clearly indicated the shift that was taking place

* *Sertanista* (not to be confused with "Sertanejo," a native of the
Sertão) sometimes means, as here, a pioneer or explorer of the backlands,
or at other times a person with extensive firsthand knowledge of the
Sertão. Fernão Dias (Pais) had led the *bandeiras* from São Paulo which
traversed the region that became Minas Gerais in the 1670's and 1680's
in search of emeralds.—Translator.

in Minas Gerais from mining to agriculture and stock rearing. The Rio das Mortes district was primarily agricultural and the new route established an easier and more direct link with the chief market for its produce, Rio de Janeiro.

Several new roads were being built between the seaboard and Minas Gerais in the period with which we are now concerned. They reflect the phase of greater liberalism in the mother country's colonial policies and indicate that she was no longer so exclusively preoccupied with collection of the royal fifths and control of gold smuggling.[10] An attempt was being made to instill new life into the moribund captaincy, and the establishment of communications with the seaboard was therefore encouraged. Routes were opened up in areas hitherto closed off, referred to in a previous chapter: the captaincy's eastern valleys. The Jequitinhonha began to be used by canoes which were employed to ship cotton produced in Minas Novas downriver to Belmonte, situated at the bar of the river, whence it was conveyed to Bahia for export.[11] The river journey was first made in 1764 by the Captain-Major of Belmonte, João da Silva Santos, who was the first person to identify what had hitherto been known as the Belmonte River as the lower course of the Jequitinhonha itself.[12] Regular navigation of this river, however, was undertaken only at the beginning of the nineteenth century. To facilitate communication a road was built along the riverbank from Minas Gerais to the military post of Salto on the border of the captaincy; the rapids having thus been circumvented, the cargoes were taken downriver by canoe.

An overland trail for use by cattle driven down to the Campos dos Goitacases was opened in 1811 to replace the longer and more difficult trail through Rio de Janeiro hitherto used to reach the Campos market.[13] More important than any of these new connections between the coast and Minas, however, was the line of communication offered by the valley of the river Doce. The authorities became seriously interested in opening up this route because the natural outlet for the captaincy was really through Espírito Santo and not through Rio

de Janeiro. At first, political and fiscal interests and, later, the
fact that an alternative route had been pioneered by Garcia
Rodrigues prevented the Rio Doce from developing into an important line of travel, and the old route continued to be used.
But the most direct way, and by far the easiest in terms of
grades, was that along the Doce valley. As a preliminary to
opening up this desirable route, the border country between
the captaincies of Minas Gerais and Espírito Santo was properly explored for the first time and the dividing line between
them officially fixed in 1811.[14] Military posts were established
along the Doce at Sousa and Lorena to hold off the numerous
hostile tribes infesting the forests which lined its banks.[15] The
accounts given of these initial attempts clearly indicate the
practicability of navigating the river, and within a few years it
began to be utilized. Later an overland trail along the valley
was opened up as a cattle road between Minas and Espírito
Santo. Indeed, one of the main reasons for establishing a connection between the two captaincies was to enable cattle to be
sent from Minas to the coast. The road was built piecemeal
from Minas Gerais: first, the Minas stretch, then the portion
running through Espírito Santo built in 1812 on the initiative
of this captaincy's Governor, Francisco Alberto Rubim. It was
interrupted above the rapids on the Santa Maria River, where
the present Pôrto do Cachoeiro is situated, but continued to
Pôrto Velho opposite Vitória and then followed the valley eastward, crossing the Guandu, Manhuaçu, and Casca rivers, to
reach Mariana and Vila Rica by way of Ponte Nova.[16]

In addition to these routes, roads from Minas to the coast
were also built in other directions at the period which we are
considering. One led from Minas Novas to São José de Pôrto
Alegre by way of the Mucuri River.[17] Another started from the
Ilhéus coast, followed the Cachoeira River to São Pedro de
Alcântára—an Indian mission village founded by the Franciscan friar, Ludovico de Liorne, whose work has been referred to
in a previous chapter—and then joined up with the Conquista-
Rio Pardo route described above.[18] This route, which was
destined chiefly for the cattle droves sent from Minas Gerais to

Ilhéus, was never very popular in spite of its magnificent construction; by the time Prince Maximilian traveled along it toward the end of 1816, it had already been almost abandoned, the bridges had crumbled and the surrounding forest was beginning to invade the highway.

Let us now turn to communications with Goiás. This captaincy was also served by three routes. The original route from São Paulo was the one pioneered by Bartolomeu Bueno, nicknamed the *Anhangüera* * in the eighteenth century, when he discovered gold in Goiás. This was the "Guaiases Trail," famous in the history of São Paulo and the *bandeiras,* which is more or less followed by the modern railroad lines of Mojiana and São Paulo-Goiás. Fiscal interests, political contingencies, and the advantages offered by the more direct link with Rio de Janeiro meant that the Minas route was early utilized in preference to this old trail. This is true in spite of the fact that the Minas route was geographically not an easy one, and travelers had to contend with the obstacle of the Serra da Mata da Corda.[19] The Goiás-Minas route passed through Paracatu and entered Goiás through the ravines that intersect the São Francisco-Tocantins watershed: São Marcos and Arrependidos.

Further northward, the Bahian route—the third of the routes connecting Goiás to the coast—was also crossed by the São Francisco-Tocantins watershed. There were several variants to this route. We have already seen two of these variants: they were branches of the road from Piauí that entered Goiás through the registos at Duro and Tabatinga. A third variant was simply a prolongation of the Bahia-Minas route described above leading to the São Francisco; a sideroad branched off from this route, crossing the São Francisco at Malhada, where a registo had been established, and thence following the banks of the Carinhanha and Paraná rivers into Goiás.

In addition to these traditional connections with Goiás, it

---

* *Anhangüera*—from the Tupi Indian word *anhangá,* meaning "evil spirit" or "devil." Bartolomeu Bueno da Silva, the "Old Devil," was the Paulista bandeirante who discovered the mines of Goiás in 1725.—Translator.

had been proposed to take advantage of the line of communication offered by the Araguaia-Tocantins rivers since the third quarter of the eighteenth century.[20] The idea was to find a new outlet to the coast, to avoid the long and difficult overland journey, hitherto the only one feasible, and thus to help the captaincy to make a recovery from the economic depression into which it had been plunged as the result of the decadence of its mines. However, it was only toward the end of that century that practical and effective measures for the utilization of the river system were undertaken. Up to then official plans had never materialized, and the rivers had only been explored by adventurers.

In 1792, three Pará merchants, encouraged by Governor Sousa Coutinho, organized an expedition and shipped a cargo of merchandise to Vila Boa by way of the Tocantins, Araguaia and Vermelho rivers.[21] In 1799, D. João Manuel de Meneses, the newly appointed Governor of Goiás, chose the river route to travel to his captaincy from Pará.[22] The presence of hostile Indians along the river banks and the lack of resources along the uncolonized stretches were the greatest obstacles to the development of this route. Even the Tocantins region, the only one to have been penetrated by colonization, since the Araguaia was still deserted, was only very sparsely populated along the river banks. To help overcome these difficulties, the Governor of Goiás, Tristão da Cunha Meneses, founded Pôrto Real on the Tocantins in 1791 to act as the point of departure for the river journey. But this was not enough, and in the early years of the following century more effective measures were taken. The royal letter of January 7, 1806, created the northern comarca, detaching it from the southern one to enable the magistrate appointed to administer the new district to devote himself to the problems of opening up navigation on the Tocantins-Araguaia system, and stimulating an increase of traffic carried by this route. The letter also provided for the seat of the comarca to be set up at the junction of the Tocantins and Araguaia, where there was already a registo and a presidio, which had been established to protect travelers from the attacks of hostile Indians. At around the same time, two more forts were built and garrisoned, one at the mouth of the Manuel Alves Grande River and the other halfway between Pôrto da Piedade and the Tocantins-Araguaia confluence.

The success of these and other measures, which it would be tedious to enumerate, is demonstrated by the report that in 1810 a Goiás merchant, Francisco José Pinto, was making regular use of the Tocantins River route for shipping goods to Pará. It was he who established the township of São Pedro de Alcântara on the banks of this river, as I have already had occasion to mention.[23] Situated in territory included in Maranhão, this township was connected to other settlements in Maranhão by way of the Pastos Bons, which were beginning to be penetrated by the rapid establishment of cattle ranches. A new internal link was thus being forged; and its commercial utilization was suggested and recommended at the time, although little came of these recommendations and traffic continued to be light in this period.[24]

The last and most remote of the interior captaincies, Mato Grosso, was served first by the classic and famous Tietê River route, used by the pioneers who discovered gold in the territory of the future captaincy in the early years of the eighteenth century. This route was still in use at the beginning of the last century. Travelers embarked at Pôrto Feliz in São Paulo, situated below the worst stretch of rapids. They then journeyed downriver along the entire course of the Tietê, continued down the Paraná to its right-bank tributary, the Pardo, and thence proceeded upriver to the village of Sanguessuga. Here navigation of the Paraná basin came to an end, and there was a portage of two and a half leagues (some ten miles) to the Paraguay system. Fortunately the country through which the travelers had to pass was not very rugged, and the canoes and cargoes were transported by oxcart to the Camapoã River, where a fazenda of that name (the origin of the present-day town) had been established to furnish men and animals for the overland stretch. The Camapoã fazenda also had a garrison to counter the incursions of the warlike Indians present in the vicinity and to defend voyagers from their attacks. The canoes then proceeded downriver via the Camapoã-Poxim-Taquari, crossed the Grande Pantanal (Great Swamp), then known as the Xaraés lagoon, a vast, semiaquatic territory, under water for part of the year, and continued along the perennial Taquari to its junction with the Paraguay. Thence they proceeded upriver to its affluent, the Porrudos or São Lourenço, finally reaching the Cuiabá River and the capital of the captaincy.

The whole voyage took from four to five months; merely to trace its course on the map is tiring. It was truly an epic undertaking, almost unbelievable when one considers that it was not simply an occasional adventure but a regularly utilized commercial route in common use for more than a century. The volume of traffic was, however, already very small at the beginning of the last century, and only about a dozen canoes still set out annually from Pôrto Feliz.[25] The dugout canoes employed were large and substantial enough to take 400 arrobas of cargo in addition to the provisions, arms, and munitions used on the voyage; they were 50–60 feet long, 5½ feet wide, and 3–4 feet deep, and were manned by a crew of eight who used short oars and punting poles.[26]

This original route to Mato Grosso was gradually neglected in favor of the overland route leading from Vila Boa, the capital of Goiás, to Cuiabá. The land route ran eastward via the mining camp of Pilões, passing through territory which, although largely uninhabited, afforded easy going because of the flatness of the terrain. Mato Grosso thus established overland contact through Goiás not only with São Paulo but also with Minas Gerais and Rio de Janeiro, the road to the latter being the most direct and thus the one preferred.

The last of Mato Grosso's lines of communication with the outside captaincies was also a waterway. This was the link with Pará, via the Amazon's great tributaries, the Madeira and the Tapajós. The Madeira-Mamoré-Guaporé route had been utilized for this purpose since the middle of the eighteenth century. Before then, the inhabitants of Mato Grosso had made contact with the Jesuit mission downstream on the left bank of the Madeira, which today falls within Bolivian territory. At the same time, colonists from Pará and Rio Negro regularly went upriver as far as the first rapids to collect cacao and other forest produce. The two currents of penetration, setting out from opposite directions, had gradually met and mingled, and in 1742, the first pioneers from Mato Grosso reached Pará.[27] In 1769, 85,963½ drams of gold left Mato Grosso by the Madeira route, which proves that there must have been a considerable volume of trade between the two regions. Later, competition from the overland route, favored by the attractions offered by the large centers of Rio de Janeiro and Bahia, together with the decadence of mining, which had been the captaincy's only industry, reduced the volume of traffic carried by the river route.

We have a long and detailed report on the state of navigation on the Madeira, written in 1797 by the Governor of Pará, D. Francisco de Sousa Coutinho.[28] We learn from this report that there was still some traffic along the river at this period, but only for the trade carried on with the establishments along the Guaporé (Vila Bela). Cuiabá preferred direct communication with Rio de Janeiro, Bahia, and São Paulo.

The greatest obstacle to the growth of river traffic was the complete lack of resources along a large stretch of the route, the 283 uninhabited leagues from Borba to the fortress at Príncipe (on the Mamoré). There were also 70 leagues (about 200 miles) of rapids along the same stretch. Another obstacle was the difficulty of finding Indian rowers, since not many were willing to undertake the arduous task of navigating such long distances. The governor recommended the use of Negro slaves, since the forced enlistment of Indians as crews for the river voyages was depopulating the mission villages and proving very harmful to colonization. His plan for stimulating navigation on the Madeira was carefully thought out and presented, and the authorities thought highly enough of his suggestions to incorporate the plan almost unaltered in the royal letter of May 12, 1798. On the same date, other royal letters were addressed to the governors of Maranhão, Goiás, Mato

Grosso, Piauí, and Ceará, requesting that they do whatever they could within their respective jurisdictions to encourage navigation on the rivers leading to the Amazon, with a view to carrying out Sousa Coutinho's project for the commercial utilization of these river communications.[29] This clearly revealed the mother country's intention of using the Amazon Basin as a vast general outlet for the colony's upper interior. It was a grandiose plan, and was certainly the right answer, since the geographical determining factors made this part the natural focus of routes for the future Brazilian system of communication. But it made no progress at the time, and indeed even today what has been achieved amounts to but little.

In 1820, Martius wrote an account of navigation on the Madeira based on personal experience; he found it decadent but not yet entirely abandoned. The river still carried a certain amount of traffic, enormous canoes being used to transport 2,000–3,000 arrobas of cargo and manned by crews of twenty men, including rowers, fishermen, and hunters. Heavy goods which would have been difficult to transport overland, such as metals, tools, glassware, crockery, salt, and so forth, were sent by river. The lighter merchandise, such as clothing, hardware, and odds and ends, as well as slaves, were sent overland from Rio and Bahia. Merchandise exported from Mato Grosso by river included not only contraband gold and diamonds, but also high-quality sugar, which was not produced in the Amazon Valley, rough cotton cloth, Indian handicrafts, and forest produce, such as tamarind pulp, clove bark, and Pichurim beans.[30]

The Tapajós had only begun to be used as a means of communication between Mato Grosso and the outside world in the period with which we are here concerned. Its utilization had been stimulated by the opening up of the mines along the upper Paraguay, in the region of present-day Diamantina, referred to in a previous chapter. These mines were readily accessible from the Amazon Basin by way of the Arinos, which flows into the Tapajós; and thus when Governor Abreu e Meneses lifted the ban on mining in this region in 1805, he also sent an expedition up the Arinos to Belém do Pará.[31] But the upper Paraguay mines were not the success expected, and since the mines alone were unable to animate communication by way of the Tapajós, navigation on this river ceased to attract attention. Another attempt was made in 1812 by Governor Carlos Augusto de Oeynhausen, who managed to persuade a number of merchants to send their goods via this route. The venture proved successful, and the expedition reached Pará and brought back a large cargo of goods on its return voyage.[32] From then on, the Tapajós began to carry more traffic, but according to one contemporary account, this trade route was not very successful.[33] Martius affirmed, however, that in his time the river was regularly used, to the great profit of merchants in Belém.[34]

The fourth and last sector of the colony's internal communications is that of the extreme south. It was the most poorly developed and also the least important historically, at least up to the time we are considering. This sector consisted of a single trunk, running through the plateau more or less parallel to the coast and connected to the seaboard by a number of branches. The trunk road started in São Paulo, from the market town of Sorocaba, and proceeded southward through the Campos Gerais—now falling within the territory of Paraná but at that time within the captaincy of São Paulo—via Castro, Curitiba, Vila do Príncipe (Lapa); it then crossed the Rio Negro at the point where the present-day town of this name was later founded. In Santa Catarina it continued to Curitibanos, which was still only a supply station, then followed the Lajes route and entered Rio Grande after crossing the Pelotas River at the registo of Santa Vitória, whence it reached the capital of the captaincy.[35] Two of the coastal connections started from Curitiba; one led to the little port of Paranaguá and was described by St. Hilaire, who traveled along it in 1820, as a "wretched track";[36] the other, leading to the garrison town of São Francisco, was, according to the same author, almost impassable and little frequented. Both were used as trails for the cattle sent down from the grazing regions to the coastal towns, but the first route was also used to send export commodities from Curitiba to the ports, the chief product being, as we have seen, maté. Another road, opened in 1787, ran from Lajes to the parish of São José opposite the island of Santa Catarina.[37] This road, which at first carried some traffic, particularly cattle droves moving from the plateau to the coast, was later abandoned because of the poor condition into which it had been allowed to lapse. One of the settlers in the neighborhood wrote a letter to the *Patriota* in 1813 protesting against its neglect and asking the authorities to take steps to repair it.[38] We must also recall the coastal road leading from Paranaguá southward and made up of small stretches of a local character, more or less interlinked, as far as Laguna, where it became a continuous road traversing the whole of Rio Grande down to the "Colony of Sacramento" on the Plata. I have already noted that the first colonists to enter Rio Grande had pushed southward along the coast from Laguna. For strategic reasons, Governor Sousa Meneses (1765–1775) built up the road from Laguna to the town of Colônia (Sacramento), a road of considerable military importance in the struggles over boundaries between Spaniards and Portuguese. It was also to serve as a cattle road for the animals driven from Rio Grande to the Santa Catarina coastal settlements.

The São Paulo-Rio Grande road played an important historical role. It served to integrate into the rest of the colony the southern territories so long disputed by Spain and Portugal, which otherwise would probably have become detached from Brazil. The difficulties of maritime communication contributed to the south's isolation, the Rio Grande coast being unsuited to the maintenance of connections by sea. It was in fact because the administration recognized the dangers of this isolation that the overland connection was opened up in the third quarter of the eighteenth century. This enabled a current of settlement, originating mainly from São Paulo, to penetrate southward along this route and to occupy the territory that was later to become Rio Grande do Sul for the Portuguese. The route continued to fulfill this role in consolidating the Luso-Brazilian hold on the south for as long as the Spanish threat remained active, a role it was destined to play for a long time to come, since the claims of the Spaniards were taken up by their Spanish-American successors after their colonies gained independence. For almost another century it was to be used by the troops periodically recruited—mainly in São Paulo—to defend the southern frontiers against aggression and to carry on the wars with Brazil's neighbors which lasted well into the empire period.

More modest and more obscure, but perhaps no less significant, was the other role played in Brazilian history by this southern route. While the settlers and troops were entering the south, a steady stream was flowing in the opposite direction: the convoys of mules which for more than a century were the chief means of transport and travel in the colony and even in the independent empire. Without the mule, Brazil would have moved even more slowly; the horses bred in the northeast were not sufficient to supply the whole country, and up to the middle of the eighteenth century most of the traveling in the captaincies of the central-south, which mining had brought to the fore, was still done on foot and goods were transported on the backs of slaves.[39] The humble, sturdy mule was to solve this great problem. Bred in Rio Grande, or brought in from the Plata, young mules were sent northward to the rest of the colony. The convoys were organized in Rio Grande; often there were hundreds of animals and not infrequently as many as a thousand. The convoys began the journey northward in September or October, after the rains, when the pastures along the route were at their most succulent. They sometimes headed straight for Sorocaba, the market town for which they were ultimately destined, but frequently went first to Lajes, to continue their journey only in the following year.

Sorocaba was the scene of the great annual mule fair held from April to May, attracting buyers from all over the colony. Here, at the beginning of the last century, as many as 30,000 mules were traded annually. This trade gave Sorocaba, a sleepy, peaceful little town for most of the year, the animated intensity of a great, bustling center. During the fair its numerous inns were crowded with people; the streets and squares were thronged with buyers arguing and clinching deals; there was a continual to and fro of merchants and animals; and at night, the town was given over to the no less lively pursuit of pleasure. Gambling, drinking, and whoring were rife in this casual hodgepodge of muleteers, traders, prostitutes, and adventurers of all sorts, lured by the prospect of profit or debauchery.[40] From Sorocaba the mules were distributed to all parts of the colony, to the central-south in particular but also to the north. Martius saw mules in Bahia, "very depressed" by their long journey along the São Francisco.[41]

Having thus completed our survey of the colonial lines of communication, let us now turn to a consideration of their quality and condition. For this, we have more or less complete records for the first years of the last century, the diaries of foreign travelers who visited the colony at this period and left detailed descriptions of the courses they traveled. They covered, among them, the whole colony; and if we combine the accounts of St. Hilaire, Martius, Koster, Luccock, Prince Maximilian and Pohl, the most noteworthy travelers in this respect, we will have a detailed description of all the more important routes, since all of them have left minute accounts—often a result of the bad moments they lived through on account of the colony's wretched roads. Their diaries were the repositories of their ill-humored outbursts against the difficulties of colonial travel.

Colonial roads were, in fact, almost without exception beneath criticism; they were no more than passable even by travelers on foot and animals in the dry season, and in the wet season they became muddy quagmires often defeating all hope of passage. As for the waterways, these were also affected by the seasons but in the opposite way. In the dry period, when the rivers tended to run low, baring the rocks which, dotted all along their courses, presented dangerous and often impassable obstacles, the waters frequently became too shallow to permit traffic. Stone-paved roads were so rare in the colony that they were regarded as veritable marvels; the stretches of surfaced road can be counted on the fingers of one hand and measured in palms.[42] The most that was done to surface roads that were well traveled and subject to heavy rains was to place sticks across the path at particularly muddy points which, although it made the surface a little firmer, offered pretty rough going, especially for the animals. The sun was still the greatest ally against mud, and to help it in its task the roadbuilders and repairers sometimes went so far as to permit themselves the luxury of clearing away some of the bordering vegetation. But not even this practice was very common.

The courses chosen for the roads were those that avoided too much work, the criterion followed being economy of effort; only the bare minimum needed to make the road passable was put into its construction. It was easier to go around the minor obstacles to travel than to remove them, and since the steepness of a climb meant less than the directness of the road, the courses turned away from the most direct route only when the slopes were beyond all doubt impossible to climb. Traveling across the colonial passes was a real "Alpine" expedition, and the way in which the animals, heavily laden as they were, managed to keep their footing arouses one's admiration and wonder. Apart from the petty and self-defeating economics that guided the courses followed by colonial roads, the ignorance and empiricism of the roadmakers often led them to extend roads quite unnecessarily through their gross blunders in plotting directions and making their reckonings. "It is hardly surprising," wrote Eschwege, "that they go round in circles for many days, getting hardly further than the point of departure." [43]

The width of the road, when not determined by natural conditions such as levelness of surface or absence of obstructive vegetation, was always kept to the strict minimum; convoys and travelers on foot had to march in single file, and the goods on the backs of the mules or the legs of riders often brushed against the roadside trees or cliffs. When convoys coming from different directions met at such points, the ensuing difficulties

were of no mean order. Such encounters are frequently noted
by St. Hilaire, who used them to expand on the courtesy and
consideration of Brazilians compared to the uncouthness and
violence of Europeans.

Bridges were rare, and even St. Hilaire wonders if this type
of construction had ever been heard of in Brazil. Rivers generally had to be forded, often forcing travelers far out of their
way; when there were no possible fords, the rivers were
crossed by canoe, travelers and merchandise being rowed
across while the animals had to swim.[44] Very rarely, where
rivers were too deep and traffic heavy, ferries were used, as at
Juàzeiro on the São Francisco, and the Paraíba crossing on the
Rio Minas route.

In short, roadbuilding techniques in the colony were of the
most summary and backward sort, and if the roads were
passable at all it was due more to the caprice of nature than to
the arts of man. The first practicable roads for carriages were
built only after the Regent's arrival in Brazil. They were constructed in Rio de Janeiro on the initiative of Paulo Fernandes
who, although only the Royal Intendant of Police, undertook
tasks connected with public administration that had nothing to
do with his office. It was he who built the road from Praia
Grande (Niterói) to Maricá, used by Dom João's carriages;
and the road from the capital to Iguaçu, later extended to the
Rio Prêto.[45]

Waterways were even more neglected. The colonists depended solely on nature, and even on important river highways
like the São Paulo-Cuiabá route, no attempt was made to facilitate navigation by removing some of the obstacles and dredg-
ing the more difficult stretches. The most that was done in this
direction was to make arrangements for helping passengers at
the portages, as in the case of the Camapoã fazenda already
mentioned, which was established on the São Paulo-Cuiabá
route. But this was an exceptional case, and passengers had in
the main to fend for themselves.

There is, of course, no mention of artificial canals and link-
ages. The swirling waters of rapids and whirlpools were nego-

tiated at great risk, and there were not infrequent disasters. The crews of the canoes had to learn to gauge the depth of the water so that they could pass along the channels where the water was deepest, or to steer their way through the intricate and tortuous passages between the projecting rocks. Before negotiating the shallower rapids, the cargoes had to be unloaded, in whole or in part, to reduce the draught of the canoes, and when even this proved ineffectual, the passengers had to disembark and, carrying the canoes on their backs, plunge overland as far as the next stretch of navigable water. Quite apart from the fact that the lack of resources and help along stretches running through uninhabited land and the frequent attacks of hostile Indians had to be contended with, in such conditions navigation on the colony's rivers became a major feat. Unfortunately, very few of the Brazilian watercourses useful to colonization offered even passable conditions for navigation. With the exception of the Amazon and its tributaries—and even these are all broken up by falls and rapids immediately above their lower courses—the easily navigable and useful water networks are few and insignificant. The Itapecuru and the Parnaíba, and to a certain extent the Guaibá and Jacuí in Rio Grande do Sul, practically exhaust the list. The others are merely unimportant stretches of navigable water unintegrated into any system. The São Francisco appeared to offer a major line of communication, but proved to be of little value commercially because it flowed through regions where trade was largely restricted to the interregional traffic in cattle, which could not easily be transported by water. The São Francisco was used mainly for transporting salt produced along its middle reaches and shipped to São Romão, whence it was distributed to Minas Gerais and Goiás.

Only in the last years of the eighteenth century was utilization of the rivers as lines of communication seriously contemplated on any scale. The most noteworthy attempts to facilitate navigation have been summarized above. But few of the suggestions put forward were ever carried out. Grandiose plans were later made for connecting up the great basins, linking them by means of canals and thus integrating the rivers into a system of interior waterways serving the whole country.[46] We shall see below why—apart from the physical obstacles to such major undertakings—these projects failed to materialize.

Let us now see what means of transportation and travel were available to the colonists for use on these land, river, and sea routes, with the enormous distances they covered, measurable in the hundreds and hundreds of leagues. They were best equipped for navigation, particularly of the rivers. The blood of two navigating peoples ran in their veins, the Portuguese and the Tupis. But it was to the latter that the colony owed its finest achievements in this sphere. Thanks to the Tupis, it could boast of an enormous variety of craft of all types and sizes admirably adapted to their different functions. From the native canoe to the seagoing *jangada* (which was, in fact, used for deep sea fishing and only in exceptional cases for cargo) and the *ajoujo*, that ingenious hybrid of the two, we find a multitude of types: the *barcaça*, the *saveiro*, the *lancha* and many others, each further subdivided into a large number of subtypes.[47] * But all these vessels were used for river or coastal navigation along bays, estuaries, and offshore waters.

For coastal shipping proper, the colonists were very ill-equipped, particularly in view of the length and difficulty of Brazil's coastline. The vessels used as coasters, *sumacas* (smacks) and large launches, were generally poorly outfitted; the rigging was usually made of twisted leather thongs and the sails of poor quality light cotton cloth. Hardly any navigation aids were used; even the ordinary, indispensable instruments like the quadrant were frequently lacking, and more often than not there was not even a compass on board.[48] In such conditions, navigation beyond a minimal radius was always perilous. The vessels had to hug the coast, even at the risk of being stranded or coming to grief on the rocks; they were driven into

---

* *Jangada*—seaworthy catamaran; *ajoujo*—canoes lashed together; *barcaça*—large barge used as a coaster or lighter; *lancha*—a launch of a special type, constructed of hardwood; *saveiro*—a kind of long, narrow fishing boat.—Translator.

port at frequent intervals because of some slight setback in the weather, and these holdups often prolonged themselves indefinitely. Only after the transfer of the Court was there any progress in this sphere, as a result of the stimulus to trade provided by the opening of the ports, as well as of the example of navigational techniques set by foreign competitors.[49]

Means of freight transportation and travel by land were, of course, restricted by the limitations imposed by the roads. For two of the colony's chief items of trade, cattle and slaves, the solution was easy: they were made to transport themselves. In the case of cattle, I have noted that it was this solution that made it possible to cover the vast distances involved. For the rest, pack animals were used. Wheeled vehicles were seldom used. St. Hilaire mentions that there were a few oxcarts for local use in some districts of southern Minas; in São Paulo oxcarts were used for traveling the flat and easy road to Guaiases, and settlers from Franca habitually used carts for taking their produce to the captaincy's capital.[50] But only in the colony's extreme south, Rio Grande, where the topography and other natural conditions spared the necessity for constructing roads for wheeled vehicles, were carts used to any general extent. Here, large four-wheeled vehicles, which later developed into wagons, protected by a covering of cloth fixed over a curved wooden framework, were used. They were drawn by oxen, sometimes as many as four yoked together.[51]

Pack animals in the colony were, as has been noted, mules in the south and horses in the north. On the whole, the role played by the mule was much more important, since there was a great volume of overland traffic in the captaincies of the central-south, particularly Minas Gerais, São Paulo, and Rio de Janeiro. In the north there was very little freight transportation by land, since the most populated centers were all clustered along the seaboard and only droves of cattle traveled through the interior.[52]

The colony's freight transportation by land was not left to chance or to the improvisation of the moment: on the contrary, it was a properly organized business undertaking, particularly

in the captaincies of the central-south.[53] In this respect, cattle
droves, slave gangs, and pack trains are to be distinguished. A
drove might contain from 100 to several hundred head and
was obtained from the ranches by the *boiadeiros* (cattle traders), who hired an overseer and a number of drovers, one for
every twenty animals, to drive the beasts to the markets. Once
organized, the drove set off on the road, covering an average of
three leagues a day. In Minas and in the south there were no
rest days on the journey; but from Bahia northward, alternate
days were spent resting. Pigs were driven in large herds from
Minas to Rio in the same way.

Slave gangs marched in smaller groups of twenty to thirty
slaves, accompanied by a heavily armed escort. There is a contemporary engraving by Rugendas, illustrating one of these
slavetrains. The same artist also illustrated the gold and diamond convoys.[54]

The mule trains and caravans of packhorses are more interesting. There were many enterprises engaged in the business of
supplying packhorse and mule transportation to the general
public. They were owned by a *tropeiro* (literally, a driver of
pack animals), often a wealthy man owning a number of
teams. There was a schedule of arrivals and departures and a
fixed table of freight charges. In short, it was a properly organized business. The typical mule train or packhorse caravan was
made up of 20 to 50 animals under the general leadership of an
arrieiro, as he was called in Minas, or *arreador* in São Paulo.
This leader was in charge of the drivers and rode in front on
horseback, while the drivers, who were sometimes slaves, generally followed on foot, each being assigned seven animals.

The arrieiro's functions were numerous. Apart from acting as
team leader, he was responsible for saddling the animals and
packing the loads, a delicate task that is much more complicated than appears at first glance, since the animal's health and
efficiency largely depended on the way it was saddled and the
method of distributing the pack. If this was not properly done,
there was a risk that the animal would suffer injury on the long
and difficult journey it had to undertake. Problems of saddling

and packing the loads were so important that there were considerable differences in the arrieiro's skill from region to region. St. Hilaire considered the most competent to be those of Minas; the São Paulo arrieiros gave him a great deal of trouble. The leader's other functions included grooming the animals, seeing to their rations, and veterinary attention.[55]

Mules could generally carry loads of seven to eight arrobas in the southern captaincies; but according to Martius, they could carry no more than four arrobas in the north (Bahia). In Argentina and Chile, mules carried as much as four *quintais* (16 arrobas), and the contrast led the naturalist to conclude that climate was a decisive factor in the mule's resistance and carrying capacity, which was lowered by heat.[56] We must also bear in mind that the mule trains moved slowly, covering no more than an average of five to six leagues a day.

The use of pack animals for freight transportation gave rise to a number of problems that are worth mentioning for their impact on the interior's trade and way of life generally. One of the more serious problems was the volume of the merchandise. The packs could not be made up in large units or weigh more than half the full load the animal could carry, since the *cangalhas* (pannier frame) had to be evenly weighted on either side of the animal. The merchandise, therefore, had to be reduced in bulk or divided up; and when this was not feasible, it became impossible to transport. The consequences of this limitation showed up clearly in the colony's mercantile trade; large articles were relatively devalued, and there was a greater demand for small ones. This was especially important in the case of metals, one of the chief items of the colony's domestic trade. This has already been noted, and I also showed how the consequent rise in the prices of metals provoked by the difficulties of transportation influenced the economic life of Minas Gerais. The problem of heavy loads and large packs was sometimes solved by suspending them from poles slung between a pair of pack animals. But this could not become a regular solution in view of the inadequacy of the roads, their condition making this system difficult and even impossible over certain stretches.

It was more commonly used to carry hammocks, litters, or sedan chairs, in which self-indulgent gentlemen or their wives were wont to travel.

The colony's public transportation business was completed by the establishments set up along the routes to provision the pack trains and cattle convoys. These were the *ranchos,* great tile-covered sheds where travelers halted on their journeys for rest or shelter from bad weather. The ranchos were generally built and exploited by fazendeiros whose lands bordered the route, and although they made no charge for their use, they made a profit from the sale of maize for the mules. There were also, in fewer numbers, *ranchos reais* run by the public authorities. St. Hilaire found these "Crown Inns" on the São Paulo-Jundiaí route. Alongside the ranchos were the *vendas* (trading posts) where all sorts of articles needed by the travelers were available, notably, of course, alcoholic beverages. This was another profitable business for the fazendeiros established along the routes.

The transportation industry thus played a major role in colonial life, particularly in certain regions. We have already seen the role it played in Sorocaba in the south, where the trade in mules destined for use in the transportation business can be said to have been the region's lifeblood. But this was not the only part to feel its influence. In São Paulo, the region comprehending Moji-Mirim, Campinas, and Jundiaí, the supply of pack animals to the general public was one of the region's chief resources, since it was here that the drivers were recruited for the numerous mule trains traveling between Goiás and Mato Grosso. Jundiaí was intimately connected with this activity. It was in this town that the mule trains were organized, destined not only for the two captaincies already mentioned but also for the city of São Paulo and thence to Santos, carrying products from the backlands beyond Jundiaí, which were, as we have seen in a previous chapter, becoming a fairly important exporting center. Hence, there was great commercial activity in this town. Mules bought in Sorocaba were pastured in the winter pastures on the outskirts of the town and sold to the tropeiros, who then organized the mule trains and recruited the necessary drivers.[57]

We can now summarize and distinguish the more general trends in the evolution of the colony's communications and transport at the beginning of the last century. At the beginning of this chapter I tried to give a brief survey of the development of its transport system and the point this had reached at the period with which we are concerned. Colonization, having moved into the heart of the interior (Minas Gerais, Goiás, and Mato Grosso) and established links with the eastern seaboard, now sought to open up outlets to the extreme north, utilizing the tributaries of the Amazon basin. The determining factor behind this attempt was the advantage of river transport, since nature had supplied Brazil with rivers which afforded natural highways in many ways preferable to the overland routes, the inconveniences of which have been partly analyzed above. But the cost of overland transportation was another determining factor. The Governor of Espírito Santo, Manuel Vieira de Albuquerque Tovar, made a study of costs in 1810 and gave the following figures, which can be used as a basis for comparison: a small canoe could carry the load of 10–11 mules, that is, 70–90 arrobas, and cost 16,000–18,000 reis; whereas the cost of transporting this freight by mule train would have been 40,000–50,000 reis, not including the cost of feeding the animals. Canoes also lasted longer.[58] The governor was referring particularly to navigation on the river Doce, but we have seen that in other places canoes could transport as much as 2,000–3,000 arrobas.

It seems, then, that river transportation offered more advantages, at least for certain types of merchandise. Martius mentions that in Mato Grosso heavy merchandise cost less than half when transported on the Madeira than when brought overland from Rio or Bahia.[59] The chief factor in diverting transportation from the river routes was the attraction offered by large centers like Bahia and Rio de Janeiro, which were not situated close to a readily accessible waterway. These centers were sufficiently important to become a focus for the colony's internal trade, and overland freight transportation therefore became indispensable. Another factor in the greater use of overland routes was, of course, the poor conditions for navigation on the river routes. We have seen, however, that some attempts were being made to remedy this situation at the end of the eighteenth and beginning of the nineteenth centuries.

By turning its efforts in this direction and developing navigation on the major tributaries of the Amazon in particular, colonization was completing its integration of an internal communications system in Brazilian territory. The scattered population clusters of the interior were being linked up, and communication by sea, originally the only connection between different parts of the country, was gradually being supplemented or replaced. In the northeast, integration had already been achieved a century earlier by means of the circuitous overland routes linking the northern and eastern coasts. But the interior still had to be integrated into the network; the heart of the continent, still linked to the seaboard only by means of parallel routes, one for each region, had to be opened up to intercourse with the world at large. The utilization of the great left bank tributaries of the Amazon thus completed the lines of circulation. And this was the end toward which the evolution of Brazilian communications had been moving.

Communication by sea was, of course, to remain paramount for some time to come, and even offered many advantages. The fact that most of Brazil's population was concentrated along the seaboard and that its most economically advanced centers were on the coast ensured the continued importance of maritime links. But in spite of this, the trend toward establishing a system of internal communication encompassing the whole country was already clearly discernible at the beginning of the nineteenth century. It was most significantly so in the lines chosen for the establishment of postal services, which began to be organized in the last years of the eighteenth century. It was the inland routes that were chosen. I have already referred in passing to two of the postal services established: Maranhão-Pernambuco, and Ceará-Bahia, both of which ran through the interior. In 1808, Judge Luís Tomás de Navarro was appointed to study the opening up of another overland postal service between Bahia and Rio de Janeiro.[60] Even more interesting from this point of view is the postal route between Rio de Janeiro and Pará, which clearly illustrates the point we have made. When a postal service was organized in 1808, the coastal route was considered too slow and an inland route was chosen, running through the center of the colony via Goiás, and utilizing the Tocantins waterway. The route covered approximately 280 leagues overland and 250 leagues along the river.[61]

In the course of the nineteenth century this trend was decisively countered by the advent of the steamship. Coastal navigation once more became the only general line of communication in Brazilian territory. This was a return to the original system of the colony: sea routes were the backbone of the country's communication system, with lines of penetration running in from the coast and entirely cut off from one another. Thus the territorial structure was broken up again, although with less dire consequences than before since the steamship improved the precarious maritime routes of the past. But the task of integrating the country, the task of the long colonial past, was interrupted. The railway built round the Paulo Afonso Falls, on the São Francisco between Piranhas and Jatobá, and the Madeira-Mamoré railway round the rapids on the Madeira— the latter built, however, as the result of international political factors *—are like distant and muffled echoes of this great work. Neither of these lines has been successful and both have stagnated in an obscurity which, for the time being, offers no prospect. The time has not yet come to resume the task, of such far-reaching consequences for the nation, of developing internal communications—so paradoxically arrested by the steamship.

---

* The Madeira-Mamoré line was built to give the produce of the northern Bolivian lowlands an outlet to the Amazon navigation below the Madeira rapids in exchange for territorial adjustment in favor of Brazil.— Translator.

PART THREE—SOCIAL AND POLITICAL LIFE

Social Organization

What first and foremost characterizes Brazilian society at the beginning of the nineteenth century is slavery. Wherever this institution has existed, its influence on social life has been unequaled and the role it has played in all sectors has been a major one. Economic organization, material and moral standards—everything is affected by the presence of slave labor when it reaches the proportions it assumed in Brazil; and its repercussions, direct or indirect, are profound. I shall not dwell on the general material and moral influence of slavery as an institution. Historians and sociologists in many different periods and countries have gone into these aspects, and there is a vast literature on the subject. I could add nothing that would not be a mere rehash of familiar material already thoroughly discussed. I shall therefore confine myself to what was peculiar to Brazil. For slavery in Brazil did possess individual characteristics, and although it shared its most prominent traits with all the American tropical colonies in the same position, it was the characteristics peculiar to Brazil, perhaps even more than those common to slavery in general, that molded Brazilian society.

Slavery in the Americas was not affiliated, in the historical sense, with any of the forms of servile labor deriving in Western civilization from the ancient world or the centuries that followed; it derived from an order of events that was inaugurated

313

in the fifteenth century with the great maritime discoveries and belonged entirely to this order. I have already mentioned in passing in a previous chapter that slave labor, which had reached considerable proportions in the ancient world, had first declined and been replaced by an attenuated form of slavery—the serf attached to the soil—later to disappear almost entirely from the Western world. With the discovery of America it was reborn with a vigorous new life. This circumstance should be particularly stressed. The fact that in the case of American slavery there was a rebirth of an institution that appeared to have been abolished forever in the West is of paramount importance. It gave rise to a number of consequences that were to make of the institution of slavery in the Americas an original and singular process with repercussions that can only be fully grasped when seen from this particular angle.

This is evident from a comparison of slavery in these two historical periods, the ancient world and the modern. In the first, for all the importance of the role he played, the slave was no more than the result of a natural evolutionary process with its roots in the remote past, and thus fitted perfectly into the material structure and moral physiognomy of ancient society. He figured as spontaneously—and appeared even as inevitable and justifiable—as any other element that went to make up this society. It is in this sense that the often-cited and much-discussed attitude to slavery of a philosopher like Aristotle can be understood, and, leaving aside any appreciation of his work as a thinker, we must remember that he represented in its highest form the temper and thought of his age. In Greece and Rome the slave was what the wage earner is to our own time; although much discussed, and its legitimacy seriously challenged by some, in the eyes of our society as a whole, working for a wage appears an inevitable, necessary, and irreplaceable condition.

Modern slavery, that is to say, slavery in the Americas, was a quite different phenomenon. It came into existence abruptly, without any link with the past or a long tradition. It merely brought back an institution at the very moment when it had

completely lost its reason for existence, having been replaced
by more evolved forms of labor. Thus, it was like a foreign
body insinuating itself into the structure of Western civilization
where it was completely out of place. And it went against all
the moral and material standards already established. It
brought about a revolution for which nothing had prepared the
way. How did this come about? Nothing could be more restricted, petty, or one-sided. Unlike slavery in the ancient
world, which arose naturally out of the social, material, and
moral life of the time, modern slavery was no more than an expedient resorted to by the countries of Europe in their desire to
exploit commercially the vast territories and riches of the New
World. It is true that slavery in America had an immediate
precursor in the captivity of the Moors and later that of African Negroes brought back by the first Portuguese expeditions
overseas as prizes of war or the fruits of ransom. But this was
only a first step, prelude to the great drama that was to unfold
on the other side of the Atlantic. And it was there that was
really reborn, in proportions undreamed of in the ancient
world, an institution already condemned and practically abolished.

For this expedient to which Europe greedily resorted, she
was to pay a heavy price. We can only repeat what John Kellis
Ingram has said in this respect: "Not long after the disappearance of serfdom in the most advanced communities, comes into
sight the modern system of colonial slavery, which, instead of
being the spontaneous outgrowth of social necessities, and sub-
serving temporary needs of human development, was politically as well as morally a monstruous aberration." [1]

It is neither necessary nor appropriate to judge modern
slavery from the standpoint of absolute morality. Without even
taking into account the havoc it wrought among the indigenous
peoples of America and those of the Dark Continent, the grav-
est effects of slave labor for the colonizing nations, particularly
in their New World colonies, were due to the fact that it was
not, as in the past, accompanied by any constructive element
except, that is, in a very restricted sense, the purely material

advantages it offered in the realization of a commercial enterprise, a mere business venture yielding fat profits to its promoters. And for this, for so narrow an aim, the nations of Europe abandoned all their principles and the basic precepts on
which their civilization and culture had been founded. What
this represented in the course of time, in terms of degradation
and corruption, with repercussions that ultimately affected the
very course of progress and material prosperity, has never yet
been fully evaluated; nor is this the proper place to go into this
aspect of the subject. But this must have been one of the chief
causes of the tragic shipwreck of Iberian civilization, both for
Portugal and for Spain. These two nations were the ones most
firmly set on this course and were also its two chief victims.[2]

Even more serious were the effects of slave labor on the
nascent American colonies. Their formative years were marked
by the corrupting atmosphere it creates; slave labor even
became the cornerstone of their structures, the cement which
held together the elements that went into their building. They
therefore presented a sorry human spectacle; and the example
of Brazil, which will be considered below, was more or less followed in all the other colonies.

There is yet another consideration that rendered modern
slavery even more damnable: the elements it seized upon to
keep it alive—the American native and the African Negro, peoples of a lower cultural level than their exploiters.[3] In this case,
too, comparison with the ancient world is illuminating. Slaves
in the ancient world were supplied by peoples and races whose
culture was often equal, if not superior, to that of their conquerors. They thus contributed cultural values of a high standard to the civilizations they served. Rome would never have
become as great had she not received this contribution from
her slaves, brought from all parts of the known world and con-
centrating in Rome the finest and most advanced culture of the
age. Roman civilization owed much to its slaves, from whom
much was learned. In Rome the slave was never simply the
brutal and mindless labor machine that his American successor
was to become.

In America we witness the very opposite, the recruitment of barbarous and semibarbarous peoples, torn from their natural environment and placed without transition into a completely alien civilization. And what awaited them in this civilization was slavery in its basest form—man reduced to his lowest, little more than an irrational animal, "A living tool," as Perdigão Malheiro has expressed it.[4] No more was expected of him, no more asked, and no more given than his brute strength, primitive muscular effort under the lash of the overseer; and of the woman, in addition to her work, the passive submission of the female to the sexual embraces of her master. In both cases, only the physical act counted, any spiritual or moral accompaniment being excluded: man's "animality" not his "humanity."

Apart from this physical exploitation, the contribution of the Indian or Negro slave to the formation of Brazil was practically nil. They did, of course, contribute to our "culture" in its widest anthropological sense, but it was a passive contribution, the result of their presence and the widespread diffusion of their blood rather than of an active and constructive intervention. The cultural heritage they brought with them from the American or African jungle—which I do not intend to underestimate —was smothered, if not debased and annihilated, by the social, material, and moral status to which they were reduced. And thus it emerges only very slightly here and there in the general cultural pattern. It acted more as a corrupting ferment to the other culture, the culture that the white master superimposed upon their own.[5]

In fact it was this passive role of the Negro and native cultures in Brazil that enabled the white man to impose himself with such force and to become undisputed master, although his contribution to the size of the population was relatively small compared to the other races. The Negro and the Indian would certainly have played a quite different role in the formation of Brazil if colonization had taken another course, if it had attempted to accept a less one-sided contribution from the two dominated races, something more than mere physical effort. But Brazilian colonization unfolded within a narrow frame, its

only objective the utilization of the territory's natural resources
for the extensive and precipitate production of a small number
of highly profitable commodities for the international market.
It never swerved from this course, fixed from the very outset of
conquest; and it seems that there was no time to lose and no
thought could be spared for a more solid, stable, and carefully
planned undertaking. One prospect and one only was envisaged, big returns for the capital Europe had invested. The
land had not been exploited; its resources accumulated over
the centuries lay near the surface. No great plans were needed
to extract them, nor did their exploitation present any great
problem. All that was needed was simple physical effort. And
this the Negro and the Indian perforce supplied.

This duty exacted from the subject races was paralleled by
another, a by-product of slavery, of which the master race took
full advantage: the docile caresses of the female slave to satisfy
the sexual needs of colonists deprived of women of their own
race and class. From the moral and humane point of view these
two functions are on a par, and the way in which they were
performed excluded anything the Negro or Indian might have
brought by way of positive and constructive cultural value.

One last characteristic distinguished slavery in the Americas,
the profound racial difference between slave and master. In
some parts of America this difference proved an insuperable
obstacle to any approach between classes and individuals and,
hence, considerably reinforced the rigidity of a structure which
the social system itself had already rendered inflexible. I do not
intend to consider these other colonies, and in any case in Brazil there was in fact such an approach which, as I have noted in
a previous chapter, took place on a considerable scale. Nevertheless, contacts were made only within limits that were narrow in spite of all, at least up to the period which concerns us
here. Strong racial prejudice always existed, and although
there was a fair amount of tolerance and a blind eye was often
turned to the telltale signs of mixed racial origin—a calculated
hypocrisy—there was nevertheless still a pronounced racial
barrier to social integration in the colony, creating serious

obstacles to the formation of a whole which would be, if not racially (which would still take a long time), at least morally homogeneous.

I shall not go into the question of race and color prejudice and its origins—whether it stems from innate psychological characteristics of an aesthetic or some other order or whether it is simply due to particular social situations and conditions. Whatever point of view is accepted, one thing remains certain: racial differences, particularly when manifested in such clear somatic traits as color, will, if not create—an opinion open to well-founded doubts, and in my view one which has been incontestably controverted—at least accentuate a discrimination already made on the social level. The reason for this is that the racial features give an unmistakeable stamp to existing social differences. They label the individual, helping to raise and strengthen the barriers that separate different classes. Any approach or blending of the classes thus becomes much more difficult, and the domination of one over the other is accentuated.

This does not preclude—and in Brazil it certainly did not do so—a degree of social mobility. Already in colonial times, individuals clearly of Negro origin rose to prominent positions. The same, of course, was true of persons of Indian origin, but it is less noteworthy than in the case of the Negro and his mixed descendants, because prejudice against the Indian was not as strong. But the fact that colored men did manage to rise in the social scale does not signify that prejudice did not exist. It was circumvented by the hypocrisy of allowing them to pass as white. The situation created when a mestizo's exceptional ability or talent enabled him to attain higher social status was accepted, but prejudice continued to be respected. Indeed, only persons who were of not too dusky a hue, the so-called *brancarrões* (light-skinned mulattoes), were allowed to rise in this way, when the polite fiction was not too blatantly absurd. Dark-skinned mulattoes and Negroes found that the color bar was too strong and that however talented or well qualified, they had little hope of surmounting it; they were indelibly marked by the stigma of a race for so long confined to the lowest rungs of the social ladder that it had finally become altogether identified with them. "Negro" or "Darkie" was still a pejorative term in the colony and would so remain for some time to come. These words were even used as synonyms for "slave," and dark-skinned people were treated as slaves even when they happened to be free.

Luccock recounts a revealing incident in this respect. On one occasion when he needed the help of two free Negroes who happened to be with him at the time, he forced them in spite of their obvious reluctance, but aided and abetted by other people present, to supply the help he needed. He tries to justify himself by explaining that extreme circumstances had obliged him to act in this way. But his scruples were not shared by the Brazilians who encouraged him and took the whole thing for granted, as if they had an unquestioned right to make such demands.[6]

The role of color in class distinction and class relations was reflected in the customary practice of the law. Perdigão Malheiro observes that during the slave auctions, bids made "with a promise of freedom," that is, on condition that the slave would be allowed to buy his freedom if he could find the necessary money, were generally supposed to override any other bids. But only in the case of light-skinned slaves was this strictly adhered to.[7] He adds that the lighter-skinned mulatto's loathing of slavery was common knowledge and even comes to the exaggerated conclusion that, had it not been for the dark skins of the slaves, Brazilian custom would have made it impossible for slavery to survive. It should be remembered, however, that he was writing in 1867 when slavery had lost much of its moral respectability, and that the views expressed clearly reflect his well-known sympathy for the abolitionist cause; his great work on slavery is in fact simply an apology for abolition. His evidence must nevertheless be regarded as valuable, and it clearly demonstrates the effect of color in keeping down persons of the subject race; it also shows how much harsher slavery must have been when social discrimination was reinforced by a corresponding color bar, with its indelible and inescapable imprint.

In sum, we can see from the foregoing remarks that slavery as established in America and more particularly in Brazil was the result of a number of special circumstances which accentuated its negative characteristics, aggravating the morally corrupting and debasing features it already exhibited as an institution per se. It brought into the colony from the very beginning and in an overwhelming proportion an alien and heterogeneous contingent of races still on the fringes of a barbaric state and who, on contact with the superior culture of the dominant race, became completely degraded. And this contingent was ingested at one gulp in its raw state, with no preceding transition stage.

In the case of the Indians there had been some preparation in the form of the education provided by the Jesuits and other orders which, for all its defects, gave them some kind of a start. Even after the expulsion of the Jesuits, which seriously handicapped missionary work since the other orders were unable or lacked the knowledge to fill the gap, the status of Indians, although still far from what it should have been in view of the existing legislation, which aimed to support and educate the savages who wished to become integrated into colonization, still helped to keep the natives away from the more depressing forms of slavery; and even if it offered them no great advantages or material progress, it did give them a minimum of protection and encouragement. But there was nothing comparable for the African Negro. So zealous in upholding the freedom of the Indian, the religious orders were the first to accept and even to encourage Negro slavery to keep at bay the colonists who needed laborers and so have a free hand in the running of their missions.

In Brazil the Negro found no one to protect him. A virtual pariah, no finger was raised to defend him. And if it is true that in Brazil custom and even laws were more benign, in spite of their brutality, than in the other slaveholding American colonies, it is also true that here the Negro received no moral or intellectual preparation for the society into which he had been brought by force. His education was utterly neglected. He was baptized and given a little religious instruction, but no more. And even the rudiments of the Catholic faith were parroted rather than learned, and then only enough to give rise to that picturesque but thoroughly perverted mixture of their own superstitions and beliefs with Catholicism, an inchoate hotchpotch completely lacking in any cultural value, which parades under the name of "Catholicism" and is the real religion of millions of Brazilians. Manuel Querino, Nina Rodrigues, and more recently Artur Ramos,* have revealed the more extreme characteristics of this religion, which a hypocritical and absurd "shame" had hitherto kept in the dark.

The enslaved races thus taken into colonial society, ill-prepared and ill-adapted, constituted an uneasy foreign body within it. The process of absorption has gone on up to the present day and is still far from complete. It is not simply a question of that ethnic elimination that so troubles the Brazilian "racists"—which, although slow, proceeded and is proceeding in a progressive and normal way with no great obstacles. This is not the most serious aspect of the problem; in fact it is an aspect that matters more from the point of view of "façade," or aesthetics, if one wishes to look at it in this way. In itself, racial intermixing is of practically no importance in Brazil, and in many ways is even an advantage. What really mattered in the formation of Brazil was the low level of the enslaved masses, who were to constitute the greater part of the country's population. In the period under consideration, the

---

* Artur Ramos's *Culturas Negras no Novo Mundo* is listed in the Bibliography, as is Nina Rodrigues's *Os Africanos no Brasil*. (Manuel Querino's article, "A raça Africana e seus costumes na Bahia" is not listed. It was published in *Revista da Academia de Letras*, No. 70, and describes the customs and religious rituals of Africans in Bahia, which reveal a strong Mohammedan influence in the religion of the slaves.) Ramos is an internationally known anthropologist, and his work, like that of Nina Rodrigues, throws new light on the origins and customs of the Negroes in Brazil. Nina Rodrigues also wrote an exhaustive study of fetishism, totemism, and African animism, *L'Animisme Fétichiste des Nègres de Bahia* (Bahia, 1900).—Translator.

problem was of course much more serious. The slave trade
was still flourishing and was even growing in volume, bringing
into the colony a constant stream of massive contingents of
semibarbarous people. The result could only have been the incongruous agglomeration, resting on a precarious foundation,
that was Brazilian colonial society. Certain consequences were
to stand out more clearly. One was the prevailing laxity of
morals, verifiable in the general relaxation of standards commented on and deplored by all contemporary observers, Brazilian as well as foreign. Another was the low level and inefficiency of labor and production, left to the "raw" Negroes
(*Negros boçais*) and the apathetic Indians. This was one of the
main reasons for the sluggish tempo of the colonial economy.

These and other results of slavery and the elements used to
keep it alive, together with other aspects of colonial life and
social customs, will be analyzed in a later chapter. I shall confine myself here to the structure of Brazilian society. As far as
the slave and his legal and social status is concerned, I feel that
there is no need to go into what has already been discussed in
other works.[8] On the matter of slavery the colony followed
Roman law, in which the slave was a "chattel" of his master,
who could dispose of him as he saw fit. Relaxations of this rule,
which afforded the slave some protection, were not very numerous. Indeed these cases were decided *de facto* rather than
de jure, since the slave was generally unaware of his legal
rights.

If there was any redeeming feature in the rigors of slavery as
practiced in consequence of the absolute and unlimited ownership granted to the slaveholders, this was more the result of
custom than of law, since the custom of the land was relatively
mild in this respect. It was not as mild as current opinion
would have us believe, however, since the common belief that
the Brazilian was an exceptionally kind master is applicable
only to nineteenth-century slavery, after the abolition of the
slave trade, when the scarcity and high price of slaves made it
uneconomical for slaveholders to neglect or maltreat their
slaves. The testimony of eyewitnesses for the colonial period

contradicts this belief, based on a tradition still close in time
and thus still alive and dominant. We find in these testimonies
nothing to persuade us that the Brazilian slaveholders were humane and tolerant; on the contrary, what we learn leads us to
form a quite different opinion.[9] The kernel of truth in this belief is that Brazilian slaves seem to have been better treated
than in some of the other American colonies, particularly the
English and French colonies. One reason for this better treatment of slaves was probably the natural indolence of the Portuguese, especially when softened by the tropics and the
general lassitude that characterized Brazilian life.[10] The patriarchal regime, which will be considered below, also played its
part in smoothing the relationship between master and slave,
the master having something of a fatherly and protective attitude toward his slaves. The proof of this is that in the regions
which had been more recently developed and where the
patriarchal way of life, fruit of a lengthy process of consolidation, had not yet been established, there was greater harshness
in the treatment of slaves. In the period we are considering,
this can be seen in the two regions, Maranhão and Rio Grande
do Sul, where prosperity and hence the influx of slaves was of
recent date, that is, the second half of the eighteenth century.
These two captaincies contrasted with those where colonization and progress had been longest established: Bahia, Pernambuco, and Rio de Janeiro.

As for the functions performed by slaves, I need hardly state
that these were numerous. In the chapters on the colonial
economy we saw that practically all the labor in Brazil was
servile. But we must distinguish between two sectors with
clearcut differences and consequences, the functions connected
with production and those connected with domestic service.
Despite the scope and economic importance of the first sector,
the second should not be forgotten or underestimated not only
because of the large numbers of slaves engaged in this sector
—the vanity of the master contributed as much to this as the
needs of the household, for he liked to surround himself with a
swarm of servants [11]—but also because it played an enormous
role in the colony's social life and exerted a strong influence on

all its aspects. In this sense, if we exclude the economic element, its importance easily surpassed that of the other sector. Contact between the domestic slave and his owner and white society in general was much greater and far more intimate. And it was undoubtedly through the domestic slave that most of the evils of slavery were channeled into Brazilian life. The few favorable contributions it made were likewise channeled through the household slave: the tenderness and warmth of the "black mammy," the delicious dishes of Afro-Brazilian cuisine.[12]

Thus in the fields as in the city streets, in trade as in the home, the slave was omnipresent. Slavery had taken such a hold that free labor became restricted to a very small field. And the universal use of slaves in the different trades and occupations of economic and social life ended by influencing the attitude to work, which came to be regarded as contemptible and degrading. "As all servile tasks and mechanical arts are performed by slaves," wrote that perceptive observer, Vilhena,

few are the mulattoes and rare the whites who wish to work or practice any handicraft, not even those same paupers who in Portugal were nothing but servants, and waited at table, or wielded the hoe . . . The servants [who came from Portugal] deem it a better fortune to be vagrants or to die of hunger, to end up as soldiers or even as thieves, than to serve an honest master who would pay them well, feed and care for them, and all this not to do what Negroes do in other houses; the daughters of this land are of such a stamp that even the daughter of the poorest and most abject man, the most destitute little mulatta, if she be free, would sooner go to the gallows than serve even a Duchess, if any such existed in this land.[13]

The same deeply engrained prejudice against manual work prevailed in the rural areas; no free man would take up the hoe without feeling that he had tarnished his reputation. And for this reason, as Vilhena says, "Although there is abundant land, there are few who own it, since even those who could do so, lacking the 150 reis to buy themselves each a Negro to do the work, would deem it the same, to have it or no." [14]

In such conditions it is hardly surprising that so few occupations were considered worthy of a free man. If he could not become a landowner or *fazendeiro, senhor d'engenho,* or sharecropper, only a few rural occupations were acceptable to him—overseer, *mestre d'engenho* (foreman), and so forth.[15] He could also practice some mechanical trade which had not been monopolized by slaves and which was not too unworthy of the whiteness or lightness of his skin. He could go into public service if, on the contrary, his skin was not of too dusky a hue; or he could take up soldiering or go into commerce, either on his own account or as a cashier or shop assistant. In the latter occupation, however, he came up against another barrier: commerce was monopolized by the *reinóis* (natives of the realm). Colonial-born aspirants usually found the doors of commerce closed to them, not on account of any legal disposition or prejudice of any nature, but on account of long-established practice; the original emigrants jealously guarded their monopoly of commerce and by tacit agreement rigorously adhered to the custom of employing newly arrived immigrants or compatriots. "Immigrants from the realm," wrote the Marquis of Lavradio, Viceroy of Rio de Janeiro, "are concerned only to make themselves the lords of commerce in this land, and they will in nowise allow the sons of the land to become cashiers or sales clerks, for fear they may some day become established on their own, and thus they have taken all the trade to themselves." [16] This situation was very serious, and gave rise to a number of grave consequences, which will be seen below.

The other occupations open to free men were the liberal professions: law, medicine, and so forth. These were by nature restricted to the few. They called for special qualifications and studies that were not available in the colony, and hence would-be practitioners had to be persons of means. There were, thus, very few professionals. In 1792 there were in Rio de Janeiro only 32 advocates and 24 solicitors.[17] Doctors were rare. Martius observed that in 1818 in the entire captaincy of São Paulo there was not a single genuine doctor or surgeon.[18] The same was true of engineers; the colony could count on only a few military engineers.[19]

There still remained the Church. And the Church certainly offered better opportunities. Most of the studies required could be undertaken in Brazil and even completed in the case of the secular offices. Seminaries were the first institutes of higher education to be established in the colony. Indeed, candidates for the priesthood who showed especial aptitude were always encouraged, and there was no lack of persons willing to finance their training in the colony or in Europe.

It is true that here also color prejudice raised its head, and if the aspirant was not pure white he needed a special dispensation.[20] But this was more a matter of form; for really promising students managed to surmount this barrier. Was this not the case of Luís Antônio da Silva e Sousa, who later made a name for himself as poet and historian, and who, in spite of having found the doors of the Church barred to him in Brazil, succeeded in getting the necessary dispensation in Rome, with the backing of the Portuguese minister to the Vatican?[21] Indeed, there were numerous priests of mixed blood in Brazil. The Church in Brazil always honored its democratic tradition, its greatest strength in the spiritual conquest of the West.

What had happened in mediaeval Europe was repeated in the colonization of Brazil: the cassock became the refuge for intelligence and culture, especially since these were the qualities on which selection for the priesthood was based. The Church thus became in the colonial period the intellectual career par excellence and the only one that offered bright prospects; and when, after independence, native-born Brazilians were sought to fill the colony's political posts, it was chiefly from the Church that candidates were recruited.[22] The Church therefore played an important role in the colony as an outlet for any individual seeking a professional opening. In the eighteenth century this was recognized and not only stated but also justified by an ecclesiastical authority as eminent as the Father-Superior of the Franciscan Province in Rio de Janeiro, Frei Antonio da Vitória: "Today there is no longer a true vocation for the religious state, nearly all seek it as a profession, particularly in Brazil where there is a shortage of jobs in which fathers can place their sons. In accordance with this principle, it would be unjust to Brazilians to deprive them of this benefit, when it is their fathers who feed and clothe all the religious of that continent and repair their convents." [23]

In sum, it can be seen that for persons destitute of material means, openings in the colony were few. There was, thus, an enormous empty space between the two extremes of the social scale, the masters and the slaves, the tiny minority of the former and the overwhelming majority of the latter. These two groups were clearly classified in the hierarchy of the colony's social structure. The masters were the directors of colonization in its various sectors, the slaves were the working masses. Between these two neatly defined categories, geared to the general aims of colonization, was sandwiched the growing number of unclassified individuals, the useless and the ill-adapted—individuals whose occupations were more or less uncertain or shifting or who could be regarded as the "vagrant poor." This large contingent Couty later saw as "the Brazilian populace," describing it as "nonexistent" because of its general uselessness and summing up the country's social situation in a pithy sentence that was to become famous: "Le Brésil n'a pas de peuple." [24]

This socially undefined element was large and steadily increasing since the causes that led to its appearance continued to exist. Couty estimated that out of a population of 12 million, no fewer than half were socially unclassified. The proportion among the three million that made up the population at the beginning of the century must have been smaller but nevertheless certainly included the great, indeed the overwhelming, majority of the colony's free population. Most of the members of this large element were freed Negroes and mulattoes or runaway slaves; Indians who had been removed from their native environment but had not yet adapted themselves to the new society into which they had been drawn; mixed-bloods of all shades and categories who, being neither slaves nor able to be masters, were excluded from any stable situation either because of the prejudice against them or because no openings were available; and even whites, pure whites, including descendants of illustrious Portuguese families like the Meneses, Barretos, Castros, Lacerdas, and others whom Vilhena encountered in Cairu, reduced to poverty: [25] the "poor whites," * human flotsam and jetsam stranded by the slavocratic and rigid society whose victims they were.

Part of this category of the colonial population was made up of people who vegetated in obscurity in some remote and cut-off corner of civilization, living from hand to mouth, brutalized and morally degraded. This was true of a great part of the Amazonian population, of the *Tapuyas,* who had ceased to be pure forest dwellers and had not become colonists,[26] and of the *Caboclos,* pure or almost pure Indian, in other parts of the colony in more or less the same position, isolated from the surrounding civilized world that rejected them and dependent on a miserable natural economy which provided them with only the bare necessities of life. Similarly placed were the Negroes or mulattoes who, excluded from active society, tried to imitate the way of life of these sons of the continent. Runaway slaves founded the dreaded *quilombos* in the backlands which so worried the authorities because they could sometimes become dangerous to the social order.[27] More or less pure-blooded whites also often fled or were expelled from society and took advantage of the vastness of the territory to find refuge in the wilderness, shunning any contact with civilization.

Another part of the more or less vagrant section of the colony's population was made up of individuals who, in the cities but above all in the rural areas, leaned on some powerful patron who, in exchange for small services or sometimes merely to add one more member to his retinue to feed his vanity, allowed them to live in his shadow and receive his protection and support. These individuals were then called *agregados* (tenants) or *moradores dos engenhos* (plantation sharecroppers). Their duties as vassals were later proclaimed and justified in Pernambuco at a difficult moment in an acute political crisis.[28]

---

* The author uses the English term.—Translator.

Finally, the last part of this unclassified element—and the most disreputable, troublesome, and obnoxious—was made up of homeless beggars, vagrants, and vagabonds, permanently unemployed, wandering from place to place in search of a way of maintaining themselves and who, when opportunity presented itself, went in openly for crime. This unruly swarm of pauper-vagrants in the rural and urban areas became one of the authority's chief concerns, and was the leitmotiv of their reports. Their presence is constantly deplored by contemporary observers of colonial life. Viceroy Luís de Vasconcelos complained bitterly of the evils of this situation and insisted on the need for measures to be taken to grapple with the problem when he handed over the vice-regency in 1789.[29] Vilhena devoted many pages of his letters to the problem [30] and Brigadier Cunha Matos considered the vagrant element to be one of the chief curses of the captaincy of Goiás,[31] while the President of the Board of Inspection of Rio de Janeiro, Judge Rocha Gameiro, pointed out that one of the obstacles to agricultural development in the colony was the presence of these vagrants.[32] Nor did they escape the notice of foreign travelers. St. Hilaire and Martius made detailed references to them and clearly realized that it was no temporary state of affairs but an endemic social disease.[33]

The roving bands that infested the backlands were recruited from this unclassified section of Brazilian society. Under the protection offered by a weak or distant authority, they attacked and plundered the peace-loving and sedentary population or, in the service of powerful local "bosses," served their whims and ambitions in the frequent wrangles that arose between different masters. The Feitosa gang of Ceará for years terrorized the interior of the captaincy and was only finally defeated and captured by a ruse of Governor Oeynhausen's.[34] But despite such extreme cases, the recruitment of down-and-outs for the private armies of the great landowners and local bosses was a way of ensuring some security and peace, since it channeled the natural turbulence of this feckless element and imposed a minimum of organization and discipline. Left to their own devices, these roving bands would have terrorized the unprotected backlands, crime would have become more commonplace, and there would not have been, in these vast areas where there were no police or troops to maintain law and order, the relative security which St. Hilaire was so surprised to discover and of which his personal experience gave so striking an instance. In all the years that he wandered around the interior of Brazil, he was never once molested.

In the cities the vagrants were more dangerous and delinquent, since here they did not encounter the hospitality of the rural areas; nor were there any sertanejo bosses to take them on and provide them with an outlet for their aggressive feelings. In Rio de Janeiro it was dangerous to travel in secluded parts alone and unarmed, even in broad daylight. The city's first chief of police, appointed after the arrival of the Court, was Paulo Fernandes, who made an energetic attempt to grapple with the problem. But the social evil continued, and only in the Republic were the notorious *capoeiras,** offshoots of the colony's vagrants, eliminated from the capital.

As we can see from the foregoing, this stratum of the colonial population clearly made its presence felt. It was to do so even more markedly during the agitations preceding independence and continuing up to the middle of the nineteenth century, keeping the country in a constant state of near anarchy. In the whirlwind of passions and claims and counter-claims unleashed by the breaking up of the social and political balance brought about by the transition from colony to independent empire, members of this category of the population—displaced, undefined, maladjusted to the social order, and in fact both product and victim of this order—plunged headlong into the struggle with all the violence of instincts long held in check and with touches of the barbarism that still ran so freely

---

* *Capoeira*—a ruffian bandit or highwayman. Capoeira (the term is untranslatable) has become an athletic pastime in which the participant, armed with a razor or a knife, goes through the motions of criminal acts, obviously miming the real-life assaults committed by the *capoeiras* of the past.—Translator.

in their veins. There is not the slightest doubt that the disturbances preceding and following independence—the agitations of the troubled Minority * and the first decade of the Second Empire, all of them still awaiting proper research—were largely a consequence of the situation we have just analyzed. It was from this shiftless element of the Brazilian population that the political factions which sprang up recruited the greater part of the armed forces they used against each other, and it was to serve as the battering ram for driving the claims of the people against the solid structure of the empire, which in spite of the siege continued to withstand all assaults. The subject is therefore one of great historical interest and is worth analyzing further, since it was in the period with which we are here concerned, immediately preceding the events mentioned above, that we find the situation ripe but not yet disrupted by the struggles that later arose. The task of the observer is therefore an easier one.

We have seen the general conditions which gave rise to the swarm of people living more or less on the fringes of the social order: the shortage of regular and stable employment capable of absorbing the great mass of the colony's free population and providing a secure basis for its existence. This situation sprang from deep-rooted causes, the chief and most immediate of which was slavery, which excluded free men from the majority of occupations and forced them into situations where idleness and crime became almost inevitable. But it was allied with the same effect to another circumstance which was in fact intimately related to the first, the economic system governing colonial production. In the stifling atmosphere of plantation agriculture, there was no room for any other major activity. Anything that was not connected to the large-scale production of a few commercially valuable commodities destined for export was doomed to be a miserable, small-time, secondary activity. It did not and could not offer prospects for lucrative

---

* Minority—the period lasting from Pedro I's abdication (1831) until Pedro II was considered old enough to ascend the throne at the age of 14 (1840).—Translator.

employment on a higher level. And thus anyone who remained outside the narrow circle of plantation agriculture, and in practice this meant nearly everyone except the masters and the slaves, was condemned to dismal prospects.

A final factor which contributed considerably to the growth of this useless social residue was the lack of stability that characterized the Brazilian economy, the failure to find a solid and permanent basis for production. We have seen how the economic history of the colony was dominated by a series of short-lived cycles, alternating from region to region and consisting of a period of prosperity followed by collapse and decadence. The social repercussions of this history were disastrous. With each period of decadence, part of the colony's structure crumbled; the population hit by the crisis was left stranded. More or less large numbers of people were rendered useless, cut off from their roots and the vital basis for their existence. They survived in a condition of poverty, outside the established social order. At no time was this more catastrophic in its proportions than in the period we are dealing with here, and nowhere was this crisis more profound and far-reaching in its effects on the colony as a whole than in the mining districts. Here we find large numbers of destitute and stranded individuals for whom there seemed to be no future, with no proper means of livelihood, no fixed or decently paid employment, or else completely unemployed, maintaining themselves by begging or driven to some disreputable and dishonest way of making a living, alternating between charity and crime—vagrants and vagabonds in the truest sense. In the gold districts of Minas Gerais, Goiás, and Mato Grosso, the problem reached such alarming proportions that all contemporary observers were horrified. A substantial part of the population of these captaincies had been left in this miserable condition, and the future looked very bleak.[35]

These were in brief the basic reasons for the existence of these fringe elements in Brazilian colonial society. Let us now consider the organized elements of this society. The aspect that immediately strikes us—and one that, together with slavery, which formed the basis of colonial society, dominated the

scene in the colonial period—is the existence of a "patriarchal
clan" (a term already consecrated by usage). Much of the Brazilian population was gathered into these patriarchal units centered on the large estate; these units included all the individuals who participated in the activities of the plantation or were
attached to it, from the plantation owner who lorded it over
this miniature world to the humblest slave and *agregado* (tenant) who formed part of his large retinue. They formed economic, social, administrative, and in many respects religious
units. When I come to deal with the colony's administrative
organization, we shall see how this truly sovereign power of
the great landed proprietors, together with the units over
which this power extended, fitted into the structure of colonial
administration. For the moment we will consider only the social and economic characteristics of the patriarchal system.

We could trace the origins of this singular unit in our social
structure back to its Portuguese roots, and find that it stemmed
not only from the kingdom's organization and close-knit family
relations but also from the paternalism of the monarchical regime. But we need not go back so far, since there were more
than enough causes closer at hand: the circumstances of the
Brazilian environment. If the patriarchal system is found in
embryonic form in Portuguese institutions—a question I would
prefer to leave open—what really determined its splendid flow-
ering in Brazil was the local background from which it
emerged. The form assumed by the patriarchal clan was something peculiar to Brazilian organization.[36] It sprang from the
economic regime, from the plantation system that absorbed
most of the colony's production and wealth. Around the lords
and masters, the plantation owner and his family, were
grouped the other members of the clan, some because they had
no choice in the matter (the slaves), others drawn by the only
real and effective center of power and wealth. The domain was
vast enough to make it difficult for what happened within its
limits to be spread abroad. It was therefore completely under
the sway of the plantation owner, and his power extended over
the neighboring population which revolved within the orbit of

the domain. Public authority was weak and remote; it was not only unable to counterbalance the effective power established by the local senhor d'engenho, but was obliged to count on his help if it wished to function in the greater part of the territory falling within his sway, where on its own it would have proved feeble if not ineffectual. Real authority and prestige were in the hands of the great rural landlord, the lord of the domain. The administration was forced to recognize this and, as we shall see, did so effectively.

Even the Church and the priests, the second of the colony's administrative powers, were partly dependent on the great estate. The plantation or fazenda chapel and its chaplain, the nearby parish church and its priest, whose flock came mostly from the estate—were not chapel and chaplain, church and priest, accessories and servants of the great estate which provided almost all the faithful? [37] The only independent power, free of any shackles, was thus the large estate. It was the only provider of a means of livelihood and protection and all sought shelter under its great accommodating wing.

Built thus on a solid economic foundation and centralizing the colony's social life, the great domain gradually acquired all the other features that came to characterize it. From straightforward unit of production it soon became the organic cell of colonial society, and from this it was but a step to the "clan" of the great patriarchal Brazilian family. The process was not one that happened overnight, it unfolded slowly as a result of the peculiar conditions in which the large number of individuals concentrated on the estate lived out their lives, in a forced communion strictly limited to the confines of the estate.

Comparative analysis reveals that different stages of this development coexisted at the period we are considering, reflecting the length of time the regions had been settled. In the longest-established traditional centers of the north, Bahia and Pernambuco, with the long and sedentary past in which a stable way of life had been achieved, the patriarchal system had flourished and borne all its fruits. In Rio de Janeiro it had not gained so strong a hold; and in the northern regions newly

opened up in the second half of the eighteenth century,
Maranhão and the Campos dos Goitacases, it had hardly taken
hold at all. It was prolonged contact, repeated over successive
generations, that slowly molded the internal relations of the
domain, clothing them in such a way as to conceal the original
harshness of the slavocratic estate. The master ceased to be
simply the owner who exploited his lands and his workers for
commercial ends; the slave ceased to be only the manpower exploited. If he was made to work, even under the lash of the
overseer or the threat of the stocks set up in the *senzala* (slave
quarters), he was likewise entitled to count on the master's
protection, depending on him for all the other aspects and
needs of his life. The slave lived and died, as did his offspring
for successive generations, within the orbit of the master and
his domain, the small self-contained world which was the setting for his joys and griefs. Thus, the bonds between master
and slave were gradually strengthened; the force that bound
them together became more powerful despite the distance
between them. The same thing happened with the free workers
or tenants. They enjoyed a relative freedom which in practice
did not extend beyond the choice of exchanging one master for
another, and then not always. A little more detached from and
independent of the estate were the sharecroppers or copyholders, known as *obrigados:* there was greater friction in the relations between the smallholders and the senhor d'engenho and
several crises arose, but the rougher edges were eventually
smoothed by continual contact over the years.

Relations within the domain were therefore no longer confined to the master-slave relationship in a slaveholding and
commercially exploited estate. They became more humane and
more friendly, and embraced all kinds of emotional attachments. And if on the one hand these new relationships moder-
ated the master's absolute power and the strictness of his authority, on the other they reinforced them by making them
more acceptable. The master became the protector, almost the
father. Even the Catholic relationship of godfather to the child
sponsored, or the bridal pair whose marriage was witnessed,
was used to sanction the situation created by the new relation-

ships; and the terms *padrinho* (godfather), *afilhado* (godchild), and *compadre* * were the official titles used to designate the new relationships created.

Placed, then, at the very center of the colony's social life, the great landowner began to aristocratize himself. He could command the elements that constitute the basis and origin of all aristocracies: wealth, power, authority. To these was soon added tradition, continuity being assured by the patriarchal family with the absolute authority of the head of the household, who could arrange suitable marriages for his children. The great rural landowners were aristocratized not merely in name—fruit of the vanity and pretension of the titled—but in a real sense; they formed a separate and privileged class surrounded by respect and prestige, universal recognition of the eminent position they occupied.

A contemporary writer, who was no base flatterer but an enlightened and critical observer of Bahian life at the end of the eighteenth century, said of them: "They form in that Comarca a respectable Body per se, so noble by nature that in no other corporation, no other Country, is its equal to be found: it comprehends the best families of this or any other Continent; they are persons who do most honor to the Motherland, who give it greater wealth, brilliance and power, by the solidity of their establishments and their natural possessions." [38] Almost a century previously Antonil had made similar comments.

Having originated in this way, the colonial aristocracy assumed the characteristics of all aristocracies: pride and a respect for tradition, at least the tradition of the family and the blood that ran in its veins.[39] But this did not make it arrogant;

---

* *Compadre—* When a child was baptized, the parents of the child and the sponsors became *compadres* (lit. coparents) and considered themselves spiritually related. Similarly, witnesses at a wedding were called "godparents" by the couple, and the two sets of godparents became "compadres" to each other—hence *compadresco*, a ritual kin system implying relationships of mutual aid and support as strong as those of consanguinity. The institution of *compadrio* (or *compadresco*) also gave rise to a system of oligarchic nepotism and patronage known as *compadrismo*, in which the pseudo-kin relationships were used as political weapons.—Translator.

the general tone of Brazilian life, its indolence and easygoing
approach to human relationships did not encourage such an attitude. Nevertheless, it shared the weakness of all short-lived
privileged castes: the desire to ally itself with members of an
older privileged class. Vilhena satirized the colony's aristocrats
and referred to their coats of arms as having been "despatched
from the Court for the sum of 20,000 reis or so." [40]

All this applied particularly to the plantations in the colony's
major agricultural sectors: the sugar and tobacco plantations of
Bahia, Pernambuco, and Rio de Janeiro and the cotton plantations of Maranhão. *Mutatis mutandis,* the same pattern was repeated in the mining districts. And a similar development took
place in the pastoral centers, although on the cattle estates the
features of social life were somewhat altered by the peculiar
conditions in which pastoral activities were carried on. This
was most true of the backlands of the northeast. The limited
number of workers on an estate, the small proportion of slaves,
the system of labor in which the independence and self-
sufficiency of the *vaqueiro* was a prominent feature and in
which the workers employed had greater freedom of movement, the scattering of ranches and corrals that made up the
estate—all these factors limited the absolute authority of the
estate owner and restricted his power as compared to that of
the senhor d'engenho in the coastal areas. Absenteeism also
played its part, and was more prolonged and accentuated than
in agriculture. The classes were therefore more cut off from
each other, and the feeling of community we find in the other
sectors was more difficult to foster. [41] Nevertheless, the same
patriarchal and aristocratic features, although with individual
characteristics, were present in the pastoral regions.

Cattle raising in southern Minas was, however, slightly
different. I have already cited St. Hilaire's observation that he
found a democratic tendency in the social customs and habits
of the upper classes of this region, and this despite the presence of numerous slaves. The estate owner and his family were
more uncouth and less haughty; they were more like prosperous European peasant farmers than aristocrats which they
tended to be in the mining districts. The fazendeiro and his

sons took an active part in the management of the estate, tended the cattle, and cared for the crops. They even became leaders of the cattle droves or mule convoys sent to the markets on the coast. Work was thus held in greater respect and was not considered discreditable or degrading.[42] In the campos of the extreme south the way of life was also conducive to this more democratic tone; there was greater equality, fewer absentee landowners, more contact between *estancieiros* (estate owners) and *peões* (ranch hands). It should be pointed out, however, that in the south, as in the northeast, slaves were rare. In any case, the character and way of life of the southerners was rather special and possessed individual characteristics.

But in spite of all these differences and attenuating circumstances, the existence of pronounced social distinctions and the absolute and patriarchal domination of the owner and master were elements invariably associated with all the colony's large landed estates. And with greater or lesser differences, the social group centered on these estates performed the same function and occupied the same place in the economic, social, and administrative life of the colony as in the purest and most complete form of the system described above.

The situation was, of course, quite different in the other sector of the colony's economy, comprising the small-scale agriculturalists and the smallholders. For the humble independent copyholders and small-time sugar planters, tobacco growers, or cotton planters—and we have seen that there were large numbers of these—and even for the farmers raising food crops on the outskirts of the great agricultural centers, the situation was not really so different. They lived, so to speak, in the pockets of the great estate and revolved within its orbit. The scope of the small units they formed was nowhere large enough to give rise to the characteristics of the great estate, but neither was it enough to make them completely self-sufficient. They suffered from the overpowering proximity of the big landowner and participated in the regime he established in almost the same way as the tenants and sharecroppers.

In regions where the large landed estate had either never

been established or for some reason had not managed to survive, a distinctive pattern emerged. Such regions included the southern coastlands of Bahia, Espírito Santo, and other parts of the colony. The districts colonized by Azoreans in Santa Catarina also come into this category by reason of their special circumstances. Rio Grande do Sul can be omitted because it had already turned to cattle raising and the charque industry.

Most of the population of these regions, or at least in a good part of them, fell within the unclassified category of colonial society analyzed above. The agriculture practiced was backward and primitive, and followed the indigenous or *caboclo* pattern. If it managed to contribute any surplus to trade, this was in relatively small proportions and generally only sporadically. The social relations established in these regions of low economic level were, thus, profoundly different from those in which commercial agriculture was practiced, stemming as they did from an activity carried on in such contrasting conditions. Here there was nothing remotely like the great patriarchal landlord, aristocratic and powerful, dominating his vast circle of slaves and retainers. There were greater uniformity and equality and hence greater independence and less of a hierarchy. But these were negative characteristics, arising from the low standard of living, the slack pace and backward nature of the activities; they were reflections of the lack of organization rather than distinctive and individual social institutions.

Azorean colonization of Santa Catarina should be considered apart. Here, there was something completely different, a singular feature in the physiognomy of Brazil. We have already seen that here slaves were rare and the population was ethnically homogeneous. There was no dominant group or caste, no marked hierarchy of class. In short, here was a community whose parallel was to be found only in the temperate colonies of America, a pattern outside the norms of tropical colonization, forming an island in the Brazil of slaveholding landed estates and their derivatives.[43]

The patterns we have been considering all apply to the rural areas, but having originated and developed in these areas they were transferred almost untouched to their urban centers. Most of these centers were in fact no more than rural appendages, a simple reflection of the rural way of life. They grew up around the parish church and the small shops.[44] Nearly all the inhabitants of such an urban community were small farmers or sharecropping agriculturalists living in the neighborhood, sometimes at considerable distances from the town, who came to the center only on Sundays and holidays. On these days the centers were animated, active, full of noise and bustle, but on other days they were empty, silent, and dead. This was because the population was engaged in rural activities during ordinary working days and only went into the town on Sundays and holidays to fulfill their religious obligations, to buy and sell, to meet their friends, or to participate in celebrations and festivals—in short, to lead a "social life" after the long days of segregation on the farm.

The fixed population of these small towns was made up of a few traders—and even these were often local fazendeiros who added to their income by keeping a store as well as practicing their rural activities—occasionally an artisan or two (since who was there to employ them when the fazendas had nearly all they needed and employed their own workers?), and a larger number of vagrants and prostitutes. There were so many prostitutes, even in the smallest villages and mining camps, that the leaders of cattle droves and pack trains always tried to give them a wide berth, pitching camp in the open fields rather than run the risk of having the drovers and drivers fall into debauchery and dissipation. In these small towns even the priest was not always a fixed resident. He generally added to his priostly functions the more earthy function of the fazendeiro or miner, a fact which astonished and horrified the pious St. Hilaire, who saw the spiritual neglect to which the pastor's flock was abandoned.

The larger the town, the greater the size of the fixed population. Functions became more specialized: the trader was exclusively a trader and did not run his store only in the hours when he was free of his agricultural commitments; artisans and craftsmen were detached from rural activities and set up on their own. Fixed permanent authorities began to appear; the judge was no longer simply a fazendeiro appointed to perform judicial duties in his spare time. In the more important *jul-gados* (local courts) there were even educated judges sent from outside the district—the *juiz de fora*. There were also public servants who could keep themselves on their salaries and who no longer had to supplement their incomes by engaging in other activities: notaries, clerks, bailiffs, and so forth.

But even in the colony's largest centers the population of rural origin continued to predominate, if not in numbers at least in prestige and wealth. The cream of society in the large centers was drawn from the fazendeiros, the senhores d'engenho and the wealthy copyholders. They lived on their fazendas and engenhos during the busiest season, or at harvest time—if they were very conscientious, which was not always the case—but for the rest of the year they preferred the pleasures and diversions of the city. Absenteeism was the rule among the big landed proprietors, and this fact was deplored by all who wanted to see an improvement in agricultural production, usually left to negligent or incompetent managers. "The big landowners of Brazil," wrote Councillor Veloso de Oliveira in 1810, "particularly those of the seaboard, almost all live in the cities and towns, abandoning the culture and management of their lands to the crass ignorance and senseless acts of yokels from the Azores islands or poor emigrants from the north of Portugal. . . ." [45] And the President of the Rio de Janeiro Board of Inspection, Judge Rocha Gameiro, writing in 1798 to Minister D. Rodrigo de Sousa Coutinho, described the state of agriculture in the colony as largely due to the absenteeism of the landowners, one of the greatest evils with which it was afflicted. [46]

Urban centers were thus a reflection of the prevailing rural conditions. Here, too, the rural senhores formed the upper class. But they were no longer alone. They were joined by the higher officials of the military, civil, and ecclesiastical administration, who even enjoyed social precedence over them: viceroys, captains-general, governors, commanders, high-ranking army officers, judges, bishops. And there were also the professional men: advocates and solicitors in particular, who were effective members of the judiciary.[47]

Commerce gave rise to a distinct and well-defined class in these large centers. I have already referred to the virtual monopoly of commerce held by the natives of the realm. But even if we do not confine ourselves to the small retail merchants or purveyors of necessities who, according to Vilhena, were legion in Bahia [48] and were of course of little social importance, the scope of commercial enterprise seems to have been small. We must distinguish two branches of commercial activity: the merchant proper, officially registered and licensed, and the simple *comissário,* whose rights and activities were limited. The comissário corresponds to the modern commercial agent or concessionaire who always acts on behalf and in the name of a third party. According to the Marquis of Lavradio, true merchants were few in number even in the colony's largest commercial center, Rio de Janeiro:

Most of the people who are here given the name of merchant are nothing but humble agents . . . ; the only firm that comes within the merchant category is that owned by Francisco de Araújo Pereira, in association with his cousins and a few partners in Europe. Those merchants who are here considered wealthy, such as Brás Carneiro Leão, Manuel da Costa Cardoso, José Caetano Alves and some others, have amassed their wealth from the large number of commissions they have been given, from the goods or ships consigned to them. . . . These men, although they are persons of means, honest and true, I cannot consider merchants because it must be confessed that they know not what this profession means, nor the books that they need, nor how to order their bookkeeping and accounts.[49]

With all its limitations, commerce played an important role in the colony's social life. The social standing of merchants was not, however, very high. On the contrary, they were looked down on and commerce was even considered somewhat de-

grading. This attitude stemmed from the mediaeval prejudice
against merchants brought over from Portugal and was preserved until very recently in Brazil.[50] Many persons of means
in the colony consequently kept secret their commercial interests and activities by sheltering behind a figurehead appointed
to handle their affairs.[51] Nevertheless, the merchants became
the creditors of the planters, and it was they who financed
commercial agriculture. Senhores d'engenho, copyholders, and
fazendeiros were all indebted to the merchants and found it
difficult to keep out of debt, since their social position, vanity,
and prodigal upbringing led them to become extravagant
spenders, and they often found themselves in serious difficulties as a result of their feckless and spendthrift ways.[52] Officially the merchant was not subject to restriction and was on
an equal footing with the other proprietary classes. The old
Portuguese laws which had barred merchants from holding
office in the municipal senates (town councils) had fallen into
disuse in Brazil, and there were merchants on all the municipal
councils of the colony's cities and towns.[53] They even formed a
recognized and officially esteemed category, and in this capacity participated in the deliberations of the public administration. Thus, on the boards of inspection created in 1751 for
the colony's chief commercial centers to supervise the sugar
and tobacco trade, merchants were allowed two official representatives, in the same way as the senhores d'engenho and the
tobacco planters, who were also allowed two each.

In these conditions commerce occupied a prominent position, in spite of the ambiguous social standing of the merchants. They were able to make a stand against the colony's
other proprietary class, the landowners, and dispute their
preeminence. And this is precisely what happened. The hostility that arose as a result had profound political repercussions.
There was a repetition in Brazil of the traditional rivalry between noblemen and bourgeoisie which fills the history of Europe. And in Brazil the ill-feeling was sharpened by national-
ism, since, as we have seen, the merchants were nearly all
European-born Portuguese, whereas the planters were descend-

ants of the country's first settlers and pioneers. They felt, therefore, that they had stronger claims.

The mother country's policy and administration had, of course, to placate both factions, which were equally powerful. Her true sympathies lay, at least in the persons of her representatives in the colony the great majority of whom were likewise European-born, with the merchants. And bitterness increased as the "national" characteristics of the contending factions became more and more clearly defined. The distinction between European-born and Brazilian-born colonials was at first blurred, was felt rather than expressed. It was a secondary issue, the distinction being made de facto rather than de jure. But with time it became a passionate and fundamental issue. This distinction had already started to become an important one in the period we are considering and to be overtly expressed: colonials had become "Brazilians" rather than "Portuguese," whereas hitherto all persons in the colony, both European-born and colonial-born, had been known as "Portuguese." "Brazilian" had up to then been restricted to residents in the colony or persons who had amassed their fortunes in the colony even when they were European-born.

The rivalry between landowners and merchants, exacerbated by this nationalistic element, had long been manifest in the colony and had expressed itself in violent outbreaks such as the Beckmann revolt in Maranhão and the War of the Mascates (or Peddlers' War) in Pernambuco.* As time passed it was further sharpened and prolonged by the participation of other groups. Monopoly of commercial opportunities by the *reinóis* affected other classes of the colony's native-born population, barring them from positions they might otherwise have filled

---

* The Beckmann revolt was an anti-Portuguese riot which took place in Maranhão in 1684 under the leadership of Manuel Beckmann, a sugar planter of São Luis. The War of the Mascates took place between Olinda, the provincial capital of Pernambuco, and its neighboring seaport of Recife. Olinda was the town of the sugar-planting oligarchs, and Recife the town of the mascates. See C. R. Boxer, *The Golden Age of Brazil*, pp. 106 et seq., for a fascinating account of the battles between planters and peddlers.—Translator.

when openings were so difficult to find. Eventually everyone became involved in this rivalry, and feeling against the *mascates* (peddlers), *pés-de-chumbo* (literally, "leadfeet," roughly corresponding to "blockheads") and *marinheiros* (sailors)— the insulting epithets applied to the Portuguese—ran high among Brazilian-born colonists. The situation became clearly defined in the agitations preceding independence and the period that followed, and was in fact prolonged for some time thereafter, frequently degenerating into ferocious armed battles.[54]

Administration

In order to understand the colonial administration we must first of all get rid of a number of concepts which have become virtual preconceptions in our own time, but which at the time we are considering had only just begun to enter into contemporary ideas and the judicial systems in force; the Portuguese administration certainly took no account of such notions. Thus, the idea of the essential distinction and separation between the "functions" of a state and its "powers"—the legislative, executive, and judicial branches of government—was completely ignored, as were the parallel spheres of the different state activities, general, provincial, and local. Finally, no distinction was made at the individual level between the two different spheres of a man's obligations, each different in origin and now differently regulated: his legal obligations, stemming from his external and judicial relations, and his religious obligations, arising from the intimate claims of his religious beliefs and the complex of practices and rules of behavior to which they bound him—a moral and sacramental code regulated by religion. Lacerda de Almeida was to call this distinction "the dividing of a man into two distinct beings: the citizen of the Republic and the son of the Church." [1] Today, all these notions are regarded as "scientific principles"; that is to say, inherent and universal absolutes. To reject them in practice in the judicial organization of a society in what is

347

called "positive law" would be considered "an error" in the modern "science" of jurisprudence; an error of the same order and magnitude as designing a building without allowing for the law of gravity. But the fact is that such notions were not regarded in this way by the Portuguese monarchy of the eighteenth century, of which Brazil was a part. Whether this is today considered an "error," the result of ignorance or backwardness, as the progressives would say, or whether, as I personally believe to be more accurate, it is considered the result of a particular "historical moment," I shall not here pursue.

What concerns us here is that in the period we are considering, the Portuguese administration and hence its colonial administration was guided by quite different principles in which these concepts played no part. The state was regarded as an undivided whole, functioning as such and embracing all aspects and manifestations of its individual citizens. There was, of course, a division of labor, since the same organs and representatives of the state could not simultaneously exercise their functions in all branches, nor was it convenient unduly to increase the individual power of each. The only complete embodiment of this power, the synthesis of the state, was the king; the division of functions stemmed from the necessary delegation of his power. But this division was formal rather than functional: it corresponded to a practical necessity rather than to any essential division between the specific functions of the state. Even the clear and absolute distinction between "public" law, which affected collective relationships, and "private" law, affecting the individual, a fundamental distinction on which the entire structure of modern law is based, must be understood in a sense quite different from its modern one.

It would be impossible for me to embark here on theoretical development of these questions, since this would mean going into the historical philosophy of law which calls for special treatment and would lead us far from the subject at hand. The foregoing observations—observations, not a statement of principles—were intended merely to clarify the historical, and purely historical, analysis of colonial administration which follows, to prepare the reader, who is more accustomed to concepts which must in this context be set aside, and to provide a point of departure for this analysis. The only broad and general concept that effectively governed colonial administration was the concept of the Portuguese Monarchy as a vast, organic body with the King as its head, leader, father, representative of God on earth, supreme dispenser of all graces and favors, rightful regulator of all activities, or, more precisely, of all personal and individual "expressions" of his subjects and vassals. All, down to the meanest vassal, who had his role and performed his function, however humble, were recognized and effective parts of the organic whole, the political organism of monarchy. Having thus rid ourselves of all the concepts which arose after the period with which we are concerned, we shall not run the risk of falling into glaring anachronisms, so frequent in this field and so misleading.

One further point should be borne in mind: the colonial administration displayed little or nothing of that uniformity and symmetry we are today accustomed to expect from administrative institutions. By this I mean clearly distinguished functions, well-defined division of authority, organized arrangement, based on a uniform principle of hierarchy, of the different administrative bodies. In the public law of the Portuguese monarchy, general rules for the division of authority, the formal structure of the administration and its various departments were few or nonexistent, and there was no definitive or overall regulation of these matters of the modern type. If we study the colony's administrative legislation, we find a mass of enactments, subject to continual modifications often of a contradictory nature, which appeared to be entirely unconnected and to pile up with no guiding plan whatsoever. A labyrinth in which a modern jurist, accustomed to neatness and clarity of general principle from which, with "Aristotelian logic," all special rules and concrete applications follow with absolute rigor, would find himself lost.

Since the last codification of laws known as the *Ordenações filipinas* (the Philippine Code), promulgated in 1603,* which was the basis of Portuguese law, there had been one and a half centuries of decrees, edicts, instructions, letters royal, royal provisions, orders, and other enactments which formed a complicated and copious body of law known as *legislação extravagante* (supplementary legislation). But not all the legislation preceding the basic code had been repealed, particularly legislation relating to the administration of the colonies, and much of it continued in force after promulgation of the code and even up to independence—and how many laws remained in force, indeed, even after that—including decrees dating from the first century of colonization.

The code itself was far from what is understood by a modern codification—a logical, systematic, and accurate collection of statutes. And it was this chaotic jumble that constituted the colony's administrative law. Finding one's way through the tangled mass is a formidable task. The administrative organs and functions mentioned in one place disappear in another or appear under different names and in different forms; persons to whom authority had been delegated often received their instructions in the form of letters which became law, and which frequently established new rules or a different allocation of functions and competence from those previously in force. When a new administrative organ or function was created, the law made no attempt to harmonize it with existent bodies or functions; minute and often contradictory instructions were issued for the matter at hand, only the immediate needs being provided for. Even when one of the administrative organs or functions, or something similar, existed elsewhere, the new regulations took no account of the fact and laid down special provisions.

* During the reign of Philip III of Spain and II of Portugal (1598–1621). The union of the two crowns lasted from 1580–1640, covering the reigns of Philip II of Spain (I of Portugal), 1580–1598; Philip III of Spain (II of Portugal); and Philip IV of Spain (III of Portugal), 1621–1665. Dom João, Duke of Braganza, was proclaimed King John IV of Portugal in 1640.—Translator.

All this was further complicated by the general practice of reinforcing all previous orders, or frequently appealing to the "usage of the kingdom," making it difficult for even those contemporaries well versed in law to pick their way through the confusion and to know exactly how matters stood. Consequently, application of the law was seldom uniform, but varied in accordance with the place and the time, and was often ignored in practice, some reason always being found should one prove necessary to justify this disobedience. Hence, the relationship between what we find written down in the legal documents and what we find in actual practice is often vague, if not downright nonexistent. We have thus to be extremely cautious when considering the legal texts, since what concerns us here is the practice rather than the theory, and we should seek other sources for a true picture of the colony's administrative life. Unfortunately, such sources are few. Copies of official documents have been published, but only for a limited number of the country's administrative regions: Rio de Janeiro and São Paulo; fewer for Minas Gerais, Bahia, and Pernambuco; and almost none for the others. And given the unsystematic nature of colonial administration, even with these sources at our disposal, we are left in some uncertainty as to the rest of the colony and hence in doubt about the system as a whole.

For all these reasons we should approach our survey of colonial administration prepared for all kinds of incongruences. Above all, we must not expect to find the order and architectural harmony of modern governmental institutions, which it would be vain to attempt to project onto a past by nature chaotic.

By and large, it can be said that the Portuguese administration extended its organization and system to Brazil, and created nothing new for the colony. The *donatárias* (proprietary captaincies) * were an exception, but the "captains-donatory" very early disappeared and were replaced by governors and

---

* *Donatária*—the captaincy commanded by a donatário, or proprietary landlord.—Translator.

captains-general. Nevertheless, although their functions did have an individual stamp, they confirm rather than invalidate the observation about the mother country's lack of originality in her administrative organization of the colony, her inability to create different administrative bodies especially adapted to the conditions prevailing in her colonial settlements. For the governor was a hybrid figure, who combined the functions of the military governor (*governador das armas*) entrusted with military and defense matters in the kingdom's own provinces, with some of those of other officials, such as the governor of justice (*governador da justiça*), and even some of the functions of the king. His duties were never clearly defined, and his authority and jurisdiction always varied widely from captaincy to captaincy and from governor to governor. They varied, above all, in accordance with the personalities and capabilities of the men appointed to the office. And since the closest model for the office existing in the kingdom was that of *governador das armas*, the colonial governors tended to be primarily military governors, with adverse effects on the proper functioning of the colonial administration.

Apart from this, innovations were insignificant, and there were no alterations to the system and character of the administration which was a perfect copy of that of the kingdom. The differences that arose were due to particular local conditions, so profoundly different from those of the mother country, to which the colonial administration was obliged to adapt itself; but this adaptation was carried out in practice and not provided for by law. It was a spontaneous adjustment, forced on the colonial authorities by circumstance and always made on their initiative. Laws framed with special reference to conditions existing in the colony were few and far between, and there was certainly never any systematic or deliberate attempt to understand the differences and to embody them in concrete provisions. Only in the matter of taxation, when the problems of imposts, tolls, and taxes and the best methods of collecting them came up, did the Portuguese administration make some attempt to depart from its routine practice. But even then, what lack of imagination was displayed! The checkered history of the royal fifths shows this clearly enough. But apart from this, practically all the institutions we find in colonial Brazil are no more than straight copies of those in Portugal. The best institutions, those that appear to be most original, turn out to be no more than poorly disguised imitations or borrowings. We could give many instances of this, and indeed it would be easier and quicker to list the few original creations.[2] But, not to dwell too long on the subject, we will recall only the most flagrant instance, and perhaps the most harmful in its effects, of this set practice of servilely copying the kingdom's systems for application in the colony: the centralization of power and concentration of authorities in the capitals and seats, leaving the rest of the territory practically ungoverned, authority being merely nominal in the remoter regions which were often separated from the nearest administrative center by hundreds of leagues.

The size of the country, the scattered pattern of settlement, and the lack of resources naturally made the problem of extending authority in an effective manner to all parts of the territory a difficult one to solve. But instead of getting round these difficulties by dispersing the local authorities over as wide an area as possible, the crown adhered to its usual administrative procedure, evolved for a tiny kingdom, and concentrated most of its authorities in the principal centers, where their control was severely limited by their distance from the majority of the settlements they were appointed to administer. The high courts of chancery (*relações*) of Rio de Janeiro and Bahia, for instance, each disposed of more than thirty officials, including royal judges, crown lawyers, notaries, and other officials, all handsomely paid; whereas in the greater part of the colony no judicial authority was present or accessible, or, in more favored cases, the administration of justice was in the hands of ignorant and incompetent lay judges known as *juizes ordinários* (justices of the peace), who were ordinary citizens chosen by popular election and performing their services free.

A similar pattern was repeated in the colony's territorial

administrative divisions. The authorities—*ouvidores* (royal judges), justices, senators,* and other officials—were concentrated in towns which were the seats of municipal councils and districts (*comarcas*). This was the model for the kingdom, and no one thought of adapting it to the requirements of the colony. If a settlement had the status of a town, all these authorities had to be present; if not, there was simply no local authority. This system led to two extremes of equal absurdity and both detrimental to the colony's administration: towns which acted as official administrative centers for an immense tributary neighborhood, often inaccessible to the officials concentrated in the seat; and nominal "towns" which had populations so small that there were not even enough townspeople to fill the public offices.[3] There was nothing between these two extremes.

The difficulties of administering such vast areas were partially overcome by the practice of sending out *correições* and *visitações*, a kind of administrative expedition organized by the crown authorities as a means of visiting the outlying settlements falling within their competence. But these visits which, given the prevailing system of centralizing the authority, should have been current practice, were only undertaken by the more diligent authorities. And even in these cases, the administrative expeditions did not serve the purpose intended, because their chief objective, like that of similar expeditions in the kingdom, was inspection, general supervision, and the hearing of appeals; whereas in reality there was less need for this than there was for direct and effective administration.

But we will leave aside these criticisms of the colonial administration for the moment, as they will be considered later in the context of a general critical analysis of the system as a whole, and turn now to the colony's administrative structure. For the purposes of administration, Brazil did not form a whole

---

* The senators were members of the *senado da câmara* (municipal council), usually comprising two justices of the peace (*juizes ordinários*), three councillors or aldermen (*vereadores*), and a procurator or attorney (*procurador*). All these members were known as *senadores*.—Translator.

in the eyes of the crown. What existed on the other side of the ocean was, for the mother country, a number of colonies or provinces, even "countries," as they were sometimes called, which under the official designation of "captaincies" were integrated into the Portuguese monarchy and were as much a part of it as were any of its other parts: the provinces of the Kingdom of Portugal, those of the Kingdom of the Algarve,* and the establishments in Africa and the East.

The monarchy formed a heterogeneous complex of kingdoms, states, European and overseas provinces, captaincies, and other administrative divisions of no fixed title, something like the British Commonwealth of our own time. What is today known as Brazil consisted of a number of such divisions, and for the purposes of analyzing colonial administration we should bear this in mind. Geographically and in general popular opinion, Brazil formed a unit, but officially it appeared as such only in the honorific titles of "Viceroy of Brazil" (and even then he was more often currently known as "Viceroy of Rio de Janeiro," the seat of the vice-regency) and "Prince of Brazil," the title of the heirs to the throne of the Braganza dynasty. "Brazil" also appeared in what was called the "state of Brazil," to distinguish it from the "state of Pará and Maranhão." These "states" nominally comprised respectively the southern captaincies and the captaincies of Maranhão, Pará, and their subordinate captaincies, Piauí and São José do Rio Negro. But these names had long since lost their practical significance.

There was great confusion between these two pseudo-states, and even in the text of a legal enactment as important as that of the decree of August 17, 1758, which approved the *Diretório* or Code governing the Indians, we find the designation "state of Brazil" used in two different ways, to designate the whole of Brazil and in the limited sense noted above. The only remaining trace of the former distinction of the period we are considering was the jurisdiction exercised by the *Casa de Suplicação*

---

* The Kingdom of Algarve was conquered from the Moors in the thirteenth century, and Portugal was thenceforth officially styled "The Kingdom of Portugal and the Algarves."—Translator.

(Court of Appeal) in Lisbon, which functioned as a higher tribunal for the captaincies of the state of Pará and Maranhão, whereas for the other captaincies appeals from the lower courts were made to the *relacões* at Bahia and Rio de Janeiro. Similarly, the dioceses of Pará and Maranhão were suffragans of the Archiepiscopal See of Lisbon, whereas ecclesiastical jurisdiction over the other captaincies was exercised by the Archbishop of Bahia.

The administration of the colony (and of all Portuguese possessions in Africa and the East) was controlled by the *Conselho Ultramarino* (Overseas Council) under the presidency of one of the four secretaries of state, the Secretary of State for Maritime Affairs and Overseas Dominions. The overseas councillors handled all colonial matters with the exception of those falling within the purview of the *Mesa de Consciência e Ordens* (Board of Conscience and Orders), another Portuguese administrative body concerned with ecclesiastical affairs, administration of the property of deceased or absent persons (in the legal sense), and administration of the affairs of the three military orders (the Orders of Christ, Aviz, and Santiago). These orders had been established in Brazil but the role they played was practically nonexistent.[4]

The Overseas Council's functions were not limited to the exercise of general supervisory control of the administration. It deliberated on all colonial matters, however trivial, and was concerned not only with matters referred from elsewhere but also with matters calling for direct decision. Delegates of the crown, however elevated their category, were unable to take a single step without the council's express order or agreement. The extensive and detailed correspondence of the governors and the minute orders and letters royal dispatched by the Council reveal the minutiae with which the home government's direct provisions concerned themselves. J. F. Lisboa writes:

The degree to which the mother country meddled in the most trifling colonial affairs reached almost unbelievable extremes. Petty officials had to account for themselves to Lisbon; it was at Lisbon that all the debts of absentees exceeding the tiniest minimal sum had to be cleared; minor problems arising from the collection and administration of certain tithes would wend their way up from Bahia to Lisbon. And finally, it was from Lisbon that were dispatched all the advocates licenses, passports, discharges, and exemptions from military service, together with diverse provisions concerning fireworks, the make and quality of sugar chests and, however incredible it may seem, the skirts, nocturnal excursions, and wantonness of slave girls.[5]

Everything was reported to Lisbon, and everything was of interest to the Overseas Council—at least in theory, since in practice the physical impossibility of coping with such a formidable amount of paper work not only involved delays in the dispatch of business of anything up to ten years, but also meant that a great number of dispatches were left to eternal repose in the filing cabinets of the archives.

The captaincies that made up Brazil were of two types, principal and subordinate. The latter were more or less subject to the former, as in the case of the captaincies of Rio Grande do Sul and Santa Catarina, which were subject to Rio de Janeiro, or that of Rio Negro, attached to Pará. Ceará and others were also to a certain extent attached to Pernambuco. But by and large, the powers of government were the same in both these provincial categories. Only the title of the governor differed: captain-general and governor for the principal captaincies, and captain-major (not to be confused with the military rank) or simply governor for the others. After 1763, the captain-general of Rio de Janeiro (and before this date the captain-general of Bahia) was also given the high-sounding but hollow title of "Viceroy of Brazil." His powers in principle were no greater than those of his fellow governors in the other captaincies and did not extend beyond his territorial jurisdiction as captain-general.[6]

The captaincy was the largest administrative unit in the colony. Its territory was divided into comarcas (judicial districts), generally few in number.[7] The comarca was made up of *têrmos* (counties), with their seats in one of the local towns or cities.[8]

The têrmos were further subdivided into *freguesias* (par-

ishes), an ecclesiastical division which formed the parish, seat
of a parish church, but which also served as a civil administrative center. Finally, the freguesias were divided into *bairros*
(suburbs), a rather vague division which appears to have
played its chief role in the organization of the *ordenanças* (territorial military companies), as we shall see below.

Let us now briefly consider the formal administrative structures of these various divisions. The head of the captaincy was
the governor (viceroy, captain-general, captain-major, or simply governor). His duties were primarily military. This did not
necessarily involve the appointment of a professional military
man to the post—in fact, such appointments were few. But the
governor was considered supreme commander of all the armed
forces in his captaincy and in the subordinate captaincies, not
merely nominally or only on certain occasions, but effectively
and permanently. He had untrammeled control of all military
and defense matters, and no other highranking army officer in
the captaincy was responsible for its military affairs as a whole.
The various commanders were all subordinate to the governor,
and their authority was restricted to their own corps or unit.[9]
Much of the governor's attention and energy was taken up by
his military duties, particularly in captaincies where there
were pressing military problems. This was the case in Rio de
Janeiro, whose subordinate captaincies of Santa Catarina and
Rio Grande do Sul were situated on the troubled frontiers,
where continual friction with neighbors arose. The essentially
military nature of the governor's functions were then clearly
revealed. We need only note the prominent place occupied by
military matters, and the amount of space devoted to these in
the correspondence and reports of the viceroys of Rio de
Janeiro; there was little left for any other matters.[10]

But although vested with military authority, the governor
was in charge of administration in general. There is no need to
enumerate his powers, since the authority he enjoyed was sufficiently comprehensive to cover all sectors and was subject to
relatively few restrictions.[11] In view of this it is hardly surprising that he was liable to exercise absolute power, the feature of

colonial administration which has been most strongly criticized, particularly by nineteenth-century historians who were
still close to the period when the dreaded figure of the governor cast its shadow over the land. Criticism was often exaggerated, however, since the governor's appearance of regality
—and in the eyes of his contemporaries he seemed a virtual
king—masked many weaknesses which only now, when old
passions have ceased to smoulder and the archives have
yielded up their secrets, can properly be estimated.

In the first place the governor was subject to the active
meddling of the home government, which kept a watchful eye
constantly trained on the colony. We have already seen the
lengths to which this interference went. The governor was,
thus, usually bound by precise and strict instructions, drafted
with almost extravagant attention to detail, and for which he
could seldom if ever claim prior consultation. We find a mass
of orders but hardly any recommendations (*consultas*) dispatched from the kingdom.[12] He also had to render detailed
accounts of his administrative expenditure, particularly at the
end of his term when the payment of the last year's expenses
was suspended until the accounts had been audited and approved. And the home government was only too willing to lend
an ear to complaints and criticisms, regardless of their source.
If this was of little benefit to the population as a whole, it was
because what really interested the central authorities was the
fiscal aspect, revenue, fraud, and contraband.

The other authorities in the colony must also be taken into
account. Although their official positions were inferior to that
of the governor, they acted as ponderable counterweights to
his authority. This was largely due to the curious hierarchical
structure that prevailed. In many cases, indeed in the most important, these authorities were not really inferior rungs of the
administrative ladder in the modern sense of the concept; they
were not entirely subject to the governor's authority, nor were
they expected merely to carry out his orders. The high courts,
or *relações*, for instance, were both judicial and administrative
bodies, and the governor was simply a member, although he

acted as president, since presidency of the relações automatically devolved upon the governor of the captaincy. But the
other members were in no way subordinate to him. The same
applied to the boards concerned with the collection and administration of taxes, the *juntas de arrecadação.*

The fact that these and other administrative institutions
were collective entities organized in corporate form was no less
weighty a factor in checking the governor's power. There is no
need to stress the depersonalization and diminution of individual responsibility resulting from such a system, and the im-
paired self-sufficiency and independence of its members. Nothing was more calculated to create delays in the dispatch of
business. It is easy to see how enervated the governor's actions
would be, once sieved through a hostile or antagonistic body,
as was often the case.

Finally, there were a number of important colonial administrative organs and administrative matters in which the governor was not allowed to interfere at all, at least officially. The
intendências of the gold and diamond districts and the boards
of inspection mentioned above may be cited. All these curbs to
the governor's authority were the result of the Portuguese administration's general system of checks and balances—limitation of authority, strict control, oppressive supervision of
official activities—a system that was not determined by the
laudable desire for orderliness and method, but by the general
suspicion that characterized the attitude of the home government toward all its agents. It hardly bothered to disguise its
assumption that all of them were guilty of negligence, incompetence, and even outright dishonesty. Confidence in the ability of its agents to take independent action, counterbalanced
by the assumption of full responsibility for such decisions, was
something that never penetrated the processes of the Portuguese administration.

There was yet another circumstance of a more general order
that clipped the wings of Brazil's colonial governors: the unruliness that characterized most of the country. This was the
result of geographical conditions and the way in which the

country had been formed: the vastness of the territory, the scattered pattern of settlement, the chaotic and heterogeneous composition of the population, the lack of social stability, and the failure to educate and prepare the people for any form of control. These were profound and general factors which will be considered as a whole in the following chapter. But the most striking consequence of this widespread unruliness, which was directly reflected in the administration, was the flouting of public authority, the undermining of its powers, which were severely limited and often set at naught by systematic disobedience and indiscipline.

In spite of all these limitations, however, the governor's power and authority should not be underestimated, nor should his importance in the colony's administrative life be diminished. No other colonial authorities had like powers, and none could command the whole of the captaincy's armed forces. The simple fact that the governor represented the king and embodied the royal authority, with power to speak in the king's name, was in itself sufficient, given the system of absolute monarchy found in Portugal, to ensure that the role he played was a prominent one.[13] Another factor was the colony's distance from the mother country and the inordinate delays in the latter's instructions.[14] There was thus ample opportunity for the governors to make full use, or even abuse, of their powers. And there was no lack of captains-general of this stamp.[15] But from the reports and correspondence preserved, it is also clear that even the most energetic governors had to contend with great difficulties and encountered constant obstacles to the enforcement of their authority and the attainment of their aims. The lengthy and admirable *Relatório* presented by the Marquis of Lavradio—one of the greatest administrators of Colonial Brazil —to his successor after a decade in office (1769–1779), makes this amply evident.

Let us now consider the other administrative organs. These can be divided into three groups: military, general, and fiscal. Other organs of a special nature will be described last. The captaincies' armed forces were made up of the *tropa de linha* (regular troops), the *milicias* (militia), and the *corpos de ordenanças* (territorial units). The first were the regular professional troops permanently under arms. These tropa de linha were invariably made up of Portuguese regiments, which retained the names of the places where they had been raised, such as the *Bragança* and *Moura* regiments, stationed at the end of the eighteenth century in Rio de Janeiro, or the *Estremós* Regiment, quartered in Santa Catarina, Parati, and Angra dos Reis.[16] Reinforcements for these permanent troops from the kingdom were recruited in the colony itself. In principle, only whites were eligible for enlistment, but this naturally proved unenforceable in Brazil, with its mixed population. There was, therefore, a good deal of tolerance of the enlistment of colored men, but Negroes and dark-skinned mulattoes were generally excluded.[17] Apart from voluntary enlistments—and these were few—there was the enforced "enlistment" of criminals and other undesirable elements of whom the authorities wished to be rid. When sufficient "volunteers" were not forthcoming, the authorities resorted to conscription.

The prospect of military service during the colonial period —and even in the empire—was dreaded, and "conscription" was the greatest popular bogey; oral tradition has kept alive the memory of this fear in many places even today. And it was quite justified. There was scarcely any standard for the recruitment of men, and no formal organization. It depended on the needs of the moment and the arbitrary decision of the authorities. Once the quota had been settled on, recruiting sergeants sallied forth in search of victims; nowhere and at no hour of day or night was there safety from their marauding. They broke into private homes, forcing windows and doors, and even marched into schools and colleges, interrupting classes to tear away the hapless students.[18] Anyone judged fit to bear arms was instantly bundled off to the recruiting post in total disregard for any pleas or protests. We learn from Vilhena that a whole regiment was often dispersed through the city (Bahia) with orders to take into custody anyone within reach at an appointed hour, provided they were "white" and not already in the forces. All the individuals captured in this way were taken to the army guardroom, and only there were those fit for military service selected. In some cases, out of hundreds of captives only a couple of dozen were found to be suitable. Even priests suffered this outrage—and this in a country in which the cassock was held in such universal and profound veneration.[19]

At the least suspicion that a recruiting drive was afoot, the populace abandoned their homes and fled into the bush. Vilhena observed that in Bahia, as soon as recruiting began, there was invariably a crisis in the city's food supply because the farmers deserted their *roças*. In 1797 there was a population exodus from the regions of Atibaia and Nazaré in São Paulo when people got wind of recruiting agents in their midst; and the alarmed São Paulo municipal council asked the governor for help, since these were the two regions that produced the captaincy's food supply (*Reg.*, XII, p. 148). These are merely a few of thousands of instances of the periodic upheavals provoked throughout the colony by the recruiting drives.

The *milicias* were the auxiliary forces; like the regular troops they were generally organized into regiments, which had replaced the former *terços*. Recruits for the militia were conscripted in the colony and received no pay. The units were commanded by officers chosen from the civilian population who, like their men, could not refuse to serve and were expected to do so without pay, and by a few professional officers appointed to organize and train them. The militia units were instituted on a territorial basis (the parishes), as well as on the basis of the trades or occupations of the recruits. Practice varied from captaincy to captaincy; in Bahia, for instance, the militia, known as the "urban troops" (*tropas urbanas*), consisted of the following regiments: *Úteis* (service units), made up of merchants and their cashiers; *Infantaria* (infantry), made up of artisans, shop assistants, taverners, and others, all of whom had to be white; the *Henrique Dias Regiment*, composed of freed Negroes;[20] and finally the Fourth Regiment, also known as the *Auxiliar de Artilharia* (auxiliary artillery), composed of mixed bloods and mulattoes. There were in addition a few independent companies entrusted with special duties: one company of *familiares* (orderlies) and two companies of *capitães de assalto* ("spearhead" companies) made up of Negroes and used as scouts and runners in time of war (these correspond to modern communications companies), and in peace time to hunt down runaway slaves and fugitive criminals. These companies, which also existed in the other captaincies, were those commonly known as *capitães-de-mato* (bush captains), whose reputation was so appalling. In Rio de Janeiro the militia was organized along quite different lines. The units here were still terços, the old Portuguese unit replaced in the second half of the eighteenth century by regiments based on the French model. There were three terços, which took their names from the parishes in which they had been formed: Candelária, São José, and Santa Rita, with a further company made up of colored free men.[21]

The last category of the armed forces, the Third Division, to use current terminology, was that of the *ordenanças* (territorials), drawn from the rest of the colony's population, men between 18 and 60 years of age who had not been conscripted or enlisted for the regular troops or the militia and who had not been exempted from military service for some special reason. Priests, for instance, could claim statutory immunity. Unlike the militia, the ordenanças were a local armed force, that is, they could not be transferred from their place of formation where the majority of the recruits normally lived. There was no conscription for the ordenanças, only "enrollment," since all eligible members of the population within the limits stipulated were considered to be automatically enrolled. Their military activities were, however, limited to periodic parades and exercises, but they could be called up for local duty in time of trouble: internal strife, defense, and so forth.

The ordenanças continued to be organized into terços, divided into companies, and this organization was to continue right up to the final abolition of ordenanças during the Empire period (1831). Each terço, commanded by a captain-major, included the entire eligible male population in the district. The companies, commanded by a captain, a lieutenant, and a sergeant or sublieutenant, were made up of 250 men divided into squads of 25 men each under the command of a corporal. This was, of course, the statutory provision, since in practice there were many variants which even the law allowed in accordance with the circumstances.[22] The higher-ranking officers in the ordenanças also retained the old ranks: *capitão-mor*, which corresponds to the regimental colonel, and *sargento-mor*, corresponding to a major in regimental organization or, rather, to lieutenant-colonel, since in the terços there was no commander of a battalion, a unit which did not exist. Apart from their military function which, given the circumstances, was necessarily restricted, the ordenanças performed an important role in the colony's general administration. Before considering the nature of this role, however, we will proceed with our survey of the colony's administrative organization.

The second group of administrative organs was made up of those concerned with general and civil administration. They performed not only administrative functions proper (in the modern sense of the term) but also judicial functions. They provide a concrete example of the observation made above concerning the prevailing confusion between powers and functions which today seem to be essentially distinct. The same authorities dealt with matters falling within both spheres, and there was no substantial difference in the procedure followed for both. In the application of the law, no distinction was made between cases calling for administrative action on the part of the crown representatives and those involving legal redress between litigant parties. If the action of any authority whatsoever involved an offense against the rights or interests of any individual (and in administrative practice no distinction was made between the two), the aggrieved individual was not entitled to bring an action against the authority concerned, but could only complain of the offensive action to the relevant superior authority. In the case of offensive actions by private individuals, it was for the aggrieved party to resort to the authorities for redress, and the process would follow the same course as a modern lawsuit. But it is clear that no distinction was made between these two courses of action, at least as far as the administrative functions were concerned.

I cannot, of course, enter into any detail about this highly specialized subject; it was brought up only to provide some idea of the colony's administrative system, so different from that of today, since if we do not bear this in mind we shall not grasp the full implications of this system. We should therefore not be misled by the designations given to certain official posts in the colony, designations today used to mean something quite different. For instance, the colonial judge—whether the *juiz-de-fora* (outside judge), *juiz ordinário* (justice of the peace), or the *almotacé* (fiscal judge), *vintenário* or *vintena* (parish judges)—not only performed the functions of a modern judge, administering justice, pronouncing sentence, and deciding in litigation cases, but also performed those of an administrative agent, carrying out administrative measures and seeing that the law was enforced. And all this was done with no clear distinction in practice between the dual nature (one might almost say the "duplicity") of the functions he was performing. His duties were to enforce the law in a general way; whether this enforcement arose out of the actions of the persons within his jurisdiction, through lawsuits or their own illegal behavior, or whether it was part of his administrative function mattered little; he always acted in the same way.

In order to make it easier to follow the general system of colonial administration, we will start with the lesser institutions, since the higher organs of government generally functioned as a second resort. The most important of these institutions was the *senado da câmara,* or municipal council,[23] which had its seat in the town or city and exercised jurisdiction over its respective *têrmo* or county. It may seem strange that in this survey of the captaincy's general administrative system, I should begin with an institution that would appear to be purely local, but in this case we should once more set aside our modern notions. In the colony's administrative system, there

were no distinct and parallel administrative bodies, one general
and the other local. The administration was a whole, and the
municipal councils performed functions which would in our
own time be regarded as general rather than purely local. They
functioned, in fact, as one of the captaincy's minor administrative institutions.

The head of the senado da câmara was a judge-president,
who could be a professional judge nominated by the crown, in
which case he would be the juiz-de-fora. More commonly, however, he was simply an ordinary citizen who had been elected
to office like the other council members, in which case he
would be the juiz ordinário. There were always two justices of
the peace, who alternated with each other monthly throughout
the year for which they had been elected to serve in this capacity. Unlike the outside judges but like the other council members, they received no remuneration for their services. In addition to the president and these two justices of the peace, the
municipal council comprised four other officials (*oficias*):
three aldermen or councillors (*vereadores*) and a procurator
(*procurador*).

Councillors were elected to office by popular vote, or rather,
by a body of electors known as the *povo* (the people) but
actually composed of qualified citizens, or "good men and true"
(*homens bons*), as they were legally known. They were in fact
the county's property-owning or important citizens, and their
names appeared on the list of the povo specially drawn up for
electoral purposes. Electors were also sometimes known as re-
publicanos.[24] We have already seen how the right to vote,
which included the right to stand for municipal office, had
taken on a political coloring in certain places and had become
an apple of discord between rival factions: planters and colonials on the one hand, and "peddlers" and *reinóis* on the other. In
principle, elections were indirect.[25] The body of electors assem-
bled in the senate house, and representatives were chosen by
majority vote to act as official electors. These electors were
divided into three pairs, and each pair, separated from the two
others, drew up three lists each, containing the names of three

fellow citizens whom they considered qualified to serve on the council. The president, who was the crown judge, or in his absence the county's senior judge then collected the three lists and drew up a fourth list of the names which had gained the most votes. From this list he compiled three final rolls, which were inserted into three small wax balls known as *pelouros*.

During the "first week of Christmas" (usually December 8) of each year, the people gathered to witness the final ballot in a special council session (*vereança*). A seven-year-old boy was chosen to put his hand into the chest where the pelouros had been placed for safe keeping and draw out one pelouro. The persons whose names appeared on the roll contained in the pelouro so selected were the persons appointed to serve in the ensuing year. This procedure was followed for three years in succession, and the pelouros having all been taken from the chest, a new election was held. This form of election was known as "election by pelouro." In the event of a vacancy on the council arising from a councillor's death or his inability to serve for some other reason, a more summary procedure was followed, the councillors choosing a substitute themselves. This impromptu election was known as "a cap election" (*eleição de barrete*). The judges, aldermen, and procurator were said to be *de pelouro* when they had been elected in the traditional way, or *de barrete* when their nomination had been the result of an impromptu election.

Whatever the form of their election, the judge and the procurator had to have their appointments confirmed by the ouvidor (crown judge), who gave them their official letters of appointment (*cartas de usança*). The aldermen, on the other hand, were immediately inducted into office, the only formality required being that they take an oath to do their duty without fear or favor. From certain details of this electoral procedure we can see that authorities unconnected with the câmara intervened in its affairs.

The povo, in the restricted sense of the word given above, were convened to deliberate with the câmara on matters of great public importance or local interest and decide on the measures to be adopted (*Reg.*, XII, p. 99, and *Act.*, XX, p. 179).

Thus organized, the councillors met in session (*vereança* or *vereação*) twice weekly, on Wednesdays and Saturdays. Let us now see the matters with which they concerned themselves. It is known that in the early days of the colony their range of action was very wide. Some of the municipal councils, particularly the câmaras of São Luís do Maranhão, Rio de Janeiro, and São Paulo, had at one time even become their respective captaincy's most important authorities and had challenged the power of the governor, in some cases even succeeding in having him removed from office.[26] But in the period we are considering this former power wielded by the colonial câmaras had been lost for over a century and a half, and we must therefore consider the restricted local action they now performed and what their effective functions really amounted to in terms of the legislation in force, particularly in the exercise of their public administrative function.

The councils had their own patrimony and their own source of revenue and were not dependent on the Royal Treasury, that is, on the public funds of their respective captaincies. The patrimony consisted of lands they had been granted when the town was created, lands set aside for the *rossio* (public square), the erection of public buildings, and the creation of public parks and a common.[27] They were entitled to grant some of these lands to private individuals or to lease them out.[28] Streets, squares, paths, bridges, public fountains, and so forth, were also considered part of their patrimony.

The revenue of the câmara was derived from the rents it was entitled to collect on leasehold land and local dues (taxes) authorized by law or by special permission of the king.[29] The câmara could keep two-thirds of the municipal revenue, but one-third had to be handed over to the treasury representatives in the captaincy.

Apart from the administration of its patrimony and revenue, the câmara was responsible for appointing a number of officials: the *juiz almotacel*, who was entrusted with supervising prices of staple commodities and with keeping the town clean; the *juizes vintenários* or *juizes de vintena,* who exercised jurisdiction over the parish (each parish having one *vintenário*) and had powers similar to those of the outside judges or justices of the peace, but with a more limited range of action; and minor officials whose duties were restricted to municipal business, the *escrivão* (scrivener), *síndico* (syndic), and so forth.

The câmara was also responsible for drawing up local bylaws; acting as a tribunal in cases of verbal injury, petty theft, and bylaw infringements (such cases being known as *causas de almotaçaria*)—*Ordenações,* Book I, ch. 66, cl. 5, and ch. 65, cl. 25); and settling disputes between litigants over rights of way, paths, streams, and so forth (*Reg.,* XII, p. 393), and disputes involving the lands of its patrimony (*Reg.,* XII, p. 275).

But it is difficult to determine exactly what fell within the private competence of the câmara. Crown officials seemed to intervene in all its affairs, their authority in council matters being greater or equivalent to that of the câmara itself. The comarca's crown judge and its *corregedor* (chief magistrate) constantly interfered in routine municipal business. Thus, in the São Paulo Council, they verified the accounts, decided on the system of collecting municipal taxes (*Reg.,* XII, p. 194), authorized the levying of certain dues (*Reg.,* XII, p. 477), authorized expenses (*Reg.,* XII, p. 199), agreed that the câmara could allow a reduction on its credits (*Reg.,* XII, p. 206), and decided on the disposal of its patrimonial lands (*Act.,* XX, p. 406). The crown judge even meddled in the câmara's composition, not only by his power to confirm the appointments of the justices of the peace and procurator through the *cartas de usança,* without which they were forbidden to take office, but also by his power to decide whether candidates for municipal office were eligible and did not suffer from some "impediment." He was also responsible for granting leaves of absence (*Reg.,* XII, p. 11). He attended council meetings and the special session at which the list of candidates for the post of captain-major of the territorials was drawn up. Finally, he was empowered to appoint the parish judges himself and could nominate other municipal officials (*Reg.*, XII, p. 410).

The governor also meddled in municipal affairs. Although the câmara was responsible for making appointments to a number of official posts, it was the governor who nominated certain officials, such as the secretary, the câmara being merely ordered to administer the oath and induct him into office (*Act.*, XX, p. 264). There were even cases where the governor extended the term of office of the justice of the peace and the council's other members beyond the period for which they had been elected, as happened in São Paulo in 1799, when all the newly elected councillors requested, and were granted, exemption from office. An impromptu election was arranged—the *eleição de barrete* prescribed in such an event—but the governor canceled the election and made his own decision, extending the term of office of the time-expired councillors (*Act.*, XX, p. 153).

The governor also interfered in purely local matters, initiating public works and ordering the câmara to collaborate with his plans. This happened in the case of fountains erected in São Paulo in 1800 with no prior consultation with the câmara (*Reg.*, XII, p. 601); he issued instructions regulating trade in staple commodities (*Reg.*, XII, p. 248) and took measures on the administration of the *casinhas* (*Reg.*, XII, p. 601).

On the other hand, the câmara dealt with other matters that were by no means of a local nature—the nomination of inspectors for the Intendency of the Gold Mines, for instance. In short, there was no clear distinction between local government and general administration. Appeals from all the câmara's decisions could be made to a higher authority: the crown judge, governor, high court, and even direct to the crown. At the same time the councils acted as local executive organs for the administration in general. The governor dealt with them in this capacity, holding them responsible for the execution of his written orders (*Reg.*, XII, pp. 248, 256). In this sense, the câmara functioned as an executive department subject to the governor's authority, and as such played an extremely important role. Its direct contact with the local population enabled the distant higher authorities, who had no other appropriate instrument at their disposal, to enforce their decisions through the medium of the council's authority. The câmara was even responsible for promulgating edicts of the governor on matters affecting the public weal (*Reg.*, XII, p. 483). The Treasury also had its edicts on contracts and trades promulgated through the câmara (*Reg.*, XII, p. 589), and certain taxes levied by the crown were collected by the câmara in the crown's name (*Reg.*, XII, p. 508, and *Act.*, XX, p. 427).

Its function as a purely administrative department subject to the government and intimately related to it is clearly evident from the terms in which the governor's reports refer to the "Senado da Câmara." The viceroy of Rio de Janeiro in his report on the administration deals with the local council and its affairs in the same way as he deals with the other administrative organs, referring to its proceedings as if they fell within the province of his office (see, among others, the *Relatório* of the Marquis of Lavradio). Similarly, enumerating and analyzing Bahia's public administrative departments, Vilhena makes no separate mention of the senado da câmara, lumping it together with the other administrative bodies under the general heading of "Judicial and Treasury Departments" (*Recopilação*, Letter X).

Thus, although the municipal councils had special features —indicated chiefly by the fact that they possessed their own patrimony and sources of revenue and were entrusted with a certain judicial authority, which was not the case with the colony's other administrative bodies—they really functioned as departments of the central government and fitted into its organization and administrative hierarchy. But since they did possess the individual characteristics indicated, and since councillors were elected by popular vote and maintained an intimate contact with the people, they played a special role. The São Paulo Council referred to itself as the "head of the people" in the representation it made to the bishop in 1798

(*Reg.*, XII, p. 291), and it was through the councils that nearly all the people's claims and complaints were transmitted to higher authority (*Reg.*, XII, p. 289). This was the source of their strength, and this was what empowered them to intervene —as they did intervene—and to take effective and often decisive action in the successful implantation of independence, the drafting of the Constitution and the founding of the Empire. The municipal council was the only administrative body that survived the wholesale destruction of all the colonial institutions, retaining all its powers and perhaps even augmenting them.

In addition to their functions as members and presidents of the councils, the *juiz ordinário* and the *juiz-de-fora* performed other duties which were both judicial and administrative. It will be recalled from the description of the functions of colonial judges given above that apart from their jurisdiction in litigation cases they were also administrative agents, responsible for the execution of administrative provisions.[30] In both instances, the juiz-de-fora or juiz ordinário was a higher authority than the parish judges, but lower than the ouvidor, or crown judge, who was the senior judicial authority in a comarca.

The ouvidor, who as a rule combined his judicial functions with those of corregedor, that is, administrative duties, was immediately above the organs of government we have just considered in the administrative hierarchy. His jurisdiction extended over the whole comarca and all its counties. There is no need to specify his powers, since they were of a general administrative nature, although his jurisdiction was of a higher instance than that of the câmara and the "judges" described above. We have already seen a number of cases in which he exercised his power.[31] Ouvidors were appointed by the crown for a period of three years. In the more important comarcas, Bahia and Rio de Janeiro, there was a second ouvidor, with criminal jurisdiction of the first instance, in addition to the civil ouvidor. Both were members of the relações, or high courts, established in these cities. The relações of Bahia exercised jurisdiction over the northern captaincies (with the exception of Pará, Maranhão, Piauí, and Rio Negro which transferred appeals from the courts of first instance to the Court of Appeal or *Casa de Suplicação* in Lisbon). The Relação of Rio de Janeiro was the court of final judicature for the southern captaincies from Espírito Santo southward, including the interior captaincies. The presidency of the relações devolved upon the governor (the viceroy of Rio de Janeiro) and their members included, in addition to the ouvidors: *agravistas* (appeals judges), *procurador* (procurator), *juiz da coroa* (crown judge), and so forth, all of whom were known as *desembargadores* (crown lawyers). The relação, like all other government organs, exercised administrative as well as judicial functions. But since it functioned solely as a higher tribunal and court of appeal, taking no direct action, its role in the administration was somewhat restricted and it was closer to the modern tribunal of justice.[32]

We shall now turn to the Treasury organs. For the supervision of the Royal Exchequer in the Brazilian captaincies,[33] the collection of taxes, and the administration of revenue and disbursements, there were a number of separate organs whose functions were more or less specialized. These organs were not subordinate to one another or to the governor, and there was no structural hierarchy in the modern sense of the term. It was in this field that the lack of a balanced hierarchical structure, which I have pointed out as one of the most characteristic features of colonial government, was most striking. The most important government organ dealing with matters of revenue was the *junta da fazenda* (board of revenue), presided over by the governor.[34] As its name implies, the junta dealt with financial concerns in general, but there were numerous exceptions, particularly in the more important captaincies, where there were a number of separate organs charged with functions that also fell within the general province of the junta: the *Junta de Arrecadação do Subsídio Voluntário*[35] (Board for the Collection of Voluntary Subsidies), also presided over by the governor; the *Alfândega* (Customs), which collected import duties; the *Tribunal da Provedoria da Fazenda* (Tribunal of the Crown Purveyor), which not only performed functions which are today the province of the procurator's office, that is, the collection of taxes, but also dealt with other financial matters.[36] There was also a body for administering the various monopoly contracts farmed out by the crown, such as the contract for the collection of tithes, contracts for the provision of such staple commodities as salt, olive oil, and so on, which was known as the *Juízo da Conservatoria*. Other Treasury departments were: *Juízo da Coroa e Execuções*, dealing with foreclosures; *Juízo do Fisco*, for the general administration of fiscal matters; *Juízo das Despesas*, charged with official disbursements, and so forth. All these different bodies, as usual, exercised mixed administrative and judicial functions which would today be divided into two distinct branches.

The principal colonial tribute exacted was the *dízimo*, or tithe, an ancient ecclesiastical privilege which the Church had empowered the king of Portugal to collect in his capacity as Grand Master of the Order of Christ. In theory, the tithes were supposed to furnish the stipends of the clergy, but the privilege had become confused with the regalia of the crown and was known as the *dízimo real* (royal tithe). As the name implies, tithes comprised a tenth part of all products of the land. Next came the customs duties; the tolls levied at the principal river crossings and registos (dry customs); the duties levied on all merchandise, slaves, provisions, and cattle entering Minas Gerais, known as the *entradas;* and special taxes on mules from the south, levied at Sorocaba in São Paulo. In addition there were the *donativos* or voluntary contributions, the *terços* (thirds), and *novos direitos* (new duties) levied for the services of law officials—scriveners, bailiffs, solicitors, and so on— and fees payable on nominations to public office, known as *provisões* and *patentes*. Apart from these standard contributions, the crown also collected special contributions to defray extraordinary expenses—the literary subsidy created in 1772 in all the captaincies and in the kingdom to raise money for the provision of public education, and other "extraordinary subsidies" periodically raised to meet emergencies.[37] These were generally collected in the form of special duties on cane spirits, animals slaughtered in the public abattoirs, foodstuffs, and a capitation tax on slaves.

Collection of all these dues—and this applied both to the numerous taxes levied by the crown and to those levied by the municipal councils—was operated on a monopoly contract basis; that is, contracts were farmed out for a fixed period, usually three years, to private contractors who, in return for a fixed payment to the Treasury, collected the dues in the crown's name and were entitled to keep the surplus after the needs of the administration had been satisfied. Contracts were put up for public auction and went to the highest bidder. When the Treasury collected taxes directly—which happened only rarely, since it was not equipped for this—it was said to "administer" collection or that the contract was "under administration."

This system of collecting taxes was one of the colonial government's most evil practices. All that can be said in its defense is that all nations at that time included collection by contract in their fiscal systems and that it stemmed from a long tradition dating back to Roman times. But the fact that the system was a time-honored one was no consolation to the populace who suffered from the onerous burden it imposed on the colony. Inspired only by greed and the profit to be reaped, the contractors were pitiless in their methods. The public authority would, or should, have been moved by considerations other than the unscrupulous collection of taxes; but the private contractor's only interest was to cover the amount he had paid for his contract and pocket a substantial profit. And the extortions which the contributors were obliged to suffer did not even benefit the Royal Exchequer; for if, on the one hand, the monopoly contract system simplified tax collection, on the other, cases where the contractor went bankrupt and could not pay the agreed price of his contract were not infrequent. This was because, in their eagerness to get the contracts—considered one of the colony's most lucrative businesses—bidders often contracted for a higher sum than they could possibly make from the dues collected, and this meant that not only were they themselves ruined but the Treasury did not receive its portion. There was, besides, the favoritism exercised by crown officials, who took handsome rake-offs from contractors and overlooked their failure to make the payments due to the crown. This kind of thing was almost the rule.[38]

Tithes ran neck and neck with conscription as one of the great scourges inflicted on the population by the colonial administration. What the people suffered from this crippling burden beggars description. The duty in itself was bad enough —ten percent of the total product was payable to the crown. But onerous as was this exaction, it was nothing compared to the way in which it was collected. In the first place the tithes had to be paid in cash instead of in kind, as they should have been and in fact had been in the remote past. The producers were thus obliged to raise money on a substantial part of produce not yet sold, a sum more or less arbitrarily determined by the *dizimeiros* (tithe collectors).

We can readily judge the catastrophic effect of this extortion in an economy such as that of the colony, where money was scarce and credit practically nonexistent, at least for the majority of essential commodities and for most people. Except on the commercial plantations, which were highly profitable and provided considerable security, no one dared to produce more than was strictly needed to meet his own individual requirements or to sell to a guaranteed market. But the exigencies of the dizimeiro did not stop at this. To save himself the trouble of undertaking arduous journeys, he stopped collecting the tithes annually and demanded the total due for the period of his contract in one lump sum. This sum was estimated on the basis of the prices obtaining at the time the tithe was collected, and if this happened to be a bumper year for production or if prices that year were high, the contributor was obliged to pay an average amounting to far more than the legal ten percent of production.

For these and other reasons, when the dizimeiros descended

on the population in search of their tithes, they left a sinister trail of misery and ruin in their wake. Since they were empowered to recover debts due to them by distraining the property or imprisoning the persons of their debtors, and since they used these powers ruthlessly, they ruined farmers and paralyzed production as they scoured the country. St. Hilaire was an eyewitness of the activities of the dizimeiros and held them largely responsible for the scattering of the rural population, who fled to remote and inaccessible spots, condemning themselves to a life of poverty to escape the disastrous attentions of the tax collectors.[39]

After this melancholy excursion through the colony's fiscal system, let us now turn to its administrative departments, the last group of government organs which I indicated as having a special nature. Some of these have already appeared in earlier chapters: the *Administração dos Indios* (Indian Administration) and the Intendências for Gold and Diamonds. The other administrative organs were: the *Intendência da Marinha* (Intendancy for Maritime Affairs) which, as its name implies, administered the seaports in the seaboard captaincies and supervised all coastal shipping as well as being in charge of shipyards and warehouses; the *Mesas de Inspeção,* which supervised the sugar and tobacco trades (there were boards in Bahia, Rio de Janeiro, and Pernambuco); and finally the *Conservatorias de Cortes de Madeira,* created in Alagoas and Paraíba by the royal letter of May 13, 1797, and in Ilhéus (Bahia) by that of July 11, 1799, and presided over by the ouvidors of the respective comarcas, who acted as conservators charged with the administration of the lumber industry being fostered in the colony to provide timber for naval construction.

In addition to these regular departments, the colonial administration also counted on the territorial units (*corpos de ordenança*) referred to above to carry out some of its functions. Although not intended for this purpose, these ordenanças came to play a significant role in the administration of justice. From a military point of view, as we have seen, the ordenanças were of minor importance; they were local service units and could not be posted away from their home districts to other parts of the colony. Being generally ill-equipped and badly trained, they were as troops of little or no use. In principle they were supposed to provide local auxiliaries for the regular troops or militia in cases of external aggression or civil strife. But no such emergencies arose in the period with which we are concerned; indeed, they belonged to the remote past. The only military problems in this period were those of the southern frontiers and minor conflicts in Mato Grosso. But the ordenanças had played no part in these affairs: both were scantily peopled regions where ordenanças had not been formed, and they had therefore to depend solely on external aid, and the armed forces involved were all regular troops or militia conscripted in other captaincies.

But if they played a minor role as armed forces, the ordenanças played a major one in another sphere, one not foreseen when they were originally created. Without fear of exaggeration it can be said that the ordenanças made possible the maintenance of law and order in this vast territory, with its scanty population and paucity of proper officials. It was impossible, with the enormous tracts of territory assigned to them and their concentration in the capitals and larger centers, for the authorities to cover adequately the territories within their jurisdiction; and the ordenanças alone made this feasible.

The idea of using the ordenanças for this purpose can be traced back to the last quarter of the eighteenth century, and I am paying just tribute to the foresight of one of the greatest administrators of colonial Brazil in attributing it to the oft-cited Marquis of Lavradio. It is in that detailed and precious source of information, the *Relatório* to the viceroy who was to succeed him in office in 1779, that we find the matter clearly and consciously formulated for the first time. The Marquis reveals his understanding of the usefulness, even necessity, of organizing the colony's population into a number of units, instituted along territorial or local lines, in order to bring the population more easily within reach of the administration, thus making it possible to extend royal authority to the remote and intractable backlands. The passage in which he refers to the problem is a lengthy one but worth quoting in full since it clearly reveals the nature of the project and covers the ground so thoroughly that little remains to be added:

For me there is a strong reason to institute auxiliary *terços* (*milicias*) in all the settlements comprising all the inhabitants who are of proper age and have the strength and agility to take up arms, and to form ordenanças with all those who are less suitable; and this reason is that in this manner, if the populace is divided into small groups subject to a certain number of persons, who should always be chosen from among the most capable to act as officers, it will gradually become accustomed to obedience and will finally recognize authority in the person appointed by H. M. to govern it. The population in a country so wide, so abundant, so rich, being composed for the most part of persons of the lowest education and the most dissolute characters as are the Negroes, mulattoes, cabras,* Indian half-breeds and other such persons, being subject only to the governor and the magistrates without first having been separated and accustomed to know more intimately the authority of other superiors who would gradually set the example of obedience and respect and show that they are representatives of the sovereign's laws and order, it becomes impossible to govern such persons unless peace and authority be established. Experience has proved this, since in all places where there has been failure to establish order among the people there has been much disorder and unrest, and even though those entrusted with administering justice have proved themselves tireless in their efforts, and have ordered the execution of those condemned by their crimes, this has been of little avail in bringing the people to order and, on the contrary, in those parts where the people have been brought to order, all has remained much more peaceful, and disorders are less frequent, for the laws are held in greater respect.[40]

The Marquis's proposals for the militia (which he calls the "auxiliary terços," the term used in his day) were the least prac-

---

* *Cabra*—bandit, ruffian, or backwoods cutthroat; a term used to designate half-breed Negroes.—Translator.

tical. This is because the militia units, as auxiliaries to the regular troops, had an important military function and therefore had to be properly trained, exercised, and equipped. Apart from this, only persons completely fit for military service were enlisted in these units, and hence they could not have the wide range of action of the ordenanças raised throughout the territory, whereas the militia comprised only a limited number of units. For the functions envisaged by the Marquis of Lavradio, the ordenanças were the better fitted.[41] These functions, which in the Marquis's time were already performed by the ordenanças, although without the full awareness of their scope displayed by a politician as astute as the viceroy, later became part of the administrative machinery, perfectly defined and working smoothly, as can be seen from the references to the ordenanças made toward the end of the nineteenth century. We shall not seek such references in the works of contemporary writers, wherein the personal attitudes of the authors may have influenced their observations, but in the ordinary everyday administrative documents of the time, those dealing with routine matters in which the authors are simply repeating unquestioned and commonly held opinions.

The senior officers of the ordenanças—captain-major, sergeant-major, and captain—were chosen by the governor from three lists drawn up by the senado da câmara of the respective counties. As we can see from an official letter addressed to the Câmara of São Paulo, on the occasion of his decision to institute new units in one of the capital's parishes, the governor asked the Câmara to draw up these lists of nominations for the posts of officers in the ordenanças in the following terms: "The large number of people who live in the undermentioned parish cannot be properly governed, nor disciplined to the requirements of the Royal services, unless two more companies are created, so that their respective officers can look after the interests and carry out the necessary provisions of the said Royal services" (*Reg.*, XII, p. 35). Similar language was used in the letters patent conferred upon the officers appointed: "to form a company for the better provision of aid to and the maintenance of due order among the settlers" (Reg., XII, p. 54). These are only two out of hundreds of similar instances and, in the matter-of-fact tone employed, clearly reveal that these administrative functions were taken for granted, and that the use of the ordenanças for this purpose was not a matter of opinion but an established fact and everyday occurrence.

The administrative powers of ordenança officers are constantly referred to in routine administrative matters. Let us select at random a few of these references from the ample material provided by the *Registo da Câmara de São Paulo*. In a letter from the governor to the câmara in which he discusses a number of points concerning the jurisdiction of various authorities (he was specifically dealing with the jurisdiction of the ecclesiastical authorities), he states that the only persons empowered to "compel" the "civilian settlers" are the judges and the "officers of the ordenança" (Reg., XII, p. 473). In dealing with the construction of an embankment along the Rio Pinheiro, the câmara on the governor's instructions, ordered the local ordenança captain to detail members of his company, with a sufficient number of corporals, on a certain day and at an appointed time to the site, in order to carry out the requisite work under the supervision of the council's overseer (Reg., XII, p. 175).

Another reference reveals that the captain of an ordenança was charged with collecting from the settlers in his parish the dues levied by the council for construction of a bridge (Reg., XII, p. 277). From yet another reference in the *Registro* we learn that the governor issued instructions for the officers of the parish of Atibaia to take action to prevent the settlers from abandoning their lands—as they had been doing in fear of the conscription drive—since this was threatening the capital's food supply (Reg., XII, p. 150). One final example of the ordenança officer's functions: in a matter of public interest concerning the parish of Sant'Ana, the local ordenança captain addressed himself officially to the governor, asking him to take measures (Reg., XII, pp. 252, 275).

It should be noted that none of these functions was determined by law. The use of the ordenanças for administrative purposes arose out of the pressing needs created by the vastness of the territory and the scattered pattern of settlement, which made it impossible for the authorities, ill-equipped as they were to administer the huge areas assigned to them, to perform their functions adequately. It was a situation sanctioned by custom rather than law; but thanks to this possibility, the colony became governable. What made it easier for the ordenanças to perform their functions and enabled them to carry out their duties in an effective manner was the existence in colonial society of an established and universally recognized social hierarchy.

I have indicated in a previous chapter the nature of this social organization, the system of the "patriarchal clan" grouped around the powerful territorial magnates and local "bosses"— the senhores d'engenho, the great landowners, and the wealthy fazendeiros. This social structure paved the way for the establishment of the ordenanças; in fact, they did no more than provide official recognition of the existing social situation, by using this "clan" to form the ordenanças. And this in effect was what happened. Local bosses and leaders were given command of the ordenanças. Armed with their "letters patent" and the public authority they conferred, these magnates not only gained in power and prestige but also became guardians of law and order in their home districts; and the administration, while perhaps maiming itself by this more or less enforced delegation of power, nonetheless gained a weapon of wide range: it enlisted on its side a power it was unable to match and that otherwise would have proved impossible to control. And with this power, the administration penetrated the mass of the people and succeeded in effectively extending its authority over the colony.[42]

The ordenança system came to the aid of the administration in another sphere: the problem of the Indians, this poorly assimilated group living on the fringes of colonization who, after the Pombaline laws, had been promoted to the status of "citizens" like all the other colonists. The task of governing them and of gaining the obedience and subjection that only the missionaries, with their limitless patience and absolute dedication, had managed to achieve in a wholehearted and spontaneous way was a difficult one, since neither the lay colonists nor the European-born bureaucrats enjoyed the priests' knowledge of human nature, or had their tact and ability in handling Indians. The ordenança system replaced, although only to a limited extent, the authority of the priests and in some measure obviated the brute force generally used in dealing with the Indians to maintain order. They took advantage of the vestiges of hierarchy, the consideration or respect which had once existed among the native tribes and which, in spite of the breaking of their original social and political ties through long persecution, subjection, and slavery, still survived in latent form. And in the Indian villages or "towns," as they became after the Pombaline laws, military appointments in the ordenanças were conferred on Indians who enjoyed real ascendancy or prestige among their fellows. Koster makes sardonic comment on these "seminaked officers" with their gold-encrusted batons, the symbols of their authority; what he failed to realize was the system they represented, a sounder basis for the colony's administrative and political order.[43]

The military and civil government organs we have analyzed above do not exhaust the subject of colonial administration. Inappropriate as its inclusion may seem at first sight in this context, religion and the clergy belong in this chapter for all sorts of reasons. The position of the Church differed greatly from that in our own time and we cannot really fully grasp it by drawing parallels. We must transport ourselves in imagination to a completely different environment and make the effort to participate in the priest-ridden and religious atmosphere of colonial life. This does not mean that there was then a stronger and deeper religious feeling. Or, if there was, it is not this aspect that concerns us here. Of far greater import was the all-pervading complex of beliefs and practices that dogged a man's footsteps from cradle to grave, confining all his deeds within the framework of their constant and powerful influence. He participated in religious activities and the ritual of the Church with the same naturalness and conviction he brought to all the activities of his mundane daily life, and it never entered his head to set himself against them. He was baptized; he went to confession and received Communion at the prescribed times; he was married in church; and he performed all his religious duties and attended religious festivals and ceremonies in the same spirit that he performed the actions of what we would today call his civil life, as distinct from his spiritual life. It was all as natural and inevitable as wearing clothes, eating meals at certain hours of the day, and following the conventional routines of life that were the same for everyone else. The colonial citizen lived out his life without for one moment thinking that such acts might be dispensable. There were unbelievers and skeptics—and the period we are considering was propitious to the spread of such skepticism—but doubts were confined to the small, closed, and isolated circle of Freemasons and freethinkers who carefully disguised their true attitude. In the eyes of the world about them, they were thought mad, more dangerous than criminals. Religion was never questioned; it just "was."

This attitude meant that spiritual needs were placed on the same footing as the demands of civil life. Participation in religious activities was no less important than participation in those of the latter. Attending mass, receiving the sacraments, and taking part in Church ceremonies were duties as pressing as those required from a citizen in the other spheres of his life: respect for the law, the maintenance of order, and obedience to the decrees of the public administration. The state could not shirk its duties in this respect. On the contrary, it always contested with the Church the right to minister to its subjects the spiritual nourishment they needed. It never lost sight of the political importance of these spiritual needs.[44]

But even for the colony's confirmed atheists and agnostics, existence outside religion and the Church was not only inconceivable, it was also frankly impractical. Regardless of the religious implications involved, certain indispensable legal acts could only be done through the Church. Births could be registered only through baptism; marriages could only be performed by priests. And ecclesiastical jurisdiction went further than this, being exercised over many matters of basic importance. All matters pertaining to marriage came within the province of the Church: divorce (or "repudiation," as it was termed), legal separation, and annulment, as did all cases involving sin.[45] These were stipulations laid down by the Council of Trent, which Portugal had been the only Catholic nation to approve without restriction, the essential features remaining in force in Brazil right up to the Republic.[46]

If this was the Church's judicial position in positive law, its position in the everyday life of the colony was no less prominent. Its authority was universally accepted; and this acceptance was extended to its ministers. Individuals not only participated actively in the external manifestations of the Catholic faith, but also subjected their intimate lives to the Church's scrutiny. There is no need to go into the age-old controversy about the respective attributions of Church and State, or "Pope and King" as it was customarily referred to, a controversy that has only recently lost its point. We need only note that in fact, particularly in the colonial society with which we are concerned, the interference of the Church and its ministers was considerable.

As a body the clergy was powerful and influential, being held in great respect by the majority of the laity, their right to interfere in many private matters being universally acknowledged. The priests meddled in the domestic life of married couples, concerned themselves with the "good conduct" of their lives together; they were entitled and even expected to censure their behavior and to report recalcitrant cases to the higher religious authorities. They could also intervene in the education of children, having a full right to supervise the actions of parents. By and large, the priests were regarded as the guardians of public morals, and for this they used sanctions ranging from public denunciation of the offenders to more specific penalties, including the severest penalty of all, excommunication, which excluded the accursed from the Communion of the Church. This would merely raise a smile from the modern skeptic, but it aroused quite another response from his ancestors of only a century back. Religious anathema not only consigned the individual to damnation, but also isolated him from his fellow men; he became the object of general abhorrence, a social leper banished from society. Even if in his heart of hearts he remained unaffected, the excommunicate suffered cruelly from the opprobrium of public opinion, easily controlled by the priests, who stirred up the people against the condemned man. And apart from this, in extreme cases, he was excluded from performing the indispensable legal acts controlled by the clergy, a sanction which affected his normal life.[47]

The Church's administrative activities played a prominent and, in many important cases, an exclusive role in many other departments of colonial life. Much of the social work that today would be a governmental concern was then performed by the Church, which provided social security in the form of relief to the poor and the aged, the care of orphans and foundlings, the care of the sick, and so on. Its role in education was likewise a major one. Similarly, in catechizing and civilizing the Indians, the Church continued, despite the curtailment of its temporal jurisdiction by the Pombaline laws, to perform an educational function through its regular, and in some cases even secular, missions. Finally, we should not forget the role it played in public entertainment, most festivities and popular amusements being organized under its auspices or direction.[48]

The Church was thus an extremely important aspect of public administration. It vied with the civil authorities, and it is difficult, if not impossible, to distinguish in practice in many cases between Church and State—hence the frequent conflicts between civil and ecclesiastical authorities.[49] But much more common was collaboration of a kind so intimate and so indispensable to the normal functioning of the administration that it cannot bear comparison with anything that exists today. It would be a glaring anachronism to project onto the past today's relations between Church and civil administration and attempt analysis from a modern viewpoint. There was more than a simple relationship: there was a communion, an identity of purpose, animated by the same spirit.

I shall not enter into detail about the colony's ecclesiastical organization of secular and regular clergy, nor of the tertiary orders and other lay brotherhoods (*irmandades*), which played an important role in religious activities. Nothing in this respect was peculiar to the colonial Church. In Brazil, as elsewhere past or present, ecclesiastical organization is essentially the same. We must recall only that the *padroado*—that ecclesiastical patronage granted by the pope to the Portuguese sovereign in the kingdom and its overseas possessions—enabled the crown to meddle extensively in ecclesiastical affairs, including above all the sale of episcopal preferments; the building of churches and the delimitation of territorial jurisdictions; and permission for the founding of religious orders, convents, or monasteries. Furthermore, the king, as Grand Master of the Order of Christ, had power as we have seen, to collect tithes, really an ecclesiastical tribute originally destined to be spent on the stipends of the clergy (*côngruas*).[50]

In addition to the stipends allotted by the crown, the clergy had other sources of revenue. They charged fees for their religious and judicial services—the ministration of the sacraments, dispensations, the costs of cases coming within ecclesiastical jurisdiction, and so on. Another source of income was the *desobriga*, the paschal duty paid by communicants during Lent, all Catholics over seven years of age being obliged to receive Holy Communion at Eastertide. Most of these impositions are still made by the Church, but whereas today they can be regarded as "donations" or voluntary contributions, they were then tantamount to public obligations—in modern terms, imposts or taxes—since no one could shirk payment.

The crown padroado meant that the Church never enjoyed complete autonomy or independence. The colony's ecclesiastical affairs were always entirely in the hands of the king, who controlled ecclesiastical policy through the Board of Conscience and Orders mentioned above. But Rome exercised an indirect, although decisive, influence on religious matters through the preponderance of the Jesuits at the Portuguese Court who, up to Pombal's time, used all their efforts to ensure that the kingdom remained a vassal of the Society of Jesus and the pope. After the expulsion of the Jesuits in 1759, this influence faded and Brazil's clergy and ecclesiastical affairs were entirely subject to the sovereign power of the crown. This continued even after the ultramontanistic reaction during Dona Maria's reign, which did not essentially change matters despite the fervid proclericalism and fanaticism preceding the insanity in which she ended her days. Indeed, the Papacy, already considerably weakened and preoccupied with more important matters, made no attempt to assert its rights in the kingdom and Brazil, and the colony's religious affairs were left entirely to the "Most Faithful" king. We need only peruse the official correspondence of the civil and ecclesiastical authorities relating to ecclesiastical matters to see how much freedom of movement the home government enjoyed in this respect.[51]

This concludes our survey of the administrative organization of the colony. Most of the criticisms that could be leveled at this organization are implicit in the analysis given above. From this we saw the administration's lack of organization, the inefficiency and lengthy delays involved in the dispatch of business, not to mention the harshness of some of the methods employed to enforce its measures—conscription and collection of the tithes being striking instances of the system which prevailed. The complexity of the government organs, the confusion between different functions and powers; the lack of method and clarity in the drafting of laws; the morass of contradictory regulations, further complicated by the extraordinary verbosity of the dispatches, which sometimes turn into literary dissertations; the excessive bureaucracy of the central bodies with their swarm of minor officials, who tended to "deliberate" on all matters that came within their ken and the corresponding scarcity of effective executive agents; the centralizing tendencies of the home government, which made Lisbon the only center empowered to deal with the flood of documents which made their way slowly across the ocean while the matters they related to slipped into the past—all this could have had only one result: the monstrous, awkward, and inept bureaucratic machine that was the colonial administration. And, in spite of all this complexity and the variety of organs and functions, there was no real specialization. Each organ of government embraced all the matters that came within its particular range, the most various matters being handled by the same officials, for whom it was a sheer physical impossibility to cope with the burden involved. The organs that came closest to being specialized bodies, such as the intendancies for gold and diamonds, the boards of inspection, and a few others, were in practice nothing of the sort. They accumulated powers of no relevance to their particular spheres of action and simply carried out administrative decrees and policy, ranging from stimulation of production and technical supervision to administration of tax collection and judicial resolution of cases between contending parties. They rarely employed specialists and technicians. In the various intendancies for the mines, for instance, there was never a geologist, a mineralogist, or even a simple engineer to be found. All the officials who dealt with mining were laymen, ignorant of science and mining techniques. They were expected to be primarily bureaucrats and at the same time to exercise judicial functions.

But we need not dwell on the specialized departments to uncover the weaknesses of the colonial administration. Even in the essential activities of the state it was deplorable. Justice was costly, and legal proceedings were inordinately spun out and incredibly complicated; indeed, recourse to justice was beyond the reach of most people. Professional judges were few and far between, most of the colony's "judges" being ignorant and incompetent laymen. Cases brought before the lower courts drifted up the scale to the higher tribunals: ouvidor, relação, suplicação (court of appeals) in Lisbon, and sometimes even Mesa do Desembargo do Paço (Crown Board of Appeals), meandering along for anything up to ten or fifteen years.

Public security was precarious. We have seen that its own inadequacy to maintain law and order obliged the administration to resort to use of the ordenanças for this purpose, delegating powers that would give rise to the pockets controlled by local "bosses" that lasted throughout the empire period, if not right up to the republic, and made it so difficult to extend public authority to these regions. Even with this enforced adaptation of local armed forces to administrative ends, unruliness was widespread not only in the unpoliced backlands which made up so much of the territory but even in the large urban centers, under the noses of the authorities. If banditry and crime were not the scourges they might have been, this was due much more to the temperament of the people than to the measures taken by an administration which was nonexistent in the greater part of the colony's territory.[52]

Finance was in no better state. We have already seen the methods employed to collect public revenue. Administration of the moneys so collected was hardly more efficient. All those captaincies, cities, and towns for which financial records are available seem to have been permanently in deficit. And it was a disorganized deficit at that, if I may use this qualification without being guilty of a pleonasm to characterize the colony's financial system, where the lack of revenue to meet expenses was summarily resolved by contracting debts which the authorities had no intention of repaying or which were repaid sometimes merely with good intentions only to the creditors who were protégés of the authorities. Even the troops received no regular pay, and soldiers begging in the streets were a common sight.

Deplorable as was the state of the administration's essential functions, that of the other functions was even worse. Public education was limited to a few schools for teaching the three R's and the rudiments of Latin and Greek, scattered through the most important centers, and the scanty education provided in the bigger cities by the religious orders.[53] The state provided sanitation and public health services in the major cities, Bahia and Rio de Janeiro.[54] Hospitals were few. There was a military hospital in Rio de Janeiro, in the former college of the Jesuits,[55] and there were the hospitals maintained by the Santa

Casa da Misericordia, or Holy House of Mercy,* which, although few in number were the colony's most remarkable
social institution. As to public works, we have already seen an
example of these in the miserable tracks that passed for the
colony's roads and in the other communication routes. Apart
from this, the colony has left us few public works deserving of
mention: a few mediocre fortresses and the Carioca aqueduct
in Rio de Janeiro almost exhaust the list. [56]

Development of production was entirely in the hands of the
more diligent administrators, and only a few limited edicts
were passed to stimulate production.[57] The list could be extended, but there is no point in running the gamut of inefficiency and negligence found in all spheres. One instance,
mining, will suffice to characterize the colonial administration.
For almost a century, exploitation of gold and diamonds was
the crown's greatest source of wealth, the prosperity and even
the very existence of the Portuguese throne being dependent
on this fount. Yet even this did not alter the attitude of the
authorities toward mining; it attracted their notice only as a
taxable boon, a source of revenue to be exploited to the full.
Apart from this, nothing was done, the other aspects involved
being totally neglected. The incompetence, negligence, and
inertia displayed by the colonial authorities while a source of
natural wealth was being dissipated and destroyed requires no
further comment.

If the picture of the colonial administration's efficiency is a
gloomy one, that of its moral attitude is no less unfavorable.
From top to bottom of the administrative scale, with rare exceptions, gross immorality and corruption were shamelessly
prevalent. We could without injustice repeat what was said in
the *Soldado Prático:* "In India there is nothing that is un-
tainted by corruption; all rots and festers, like enough to a

---

* The Santa Casa da Misericordia was the most famous lay brother-
hood, a charitable institution primarily concerned with the relief of
orphans, widows, prisoners, and the sick; and it founded hospitals in
many towns. The original Misericordia was established in Lisbon in the
late fifteenth century, and branches were founded throughout the Portuguese Empire.—Translator.

running sore. . . ." * The most honorable delegates of the crown administration, those of notable integrity, were those who did not pocket public funds outright or use their official position for private advancement. Diligence and the proper performance of duty could not even be contemplated. The system of taking cuts from nominations to public office naturally opened the doors to corruption. Public offices, like any other merchandise, were sold to the highest bidder. But this was still within the bounds of accepted and recognized practice. What had led Padre Antônio Vieira, S.J., a hundred years earlier to conjugate the verb *rapio* in all its inflexions (in his sermon on the "Good Thief") was this universal habit of embezzlement, graft, bribery, and all the other shades of administrative corruption.

If I were to line up all the testimonies to this general corruption the procession would be endless. And even if we allow for slander, the administration would still not be exonerated. Apart from laudatory comment made in speeches, generally of a personal nature (and their frequent repetition is in itself not without significance), in all the contemporary accounts we find not one tolerant or justificatory comment on the administration, let alone one word of praise. Whatever the source of the comment, whether made by a simple Brazilian-born colonist, or by one of the reinóis, or even by officials themselves, all are equally severe in their criticism. Add to these the observations of foreign travelers visiting Brazil at the beginning of the last century, nearly all of them persons of great integrity and conscientiousness with no special reason to depart from the truth on this subject, and we have more than enough evidence to reach the conclusions made above—unless we dispute the fundamental hypothesis of all historical research, that "it is possible to reconstruct the past."

A large share of responsibility for this—if we exclude the

---

* *O Soldado Prático* (Practical Soldier) is an early seventeenth century work by Diogo do Couto (1542–1616), who spent most of his life in Portuguese India, where he was in charge of the Royal Archives at Goa. It was an outspoken attack on the Portuguese administration of India.— Translator.

corruption which appears to mark Portuguese administration since the distant days of the Indies—must be borne by the spirit that animated the home government in its management of the colony. Even if we accept the concept expounded by the author of the *Roteiro do Maranhão* that "colonies were established for the benefit of the mother country," or that of another contemporary writer that "their primary and common effect is undoubtedly the enrichment of the mother country and the increase of her power"[58]—confessions which at least make no bones about matters in which today hypocrisy has an undisputed place—Portugal nevertheless always interpreted this primary objective, which was behind all official colonization schemes, in the narrowest way possible. She seldom saw beyond the immediate profits to be reaped from the colony in the shape of tributes of one sort or another. Silva Gama, one of Rio Grande do Sul's most notable governors, summed up this attitude in a crude, unvarnished confession that appears in one of his dispatches to the home government: "Nothing interests me more," he wrote, "than the fiscal matters of the Royal Treasury. To save on expenses as much as possible, diligently to collect all moneys owing to the crown without undue harm to its subjects, and to devise new ways of increasing its revenue, are the objects of my constant zeal."[59] It was this that animated the mother country's colonial policy in Brazil: the fiscal objective came first and foremost. The acts of the administration and its administrators departed from this rule only very rarely. Pombal, whose government was perhaps the only one after the heroic period in Portuguese history that had a wider vision, even Pombal failed to free himself completely from aims so deeply rooted in the national consciousness, or rather in the crown's policy. Gold and diamonds divested the mother country of all shreds of reason and common sense she had still managed to retain. With a rapacity hitherto unparalleled, she fell upon the gold and the precious stones like a starving dog on a bone unearthed, except that she herself had done none of the digging. For almost a century, she had no serious preoccupations other than collecting the royal dues, the fifths; the administrative history of Brazil can be spelled out in these terms.

On such a basis, the colonial administration could not have been other than it was. Anything not connected with the collection of taxes was neglected, and the greed of the crown, so crudely and cynically affirmed, and the brutal commercialization of the objectives of colonization contaminated everything. All was flung to the winds in the pursuit of profit and the attempt to gather the crumbs that fell from the royal table. The constructive aspects of the administration were relegated to an obscure and secondary plane, and only those idealists out of tune with their society found cause to rail against this.

All this refers particularly to the civil administration. Ecclesiastical administration came a close second. We must, however, make one qualification which it is only fair to point out. If the colonial clergy vied with officialdom in the moral sphere, they did at least have greater intellectual capabilities and were manifestly superior not only to the officials but also to any other category of the colonial population. It was no mere coincidence that most individuals of a higher intellectual standard than the generally low level prevailing in the colony were ecclesiastics. All the early nineteenth century foreign travelers noted this and St. Hilaire went so far as to affirm that in Goiás, the only persons of any learning were the priests.[60] Nor was it by chance that so many members of the priesthood distinguished themselves in colonial literature and science, or that it was the priesthood that supplied the principal exponents in many intellectual spheres.[61] I have already indicated the reasons why the priesthood became the colony's intellectual career par excellence; it was the only profession that opened its doors to all comers irrespective of their origins. All, or nearly all, the individuals made restless by their intelligence sought refuge in the Church.

But in another sphere, in their average moral standards, the colonial clergy as a body were little better than their lay colleagues in the administration. The commercialization of their sacerdotal functions had become a fait accompli in the period we are considering. I have already cited the observation of an ecclesiastical authority that the cloth had become "a way of earning a living," a profession like any other. And indeed the author of this remark seems perfectly reconciled to the fact.[62] And what else could one expect? The general and persistent outcry of the people against the extortionate fees the clergy charged their parishioners is a clear indication of the course they had chosen to follow. Baltasar da Silva Lisboa, a high-ranking crown official, reporting to the viceroy on his own particular functions, concluded his remarks on the clergy with the following sentence: "All they want is money, and they care not a jot for their good name." [63] In a dispatch written the following year he made a similar allegation.[64]

To gain some idea of what went on in Brazilian convents in the way of laxity and corruption, we need only read the lengthy report on the subject written by Viceroy Luís de Vasconcelos to the secretary of state, which he summarized in the report to his successor.[65] If we need still further evidence, clearly above suspicion since it came from those even better qualified to speak, we should read what the respective superiors of the convents of the Carmelites and the Capuchins had to say on the subject.[66] But was not the following text, so revealing of the concept of its sacerdotal functions held by the colonial clergy, written by no less an authority than the Bishop of Rio de Janeiro, Frei Antônio do Desterro? "As a reward and remuneration for services," he writes, "which provide so strong a stimulus for all, particularly here in Brazil, where more care is taken of material interests than of good reputation and the glory of one's name, it seems to me more just and proper that your Majesty should indefectibly remunerate these parish priests [those who had rendered services to the Indians] by appointing them as parish priests in Minas, giving each of them as many years in the said churches of Minas, *which are so highly profitable*, as they have served in the Indian parishes." [67]

We could prolong such testimonies, found in the documents of the period, which if not as abundant as those relating to the lay administration are no less illuminating and convincing. But it will suffice to refer the reader to what St. Hilaire, a devout Catholic, has to say in his long chapter on the Brazilian clergy, in which, while deploring their actions and attempting to console the pious reader, he describes in detail the many blows dealt to his sensibilities.[68]

In such circumstances, it could hardly be expected that the colonial clergy, animated by the spirit we have described, should have shown much diligence in the performance of their duties. And indeed negligence was the rule. The clergy performed its functions with zeal only in places where it could be well paid for its services, in the "profitable" parishes referred to by the bishop cited above, in the wealthy plantation chapels. The rest of the population was neglected. At most the priests said a few Masses and administered the obligatory paschal Communion, one of the chief sources of their revenue. The rest of the time they engaged in activities far removed from their sacerdotal duties: many of them were fazendeiros; the best pharmacist in São João del-Rei was a priest who made up and sold the prescriptions himself; and another priest sold cloth behind the counter of his store.[69]

And if this was the way they fulfilled, or failed to fulfill, their basic duties, what could one say of their other duties, the social aid and moral support that tradition, Church statutes, and the established division of public functions demanded? A few orders, or at least some of their members, still worked among the Indians, and I have had occasion to mention some of these rare instances in earlier chapters. Certain convents provided education and instruction, but only in the larger capitals and for small groups of the population. A few lay religious brotherhoods concerned themselves with the relief of the sick, foundlings, and the poor, like the justly respected Brothers of Mercy. There were shining examples of dedication and service and I do not wish to underestimate them; but unfortunately these were exceptions, standing out like islands in an ocean of needs that went unheeded and unrelieved. The majority of the clergy, secular or regular, from the highest dignitaries to the humblest lay workers, were completely indifferent to such matters, placidly enjoying the fruits of their *côngruas* and other revenue or making up for its inadequacy by their private business activities.

How much of the responsibility for this state of affairs should be directly blamed on the mother country's policy? With the expulsion of the Jesuits, the colony was robbed of almost the only element that had promoted social welfare on any wide scale. But the harmful effects of Pombal's measure should not be exaggerated. The days of the Nóbregas and the Anchietas * were long past, and the Society of Jesus had declined considerably. It is difficult but not impossible to hazard any opinion as to what it might have become had it not been expelled. But to estimate the extent of the loss from the standards adopted by the early missionaries would be a deplorable anachronism.

The inefficiency of the clergy in the period we are considering is the result of causes more profound than those that arose in consequence of an isolated measure taken in pursuance of the home government's policy, or even that of Rome. Some of these causes were of a general order, affecting the overall ecclesiastical structure in the period preceding the one we are concerned with; these cannot be discussed here. Others were of a local nature, peculiar to the colony. And these can be summed up in the answer to the fundamental questions: Was colonial society equipped to produce an efficient clergy of high moral standards able to meet the lofty demands of their calling? Was there in the colony the social and moral environment to promote this situation and to allow clergy of this stamp to maintain itself and flourish? The general conclusions on colonial society at the beginning of the last century, which I shall attempt to outline in the next chapter, will perhaps furnish some of the elements needed to answer these questions.

---

* Fr. Manoel de Nobrega and Fr. José de Anchieta are sixteenth century Jesuits, famous for their inspired missionary work in Brazil's pioneer days. Anchieta (1532–1597) is one of the first outstanding names in the literature of Brazil and was largely responsible for establishing the Jesuits' educational system in Brazil. Fr. Nobrega is another important name in the early literature, his *Cartas do Brasil* (1549–1560) being rich in valuable descriptions of life in the colony.—Translator.

Social and Political Life

We now have the elements needed to arrive at some general inferences about the colony's social life, inferences which will give us the general tone of this life and an overall picture of the achievements of Portuguese colonization in Brazil. We shall see the different aspects of that heterogeneous collection of races which colonization so haphazardly brought together in Brazil, with no other objective than the creation of a vast commercial enterprise to which white Europeans, African Negroes, and the indigenous peoples of the continent contributed according to the changing circumstances and needs of this commercial venture. The mixture was composed of highly diverse ingredients: three different races and cultures, of which two, semi-barbarous in their native state and whose original culture traits were to be smothered in the process, supplied colonization with its largest contingent; races brought together by force and incorporated into colonization by violence, without any preliminary attempt to prepare them for their contact with an alien society; races whose only "school" was to be the field and the slave hut.

With such beginnings, a process of formation still in progress at the period we are considering, one could only expect to find a population completely destitute of any moral nexus. Races and individuals are badly amalgamated; they do not blend into any coherent whole; they are juxtaposed, forming separate

399

groups and units that merely coexist. The strongest ties that bind them into some kind of social whole are the most primitive and rudimentary human links, stemming directly and immediately from the relationships established in labor and production, particularly the subjection of the slave or semi-slave to his master. Very few new elements had been added to this original cement of Brazilian society, a society whose framework was thus reduced to the obligatory and tenuous relationships deriving from slave labor. And in this sense, Alberto Tôrres was right when, in an apparent paradox that scandalized his contemporaries, he stood up for the slave-owning regime not as a slave owner but, for the first time in our history, as a sociologist.[1]

To prove the truth of this observation, we need only compare the sectors of colonial life dominated by slave labor and free labor, respectively. The solid and coherent structure of the first is in direct contrast to the rickety and loosely knit organization of the second. We have already seen these two aspects of colonial society: on the one hand, the master and the slave, both integrated into the organic cell of the patriarchal clan to which their interrelationship gave its characteristic quality; on the other, that immense inorganic segment of the community made up of rootless individuals drifting aimlessly on the fringes of organized colonial society and adhering to this society only in small groups, which were the nearest they could get to any form of organization. We are thus tempted to generalize even further Alberto Tôrres' remark and to see slavery as the *only* real and solid organizing element the colony possessed.

Be that as it may, the analysis of colonial society calls for the most painstaking assessment. Any generalization that covers the highly diverse situations found in this society runs the risk of leading to a serious error of judgment. To understand colonial society as a whole and in its connective links, we must see it as it was in fact composed: a central organized nucleus, whose principal element was slavery, surrounded by a number of scattered and unconnected social clusters which at the same

time occupied the gaps in the central nucleus, being influenced
in many cases by its proximity.

There is no need to stress once more the role played by
slavery in the first sector, the organic cell of colonial society.
But we should add a comment on the primary nature of the
social relations stemming from slavery, primary in the sense
that they never rose above the purely material level of their
origin, that they never really managed to create a superstructure. In fact the two functions performed in colonial society by
slaves—to meet the labor and sexual needs of the colonists—
never gave rise to anything but the most elementary social
relationships. Slave labor progressed no further than its original point of departure, compulsory physical effort. It provided
no training or preparation for a higher plane of human existence. It contributed no moral element to these social relationships; on the contrary, it led to the degradation of the slave and
any cultural content he might have brought with him from his
original state was obliterated. The master-slave relationship
was and remained a purely material one, centered on labor and
production and adding little or nothing to the colony's cultural
complex.

The other function of the slave, or rather of the female slave,
that mere instrument for the satisfaction of her lord and
master's sexual needs, produced a no less elementary relationship. This, too, did not go beyond the crude and purely animal
level of sexual contact and only remotely approached the
sphere of truly human love in which the sexual act is surrounded by such a complex of emotions and feelings that the
act itself, which after all is what gave rise to the phenomenon
of human love, is relegated to a secondary plane.[2]

In certain other respects, slavery did enrich colonial society.
The "kindly figure of the Negro mammy"—the phrase is Gilberto Freyre's—is particularly worth emphasizing. She surrounded the cradle of the Brazilian child she suckled with an
atmosphere of kindliness and friendliness that played so important a role in the growth of the sentimentalism so characteristic
of the Brazilian temperament. And if on the one hand this

made the individual soft and left him unprepared for all the reverses of life—and there is no doubt that many of the deficiencies of the Brazilian education are due to this upbringing —on the other, it contributed toward cracking the hard shell of crudeness and brutality typical of a society in the making.

But in this, as in other similar cases, it is necessary to distinguish between the pure Negro influence and that of the Negro as slave, a point which Gilberto Freyre so rightly develops.* The distinction is a difficult one: the Negro and the slave seem to be one and the same person, and the influence of the Negro was nearly always transmitted through the slave. But it is not impossible to separate the two, and by and large it would be true to say that, if the Negro did bring a positive contribution, it was canceled out or debased by the effects of slavery. The slave dominated the scene, and only rarely did he allow the Negro to appear. The role of the African in the cultural formation of the colony might have been quite different had he been given even the smallest opportunity to develop his natural aptitudes. But slavery as practiced in the colony stunted his development. It stifled most of his good qualities and released any corrupting tendencies he may have had, or whatever in him was susceptible to corruption by the system of slavery itself. And the low cultural level of the slave, compared to that of the dominant race, prevented him from forcefully asserting himself to overcome the miserable condition imposed on him, which is what so often happened in the ancient world.

In sum, although slavery was the mainstay of colonial society, the institution that enabled it to develop and the basis of its only organized social sector, the relationships deriving from it never rose above the lowest level and did not lead to the creation of a broad and complex superstructure. They served only to form for a time the social nexus of the colony's life. In

---

* In *The Masters and the Slaves*, pp. 322 ff. Cf. Freyre's observation that: "At times what appears to be the influence of race is purely and simply that of the slave, of the social system of slavery, a reflection of the enormous capacity of the system for morally degrading masters and slaves alike."

the other sector of colonial society, the sector in which slavery never took hold, the situation appears in a certain sense to be much worse. It was loosely organized and lacked any cohesive element. Its origin in large part explains this. As we have seen, this sector was made up of people who led a poverty-stricken existence on the fringes of colonial life; a segment of the population which was no more than a consequence of slavery and a replacement for it in parts where an organized system of economic and social life had not been established or had failed to survive.

For this sector, one cannot even speak of a social "structure," since it was characterized by instability and looseness of organization, tending to produce the extreme forms of social maladjustment which are so prominent a feature of colonial life: vagrancy and the *caboclo* * way of life.[3]

This, in sum, is what the observer finds in the colony's social life: on the one hand, an organization which is sterile as regards the higher forms of social relationships; on the other, a state, or rather a process, of disaggregation, more or less advanced according to the particular circumstances, which was the result or the reflection of the situation existing in the organized sector and which was rapidly accelerating. Before proceeding with our analysis, we should stress that these social aspects correspond roughly to the two sectors we found in the economic sphere: large-scale agriculture and mining on the one hand, and the activities which came into the general category of a subsistence economy on the other. This point is worth emphasizing, since it reinforces what has been said about the Brazilian economy, which was essentially devoted to the production of a few exportable commodities. Its onesidedness was clearly revealed in the colony's social life; anything outside the narrow circle of this particular form of productive activity was doomed to instability.

In the light of this preliminary glance at colonial society, it becomes possible to understand most of its essential features. It

---

* *Caboclo*—Indian; thus, *caboclizaçao* (the author's own word) implies "going native."—Translator.

can be summarized in the observation made at the outset concerning the absence of any moral nexus, the slackness of social ties. I have used the term "moral nexus" in its broadest sense: a combination of bonds or links, a complex of human relationships acting as connective forces to bring together the individual members of a society and blend them into a compact and coherent whole. Colonial society, however, was characterized by disaggregation, the operation of forces tending to segment and disperse it. But to use the word "force" is misleading; what operated in fact was inertia, and this inertia explains the relative stability of the colonial structure. The precarious balance was maintained by economic and sexual bonds which, although tenuous and primitive, contrived to hold together such diverse individuals, races, and social groups. Based on no more than this, Brazilian society survived, and the work of colonization could continue.

The external pressures brought to bear on colonial society by the mother country's authority and sovereign action also helped to weld it together. This factor should not be minimized, since, despite the limited range of the central authorities—which we have seen in the description of the colony's public administration—they played an important role in maintaining the Brazilian social structure. Later developments, the events immediately preceding and following independence, clearly indicate this. The weakening of the central power led the country to the brink of anarchy; indeed, in many cases and in various sectors, although in a small way, outright anarchy did prevail and was checked only by the establishment of a state which, while national in name and formation, was almost a faithful copy of the Portuguese monarchy it had replaced—a State which did not arise out of the intimate needs of Brazilian society, which was incapable of any such creation, but was imposed from the outside, and continued to exercise the same sort of pressure on the society as the monarchy had done.[4]

We should also take into account a certain uniformity in "attitudes"—I use the term in its widest sense—which served to bring together the different parts of the colonial whole; uniformity of feelings, customs, beliefs, and language—in a word, *culture*. This provided the moral and psychological basis for the formation of Brazil as a nation and gave it the national unity already achieved geographically and traditionally. But as a factor in the national unity, the culture only really affirmed itself later, in conflict with the mother country and later still with other nations. Before this, it was simply a political fact, and at the period we are considering its contribution to the texture of colonial society was still a minor one. The confrontation between Brazil and other countries had not yet played a social role, although it was beginning to play a political one.

We can now proceed to consider colonial life and relationships in greater detail. All organized society is founded on the regulation—however complex its subsequent results—of man's two primary instincts, the economic drive and the sexual instinct. This is not an affirmation of principle, uncalled for in this context, but a guideline for the analysis of the basic social relationships established in the colonial society. The colony's relationships in the economic sphere were defined by *labor*, a term here used in its widest sense, to mean an activity that provides an individual with his livelihood. In the other sphere, the relationships that defined it were those established between the sexes and deriving from these, in other words, family relationships.

We have already seen certain features of the colony's labor relations which indicate the form likely to be assumed by the bonds deriving therefrom—the deprecation of all forms of manual labor associated with slavery, for instance, and the stimulus slavery provided for the masters to remain idle while all the work was performed by slaves. The effect of both these influences was to create a contempt or aversion for any form of activity, complete idleness in extreme cases, or the general slackness, sluggishness, and desire to expend a minimum of energy that characterized colonial life. Everything was based on forced labor. Apart from this, the colony's activity was almost nonexistent. Where the lash, the stocks, and the other instruments invented to strengthen the human will to work were absent, activity came to a standstill. One of the proofs of this was that freed slaves generally became vagrants, in spite of the school in which they had been reared.

The attitude toward manual labor was almost universal: no free man would stoop to using his muscles. Luccock tells a revealing anecdote in this respect. Needing the services of a locksmith he went to fetch one, only to be left cooling his heels for hours while the locksmith waited for the arrival of a hired Negro to carry his tools, since to carry them himself through the streets of the city would be unworthy of a free man.[5] Nonmanual work was performed with a minimum of energy, a slowness and economy of effort that were a constant source of irritation to the energetic Europeans who visited the colony.

The only fairly active segment of the population was composed of the newly arrived immigrants who had not yet been contaminated by the example of the colonials, the *reinóis* who had come to make their fortunes in America. Avid for money, ready to do anything, hard working and ambitious, since they had been brought up in a school quite different from that of the Brazilians, they and the slaves were the only truly active elements of the population. In an interesting essay on the causes of independence written in 1823 and dedicated to the Portuguese sovereign, Francisco Sierra y Mariscal analyzed the gulf between the concepts and attitudes of Brazilians and Portuguese immigrants. Whereas the immigrants, who arrived in Brazil empty-handed and penniless, "are prepared to do anything, and by dint of hard work and thrift succeed in amassing large fortunes," the Brazilian, born to abundance, "is consumed by pride, always greater than his means of livelihood . . . he does not know the meaning of work or thrift . . . and by the time he reaches manhood, he is already poor," because, concludes Mariscal with clear logic, "no fortune will last someone who spends much and earns nothing." [6]

Since this attitude to work was shared by most of the colonial population, and was maintained over the years, it naturally ended by becoming part of the nation's collective psychology, a profound and ineradicable trait of the Brazilian character. In

Brazil, idleness and laziness became, to quote Vilhena, "as sticky as bird lime." But although the chief cause of this aversion to work was slavery, a number of other factors, more limited in scope, helped to explain its remarkable persistence. The chief of these is the substantial contribution of Indian blood. The indolence of the Brazilian Indian has become proverbial, and up to a point this reputation is deserved. The mistake made is to attribute this indolence to some vague "innate characteristic" of the savage. In his natural environment and even in civilized life when given tasks that aroused his interest, and above all whose purpose he could understand, the Brazilian savage was as active as individuals of any other race. He became indolent when uprooted from his own environment and placed in an alien world so completely different from his own. And it was only in this context that the colonist took an interest in him and passed judgment on his aptitude for work, work which the Indian was forced to perform, a sedentary, methodical activity organized according to standards he did not understand and for incentives which meant nothing to him and aroused no response in his own instincts—material gain, possessions, pleasures which for him were neither real possessions nor real pleasures. Nothing could be more ludicrous than the attempt to persuade the Indians to work for such incentives, based on European models and utterly alien to their wants.[7]

Be that as it may, for the purposes of colonization the most characteristic feature of the Indian and his mixed descendants, who followed in his footsteps and made up such an appreciable part of the population, was "a complete and utter lack of energy."[8] This was one of the chief reasons why the regions where they formed the largest contingents remained stagnant. The Governor of Pará, D. Francisco de Sousa Coutinho, after three years in office, gloomily informed the home government that "The powerful enemy of these people, and the chief cause of their backwardness, is their laziness."[9]

Along with the contribution of Indian blood to the general indolence prevailing in the colony, there was that of the economic system, which provided so few avenues of advancement and such limited prospects. It was hardly an atmosphere calculated to stimulate individual energy and activity, since there was little incentive to work.

All this led to the general inertia that characterized the colony as a whole. The atmosphere in which the colonial population moved, or rather, "rested," was contaminated by a virus of laziness and lassitude, which infected all but a few. Brazil was the picture of stagnation. After many travels and years of close contact with the life of the country, St. Hilaire could hardly conceal his admiration and was moved to glowing praise for the inhabitants of Itu and Sorocaba in São Paulo, because it was there that he found . . . a football game; in view of what he had hitherto witnessed and the state of mind this had induced in him, he considered this a "proof of energy." [10] The colonial population was apathetic even in its pleasures and pastimes.[11] Paulo Prado forgot to include apathy among the strands that make up the "Brazilian melancholy," which is the result not only of lechery and greed, but above all of a systematic inactivity that ends by taking complete possession of a man, robbing him even of his capacity for enjoyment and the energy to laugh.[12]

In such circumstances, the colony's economic standards could only have been what in fact they were, utterly deplorable. The work performed in the colony, if we exclude the badly executed production exacted from the slave, was only the bare minimum needed to survive. And this, together with the general economic conditions previously analyzed—which after all were only the indirect cause of the state of affairs described above—sufficiently explains the poverty, the low, or rock-bottom, living standards of the colonial population, the more favored classes not excepted. Of Brazil as a whole, Vilhena said that, in spite of its natural resources, it was "the abode of poverty." And the inhabitants of Bahia, the colony's second city and probably the first in wealth and importance, with the exception of the big merchants and a few senhores d'engenho and lavradores, who made a great display of their wealth but had really nothing to call their own but this outward pomp, were described by Vilhena as "a congregation of paupers." [13]

The second group of social relationships were those deriving from the sexual impulses of the colonists. There is such an abundance of material on the colony's mores that the researcher obliged to select from among these records soon loses heart. Loose living reached such proportions and was so widespread that it attracted the attention of even the least observant contemporary commentators on colonial life. The first and foremost cause of this state of affairs was undoubtedly—and I have already touched on this subject—the overwhelming preponderance of male immigrants. Only in exceptional cases did family groups come to the colony. Most of the immigrants were enterprising bachelors or married men who had left their wives and families behind, to send for them only when they had succeeded in establishing themselves. The delay in achieving this stable situation was often prolonged indefinitely, since the new colonist, even once established, ended by succumbing to the prevailing laxity and frequently preferred to live with submissive women from the dominated races he found in the colony rather than to face the restrictions his family would bring. Even when he did eventually send for his family, he had grown so accustomed to his loose way of living that wife and children proved an insignificant curb.[14]

Established on such foundations, the irregularity of the colony's sexual customs was reinforced by other factors. Slavery, economic instability—everything contributed to the weakness of the family unit, to the failure to establish family relationships on a solid and durable basis. Contrary to what is now usually affirmed, the formation of Brazil was not based on the family unit, save in the limited and, as we shall see, sadly deficient case of the upper class Big House. The mass of the people were not bound by family ties; the newly arrived immigrants and the slaves, as was only to be expected, formed only loose attachments. And the pull of the family was perhaps even less for the free population, economically and socially unstable, lacking the solid basis upon which a family could be founded.[15]

As for the Big House, if it is true that its nucleus was the family, or rather the family of the master (representing only a tiny minority of the population, a fact frequently forgotten), and if in this sense the wealthy young colonist grew up in a family atmosphere, we must nevertheless make a number of qualifications if, by the concept of family, we mean more than the simple external structure; if in fact we understand "family" to include that complex of rules of conduct, patterns of behavior and even "atmosphere" that gives the family unit in the societies of our civilization its great role in the education of individuals and the formation of their characters. In this wider sense, the Big House fell far short of its mission. The way of life to which it led, the promiscuity in the relations with slaves —and slaves of the lowest moral standards—the facilities it offered for irregular and dissolute sexual relations, the prevailing lack of discipline thinly veiled by a hypocritical and purely formal submissiveness to the father and head of the household —all this made of the Big House a school for immorality and vice, in which the child was reared from the cradle, rather than a school for the formation of character.[16]

In the Big House the family lost all or nearly all its virtues; instead of performing the function that gives it its basic moral reason for existence—the disciplining of the sexual life of individuals—it provided the opportunity for the most unbridled sexual licence. It should be pointed out that I am not regarding this from the point of view of the human feelings involved: the emotional attachment between a man and a woman, or the love they feel for their children; and that I in no way mean to deny or underestimate these feelings. On the contrary, the only accusation that could be leveled in this respect is that affection was carried to excess; too much tenderness was expressed, exaggerated attentions were lavished on the children, they were overwhelmed by the permissiveness that played by no means an insignificant part in their faulty upbringing.[17] But we should not analyze the family only from this point of view; its scope was wider than the expression of tender feelings and affection. And if in this respect the Brazilian family sinned through excess, in others it failed through its deplorable short-comings.

With the role of the family thus diminished, there was ample scope for sexual licence. In this respect we cannot confine our observations to the infrequency of lawful marriages, since marriage in itself was no guarantee of sexual regularity and discipline. Just as in sociological terms, sexual regularity is not the exclusive property of legally sanctioned unions. We must therefore consider the degree of stability shown by sexual relationships, whether formally sanctioned or not. And for the purposes of our survey of the colony's social relationships, this is particularly important, since according to the testimonies of contemporary observers, marriage was rare outside the upper classes. We should recognize, however, that the practice of co-habiting was not simply the result of sexual licence. One reason for the large number of free unions was the paucity of clergy to celebrate marriages, the parishes covering enormous areas in which only one priest, and more often than not one careless of his duties, had to cope with a population scattered over many leagues of land. Another, more common obstacle was the high fee the priest charged for officiating at marriages. There were numerous complaints about this, and the problem came up constantly in contemporary documents.[18] Yet another factor in the failure to legalize illicit unions was color and class prejudice, a prejudice so strong that it sometimes had disastrous consequences, as in the tragic case of a former governor of two captaincies, Fernando Delgado de Castilho, who, having fallen in love with a woman of humble origin who bore him a number of children, committed suicide when he was recalled to the kingdom, because it would have been socially impossible to marry her and take her back to Portugal with him.[19]

As we can see from the foregoing remarks, cases of persons living as man and wife without blessing of clergy, which cannot be considered instances of sexual licence or depravity, must have been frequent. Indeed, they were so common that they ended by being ignored in practice and were publicly accepted without any sort of constraint.[20] Nevertheless, even if we do not base our judgment of the colony's sexual climate on this widespread practice of cohabiting, we would still find enough evidence to reach certain conclusions. "The Brazilians," wrote Hercules Florence, who accompanied the Langsdorff expedition in 1828 as its official artist and chronicler, "whose amiable qualities are so characteristic and who are so much inclined to pleasure, find that the women of the country are so complaisant of custom that they rarely have to enter into the bonds of matrimony." And he adds further on that "the daughters of poor parents never even think of marriage; the chance of finding a husband without the lure of a dowry is furthest from their thoughts, and as they are ignorant of the ways in which a woman may live by honest and diligent toil, they are easily drawn to loose living."[21] Florence was repeating almost word for word what the Marquis of Lavradio had written half a century before: "The women, because they do not work, and because they lack the means of supporting themselves, become prostitutes."[22]

This brings us to a point which constituted the most alarming symptom of the immorality rife in colonial society, the widespread occurrence of prostitution. There was not a corner of the colony into which prostitution had not penetrated on a large scale. Needless to say, it flourished in the large and medium cities, as is common throughout the world. But in the smallest and most insignificant mining camps, the majority of the fixed population consisted of vagrants and prostitutes. All observers commented on this. "In the humblest settlement," testified St. Hilaire, "the most shameful licentiousness reveals itself with a brazenness not to be found in the most corrupt of the cities of Europe."[23] This state of affairs explains what became of the female part of the large contingent of the population whose male component we considered in a previous chapter: the vagabonds and the unemployed, living on their wits, one foot in vagrancy, the other in crime.

How far did religion succeed in stemming the tide of this corruption? We have already seen that religious beliefs played

an important role in the colony, and that the rituals and ceremonies of the Church penetrated deeply into its everyday life.
There is hardly a page of the *Atas da Câmara de São Paulo*
that does not contain some reference to "an adjournment of
the Council," so that the members could attend an important
Mass, or join in giving thanks for some event: Te Deums, pro-
cessions—*saimentos,* * as they were called. But from this to
true religious spirit is a far cry. The pious St. Hilaire was
deeply shocked by the religious festivals, which he condemned
as "irreverent ceremonies in which ridiculous buffoonery is
mingled with the solemn ritual of the Church." [24] And he
heartily endorsed the opinion of the colony expressed in his
presence by the Vicar of São João del-Rei, that "Brazilians
were naturally religious, but that their religion never went beyond the senses; and as for the priests, these seemed to consider sin and pardon as mere mechanical functions." [25]

It could thus hardly be expected that religious precepts
would serve to counter the widespread corruption of morals.
The emphasis was all on the external manifestations of the
Roman Catholic cult; as far as morality was concerned, there
was infinite permissiveness. This fact is not surprising in view
of the features of colonial society already revealed in the foregoing pages, which made it extremely unlikely that there
would be any deep understanding of the true meaning of religion and worship. Setting aside the deep-rooted general causes
of this failure, the priests, who were themselves victims of the
same circumstances, should bear a large share of the blame. As
a body the colonial clergy seem never to have seriously considered providing proper religious instruction; their neglect of
their duties in this respect was deplorable. They seem to have
been far more concerned with the external rites and ceremonies
of worship and with the collection of fees for their services. "In
many places," wrote St. Hilaire, "religion is preserved only by
tradition, since the faithful far from the more important centers live out their lives in complete isolation, deprived of any
spiritual aid." [26] Even where a priest was present, he was more

---

* Literally, "outings."—Translator.

preoccupied with his private and business affairs than with the spiritual welfare of his flock. The example he set was also by no means inspiring, since his life was frequently scandalously lax. All things considered, it is not surprising that religion in the colony was no more than a skeleton draped in the outward pomp of rites and ceremonies, devoid of all higher feeling.[27]

In short, the panorama offered by colonial society may be summarized as follows: settlement, scattered and unstable; economy, poor and miserable; mores, dissolute; administration, both lay and ecclesiastical, inept and corrupt. What spark of vitality, what capacity for renewal, lay concealed among the ruins, the truly catastrophic degradation into which the colony was plunged?

A reaction against this tremendous disorder was in fact gradually beginning to take shape, which, like all reactions that emerge from the very depths, was the result of the most varied circumstances. These circumstances had one thing in common; they all created an anxiety that permeated all classes and groups of colonial society from top to bottom. A deep-rooted economic and social unrest was involved, an unrest which could be explained in individual cases or in terms of the different groups by some particular and immediate circumstance but which in the final analysis stemmed from a more general and fundamental cause, the entire *system* of Brazilian colonization.

Colonization had yielded its fruits when, after three hundred years of endeavor, it had brought together in this immense and almost empty territory a population garnered from three continents, and with it formed for good or ill a social whole characterized by individual and unmistakable features—after it had explored, opened up, and settled the land and sent across the ocean to the markets of Europe chests of sugar, rolls of tobacco, bales of cotton, gold, and precious stones. Up to this time its role had been a constructive one; at the same time it was registering these achievements, however, it was piling up a considerable debit. This was not a result of the "mistakes" made, whether in moral terms or those of its achievements, but

was simply a result of contingencies it could not have avoided
and which only time would reveal as profound and organic
evils: the hasty incorporation of such diverse races and cultures, the system of slave labor, the scattered nature of settlement—all the elements that characterized and went to make
up colonization. All these elements which at the time seemed
necessary and even inevitable and hence seemed "right," now,
three centuries after the outset of colonization, clearly revealed
their negative aspects. And it is this negative side, seen in the
decomposition of the Brazilian colonial system, that we find in
the period at which we have chosen to approach Brazil's history.

But underneath all the decay, the country was beginning to
throb with new life. A change was beginning to take place. It is
obviously impossible in a situation of this nature, essentially
dynamic, to pinpoint "moments." It was a situation that hardly
yet existed; it had not yet defined its content. It was simply a
latent state, its existence revealed by certain isolated facts,
early signs that pointed the way. These facts can be traced
right back, even as far as the outset of colonization, if we wish.
And strictly speaking, they could be picked out at any point in
Brazil's historical evolution, an amusement which has whiled
away the time for a number of historians. But if we limit our
attention to the period which in a sense spans the two centuries
immediately preceding our own, and which I have chosen for
this very reason, we find that these facts stand out more
clearly. The colonial system was then in a more advanced stage
of decomposition; the seeds of self-destruction it contained, although present from the outset, were beginning to sprout. And
at the same time the forces of renewal that struggled for expression in the depths of this system—the same destructive seeds
viewed from a different angle—begin to make themselves increasingly felt, and can thus be more easily discerned.

In the period we are considering, these renovating forces already point the way to the new situation, the very opposite of
the colonial system still in force and whose outlines were already beginning to take shape. It is difficult, if not impossible,

to characterize the situation before it actually exploded. It was still vague and undefined, expressed as a formless reaction revealed only through symptoms and external manifestations often of a contradictory nature. The historian, in attempting to deal with this phase, runs a very serious risk of committing anachronistic errors, of projecting onto the past his knowledge of the outcome, the period in which the new situation became clearly defined. And this has not infrequently occurred. Since the process we are concerned with was to lead to the colony's separation from the mother country, to independence, an attempt is generally made to find manifestations that mark the pathway in this direction—a deplorable oversimplification that not only restricts the aims of research, but deflects it from its true course. The final act, or rather the first great scene of the drama that confronts us, is undoubtedly the colony's political independence. But this dénouement did not exist before it unfolded; nor was it "imminent" from the past. It was simply the outcome of a chance combination of forces, none in itself and on its own tending inevitably to such an end. It is possible that some of them may have tended in this direction, but that all of them did so is clearly untrue. But since they all contributed to the final outcome, each in its own way, none can be ignored. Besides, it is chiefly with the individual forces that we should initially concern ourselves, and not with their final effect.

This is the only legitimate attitude that can be taken by the objective researcher, an attitude far removed from the frequent tendency of the researcher to consider the situation whose historical evolution he has followed to its outcome as inevitable, regarding the end as being present in the very first stages of this evolution. In the case we are here concerned with, this would involve the presumption that the necessary and inevitable outcome for the colony was its political independence from the mother country and that this was already present in our destiny from the moment Cabral * saw the floating driftwood that led him to suspect that land was near; and from then

* Pedro Alvares Cabral who discovered Brazil in 1500.—Translator.

on it would simply be a question of seeking all the remote symptoms of this future, inevitable and necessary "independence."

Separation from the mother country had, of course, already been foreseen. The idea that Brazil would one day be an independent nation had been formulated long before the event actually took place, and a few individuals, either through intuition or because they had reached this conclusion through the example of others, were fully aware of the possibility of independence, and sometimes even worked toward this end. But this is by no means the end of the matter, nor does it in any way explain the fact of independence. No single idea, held by one individual or shared by many—and in the case of Brazil it was held by very few—was to be the "cause" of independence. Many other ideas, some of them directly opposed to independence, were held by an incomparably larger number of people, who espoused quite different causes. Ideas are never in short supply; they are tailored to suit all tastes and to express all shades of opinion. And if we stop short at ideas, without examining the facts that inspire them, we shall find it impossible to explain why, at any given moment, one and not another of these ideas should suddenly catch fire and spread, to lead to the realization of the principle or standards aimed at. Ideas by themselves achieve nothing, and for the historian they should serve only as signs, expressions, or obvious symptoms of the reality that underlies them, the concrete facts that inspire them.

Thus, before proceeding, we should forget what happened in a future which for the moment we must ignore and seek only the "forces" I spoke of above, determining the changes whose direction and purpose we cannot yet see and working against the colonial system. I must point out that I use the expression "colonial system" not in the restricted sense of a colonial regime, politically and administratively subject to the mother country, but to include all its characteristics, economic, social, and political, the combination of elements that went into the country's Brazilian policy is interesting not from the point of making of the colony and gave rise to Brazil.

The guiding thread through the labyrinth of facts with which we must deal, the thread that will lead us to the very center of colonial society where we can discover the origin of the "forces" whose most significant external manifestation was the anxiety I mentioned above, permeating all classes and groups of colonial society, is that same economic foundation described in the earlier chapters of this work. This, I shall repeat, was an economy based on exploitation, the hasty and extensive exploitation of the natural resources of a virgin territory to furnish international trade with a few tropical commodities, gold, and precious stones of great commercial value. In the final analysis, this was the essence of the colonial economy, the explanation and definition of Portugal's colonizing endeavor in Brazil. Such a foundation, with the growth of the population and the contribution of various other factors, could no longer support the structure built on it. Strong enough at first and for a long time thereafter to meet the paramount demands of colonization— the occupation and utilization of the territory to promote production and the creation of a relatively stable economic and social balance—with time this foundation proved inadequate for the social structure reared on it to continue to develop. This point was reached without any intervention from outside factors; it was simply the result of a natural unfolding on the colonization process itself.

This inadequacy was clearly demonstrated by the results achieved as colonization developed, results long accumulated, which made complete disintegration imminent at the period we are considering. The whole life of the country was grinding to a halt. The most striking evidence was the material condition of the land, which had hitherto provided the resources for that life. The most accessible sources had been used up or laid waste: lands impoverished by primitive agricultural techniques, shortsighted devastation of wide areas, mineral deposits exhausted. It should be pointed out that I am not condemning out of hand the methods of exploitation employed which, given the circumstances, were the only ones possible. They stemmed from the general system that colonization adopted in Brazilian territory; they were an integral part of this system, which could obviously not have been replaced by any other in the early stages of colonization.

Another essential outcome of the colonization process, intimately related to the material factor noted above, and due, as all else, to the same colonial system must be singled out. This was the growing number of people condemned to a marginal existence outside the normal productive activity of colonization. This activity was almost exclusively limited to members of the closed circle of the colony's basic economic and social organization: masters and slaves, the entrepreneurs and administrators of colonization and their humble tools. As long as there were only masters and slaves, as at the very beginning, everything went well. All the settlers in Brazilian territory had their proper place in the colony's social structure and its activities could develop along normal lines. But gradually other categories began to be formed, composed of people who were not slaves and could not afford to be masters. There was no room for these categories in the colony's system of production. Despite this, their numbers began to grow, a growth that was a similarly inevitable result of the system of colonization. They ended by accounting for a considerable segment of the population, tending ever to grow. Imbalance was thus inevitable.

To these more salient and fundamental features of the evolutionary process of colonization were added others deriving from or intimately related to them. There is no need to enumerate these other features here, since this would be to recapitulate material dealt with in the earlier chapters of this book, although from a static rather than a dynamic angle, which is the angle that interests us here. Briefly then, it can be stated that the system of colonization adopted in Brazil, her "colonial system," having for three centuries borne handsome fruits, which had made it possible to overlook its negative features, had now reached the last stages of its evolution, at least insofar as some of its most important aspects were concerned. And the curve it had hitherto drawn across the pages of history was beginning to trend unmistakably downward toward its completion. The system had exhausted its possibilities and would have to be replaced by another.

This need had become so obvious that none of the enlightened contemporaries who have left us their thoughts on the subject remained unaware of it. Toward the end of the eighteenth century, "reformers" and projects for reform began increasingly to appear. In the course of this work I have had occasion to refer to many of them, not for the projects they proposed, which are no longer of practical interest, but for the clarity with which so many of them analyzed the situation, providing valuable data for the reconstruction of a past which for them was a fully comprehended present. Most of these reformers advocated a "crystallization" of prevailing conditions, the perpetuation in a hothouse atmosphere of the colonial system as it had been and was still being applied. The evils they so clearly perceived were not attributed to the system itself, but to the *way* in which it was applied and, above all, to the deviations from traditional practice which had been introduced. In short, what they proposed was a reestablishment of the system in its orginally pure form. The most typical instance of this mode of thought is provided by the anonymous author of the *Roteiro do Maranhão,* a man undoubtedly brilliant, cultured, and closely acquainted with the colony.

Others, less conservative by nature, saw further than this and advocated more far-reaching reforms. Luís dos Santos Vilhena, our much-remembered regius professor of the city of Salvador [Bahia] and author of *Recopilação de Notícias Soteropolitanas e Brasílicas* (Compendium of Bahian and Brazilian News), is representative of this group.[28]

The home government also made attempts to grapple with the problem. The end of the eighteenth and early years of the nineteenth centuries saw the enactment of a mass of legislation which clearly reveals the mother country's awareness of the need to undertake reforms, or at least reveals that the crown was not oblivious to the fact that something had to be done. In fact, however, little was done that proved truly effective.[29] The measures enacted, well intentioned and apparently revolu-

tionary in relation to the traditional colonial system, such as
the permission to establish iron manufacturing in 1795 or the
reform of the Mining Code in 1803 and similar measures, were
never properly carried out in practice, because they did not alter the essential features of this system.

What explains this failure to carry out effective reforms? The
vices of the Portuguese administration and the profound decadence of the reigning dynasty do not provide a sufficient
answer. To find the complete answer we would have to go far
back in time and take a closer look at Portuguese history. But
there is no space for detailed analysis here, and this in any case
would lead us far from the subject with which we are directly
concerned. Nevertheless, we cannot afford completely to ignore this history, since many of the circumstances that concern
us here cannot be understood without it. We will therefore
take a brief glimpse at the features that have direct bearing on
our subject and in good part explain many of the facts that follow.

The first thing to consider is the general attitude of the Portuguese government toward its American colony. After the
fifteenth century, Portugal had ceased to be a small and insignificant European kingdom, and had become a great maritime
and colonial empire; and it was on the basis of this empire,
which at its height spread over vast areas of three continents
but which at the period we are considering was practically
confined to Brazil, that the kingdom had reorganized its structure and its very life, with Portugal itself as the apex and center of control. But this had been done under very special conditions, which distinguish the Portuguese Empire from the other
colonial empires, particularly the British, with which it had
once vied. The focus for the absolute Portuguese monarchy
was the person of the king and his court, the swarm of courtiers
who surrounded the throne and who formed for the most part a
togaed nobility, occupying posts and performing functions
more or less related to the monarchy's administrative structure.[30]

Portuguese policy was determined by these circumstances. It

was the king and his chosen court who enjoyed the fruits of empire, sharing in the profits of the royal ventures, and not the *Portuguese nation,* which benefited only indirectly from the vast possessions of the monarchy. This had been the case from the very beginning of Portuguese maritime expansion. It was in fact to the king that Portugal owed her conquests; the Portuguese discoveries were the result of an enterprise solely undertaken from first to last on the initiative of the Portuguese monarchs and their immediate delegates.[31] This was indeed the basis of Portuguese absolutism, the immense and incomparable power of the crown.

For this reason the Portuguese Empire was not a natural unfolding of national life, and the Portuguese nation did not figure as the basis of empire or the convergent nucleus of monarchy. Without going into further detail, which would complicate the issue, we can reach certain conclusions about the content of Portuguese policy and particularly its policy toward Brazil. It was first and foremost the king's "business concern," and all matters connected with public administration were regarded from this standpoint. Thus, the administrative and political problems that arose in the colony were always handled from a strictly *financial* angle. For the purposes of Portuguese policy, the society and the economy of the colony were nonexistent, even if these bore directly on Portuguese interests; there was merely a financial question. This is clearly evident from most of the more important official correspondence and from the legislation enacted for Brazil. Indeed, no attempt was made to disguise this fact, and the Royal Exchequer openly played the star part in Brazil's colonial history.

This was the chief cause of the failure of Portugal's policy to carry out any substantial reforms of its colonial system. For the system could only have meant one thing to the mother country: one department, albeit the essential department, of the great commercial enterprise that was the Portuguese monarchy, with the king behind the counter. This organization began with the trade in slaves, ivory, and gold along the African coast; continued with the trade in pepper and spices carried on with India; and was completed by the sugar, gold, diamonds, and cotton of Brazil. The organization had enabled the kingdom to occupy two continents and people a third, but had now become obsolete. It no longer functioned properly, and the sacrifices involved in keeping it going regardless fell heavily on its last surviving remnant, the Brazilian colony. How then could the colony be reformed if this would mean destroying the only remaining basis for the kingdom's commercial organization? It could be done only by replacing this basis with some other. This solution never occurred—indeed, could not have occurred—to Portugal's rulers, because it would have meant self-destruction. Later, it was likewise not to occur to those who toppled the absolute power of the king and attempted— vainly, as it transpired—to replace him.

As may be seen, then, the colonial system was not an arbitrary creation which could be reformed at will. It was too deeply rooted in the organization of the Portuguese monarchy of which the colony was an integral part. Their destinies were intimately entwined. How, then, could the colony be reformed short of breaking with the mother country? But although this break became the prerequisite for the reforms needed—or at least this is how it seems to us because we happen to stand at a vantage point from which events can be comfortably viewed in their historical context, whereas for contemporaries things were not quite so clearcut—the idea of breaking with the mother country did not occur so spontaneously as a sudden flash of inspiration striking some privileged mind grappling with a problem that called for solution and spreading like wildfire or an epidemic until it had gathered enough adherents energetic and daring enough to put the idea into practice with one wave of a magic wand. Historical events are unfortunately not quite so simple and cannot be explained by the sort of fairytale explanation so dear to the hearts of many historians.

It is true that, as I have already indicated, there were people who foresaw the colony's separation from the mother country. To dispose of this and pass on to consideration of the matter in its proper terms, let us name these prophets. After the independence of the English colonies in North America (1776), certain people outside Brazil, clearly inspired by their example, began to envisage the possibility of following in their footsteps. Joaquim José da Maia, a Brazilian student at the University of Montpellier (France), where there was a large number of Brazilian students,[32] wrote to Jefferson, then the American Union's Ambassador in France, asking for the new nation's support for Brazilian independence. He managed to interview Jefferson, but the matter went no further. Two other students, José Álvares Maciel and Domingos Vidal de Barbosa, the latter also at Montpellier, took their views much further.

On their return to Brazil they took part in the *Inconfidência Mineira* (The Minas Conspiracy),* and in all likelihood José Álvares Maciel provided Tiradentes with the ideological material which the fervent sublieutenant used to give color to his conspiracy and projected revolt. In this conspiracy, as well as in the later Bahian uprising known as the *Inconfidência da Bahia* (1798), although perhaps to a lesser extent in the latter, and in the plots hatched in Rio de Janeiro in 1794 which led to the imprisonment of all the conspirators, including Mariano José Pereira da Fonseca, future Marquis of Maricá and Brazil's only moralist of note, the idea of separation from the mother country played an important role. In all these schemes, the idea of national independence was openly discussed. But this never gained currency outside a small and secret circle of conspirators. Not even among the colony's more enlightened citizens did the idea gain much ground. On the contrary, those who clearly realized the need for reforms and fought for their introduction seldom, if ever, carried their convictions to revolutionary extremes. Right up to the eve of independence, even among those chiefly responsible for its implantation, there was nothing to indicate any clearly defined separationist tenden-

---

* The *Inconfidência* was a conspiracy to overthrow the Portuguese regime, organized in Minas Gerais in 1789 by a man nicknamed "Tiradentes"—the toothpuller. The conspiracy leaked out and the home government took severe action against the conspirators. Tiradentes was executed as an example and warning, and the others were exiled to the African colonies.—Translator.

cies. José Bonifácio, who became the Patriarch of Independence, was forced into this position in spite of himself. He had always envisaged not a break with the mother country, but the creation of a dual monarchy, a kind of Luso-Brazilian Federation.[33]

Thus, the explanation that the "idea" of national independence was behind the forces of renewal operating in the colony seems a risky one, to say the least. Much more compatible with events is an explanation based on the general temper of the period. The various ideas of separation, federation, the liquidation of the Portuguese merchant and taverner (the latter very much in the air), and all the other ideas present but much less prominent—abolition of slavery, suppression of the color bar, the breaking down of class barriers—were all simply reflections in the minds of the people of objective external situations. Such ideas arose out of the everyday relationships of individuals: the senhor d'engenho or fazendeiro, hounded by the Portuguese merchant to whom he owed money; the ragged colonials refused employment by the Portuguese shopkeeper; the mulatto excluded from most jobs by the white man who despised and humiliated him; the sharecropper bound by contract to send his cane to be ground at the senhor d'engenho's mill and feeling himself robbed; and the slave who longed to be free. These conflicts can also be seen from the opposite angle: the merchant who had lent his money and felt justified in wanting it back; the Portuguese shopkeeper who preferred his compatriots, more industrious and more congenial; the white man who grew up with the conviction, instilled at birth and officially recognized, that he belonged to a superior race; and the slaveholder who needed manpower and was merely conforming to the law, custom, and morality of the recognized and established order. All had reason on their side, and all formulated or adapted—and it was, of course, generally the latter—their own "ideas" to justify their positions or aspirations.

If I seem to dwell on details, this is because in this case it was the details that counted. Each of the situations enumerated above, clearly evident on the surface of events and thus

readily grasped, were related to general contradictions stemming from the very essence of the colonial system. They were
the result of what I have called the "vices" of the system,
which the colonization process gradually revealed one after the
other. In all the cases cited, as in any others of the same kind,
the individuals involved were simply creatures of the system
and suffered from the way it operated: the landowner constantly in debt, the creditor who was never paid, the raga-
muffin who could find no work or means of livelihood, and so
on. All was, directly or indirectly, a consequence of the colonial system, and all these petty conflicts mounted up to produce the restlessness and ferment of colonial society, which
prepared the way for its transformation. The impending social
change was to be oriented toward the solution of such conflicts;
it was to put a stop to the profound contradictions of a system
which had given rise to them, to harmonize these contradictions with new elements emerging fom the very process of balancing the opposites involved and removing their raison d'être.
These new elements were to constitute the hoped for change.[34]

The driving force behind the restructuring of the colony's
economic and social institutions will thus be found in the profound contradictions of the colonial system. And just as the
conflicts agitating colonial society came out of these profound
contradictions, so the resolution of these conflicts was to come
out of the synthesis of these contradictory elements, a synthesis
that was to lead to the creation of a new system that would replace the outmoded colonial organization. We must therefore
take a closer look at these contradictions.

The first, the one that played the most important role and
affected the influential and dominant classes of the social order,
was the rivalry between the proprietors on the one hand
(senhores d'engenho, fazendeiros, and lavradores) and the
merchants on the other. I have already referred to this, and
made an attempt to describe the relative positions of these two
classes, divided by antagonistic interests which originated primarily from their respective positions as debtor and creditor.
The bitterness between these two groups was exacerbated by

the chronic insolvency of the colony's finances as a result of the
more or less intense crisis affecting colonial production, particularly sugar, during the eighteenth century, which in the final
analysis was caused by the very nature of the economy—weak,
loosely organized, badly managed and viscerally dependent on
a precarious and uncertain foreign market.[35]

It was also sharpened by the profound difference in the way
of life and psychology of the classes and individuals who made
up these groups, likewise a consequence of the inherent conditions of the colonial system: on the one hand, the Brazilian
landed proprietors who regarded themselves as the country's
"nobility," brought up in opulence, accustomed to free spending, contemptuous of work and thrift; on the other, the "mascates," the immigrants who had managed to amass some
wealth, brought up in a hard school of work and parsimony
and who attempted to use their money to rival the prestige and
social position of the Brazilian gentry.[36] Hatred of the Portuguese merchant—"peddler" (*mascate*), sailor (*marinheiro*),
"lead-foot" (*pé-de-chumbo*): the insulting epithets were various
—spread because the immigrants had succeeded in monopoliz-
ing the colony's trade, both wholesale and retail, and excluded
the Brazilian-born colonists, who were thus deprived of a possible means of livelihood. The conflict between these categories
of the population thus became increasingly bitter and ever
more widespread.

Another of the contradictions of the colonial system was of
an ethnic nature, the result of the degraded position of the
black slave and to a lesser extent of the native, which led to
prejudice against any dark-skinned person. The majority of the
population was affected by this prejudice which, quite apart
from its moral effect, excluded them from any share in the good
things of life the colony could offer. The political role of this
racial antagonism, not yet fully estimated, was nevertheless
considerable. As well as the silent struggle and latent revolt
which could be sensed in the oppressed races and which contemporary accounts, in spite of their reticence on the subject,
did not conceal—Vilhena's remark on the "insolence" of the

mulattoes [37] is one instance—there were graver symptoms of an imminent clash. The testimonies given during the official inquiry into the Bahian Conspiracy and the texts of the seditious declarations which had been posted up in the city clearly indicate that what triggered off the abortive uprising was class distinction and revolt against color prejudice.[38] This is borne out by the fact that nearly all the conspirators caught were men of color or mulattoes of humble origin.

The lot of the slaves was another source of friction. Their usually passive behavior is commonly taken to indicate that they were completely reconciled to their lot, even though belied by the number of runaways, the existence of *quilombos*, and the many slave revolts like those that troubled Bahia at the beginning of the last century and the other uprisings that occurred at regular intervals (1807, 1809, 1813, 1816, 1826, 1827, 1828, 1830, and 1835).[39] There was a constant silent struggle, particularly in places where they were more numerous and more aware of their strength or where there was a larger concentration of slaves with a higher degree of culture, as in Bahia.[40] This city, the greatest center of slave uprisings in Brazilian history, was said by Vilhena to be in a perpetual state of alarm on account of the perennial threat presented by that "dread corporation," as he called the slaves.[41]

To these specific instances of social antagonism and conflict must be added the widespread ill-feeling engendered by the action and methods of the home government. These have been more thoroughly investigated: the taxation system, the methods used for rounding up conscripts, the mother country's narrow economic policy, the despotism of the captains-general, and so forth. But the role of this factor, although more obvious, was a relatively small one in the revolutionary process agitating the colony. More often than not the actions and abuses of the administration served as pretexts or justification for extreme and revolutionary attitudes, or acted merely as immediately contributory factors, the last drops before the vessel overflowed.[42] In the case under discussion, the effect of the mother view of individual measures, but from that of its general impact, its tendency to act as the chief force for preserving the colonial system intact and curbing the impending transformation.

There is no point in continuing to dissect the contradictions and sources of friction that agitated the colony and its political and social system. These are implicit in the foregoing pages, in which I attempted to analyze what colonization had achieved by the beginning of the last century. The cases singled out above as being the most obvious were chosen to illustrate the general tendency. It was the colonial system as a whole that was profoundly corroded and undermined. The outward aspects of this disintegration, the clashes and conflicts that arose, were diverse and complex manifestations and only by a process of abstraction and to facilitate exposition can they be reduced to the simple outlines I have provided, which merely reflect the total reality. The only factor common to all these contradictions of the colonial system is that they had arisen out of the same system and were clear symptoms of its disintegration. They differed widely from place to place and in the constantly changing aspects they presented. They cannot be paired off into opposing, clearly defined camps, since if in some cases their elements were plainly opposed, in others they fused and intermingled.

To illustrate my meaning I shall use the same instances as above. Thus, we find proprietors and free individuals from the lower classes joining forces against the merchants; at the same time, we find all three categories uniting against the slaves. We find the lower classes banding together against proprietors and merchants who were their overlords, and the latter driven together as the privileged against the impoverished. We find whites fighting side by side with blacks and mulattoes against color prejudice in the Bahian Conspiracy; mulattoes, blacks, and whites joining together to uphold the same prejudice. And the next moment we find they have all changed their respective positions, and the moment after that, that they are all back where they started in some other volte-face. In fact, this is precisely what happens in any similar situation wherever or whenever it may have arisen. The apparent lack of logic is naïvely explained away by making generalizations from particular cases which are in themselves insignificant, generalizations on the basis of individual or moral issues—idealism, incoherence—whatever happens to suit the taste or preference of the individual observer. The truth is that men are merely the pawns of events that move them across the board of history, for the most part hardly aware of what they are doing or of what is taking place around them.

We should add that the illogical and incongruous nature of facts makes it not only difficult to interpret them, but is also the reason why all the situations we have analyzed above are so vague and undefined—a vagueness and uncertainty that resides in the facts themselves and that no artifice of historical explanation can dissemble. The facts only stand out clearly and become meaningful as a whole when such situations have matured. It is useless to seek them before then, twisting events to fit the particular pattern which the observer wishes to impose. And even after the first clearcut facts have emerged, how many events must yet occur before the process runs its course, solving all its contradictions only for a new process to emerge, with new contradictions derived from that solution, an incessant repetition and renewal? The eternal movement of history, of mankind, of all things, a never-ending and ceaseless movement of which we, with the poor instruments of understanding and expression at our disposal, can only grasp and above all can only reproduce a minute particle, a clumsy cross-section of a dynamic reality that cannot be defined in static terms.

At the period we are considering we have not yet reached the phase of decisive and far-reaching events, whose first landmark can roughly be established as coinciding with the transfer of the Portuguese Court to Rio de Janeiro. But we have seen that in this period the latent contradictions were beginning to make themselves felt and to manifest themselves in alarming symptoms which challenged the entire colonial structure. Where would it lead, this confused, complicated, contradictory process, a process that can be likened to a whitecapped sea in which the waves rise and fall, clash and merge, pursue each other toward the shore, only to lead to the same final end as they mass themselves to crash violently against the shingle or to sweep a long line of spray across the sand? We cannot follow this process to its conclusion, since this lies outside the scope of our study. Confining ourselves, then, to the period under review, we find that there was still complete confusion; the actions of individuals, like the ideas and precepts they espoused, constantly vacillated; there were contradictions within the same currents of thought and action when not in the minds and hearts of the actors who took part in the drama that was unfolding. This was the case even for the only organizations that, in the general confusion and incoherence of the moment, were surer of their path: the secret societies and, more especially, the Freemasons.

There can no longer be any doubt as to the role played by Freemasonry in Brazilian history from the end of the eighteenth century onward, when it began to penetrate the country and to become highly organized. This role was not simply the one usually assigned to the Masons, which really amounts to what was their least significant action, that is, the part played by one of the Masonic lodges, the "Great Orient of Rio de Janeiro" and its offshoot, the "Apostolate of the Andradas," [43] which came out into the open and guided the events immediately preceding independence. It was more profound and far-reaching than that, and was also far more ancient. Above all, Freemasonry was organized, systematic, and fully conscious, with strong ties both inside and outside the colony. It was no mere coincidence that the chief architects of independence, even the future emperor himself, were all Masons, that all the cues to guide the course of events had been previously worked out in the Masonic lodges. None of this was mere chance. It was the result of systematic underground action, working in a certain direction. In other words, behind the *individuals* who played their part in all the great events of our history after the end of the eighteenth century there was an *organization*, of which these individuals were often nor more than the instruments. Or to put it even more bluntly, they were often not even aware of what they were really doing.

Through the Masons, Brazilian politics, or rather, the first stirrings of what was to become Brazilian politics, were integrated into an international movement of far wider proportions. Freemasonry was organized in Brazil either by Brazilians themselves and by newly arrived Portuguese acting on instructions received from Europe—as in the case of the first lodge established in Pernambuco in 1796 by the naturalist, Arruda Câmara and called the "Areopagus"—or by foreign agents especially sent to Brazil for this purpose, or persons who appeared to be agents, as far as we can determine from the occasional rents in the veil of secrecy shrouding Masonic activities. This was clearly the mission of a certain "Chevalier Laurent," who landed at Rio de Janeiro in 1801 and founded the city's first regular Masonic lodge, the *Reunião* (Assembly).[44] In any case, the Masonic lodges in Brazil were clearly made to order on European models.

At the beginning of the nineteenth century, there were lodges in all the colony's major cities, connected not only to each other and their European exemplars but to the lodges established in the United States and the other American colonies. The intervention in Brazilian life of a powerful organization of this type in itself shows that, over and above the individuals who appeared on the colony's political scene, there was an active will that was certainly stronger than theirs. In fact, most of the people actively involved in politics at this period were Freemasons. Conjecture becomes certainty when we scrutinize the facts that occasionally managed to break through the Masonic seal of secrecy, dragging into the light of day what had been mysteriously taking place within the lodges. The full extent of the activities of the Freemasons was then clearly revealed in all its intensity, and one feels that Freemasonry, rather than any individual or group, was behind the scenes controlling the events of our history. It is not possible here to go into detail about a subject so intimately related to all the

great international events of the eighteenth and nineteenth
centuries, which should be viewed within a larger frame than
that of the particular history of Brazil. There is, however, one
point with a direct bearing on the subject in hand and which
must therefore be clarified. This is the direction taken by this
outside intervention in Brazilian affairs, and the extent to
which it affected the issues with which we are here concerned.
It is obvious that the colonial situation, such as I described it
above, with its contradictions and internal tensions, had nothing to do with Freemasonry or with any other outside idea or
influence of any sort. The situation had arisen from the colony's
own particular conditions and was a consequence purely of the
political regime and the social and economic systems prevailing
in the colony. These and these alone had created the situation
and were the sole reason for its existence.[45]

The role of Freemasonry in this as in so many other similar
instances was to place the particular domestic situation of a
European colony within the larger framework of a general European policy, whose aim was the reform leading to the re-
alignment of European powers, and the new balance of power
established in the nineteenth century. All this is only remotely
related to our subject, since the intervention in a colony as insignificant as Brazil was of interest to international Freemasonry only insofar as it could further its attempt to undermine
one of the bulwarks of European absolutism—which was, by
and large, what the movement was aiming to achieve. Brazil
was simply the instrument for an indirect attack on the Portuguese monarchy. Indeed, the other American colonies were being used in the same way to get at the Spanish throne, hence
the interest shown by Freemasonry in gaining control of the
political situations existing in the American colonies in order to
manipulate them for its own ends.

For their part, Brazilians and all those with a direct interest
in the life of the colony, feeling rather than understanding the
need for reforms, found an ideal instrument in Freemasonry,
both because of its prestige and international connections and
because of its accumulated strength. Many of the people who

became Freemasons were, of course, merely mimicking others, and so could become puppets in the hands of the movement. But the Brazilian Freemasons, whether of the first or of the second type, could not twist the facts of Brazil's history. They could thus only take whatever advantages it offered to suit their ends, just as international Freemasonry availed itself of the Brazilian situation for its own purposes.

Masonic intervention in Brazilian politics at the end of the eighteenth and beginning of the nineteenth centuries should be interpreted in the light of what has been outlined above. Freemasonry brought about no changes in the historical facts with which we are concerned. It attempted to control and guide events in Brazil but did not essentially alter these events. Indeed, to imagine that it could do so would be palpably absurd. What deserves emphasis is the great aim behind the movement, the aim I indicated above. As for the best means of furthering this aim in the particular case of Brazil, there was room for a large number of possibilities, and even among the Freemasons there was no common accord on the subject. Any reform, whatever direction it took, would strike a blow against Portuguese absolutism, whose destruction was the major aim envisaged. Widespread unrest, even if nothing concrete came out of it, in itself was an appreciable gain. Any course was possible, provided it disturbed the stability of the Portuguese throne. This is what accounts for the struggles that went on inside the lodges or broke out between them, frequently dragging into the organization the external conflicts it was seeking to manipulate.[46]

In short, the general effective policy and activity of international Freemasonry did not concern itself with the mere detail of the colony's politics. It acted only as a stimulus and, hence, in its international and general role is of no more than indirect concern for Brazil. Brazilian Freemasons, whatever their course of action within the framework of the particular ends they had in view, were in fact acting not as "Masons" but as "Brazilians." What their membership in the society provided was the possibility of greater agreement, of concerted and

organized action which, but for Freemasonry and in the absence of any similar organization, would have been even less
coherent and more sporadic than it was. The thin thread of
continuity in the line of action that wound and twisted its way
through the confused political events of the last years of the
eighteenth century, which culminated in the colony's independence, was undoubtedly attributable to the fact that most of
the principal actors in these events were members of an organized and politically experienced body. Thus, Freemasonry lent a
measure of political consciousness to an action which, although
it would certainly have existed, would have been blind and confused without it. Or, what is more probable, political action
would have resorted to some other made-to-measure organization instead. Freemasonry was chosen for the role for obvious
reasons.

There was thus a "coincidence"—and I must pause to justify
the use of so risky a word by pleading its accuracy in this context from the point of view of the local history we are dealing
with—a coincidence of a fact in our own history and one of a
much more general nature: on the one hand, the Brazilian situation which had arisen from the particular circumstances that
determined it; on the other, an international situation, apparently unrelated but in fact indirectly linked to it through international Freemasonry and its aims in European politics.

This was not in fact the sole instance of such a coincidence.
We find that coincidences occurred in other spheres as well,
all more or less intimately related to the one considered above.
Intervention in the events we are here concerned with, in this
case not by any private organization such as Freemasonry but
by foreign powers, was clearly evident. Revolutionary and
Napoleonic France was particularly active in this respect, since
Portugal had once more allied herself with England, that age-
old enemy of France. French intervention was marked: the indirect action taken through her European contacts, especially
the Freemasons, one of the Revolution's most powerful external
weapons, was combined with direct action taken through her
agents in Brazil.

In 1809 the Portuguese government, recently installed in Rio de Janeiro, drew the attention of the provisional *junta* governing Bahia to the large number of Frenchmen living in that city, especially "a certain Abbot," whose name is not given and has never been discovered. These Frenchmen had stayed on after the visit of the French squadron escorting Jerome Bonaparte, Napoleon's brother.[47] It is also possible that the conspiracy uncovered in Pernambuco in 1801, involving Arruda da Câmara, founder of the Areopagus lodge mentioned above, and the Cavalcanti de Albuquerque brothers, owners of the Suaçuna plantation, which aimed to make Pernambuco an independent state under the protection of Napoleon Bonaparte, then First Consul, was directly inspired by French agents.[48] This has not yet been firmly established, but the incident throws a good deal of light on the confused history of the events with which we are concerned.

Nor is English intervention to be despised. The direct effects of this intervention made themselves felt less, since as Portugal's ally and protectress, England furthered her own interests at the Portuguese Court itself. But although the secret intervention of foreign powers in Brazil has not yet been fully studied, there can be no doubt that it played an important role in the underground activities affecting Brazilian politics in the early years of the last century, and that the consequences of this secret intervention were as significant as those of the more spectacular interventions recorded in the period's official history.

Finally, there was one other sphere in which Brazilian politics were linked to the international movement: the ideological sphere. The ideas and precepts espoused in Brazil both explain and justify the facts and give them the warmth of human emotions which ideologies always supply and which mankind can seldom do without. In Brazil's case, since the colonists' experience had not prepared them for the creation of original ideas and precepts, or in other words since they had failed to formulate a set of ideas which could become the foundation for a Brazilian ideology, they sought them in the great and influential storehouse of European thought or, more specifically, in the philosophy of the eighteenth century French Encyclopaedists.

The reasons why these particular ideas gained ground in Brazil are similar to those that led to the strength of international Freemasonry as a guiding political force. Indeed, the affinity between the ideas of the Freemasons and those of the Encyclopaedists is well known and this already explains a good deal. But leaving this aside we should also bear in mind the fact that no philosophy, no set of ideas, and above all no cluster of theoretical concepts gave the universal facts of the eighteenth century—and I use the word "universal" here to mean those of the Western civilization to which we belong—a clear reinterpretation, one so harmonious and so aesthetically perfect as the comprehensive ideas embodied in the general philosophy of the Encyclopaedists. Their ideas found an immediate response in the climate of the moment, echoing the intimate feelings of thinking men. The only ideology comparable in impact for the moment and the situation in which it arose was the socialism of the nineteenth century. It is thus not to be wondered at that thinking men throughout the world were caught up in the intellectual excitement that it aroused, and that it became the "official" mode of interpreting facts. Brazilians did not remain immune, and the ideas of the Encyclopaedists found a warm reception in the colony. Many representatives of the colonial intelligentsia came into direct and intimate contact with the movement, either as students in France or because they had sought this Mecca of Western philosophy for some other reason. In Portugal, commercial colony of England but intellectual colony of France, Encyclopaedist ideas had gained widespread recognition; and even the University of Coimbra, that storehouse of rancid ideas, had been affected after Pombal's reforms had opened a few windows, letting in a breeze of fresh air to be eagerly gulped down.

Thus, to the extent that general ideas, if not ideas *tout court*, managed to penetrate the thick crust of colonial ignorance, it was French eighteenth-century philosophy that dominated the colonial minds able to grasp its concepts.[49] This domination is too well known to require more emphasis. From the last quarter of the eighteenth century onward, when Brazilians began to write in earnest, all bears the unmistakable imprint of French thought: ideas, style, the attitude of mind, and the approach toward the subject. Indeed, the literature of our grandfathers, the scanty literature produced in this colony of illiterates where only a handful of people knew how to read and only a few out of this tiny minority were attracted by the things of the spirit, was almost all inspired by French models. Through official inquiries conducted by the colonial authorities into the plots and the conspiracies which had become so frequent after the last years of the eighteenth century as a result of the widespread political unrest, we penetrate the secrets of the colony's major private libraries. Lists of their confiscated contents are available to us, in the yellowed and moth-eaten pages of the official reports. The only works by philosophers, moralists, and political writers listed are French, and other French literature is abundantly represented.[50] The early nineteenth century foreign travelers in Brazil noted the pronounced influence of French culture; and the strength of French rationalist and revolutionary ideas was deplored by St. Hilaire, whose views were so diametrically opposed. Martius commented on what, even today, appears at first sight paradoxical: the unrivaled position of French culture in spite of England's complete commercial domination and the large number of Englishmen living in Brazil.[51] In fact, at this period, English culture was completely unknown in Brazil. The English had not been as successful with their ideas as with their textiles, tools, and chinaware.

The widespread influence of French thought, "Jacobin ideas" or "abominable French principles," as they were referred to in certain Brazilian circles, did not fail to alarm the authorities and all the "right people" of the period. From the official correspondence we learn of the terror these ideas aroused.[52] Knowledge of the French language was enough to excite suspicion: An uncle of Fernandes Pinheiro, future Viscount of São Leopoldo, and Canon of the São Paulo Cathedral, was horrified when he heard that his nephew was learning French and demanded, as head of the family, that these studies be terminated forthwith, since they exposed the innocent child to the "libertine, impious and atheist principles of that nation." [53]

But French revolutionary ideology overcame this opposition and was "officially" adopted with specific Brazilian circumstances in mind. Its general outline seemed perfectly suited to the colony's political requirements. "Liberty-Equality-Fraternity," the political precept which summed up this ideology, clearly lent itself to the various situations found in Brazil. Although often distorted and deformed (and indeed, what distortions and what deformations could not be covered by this blanket formula), it was the motto for all who sought to press some claim: senhores d'engenho and fazendeiros against merchants, mulattoes against whites, the barefoot against the shod, Brazilians against Portuguese—all except slaves against masters, precisely those to whom it should have been the great rallying cry. But the slaves spoke—when they spoke at all, since more often than not they simply acted, needing no ideological garb—in the more familiar and accessible language they had brought with them from the forests, the plains and the African deserts.[54]

NOTES

Notes

Introduction
(pp. 1–6)

[1] I fully understood the descriptions of the mining activities in Minas Gerais given in the accounts of Eschwege, Mawe, and others only after I had visited the area and examined de visu the processes employed, which continue, in almost all cases, to be exactly the same. In this, as in many other instances, traveling through Brazil is like going back in history a hundred years or more. A foreign professor once told me that he envied Brazilian historians, who could be personal witnesses of the most vivid scenes of their past. [M. C. von Eschwege was a German explorer who traveled in Brazil in 1811. For an account of his travels, translated from the German into Portuguese, see *Diario de uma viagem do Rio de Janeiro a Villa Rica, na capitania de Minas Gerais no anno de 1811* (Diary of a Journey from Rio de Janeiro to Villa Rica in the Captaincy of Minas Gerais, in the year 1811), São Paulo, Imprensa Oficial do Estado, 1936. John Mawe is the author of *Travels in the Interior of Brazil,* published in Philadelphia in 1816.—Translator.]

Meaning of Colonization
(pp. 7–22)

[1] From the middle of the sixteenth century, attempts were made to find a sea route to the East through the arctic regions of Europe and Asia. The first man to attempt this was the same Sebastian Cabot who had been active in America, once more in the service of the English (1553).

[2] Marcus Lee Hansen, *The Atlantic Migration, 1607–1680,* p. 13.

[3] Marcus Lee Hansen, *The Immigrant in American History.* See the chapter on "Immigration and Expansion."

[4] *História da Colonização Portuguêsa do Brasil,* ed. Carlos Malheiro

443

Dias (History of Portuguese Colonization of Brazil). Introduction, vol. III, p. xix.

⁵ The exact date of the arrival of the first Negro slaves in Brazil is not known; it is extremely probable that a number of them came with Martim Afonso de Sousa's expedition as early as 1531. In North America, the first batch of Negro slaves, brought in by Dutch slave traders, arrived in Jamestown (Virginia) in 1619.

⁶ Gilberto Freyre, *Casa Grande e Senzala*, p. 16. (The reference in the American edition, *The Masters and the Slaves*, New York, Alfred Knopf, 1946, is p. 17.—Translator.)

Coastal Settlement
(pp. 25–50)

¹ *Documentos Oficiais, Vários assuntos* (Official Documents; Various Matters), p. 456.

² For the documents relating to this treaty and an introduction by Rodolfo Garcia, see Vols. 52 and 53 of the *Anais da Biblioteca Nacional*.

³ Paradoxically, it was from the west, eastward, that the first incursion up the Amazon was made. This was Orellana's expedition of 1541.

⁴ *História do Brasil*, p. 19.

⁵ For a description of the Brazilian coast, see Alfredo Lisboa, "Vias de Communicação: Portos do Brasil" (Communication Routes: Brazilian Ports), in *Dicionário Histórico, Geográfico e Etnográfico do Brasil*.

⁶ *Recopilação*, p. 48. [The full title is *Recopilação de Noticias Soteropolitanas e Brasilicas* (Compendium of Bahian and Brazilian News).—Translator.]

⁷ *Memórias do Rio de Janeiro para Uso do Vice-Rei, Luís de Vasconcelos* (Memoirs of Rio de Janeiro for the Use of the Viceroy . . .), containing a census of the captaincy's population according to categories and parishes.

⁸ J. Carneiro da Silva, *Memórias dos Campos dos Goitacases*, p. 13.

⁹ *Ibid.*, p. 49.

¹⁰ *Almanaque Histórico*, p. 159.

¹¹ J. Carneiro da Silva, *op. cit.*, pp. 8, 53.

¹² The history of this region is admirably documented in *Mémoire présenté par les États-Unis du Brésil au Gouvernément de la Confédération Suisse, arbitre entre le Brésil et la France*, drawn up by Rio Branco, and *L'Oyapoc et l'Amazone, question Brésilienne et Française*, by J. Caetano da Silva.

¹³ Martius, *Viagem*, II, p. 560. [J. B. von Spix and C. F. P. von Martius were the authors of *Reise in Brasilien* (Munich, 1823–1831). An English translation, *Travels in Brazil, 1817–1820*, was published in London in 1824. The author here refers to the Brazilian edition of 1938, *Viagem pelo Brasil por J. B. von Spix e C. F. P. von Martius* (see Bibliography); but he later quotes from the English edition.—Translator.]

¹⁴ A. B. Pereira do Lago, *Itinerario da Provincia do Maranhão* (Itinerary of the Province of Maranhão), p. 402.

¹⁵ *Roteiro do Maranhão*, p. 64.

[16] Southey, *History,* Vol. III, p. 801.

[17] Castro Carreira, *Descrição do Ceará* (Description of Ceará), p. 129.

[18] Koster, *Voyages,* I, Ch. 6 [Henry Koster is the author of *Travels in Brazil* published in London in 1816. Caio Prado, Jr., has used the French edition of this work, *Voyages pittoresques, scientifiques et historiques en Amérique, Brésil,* traduits par M. A. Jay, published in 2 vols. in Paris, 1846.—Translator.]

[19] See the chapter, Extractive Products.

[20] Vilhena, *Recopilação,* p. 604.

[21] *Itinerário da Bahia ao Rio de Janeiro.*

[22] It must be noted that these attacks were intermittent, and hence the colonial establishments along the coast south of Bahia and Espírito Santo were given a breathing space in which to reconstruct their settlements after each assault. This intermittence, which also characterized similar attacks in Goiás, suggests the theory that, in addition to the fear that kept the Indians quiet after an attack had been repelled, there were deeper causes underlying the periodical incursions. It is possible that the physical growth of the native tribes caused the periodic relative decrease in the food resources of the forest, which provided their sole means of support. The attacks, which naturally caused a great many deaths among the Indians, may have reestablished a balance. Vicissitudes of climate may also have played their part. These points have remained obscure but deserve the attention of the historian.

[23] Cit. by Navarro in *Itinerário da Bahia ao Rio de Janeiro,* p. 431.

[24] Francisco Manuel da Cunha, *Informação sôbre o Espírito Santo* (Account of Espírito Santo), 1811, p. 246.

[25] *Voyage,* I, p. 342. [Prince Maximilian of Wied-Neuwied traveled in Brazil from 1815–1817. The Author has used the French edition of the Prince's account of his travels.—Translator.]

[26] *Notas para a história do Espírito Santo* (Notes for a history of Espírito Santo), compiled by J. J. Machado de Oliveira, p. 197.

[27] This ratio applies to 1820, if we accept the figure of 14,000 inhabitants given by St. Hilaire in his *Voyage aux Provinces de St. Paul et de Ste. Catherine,* Vol. II, p. 320. João Antônio Rodrigues de Carvalho gives the more precise figure of 15,533 inhabitants for 1824, in *Projecto de uma estrada de Destêrro às Missões do Uruguai* (Project for a road to be built from Destêrro to the Uruguay Missions), p. 508.

[28] *Voyage, op. cit.,* Vol. II, p. 332.

[29] *Voyage,* Vol. II, p. 304.

[30] Dreys, *Notícia Descritiva do Rio Grande do Sul* (Descriptive Account of Rio Grande do Sul), p. 157.

[31] *Viagem ao Rio Grande do Sul,* p. 47.

[32] Dreys, *Notícia Descritiva do Rio Grande do Sul,* p. 121.

Settlement of the Interior
(pp. 51–72)

[1] An interesting study of the expansion of colonization in Bahia, particularly the spread of the cattle estates, is to be found in the *História Terri-*

torial do Brasil, by Felisbelo Freire, who used as his source the *Cartas de Sesmaria* (title deeds of landholding).

[2] *Roteiro do Maranhão*, p. 62.

[3] Population figures for Mato Grosso are taken from the map made by Governor Caetano Pinto, *População da Capitania de Mato Grosso em 1800*.

[4] The seat of the northern comarca was to be located in the town to be built at the confluence of the Tocantins and Araguaia rivers, the *Registo*, or Registry, of São João das Duas Barras and a military fortress being already established at this point. The seat was provisionally established at the Carmo encampment, transferred to Porto Real (now Porto Nacional) in 1810, and to São João da Palma in 1814. But the district's official name continued to be that of its nominal seat, São João das Duas Barras.

[5] *Corografia histórica*, p. 291.

[6] Luís Antônio da Silva e Sousa, *Memória sôbre a Capitania de Goiás*, p. 482.

[7] This corresponds to the southeast of the present territory of Goiás, excluding the Minas triangle (Triângulo Mineiro) that then formed part of the captaincy. The latter area, situated between the Grande and Paranaíba rivers, and transferred to Minas Gerais in 1816, was thinly populated along the São Paulo route and a little more densely along its eastern extremity, where Araxá, Desemboque, and other small settlements are situated.

[8] Francisco de Paula Ribeiro, *Roteiro da Viagem*, p. 73.

[9] It is a known fact that the Indians of Goiás have not been entirely dominated even now, forming one of the last outposts of savage Indians in the country.

[10] *Corografia histórica*, p. 354.

[11] Capistrano has a very interesting theory about the differences between the populations of each Sertão. At the present stage of historical studies it is difficult to confirm this theory. However, the existence of a characteristic Sertanejo type, distinguished from the other colonial settlers, cannot be questioned. J. Capistrano de Abreu, *Capítulos de História Colonial, 1500–1800* (Chapters of Colonial History), p. 277.

[12] By virtue of decree No. 3012, published on October 22, 1880.

[13] *Cultura e Opulência do Brasil*, p. 262.

[14] An interesting description of this region, written in 1826, can be found in Accioli's *Dados e Informações estatísticas sôbre a Vila da Barra* (Figures and Statistical Records of Vila da Barra). It includes a population map.

[15] This point will be made clearer in the chapter, Communications and Transport.

[16] It was by a happy combination of circumstances that the whole of this region, lying to the north of the Amazon in what is now the state of Pará, which Portugal never occupied—and which was not occupied by anyone else—fell to Brazil. When the Treaty of Utrecht (1713) was being negotiated, and the question of the northern boundaries of Portugal's American possessions was discussed for the very first time, England

had an interest in keeping France out of the Amazon, whose strategic importance she had recognized. She therefore pleaded on behalf of her Portuguese vassal and ally, and obtained from vanquished France recognition of Portugal's dominion over the whole of the Amazon Basin. It was this claim that stood Brazil in good stead when she later disputed with France the sovereignty of the region.

[17] The figures are taken from Martius's account in his *Viagem*, Vol. 3, p. 36.

Currents of Settlement
(pp. 73–89)

[1] Reliable data that would enable us to follow these shifts from the interior to the littoral, as well as other population movements, would be furnished by genealogical studies. Unfortunately, however, this subject is for the time being studied almost exclusively to serve the fatuous vanity of a pseudo-aristocracy instead of to contribute to the legitimate aims which are the scientific research into, and clarification of, many problems which would be useful for an understanding of Brazilian history.

[2] *Corografia*, p. 303.

[3] The only gold mining enterprise of any importance that managed to succeed, the Morro Velho Mine, was established here about this time; it became a large enterprise that was later acquired by an English company. For the story of mining in Congonhas do Sabará and its development in the nineteenth century, see: *Um Município de Ouro, Memória Histórica*, by Augusto de Lima.

[4] Despite its apparent but short lived prosperity, Goiás had never really been more than a stepping-stone for the adventurers who abandoned the district as soon as the mines began to show signs of exhaustion. Cunha Matos describes the situation extremely well. It is true that in Minas the same thing occurred to a certain extent, but in a more attenuated form, and with the parallel development of the rudiments of a more stable social life, which later bore fruit.

[5] Cited by Diogo de Vasconcelos, *História Média de Minas Gerais* (History of Minas Gerais in the Middle Period), p. 258.

[6] This region formed what was later to be called the "Zona da Mata" (forest zone)—a name retained to this day and given to distinguish it from the rest of the captaincy, which had already been occupied and hence cleared of the dense covering of forest which characterized the zone.

[7] *Voyage dans les Provinces de Rio de Janeiro*, Vol. 2, p. 143. The fortress of São Miguel was one of a series of fortresses established along the frontiers of Minas Gerais in 1808 to defend the captaincy from the hostility of the savage Indians. I shall deal with this subject in the next chapter.

[8] *Travels in Brazil*, Book III, pp. 211 et seq.

[9] The dispute on the limits between Minas and São Paulo, involving lengthy debates in which various aspects of interest to the subject here dealt with were discussed, has produced a number of works. See in par-

ticular: *Resumo histórico sôbre os limites entre Minas e São Paulo,* by
Augusto de Lima (defending the Minas case); *Divisas de São Paulo e
Minas Gerais,* a collection of documents with a commentary by Orville
Derby, published in the *Documentos Interessantes;* and *Limites de São
Paulo e Minas,* a memoir by Prudente de Morais Filho and João Pedro
Cardoso (upholding the Paulista case).

[10] *Voyage dans les Provinces de St. Paul,* Vol. 1, p. 167.

[11] It is interesting to note that infiltration of the São Paulo frontier by
people from Minas has not yet come to an end. In the last fifty years this
infiltration has been directed mainly toward the eastern slopes of the
Serra da Mantiqueira and the Paraíba valley, neglected by the Paulistas,
in the last quarter of the nineteenth century. The population of this valley, the "north," as it is commonly miscalled by the Paulistas, is today
largely of Mineiro origin.

[12] St. Hilaire, *Voyage aux Sources du Rio de São Francisco.* The
French traveler traversed the region on two occasions, journeying through
different places. On the first occasion he traveled from the south, northward, passing through Araxá and Patrocinio on his way to Paracatu; on
the second, he went from Goiás to São Paulo. These journeys, undertaken
in 1819, are described in the volume cited above.

[13] St. Hilaire, *Voyage aux Sources,* Vol. I, p. 285.

[14] Cunha Matos, *Corografia historica,* p. 303.

[15] St. Hilaire, *Voyage aux Provinces de St. Paul,* Vol. 1, p. 108. We
must remember that the captaincy included the present territory of
Paraná, which became a separate province in 1853, but which at that
time was still a *comarca* of São Paulo.

[16] St. Hilaire relates that it was only by overcoming the prejudice in
favor of the *terra preta,* or black soil, of Itu that certain planters took the
bold step of establishing themselves in the lands of "deep red soil"—the
expression used by St. Hilaire—of Campinas; their success was tremendous and led to intensive settlement of the region. *Voyage aux Provinces de St. Paul,* Vol. 1, p. 206. Campinas, a small hamlet in the eighteenth century, rapidly prospered, and in 1797 was elevated to a township
with the name of São Carlos. Its former name was restored in 1842, when
it was elevated from township to city.

[17] West of the Campos de Curitiba, which had been occupied since
the seventeenth century, lay the *Campos de Guarapuava,* which had not
yet been opened up by the end of the following century. These pasture
lands had been discovered in 1771, together with the sertões of Ivaí,
Tibaji, and Iguatemi. Expeditions had then ceased, leaving only the garrison of the frontier post of Iguatemi, destroyed by the Spaniards in 1777.
These territories began to be explored again and opened up only in 1808;
and St. Hilaire found, in the pasture lands of Guarapuava the beginnings
of a colonization movement which, despite repeated attacks by Indians,
had begun to spread westward. On the exploration of the Guarapuava
Campos and western Paraná, see Sousa Chichorro's *Memória.*

[18] The region's largest and most influential landowner in St. Hilaire's
time and for a considerable time thereafter was João da Silva Machado,

who had begun life as a modest cattle puncher and having prospered and amassed a large fortune, was later given the title of "Barão de Antonina." It was he who ordered a reconnaissance party to travel through the western backlands in search of a route to Mato Grosso which would prove shorter and safer than those previously used—the Tietê river route and the long and indirect overland trail through Goiás. Concerning this, see the Baron's communication to the Instituto Histórico, written in 1848 and published in their *Revista*, p. 259. Although a native of Taquari in Rio Grande do Sul, Silva Machado settled in São Paulo and started a family there. There are still numerous descendants.

[19] See the Official Report (*Ofício*) of Viceroy Luís de Vasconcelos e Sousa on handing over the government to his successor in 1789.

[20] Three simultaneous movements converged on this area around the middle course of the Paraíba, which became the wealthiest center of the empire: the Paulista movement we have just seen, the movement southward from Minas Gerais which we shall see further on, and the movement from Rio de Janeiro. The three movements met and mingled in this region, and although it is composed of parts of different provinces, the region acquired such distinctive and individual characteristics that its formation as a separate province was at one time considered. See Melo Nogueira, *A Projetado Província de Resende*.

[21] These routes will be considered in more detail in the appropriate section; for the moment, it will suffice to point out that the two routes entered Minas through Paraibuna and Rio Prêto, respectively.

[22] On the subject of the mines of Macacu, see the Viceroy's *Ofício* on handing over office, cited above.

Races
(pp. 90–129)

[1] This problem has been tackled by Nina Rodrigues in *O Negro no Brasil* (The Negro in Brazil) and more recently by Artur Ramos in *Culturas Negras no Novo Mundo* (Negro Cultures in the New World).

[2] Some of the indigenous tribes were easily subdued, others not; some mixed freely with the other races, but there were others who did not mix on any considerable scale or who did not mix at all, and so remained relatively pure, forming isolated pockets in colonization until they were finally eliminated and disappeared altogether. Among the Negroes, distinctions can be made between those used as fieldhands for rural work and those employed in domestic service. Some Negro peoples of a higher cultural standard were concentrated in certain areas, and made a fairly important cultural contribution; others were completely passive in their attitude. All these ethnic aspects of the components that went into the formation of Brazil have already been noted. What is still lacking—and without it we cannot reach conclusions about the general history of Brazil—is a systematic study of the subject which tackles the problem as a whole from the historical viewpoint of Brazil's formation.

[3] This was also the case in the mother country. Foreigners always abounded in Portugal, whose doors were wide open to receive them. See

Gilberto Freyre, *Casa Grande e Senzala,* pp. 207 et seq. [American edition: *The Masters and the Slaves,* pp. 200 et seq.]

⁴ I am referring to the incident of Amador Bueno's acclamation. [Salvador de Sá, Governor of Rio de Janeiro, issued an edict ordering "all citizens of means" to adhere to the newly proclaimed independent King of Portugal, Dom João IV, and to "join in and contribute to the rejoicings." The southern captaincies were ordered to follow the example of Rio and Bahia. "All the townships of São-Vicente obeyed his summons, although tradition has it that some fleeting opposition was experienced in São Paulo where the pro-Spanish party tried to proclaim one of their number, Amador Bueno, as an independent monarch over the highland district. The incident was purely ephemeral and São Paulo speedily followed the example of Rio de Janeiro in declaring for Dom João IV." C. R. Boxer, *Salvador de Sá,* p. 148.—Translator.]

⁵ Handelman, *História do Brasil,* p. 698.

⁶ For a discussion of this subject, see Calógeras, *Política Exterior do Império* (Foreign Policy of the Empire), Vol. 1.

⁷ *Consulta do Conselho Ultramarino de 1732* (Deliberations of the Overseas Council).

⁸ *Legislação portuguêsa relativa ao Brasil* (Portuguese Legislation on Brazil) by Vieira Fazenda; and J. F. Lisboa, *Obras* (Collected Works), Vol. 2, p. 172. The latter analyzes in particular the most important of these laws, that of March 20, 1720.

⁹ *Relatório,* p. 452.

¹⁰ *Efemérides Paraenses,* by Manuel Barata, p. 203.

¹¹ For a historical account of this transfer and a list of the people transferred, see *Estabelecimento de Mazagão do Grão-Pará,* a contemporary record. For an account of this nucleus at the end of the eighteenth century, see Alexandre Rodrigues Ferreira, *Diário da Viagem Filósofica* (Diary of a Philosophical Journey).

¹² Alexandre Rodrigues Ferreira, *op. cit.*

¹³ The contract, *Ordens e Edital* (Order and Proclamation) was published in the *Revista do Instituto Histórico Brasileiro,* Vol. 40(I), p. 215. The transport of families of foreign nationals was authorized, provided they were Roman Catholics, and emigrants from Madeira were also provided for. But the majority of the colonists were from the Azores.

¹⁴ As may be seen from the instructions issued to the Governor of Goiás, José de Almeida e Vasconcelos, 1770, cited in correspondence with the Court, *Subsídios para a história da Capitania de Goiás* (Sources for a History of the Captaincy of Goiás), Collected Documents, p. 139.

¹⁵ It should be noted that even today, as always in the past, relations with the Indians in the United States are between sovereign power and sovereign power and are fixed by treaty. Hence this explains the federal government's authority to deal with matters relating to the Indians, to the exclusion of state authority, as has invariably been the decision of the Supreme Court. The Indians, who have been confined to fixed territories, are not American citizens but constitute legally a form of autonomous nation.

¹⁶ It must be noted that it was only the temporal power that was abol-

ished. Indeed, this was in accordance with the ordinances of the Church. The priests, whether Carmelites, Franciscans, Mercedarians, or Jesuits, were to continue in the villages as their spiritual directors. This was in fact how things stood. It was only in 1759, four years after the royal decree of July 7, 1755, that the Jesuits were expelled from Portugal and its dominions and forced to abandon their mission villages in Brazil. Up to that time they had kept their villages, but not without systematically undermining the new laws. This was probably one reason for their expulsion. As to the other orders, they retained their posts and went on with their missionary work as before. Pombal's legislation relating to the Indians is made up of the following laws: royal decree, April 14, 1755, which encouraged mixed marriages, stipulated that the Indians and their descendants were entitled to the same conditions of employment as the other colonists and could receive honors in the same way, and prohibited any mistreatment of Indians; law of June 6, 1755, which proclaimed the complete and universal freedom of the Indians, made various provisions for their relations with the colonists, and framed regulations for the organization of Indian settlements (villages and posts); royal decree, June 7, 1755, suppressing the priests' temporal power over the Indians, whose villages were thenceforth to be administered by their own headmen (this law, like the previous one, was applicable only to Pará and Maranhão); royal decree, May 8, 1758, extended its application to the whole of Brazil. In addition to these laws, there is the *Diretório*, or Code, governing the Indians of Grão-Para and Maranhão, promulgated in 1757 (May 3), a lengthy and minute codification of all the legislation on the Indians still in force, compiled by the governor of these two captaincies, Francisco Xavier de Mendonça Furtado, Pombal's brother. The *Diretório* was approved by royal decree, August 17, 1758, which extended its application to the whole of Brazil.

[17] In Maranhão, Indian labor was almost entirely replaced by Negro slave labor. This was due to the privileged Companhia de Comércio (trading company), organized in 1756, which offered credit and payment facilities for importing Africans into the country.

[18] On this subject, see: *Reflexões* (Reflections), written by the naturalist Alexandre Rodrigues Ferreira, to the Governor, Martinho de Sousa e Albuquerque, and published in his "Diary," p. 52.

[19] *Diário da Viagem Filosófica.* See in particular, p. 47, where he summarizes the causes of the general decadence of Pará and the Rio Negro.

[20] There were mission villages of some importance in Ceará, Rio Grande do Norte, Paraíba, Pôrto Seguro and Espírito Santo, but these were much less important than those of Pará and Maranhão.

[21] André Fernandes de Sousa, *Notícias geográficas do Rio Negro* (Geographical Report on the Rio Negro), p. 477.

[22] *Roteiro do Maranhão*, pp. 76, 79.

[23] *Viagem*, III, p. 356.

[24] On this subject, see the copious correspondence of the governors of the northern comarca, published in *Subsídios para a História da Capitania de Goiás.* This correspondence goes up to 1784.

[25] Capt. Francisco de Paula Ribeiro, *Roteiro do Maranhão*, p. 40.

[26] *Informações sôbre os Indios Bárbaros de Pernambuco* (An Account of the Savage Indians of Pernambuco), collection of documents.

[27] We must also bear in mind that it was in the fiscal interests of the crown to preserve the forest as a natural barrier, to prevent gold and diamond smuggling.

[28] The Indians in this particular sector began to be pacified and settled in mission villages on the initiative of Viceroy Luís de Vasconcelos e Sousa, who relinquished office in 1789. See his *Ofício* (Official Report) on handing over the governorship, pp. 35 et seq.

[29] *Descobrimento de Minas Gerais* (Discovery of Minas Gerais), anonymous work published in 1807.

[30] One of the district commanding officers was Guido Marlière, a Frenchman in the service of Portugal, who earned the name of "Apóstolo das selvas" (Jungle Apostle) for his civilizing work. He used to say that he "would rather use bullets of maize than bullets of lead" in his dealings with the Indians.

[31] Brás da Costa Rubim, *Memórias históricas e documentadas da Província do Espírito Santo* (Historical and documented memoirs of the Province of Espírito Santo), p. 263. I shall provide additional information on the navigation of the Rio Doce in the section on communications.

[32] See Accioli's *Dissertação histórica,* p. 166. See also the observations of Martius who visited the region in 1818: *Viagem,* II. João Gonçalves da Costa wrote an account of his campaign, which was published in the *Gazeta da Bahia,* July 14, 21, and 28, 1818, and reproduced in the September and October numbers of the *Correio Brasiliense* that same year.

[33] These campos, interrupted only by the fringe forests threaded along the banks of the great rivers, and which served as the refuge of hostile tribes, extend from the Paranapanema to the Uruguay rivers. The general name of Campos de Guarapuava was later restricted and in the south (Santa Catarina) new names were given to the local campos: Palmas, Iraí, and so forth.

[34] An account of this expedition and the founding of the colony is given in *Memória do Padre Francisco das Chagas Lima, capelão da tropa* (A Memoir written by the chaplain who accompanied the troops).

[35] Baron Rio Branco estimated that in 1817 it was made up of 259,400 individuals; he does not, however, quote the source of this information. *Le Brésil en 1889,* p. 152. Henry Hill, the English Consul at Bahia, estimating the Brazilian population at the end of the eighteenth century, calculated that this Indian contingent accounted for 100,000 individuals, a figure which seems somewhat small. Cit. in Veloso de Oliveira: *A Igreja no Brasil.*

[36] It is true that some of the indigenous peoples in their native state make use of alcoholic beverages and become intoxicated. But this only occurs on feast days and ceremonial occasions. It is almost a ritual, repeated at wide-spaced intervals. Colonization turned the drunkenness of the Indian into a permanent state.

[37] It is difficult to estimate the volume of the African trade, and different estimates have been essayed. Making calculations based on the num-

ber of survivors in 1820 (approximately 1,200,000 individuals) and on a rate of increase somewhat arbitrarily established, since there were no reliable figures to confirm it, Calógeras established a progression that gave him the figure of approximately 54,500 individuals per annum for the preceding 150 or 200 years. *Política exterior do Império*, I, p. 302. Veloso de Oliveira, a careful and conscientious observer and closer in time to the events he analyzes, estimated that 25,000 to 30,000 slaves had been brought in annually in the hundred years preceding his *Memória sôbre a agricultura do Brasil* (Memoir on Agriculture in Brazil), published in 1810 (p. 117). For a comparison of the different estimates that have been made see Taunay's articles in the *Jornal do Comércio* (Rio de Janeiro) for August 16 and 30, 1936.

[38] For an account of these racial contacts, see the works of Mendes Corrêa, particularly, *Os povos primitivos da Lusitânia* (The Primitive Peoples of Lusitania), p. 159.

[39] This still happens now. How much more so must it have done when the voyage itself was already a great adventure, a leap into the unknown?

[40] Gilberto Freyre asserts that Portugal also supplied shiploads of marriageable women (*The Masters and the Slaves*, p. 25). But he does not cite his source and it is therefore impossible to check his assertion. But even if we admit that this did occur, there is no doubt (and the general silence on the subject proves this) that it was not due to any systematic measures taken in this respect, as in the North American colonies, and any such event appears not to have had any significant effect on Brazil.

[41] *Voyages*, II, p. 314.

[42] *Viagem*, II, p. 290.

[43] *Viagem*, II, p. 420.

[44] *Voyages*, II, p. 317.

[45] *Esboço da Viagem de Langsdorff* (Outline of the Langsdorff Expedition), p. 238. [This expedition of naturalists traveled through the interior of Brazil between 1825 and 1829. It was undertaken by the Russian consul in Rio de Janeiro, Baron Langsdorff, and was subsidized by Emperor Alexander I of Russia.—Translator.]

[46] *Viagem*, II, p. 290.

[47] This perhaps accounts for the greater color prejudice in Maranhão, which continued to be very marked well into the nineteenth century. Aluísio de Azevedo gives us a vivid portrayal of this situation in his novel, *O Mulato*.

[48] Brigadier Cunha Matos describes the gradual disappearance of pure whites in Goiás as a result of the decadence of the mines in his *Corografia histórica*, p. 898.

[49] See the report of Arouche Rendon, who conducted a tour of inspection of these villages in 1798, *Memória sôbre as aldeias de Índios da província de São Paulo* (Report on the Indian mission villages of São Paulo).

[50] *Descrição dos Sete Povos* (Description of the Seven Peoples), in *Breve Notícia*, by Francisco João Roscio.

[51] The term "gaucho" was originally applied to these elements. The

term was originally pejorative, designating the semibarbarous and loose-living type of more or less pure-blooded Indian who had only superficially been touched by civilization.

Economy
(pp. 133–147)

[1] Coman, *Industrial History of the United States,* p. 38.

[2] Hansen, *The Atlantic Migration,* p. 41.

[3] The following definition of tropical agriculture is given in a recent book on the subject and clearly indicates the nature of the enterprise: "Commercial farming in the tropics is today one of the most distinctive types of farming, and the oldest of the modern types of large-scale, specialized agriculture. It began with the colonization of the hot, humid portions of the Americas, but its development has taken place largely during the past hundred years. This type of farming involves the growing and processing of a cash crop for export to temperate countries, chiefly those of the Northern Hemisphere." Clarence Fielden Jones, *Economic Geography,* p. 156.

[4] The presence of the slaves and the poor is, however, no more than a symptom, not the disease itself, a fact it is well to point out since it was not always remembered. The idealists who advocated abolition, for instance, thought that in liberating the slave they would achieve much more than a simple change of the legal and nominal status of the worker. What kept the mass of the Brazilian population at the miserable level of material and consequently moral existence in which they found themselves was not only the institution of slavery but also the whole basic organization of the country, of which slavery was simply one aspect and which, once abolished, was replaced by another form of labor which continued, with very little difference, to keep the worker, and hence the bulk of the population, at the same low level of existence.

[5] *Roteiro do Maranhão a Goiás.* The author and exact date of composition of this work are unknown. The last date referred to in the text is 1770, but the work appears to have been written at a later date. It was found in the archives of the Secretariat of Foreign Affairs in 1802 and a copy was made. This was reprinted in a monthly journal published in Rio de Janeiro at the beginning of the last century: *O Patriota,* in the May and December issues for 1813. The *Revista do Instituto Histórico* reproduced the document in 1900 (vol. 62, part 1).

Large-Scale Agriculture
(pp. 148–179)

[1] I have already given some figures in a previous chapter [i.e., the chapter on Currents of Settlement, pp. 73–89.—Tr.]. In 1769, there were 55 *engenhos* in the region; by 1778, another 113 had started to operate; and by 1783, a further 110. J. Carneiro da Silva, *Memória sôbre os Campos dos Goitacases,* p. 49. For the captaincy of Rio de Janeiro as a whole, which included the Campos, the increase had been from 310 *engenhos* and 166 distilleries in 1776 to 616 *engenhos* (324 in the

Campos) and 253 distilleries in 1799. *Relações que Acompanham o Relatório do Marquês do Lavradio,* p. 285; and *Almanaque Histórico,* p. 159, respectively.

² At the beginning of the nineteenth century, Santos already figures as a sugar-exporting port, although on a modest scale with its 1,000 chests per annum. It was fourth in importance to Bahia, with 20,000 chests, Pernambuco with 14,000, and Rio de Janeiro with 9,000. Varnhagen, *História Geral do Brasil,* vol. 5, p. 61.

³ *Roteiro do Maranhão,* p. 103.

⁴ *Roteiro do Maranhão,* p. 107.

⁵ The average consumption of firewood by the sugar mills was between 12 and 16 cartloads daily. Vilhena, *Recopilação,* p. 184.

⁶ The first sugar-boiling vat furnaces in Brazil to be fueled by bagasse were constructed in 1809 by Manoel Jacinto de Sampaio e Melo, owner of the Engenho da Filosofia, who published in 1816 a manual on the subject entitled: *Novo Método de Fazer Açucar ou Reforma Geral Econômica dos Engenhos no Brasil* (A new method of making sugar, or a general economic reform for the sugar mills of Brazil). On the agricultural progress made in this period, see *A Literatura Brasileira sôbre o Açucar* (Brazilian Literature on Sugar), by José Honório Rodrigues.

⁷ For Bahia, cf. *Descrição da Comarca da Bahia* (Description of the District of Bahia), p. 201; for Rio de Janeiro, cf. *Relações do Marquês do Lavradio, op. cit.*

⁸ Vilhena, *Recopilação,* p. 174.

⁹ *Ibid.,* p. 175.

¹⁰ Some authorities believe that this variety, which originated in the island of Tahiti and was thence brought to Central America and the Guianas, was introduced into Pará between 1790 and 1803. This is the opinion of Baltasar da Silva Lisboa in *Anais do Rio de Janeiro.* But in any case it was only much later that this variety began to spread to the large Brazilian sugar centers. Concerning this, see *Memório sôbre as Principais Plantas Aclimatadas no Brasil* (Memoir on the Principal Plants Acclimatized in Brazil), by Freire Alemão.

¹¹ Arruda Câmara: *Memória sôbre a Cultura dos Algodoeiros* (Memoir on the Cultivation of the Cotton Plant), p. 15.

¹² *Recopilação,* Letter 5.

¹³ A description of sugar production in the West Indies in the eighteenth century is found in Labat's book, *Nouveau Voyage,* and in other works by this author. Humboldt, particularly in his *Relation Historique,* describes the methods in use at the beginning of the nineteenth century. Vilhena recognized and deplored Brazil's backwardness in this respect (*Recopilação,* p. 198). It must also be pointed out that the sugar exported from Brazil was not yet refined in the country itself. Refining was done in England, whence sugar was reexported to Spain and even to the other Portuguese possessions. *Correio Brasiliense,* Dec. 1814, XIII, p. 785.

¹⁴ *Idéia da População da Capitania de Pernambuco e das suas Anexas.*

¹⁵ This device operates on a principle of two vertical rollers, rotating

in opposite directions, through which the lint can pass but the seeds cannot. The cotton was forced between the rollers, the lint being thus separated from its seeds. [The churcka gin was developed in India.—Tr.]

[16] A bag filled with lint was suspended, and a Negro slave was placed upright in the bag to press it down with his weight; more cotton was then added and the process repeated until the bag was completely full of compressed cotton. This method, besides being slow and inefficient, had a very harmful effect on the workers' health, the heat generated by the cotton causing serious organic disturbances.

[17] *Recopilação*, Letter 5.

[18] Vilhena, who was a Regius professor, gives a revealing account of these classes. *Recopilação*, Letter 8. [Vilhena was the Regius Professor of the Greek Language at Bahia.—Tr.]

[19] See the chapter on "Sugarcane and Water" in Gilberto Freyre's work: *Nordeste,* in which he vindicates the "little rivers" of Brazil as opposed to the "great rivers" which attract more attention but which did not play as important a role as the former. [The full title of Freyre's work is *Nordeste: Aspectos da Influencia da Cana sobre a Vida e a Paisagem do Nordeste do Brasil* (Northeast: Aspects of the Influence of Sugarcane on the Life and Landscape of Northeastern Brazil). Pub. José Olimpio, Rio de Janeiro, 1937.—Translator.]

[20] The number of mills operating in these areas were: Paraíba, 37; Pernambuco, 296; Alagoas, 73 (figures for 1777: *Idéia da População*); Sergipe, 140; Bahia, over 260 (figures given by Vilhena, *Recopilação*, p. 50; written in 1802).

[21] In 1799, according to the *Almanaque* for that year compiled by Antônio Duarte Nunes, there were 616 sugar mills in Rio de Janeiro and 253 distilleries, distributed among the sectors as follows: Guanabara Bay, 228 sugar mills and 85 distilleries; Angra dos Reis and Ilha Grande, 39 and 155, respectively; southeastern sector (Cabo Frio), 25 and 9; Campos dos Goitacases, 324 and 4.

[22] According to Martius the official figures for 1808 indicated the existence of 458 mills and 601 distilleries, most of them, however, being insignificant and of purely local importance. *Travels,* Book II, p. 15. In 1819, St. Hilaire notes that there were approximately 100 engenhos and small engenhos in Campinas and the same number in Itu. *Voyages aux Provinces de St. Paul,* Vol. I, pp. 210, 348.

[23] Vilhena, *Recopilação*, p. 181.

[24] According to Antonil, in Pernambuco the tenant paid one-fifth and in Bahia, one-twentieth or one-fifteenth. *Cultura e Opulência,* p. 162. At the turn of the century, the percentage charged in Bahia was one-fifteenth. *Recopilação*, p. 182.

[25] *Relações do Marquês do Lavradio.*

[26] Koster, *Voyages,* Vol. II, pp. 252, 264. Koster is referring to Pernambuco and probably to its larger engenhos. The only other figures for the colonial engenhos are those for Rio de Janeiro given in the *Relações do Marquês do Lavradio* in 1779. He gives a complete account of all the engenhos in the captaincy, including the number of workers and the

amount of sugar produced in each. These varied considerably from engenho to engenho. We can, in fact, make an interesting observation concerning the degree of concentration of sugar production in the various captaincies. From the figures cited above, although in the case of Pernambuco they apply to its most static period, we see that production in each of the three great sugar captaincies (Bahia, Pernambuco, and Rio de Janeiro) is inversely proportionate to the respective number of engenhos. The matter deserves a more detailed analysis which unfortunately I cannot here attempt.

27 See the interesting reconstruction by Cícero Dias of a Pernambucan engenho, published as an appendix to Gilberto Freyre's *Casa Grande e Senzala.* [In the American edition, *The Masters and the Slaves,* the plans and perspective of the "Big House of the Noruega Plantation" appear between pp. 468 and 469. See also p. xxxvi ff., for a description of the "Big House" complex.—Translator.]

28 For details of the different functions performed on the sugar plantation, see Antonil, *Cultura e Opulência do Brasil.* As I have already pointed out, although this account was written a century before the period which concerns us here, the descriptions still apply, since sugar production had continued along the same routine lines. Koster tells us that the workers responsible for skimming the sugar syrup were also free, since the work was extremely difficult and delicate and was harmful to the health of the worker—hence free workers were preferred. An interesting detail! *Voyages,* II, p. 244.

29 *Recopilação,* p. 183.

30 *Relações do Marquês do Lavradio.*

31 The chief commodity used for barter, which was the way in which Negroes were obtained, was tobacco. Rum and sugarcane brandy came next in importance. The staple of the Bahia slave trade was tobacco, that of Rio de Janeiro *aguardente* (cane spirits). Production of these spirits in Rio de Janeiro was considerable. Ilha Grande, Angra dos Reis and Parati were the chief centers, the latter producing spirits on such a scale that its name became synonymous with the product, just as in France "champagne" and "cognac" became the common name of these regions' specialities.

32 *Relações do Marquês do Lavradio.*

33 *Segunda Viagem a Minas Gerais,* p. 185.

34 Frei Francisco de Nossa Senhora dos Prazeres, *Poranduba Maranhense,* p. 106.

35 *Compêndio histórico-político dos Principios da Lavoura do Maranhão* (Historical and political compendium of agriculture in Maranhão), p. 169.

36 It was in fact produced in such small quantities that in Maranhão export of cotton seeds and raw cotton was prohibited, and cotton cloth could be sold only to Pará and the adjacent captaincies. There was not enough for local consumption. These stipulations were set out in the governor's proclamation of February 1, 1703. Cit. by Gayozo, *Compêndio . . . ,* p. 179.

[37] This had already begun to happen in the first quarter of the nineteenth century. Later, when the ruin provoked by the exclusion of Brazilian cotton was already complete, the world's greatest cotton-producing country, the United States, became involved in the Civil War and her cotton industry was paralyzed. This boosted cotton production in Brazil; and in 1861, the year after the outbreak of the Civil War, the Brazilian exports began to rise, and a breeze of prosperity once more wafted through the country's cotton regions, which had been reduced to poverty and desolation. But this favorable situation was short-lived. The Civil War ended in 1864, and the U.S. Southern states, the chief cotton producers, began to make a comeback. By 1872 they had once more ousted the Brazilian product from the market, exports began to decline, and the cotton regions relapsed into stagnation and poverty.

[38] Gayozo, *Compêndio*, p. 179.

[39] Arruda Câmara, *Memória sôbre a Cultura dos Algodoeiros*, p. 7.

[40] Maranhão was transformed not only on the economic level but also on a far deeper level. Cotton brought African slaves—or rather, African slaves were brought in with cotton—and this changed the region's ethnic features. Up to this period, the captaincy's population had been composed almost entirely but for a few white colonists of Indians and their "mixed" descendants. White cotton turned Maranhão black.

[41] In 1807 the amount of cotton imported from various sources by England, the major consumer, was as follows: United States—41,466,600 lb; Guiana—12,530,840 lb; British colonies—6,716,750 lb; India—3,650,880 lb; Brazil—3,188,808 lb; other sources—2,347,750 lb. *Correio Brasiliense*, June, 1808. In the same issue of this periodical, other figures concerning the international cotton trade are given, including prices, etc.

[42] In 1796, Pará exported cotton to the value of 71 *contos*, according to the tables published by Martius in his *Viagem*, Book III, p. 50. [The *conto* was 1,000 *mil-reis* or in modern currency 1,000 *cruzeiros*.—Tr.]

[43] *Voyage aux Provinces de Rio de Janeiro*, II, p. 107, footnote.

[44] According to *O Patriota*, No. 3, March, 1813, the amount produced by Goiás was 3,874 *arrobas*.

[45] Martius, *Viagem*, II, p. 450.

[46] Paulet, *Descrição Abreviada*, p. 127.

[47] *Voyages*, II, p. 269.

[48] For a description of these regions see the diaries of St. Hilaire and Martius, who traveled over different parts. St. Hilaire tells us that the Minas Novas cotton was known for its quality in Europe, the only Brazilian cotton surpassing it in quality being that grown in Pernambuco. *Voyage aux Provinces de Rio de Janeiro*, II, p. 5.

[49] Vilhena, *Recopilação*, p. 595.

[50] For the period January, 1816, to March, 1817, the Registry at Malhada, which registered the cotton produced in these two regions before it went to Bahia, handled 3,262 arrobas of cotton for export (tables published by Martius in his *Viagem*, II, p. 243). St. Hilaire gives an interesting account of cotton growing in Goiás, including details about its

first planting. The captaincy's chief cotton center was Meia-Ponte, present-day Pirenópolis (*Voyage aux sources du Rio de S. Francisco*).

⁵¹ According to Martius, one person could gather one to two arrobas per day. *Viagem*, II, p. 459.

⁵² *Compêndio*, p. 263 et seq. The annual cost of cotton production was approximately 2 contos (i.e., 2,000,000 reis). Gayozo's estimate of the costs involved in production is most interesting. It excludes any reference to the value of the land and any rents or interests paid on the capital invested. This throws a good deal of light upon the manner of keeping accounts and the system of financing at that time. The information is particularly valuable since this is one of the very few sources we possess for details of this type. [Tithes, or "dízimos reais," were collected on all agricultural products in Brazil, in kind or at the equivalent value in gold.— Translator.]

⁵³ The average number of slaves imported annually into Maranhão during the first years of the last century was 3,500. Martius, *Viagem*, II, p. 452. In 1783, Maranhão had imported 1,546 per annum.

⁵⁴ Bahia exported 25,000 rolls of tobacco, worth 303,100 mil-reis; Alagoas, 2,500 rolls, to the value of 41,550 mil-reis (Antonil, *Cultura e Opulência*, p. 200). Each roll, at least at the end of the eighteenth century, weighed anywhere from 20 arrobas upward (Vilhena, *Recopilação*, p. 204). Rolls weighing approximately three arrobas were used in the African slave trade (*Carta de D. Francisco José de Portugal, Gov. da Bahia, sôbre os Embaixadores do Rei de Dagomé*, 1795 [Letter from Dom Francisco J. de P., Governor of Bahia, concerning the Ambassadors from the Kingdom of Dahomey], p. 415).

⁵⁵ Martius, *Viagem*, II, p. 297. We must point out an interesting fact noted by Martius, the establishment in Bahia, just prior to his voyage of 1819, of a tobacco manufacturing concern run by a French concern. This was possibly the first such concern to be established in Brazil. The tobacco trade had always been a crown monopoly, and was operated on a monopoly contract basis through its appointed concessionaires.

⁵⁶ The total number of tobacco plantations, large and small, in these centers was 1,500.

⁵⁷ Martius, *Travels*, Book I, p. 191. Up to 1757 cultivation of tobacco in Rio de Janeiro had been prohibited in order to protect the monopolists who traded with Bahia. In that year (by virtue of the law promulgated on January 10), the tobacco monopoly was abolished in Rio, and tobacco growing in the captaincy was allowed. The tobacco growers had at first to contend with strong competition from Bahia, which enjoyed the advantage of having been longer established. See *Correspondência de Várias Autoridades e Avulsos* (Correspondence written by various authorities, and sundry papers) published in the "Revista" of the Instituto Histórico Brasileiro, vol. 63, I, pp. 85, 95.

⁵⁸ Martius, *Travels*, Book I, p. 302.

⁵⁹ St. Hilaire, *Segunda Viagem do Rio de Janeiro a Minas Gerais e a São Paulo, 1822*, p. 120.

[60] A detailed description of tobacco growing can be found in Vilhena's *Recopilação,* p. 201.

[61] *Discurso Econômica da Comarca da Bahia,* p. 322.

[62] Despite the striking contrast in opportunity that tobacco growing offered to the planter in a more modest way of business than the sugar and cotton planters, these opportunities did not offer sufficient incentive for a transformation of the basic feature of Brazilian agriculture. Indeed, it is a known fact that wherever tobacco was grown in tropical and sub-tropical America, plantation-type exploitation was the rule. Thus, in the subtropical English colonies of North America, plantation agriculture arose around this crop; rice, indigo, and cotton came much later.

[63] *Memorias de Cabo Frio,* p. 205.

[64] *Produtos Exportados do Rio de Janeiro em 1796. Mapas* (Tables of products exported from Rio de Janeiro in 1796).

[65] On the cultivation of indigo in Brazil, see the comprehensive account written by the Viscount of Abrantes, *Origem da Cultura e Comércio do Anil* (Origins of Indigo Cultivation and Trade). For an account of the introduction of the indigo plantations and the efforts of the Marquis of Lavradio, see his *Relatório,* p. 38. There is also some interesting information on this subject in the lengthy *Ofício* (previously cited), which the Marquis's successor, Luís de Vasconcelos e Sousa, handed over on relinquishing the vice-regency.

Subsistence Agriculture
(pp. 180–194)

[1] Of the 4,345 pipes of sugarcane brandy exported from Rio de Janeiro in 1796, 2,841 were used in the slave trade (*Produtos Exportados do Rio de Janeiro*). It must be noted, however, that there were in this captaincy regions specializing in the production of sugarcane brandy, as there were in regions where sugar production was of secondary importance, as in Parati.

[2] Koster, *Voyages,* II, pp. 270, 291.

[3] Luccock, *Notes,* pp. 295 et seq.

[4] *Cartas Econômico-Políticas* (Letters on Economic and Political Matters), p. 29.

[5] In Cairu, Vilhena met settlers of illustrious descent—Meneses, Barretos, Castros, Lacerdas, etc.—who had become completely degenerate (*Recopilação,* p. 517).

[6] See the accounts of Luccock and St. Hilaire, who visited the region.

[7] In this respect, see in particular the *Memória* written by José Vieira Couto and the considerations on the subject made by the anonymous author of *Roteiro do Maranhão.*

[8] Observations of this nature were commonly made by the travelers who have left us their diaries, such as Martius, St. Hilaire, and others. See in particular St. Hilaire's account of his second journey to Minas Gerais, *Segunda Viagem a Minas Gerais,* p. 200.

[9] During their occupation of Pernambuco, the Dutch had faced the

problem and sought a solution in measures designed to encourage cultivation of food crops. Wätjen, *Das Holländische Kolonialreich in Brasilien,* p. 283. [Attracted by the wealth of the sugar-producing area of the northeast, the Dutch occupied the Brazilian coast all the way from the northern border of Bahia to the Amazon for 30 years: 1624–1654. They were finally expelled by the colonists.—Translator.]

[10] Vilhena, *Recopilação,* p. 151; and Brito, *Cartas Econômico-Políticas,* p. 28.

[11] This was done in Bahia after 1788. *Memória sôbre as Sesmarias da Bahia (Fragmento)* (Fragment of a Memoir on the Land Grants of Bahia), p. 387.

[12] *Recopilação,* p. 159 et seq.

[13] *Cartas Econômico-Políticas.* Protests against restrictive measures directed at the export of foodstuffs were made by the Judge-President of the Board of Inspection of Rio de Janeiro, José Feliciano da Rocha Gameiro. Letter dated April 28, 1798, published in *Correspondência de Várias Autoridades,* p. 280.

[14] Vilhena, *Recopilação,* p. 159.

[15] *Produtos Exportados do Rio de Janeiro.*

[16] Francisco de Paula Ribeiro, *Roteiro de Viagem* (Logbook of a Journey), p. 51, and *Descrição do Territorio dos Pastos Bons,* p. 55.

[17] *Viagem,* II, p. 273.

[18] We should note here that the term "manioc" applies only to the tuberous part of the root of *manhiot,* which is the correct name of the plant. See the *Dicionário de Botânica Brasileira* (Dictionary of Brazilian Botanical Terms) by Joaquim Almeida Pinto. [Cassava flour is prepared from the manioc tuber.—Translator.]

[19] *Capítulos de História Colonial* (Chapters of Colonial History), pp. 278, 283.

[20] In the north the horse is the most common beast of burden; and according to Gilberto Freyre, the traditional forage in the northeast is molasses or boiled cane sugar syrup (*mel-de-furo*). See *Nordeste.* The absence of a widespread diffusion of maize in the north may be due to adverse physical conditions for its cultivation. Writing of contemporary conditions, Senhor Gregório Bondar, consultant to the Development Insitute (Instituto de Fomento) of Bahia, refers to the devastating effect of the grain beetle on the maize cultivated in Bahia, which can only be overcome by exterminating this pest. In the south, thanks to the climate, the grain beetle is not common. See the interesting article written by this agronomist for the *Estado de São Paulo* and published on February 23, 1941, "O Êxodo da População Nordestina e o Caruncho dos Cereais" (The population exodus of the northeast and the grain-beetle). [The *Estado de São Paulo* is a daily newspaper.—Translator.]

[21] *Travels,* II, p. 16.

[22] Martius, *Viagem,* III, p. 15. *Farinha d'água* was known locally under its native name, *farinha puba* (manioc mash), and is made by macerating the root in water and letting it begin to ferment in order to get rid of the poisonous element. The starchy mass is then dried out,

ground into coarse meal, and put to various uses in the preparation of manioc dishes.

[23] Koster, *Voyages*, II, p. 291.

[24] *Viagem*, II, p. 548.

[25] *Itinerário*.

[26] Although Brás da Costa Rubim states that in Espírito Santo, maize is the basic item of diet for both men and animals (*Memórias*, p. 310), we have reason to suspect that the assertion is a mistaken one. It is contradicted by all the other information we have on this captaincy, which furnishes a considerable amount of evidence to the contrary.

[27] Martius, *Travels*, II, p. 35, gives a table of goods consigned from São Paulo in 1807. A good deal of maize but no manioc was sent overland, which signifies that it came from the plateau; for the consignments sent by sea, the reverse situation obtained.

[28] This is indicated by the statistics of production for the year 1810, published in *O Patriota*, No. 3, March, 1813, p. 98.

[29] The country's great rice-producing areas today are Minas Gerais, Rio Grande do Sul and São Paulo. In São Paulo it is no longer cultivated on the coastlands but on the plateau, along the irrigated valley of the Paraíba. The contrast with the colonial past is in this case striking. A pity this cannot be said of all else.

[30] See the "Table of Shipments" from Rio Grande do Sul for 1790 and 1792, given in the letter written by the Governor, Rafael Pinto Bandeira. *Correspondência de Varias Autoridades*, p. 266.

[31] *O Patriota*, No. 3, March, 1813.

[32] St. Hilaire, *Voyage dans les Provinces de Rio de Janeiro*, I, p. 391.

[33] Southey, *History*, III, pp. 796, 803.

Mining
(pp. 195–212)

[1] This has been the greatest handicap to mining in Brazil. The richest mine in the country today, the only large-scale vein-mining enterprise in existence, is the famous Morro Velho mine in Nova Lima. Here there is a rich gold-bearing vein with a gold content of 10.4 g. per ton of ore, whereas the gold content in mines considered in other parts to be of profitable yield is more than twice this ratio.

[2] According to Vieira Couto in his *Memória sôbre a Capitania de Minas Gerais*, p. 289, subterranean mining had at one time been carried on, as attested by the vestiges of underground work in Vila Rica. But this was soon abandoned for the easier workings of the placer deposits.

[3] The most advanced technique employed in extreme cases was to shatter the rock by abrupt changes of temperature. The rocks were heated by fire and then doused with cold water.

[4] Vieira Couto states that horizontal veins were rare. Most were perpendicular or at an angle of 60°–80°. *Memória*, p. 304.

[5] Even today a large number of people in the former mining districts of Minas Gerais, and Goiás in particular, live exclusively by this activity. They are itinerant prospectors, moving continually from place to place,

succeeding in one, failing in another. Travelers through these districts constantly come upon these *faiscadores,* working alone or in small groups, standing in the rivers or rummaging along the banks, rotating their *bateias* in the hope of finding a miserable particle of gold for the day's meal.

[6] There are very few statistics concerning production in Bahia. The centers important enough for smelting houses to be established were Jacobina and Rio das Contas. We know that in these two centers gold was still being mined at the beginning of the last century but only on a small scale. For this we have the testimony of Martius, in his *Viagem,* II, pp. 258, 260.

[7] Navarro, *Itinerário,* p. 438.

[8] For these mines, see *Notícias e Reflexões sôbre as Minas de Cantagalo* (Information and reflections on the mines of Cantagalo).

[9] Vilhena, *Recopilação,* p. 697.

[10] These attempts are described in the *Memórias do Visconde de São Leopoldo* (Memoirs of the Viscount of St. Leopoldo), p. 49.

[11] Joaquim da Costa Siqueira, *Compêndio Histórico de Cuiabá* (Historical Compendium of Cuiabá), p. 52.

[12] Luís D'Alincourt, *Resultado dos Trabalhos e Indagações estatisticas de Mato Grosso* (Results of statistical inquiries conducted in Mato Grosso), p. 273.

[13] On this subject I have already cited the eyewitness account of Brigadier Cunha Matos, *Corografia Histórica,* written shortly after independence. Also worthy of mention is St. Hilaire's account in *Voyage aux Sources du Rio de São Francisco,* II.

[14] A detailed account is given in the *Anais da Provincia de Goiás* (Annals of the Province of Goiás), p. 54, by J. M. P. de Alencastre.

[15] Documents relating to these diggings are published in *Subsídios para a História da Capitania de Goiás.*

[16] W. L. von Eschwege, *Pluto Brasiliensis,* II, p. 34.

[17] Both laws were transcribed in full by Eschwege in his *Pluto Brasiliensis.*

[18] The modifications to this code introduced in the royal decree of May 13, 1803, were never applied, and these provisions were revoked, those of the original code being reintroduced by the royal decree of September 1, 1808.

[19] The Intendência de Minas (Intendancy of Mines). The discoveries were all made in lands not yet occupied; the problem of prior ownership of the surface, therefore, never arose. The title deeds of the land grants (*cartas de sesmaria*) had in fact specifically excluded any mines that might come to be discovered in the area granted.

[20] The *braça* was a linear measure and was measured out along the beds or banks of the rivers or streams where the gold had been discovered. This system of delimitation led to much confusion, since the datas along the river bends were arranged like the rays of a circle, the respective areas overlapping. When the diggings began to move away from the river bank, many doubts and disputes arose. [The braça was

equivalent to the fathom as a measure of length, i.e., six feet.—Translator.]

[21] There were numerous such disputes, such as those relating to the utilization of the rivers and forests.

[22] There was a certain amount of tolerance with regard to the circulation of gold dust *within the captaincy of origin,* since it was not always possible for a miner to collect enough dust to be cast into a bar. This tolerance naturally eased the way for the wide circulation of gold dust. To overcome this, a system was devised for the smelting house to issue "certificates" against small amounts of gold dust deposited, and these certificates circulated as a kind of paper currency. When enough certificates had been collected, the owner could exchange them for a gold bar. The certificates were badly printed and could easily be forged, and this naturally began to happen. The smelting houses, instead of improving the certificates, adopted the more expedient method of refusing to redeem them. Cases are cited where a certificate issued by a smelting house one day was rejected the next on the pretext that it was a forgery. It was, however, only in Minas Gerais that such certificates were issued.

[23] In some captaincies the intendant also combined his function with that of president of the board of inspection for sugar and tobacco. This, however, occurred only in the captaincies where mining occupied a secondary position, such as Bahia and Rio de Janeiro.

[24] These are the only data of which, thanks to Eschwege, we have certain knowledge.

[25] The rest of the story lies a little outside our scope but is worth recalling. In 1811 the Regent, now closer to the evil and able to perceive it for himself, decided to settle it once and for all. His first step was the judicious appointment of a man like Eschwege who, besides being a noted expert on the subject, had the qualities of dedication and energy needed to essay rehabilitation of the sorry mess entrusted to him. But as usual the administration overlooked the most important point: the man chosen for this difficult and lofty task was given no authority, no say in the matter, no active voice; he was not even given the confidence merited not only by his past record—which was recognized sufficiently to lead to his appointment—but also because, if the mission were not to be doomed to failure, such confidence was absolutely essential. He was vaguely appointed to "examine mineral production, open up mines, establish factories, etc., etc., etc." And each time he approached the administration for support or to suggest some measure, he was hostilely received by those who saw in this foreigner no more than a dangerous adventurer. In spite of all, Eschwege's achievements were enormous. And if his desperate efforts came to naught, this was really because it was already a lost cause.

[26] In the largest placer mine in Minas Gerais, which is to say in the entire colony, there were never more than 100 workers. In the tables compiled by Eschwege cited above, there is a complete list of all such mines in the captaincy with the respective number of workers in each. It

must be noted that there were many paid workers and that in one particular mine all the 34 miners were in this category.

[27] The average daily takings of the independent worker was about one-quarter *oitava* of gold, but it was more commonly between 4–6 *vintens,* the weight in gold of a *vintém* being equivalent to about one-twelfth oitava. [The vintém (pl: vinténs) was a coin worth 20 reis.—Tr.] The slaves working in the diggings were generally required to hand over one oitava of gold per week to their masters, or, more commonly, ¾ oitava. Joaquim Felício dos Santos, *Memórias do Distrito Diamantino* (Memoirs of the Diamond District), p. 260.

[28] In the mining districts the word *cascalho* was used to describe the stratum of more or less compact pebbles and gravel underlying the sand and movable earthy matter of the surface. When the cascalho was in a compact, cement-like form, it was said to be "frozen." It was in the cascalho that most of the gold was found.

[29] Even in the heyday of the mines there were cases where existing diggings had to be given up for lack of resources, and the work already started had to be abandoned or where, for the same reason, the work was badly planned and performed.

[30] Letter of July 9, 1779, to Minister Martinho de Melo e Castro, published in *Subsídios para a História de Goiás,* p. 130. This plan to divert the Maranhão called for works of some magnitude, since the river's volume of water is great. A diversion of this river had already been carried out in 1732, 2½ leagues above its confluence with the Rio Almas, above the Machadinho Rapids. On this project 12,000 people worked for a year to construct a new channel into which the flow was diverted, and to dam the river by building a dyke across its former bed. The day the work was completed the dam broke and the river flowed back along its original channel. Tradition has it that the miners had all gone to lunch when this happened and that this at least saved their lives. Cunha Matos, *Corografia Histórica,* p. 266. The Cunha Meneses project was to have been carried out on the same site as that chosen in 1732, but it never went any further.

[31] Alencastre, *Anais da Província de Goiás,* p. 54.

[32] A later governor, Manuel Inácio de Sampaio, attempted to reopen the Anicuns Mines in 1821 and formed a new company, which was even less successful than its predecessor and was soon defunct. Cunha Matos, *Corografia Histórica,* p. 293. The main cause of these failures was always, apart from the general lack of technical knowledge and the relative poorness of the deposits, the want of any team spirit. Mining companies really belong to the period following the one we are here considering. The royal charter of January 16, 1817, authorized the governor of Mato Grosso to establish the "Mining Company of Cuibá." In August of that year, Eschwege had managed to get authority to form a company, to be organized by himself, which for the first time in Brazil would make use of modern scientific techniques. The formation of companies in the true sense dates from this period, and once restrictions against foreigners had

been removed in 1824, such companies began to multiply, with an influx of foreign capital, mostly English but also French.

[33] *Ordem* (Order) of the Governor, the Count of Sabugosa, proclaimed on October 4, 1732. Diamonds occur at various points along the plateau known as the "Chapada Diamantina."

[34] Pp. 26, 46. This is the basic historical work on the subject, published in 1864 by a native of Diamantina who had at his disposal not only the official archives but also the local lore, still very lively at the time he undertook the writing of his book.

[35] Article 15 of the Regimento. The "civil death penalty" is the suspension of all the condemned man's civil rights, "as if the person had ceased to exist," in the words of Pereira de Sousa in his *Dicionário Jurídico* (Legal Dictionary). It was set against "natural" death, the only form of "death" we know today.

[36] *Viagem*, II, p. 103.

[37] The district was included in the territory of this comarca, although lying outside its jurisdiction. Even the perimeter of the district therefore suffered from its evil reputation.

[38] *Memória sôbre a Capitania de Minas Gerais*, p. 289. Asia, and Turkey in particular, were synonymous at the time with despotic and brutal regimes, hence the reference to Constantinople.

[39] J. Felício dos Santos, *Memórias do Distrito Diamantino*, p. 206.

[40] The garimpeiros are part of the lore of the former diamond district, and their deeds are still talked about. J. Felício dos Santos, who lived at a time when these were fresh in the memory of the district, has portrayed some of the most notable figures, such as the famous Isidoro, the Martyr, leader of a band of fifty runaway slaves, who lived for many years a life of adventure only to be finally captured and to die under torture. *Memórias do Distrito Diamantino*, p. 370. And this occurred in 1809, when the intendant was the mildest administrator the diamond district had ever had, the first native-born Brazilian ever appointed to the post, Manuel Ferreira da Câmara—mentioned in a previous chapter—the owner of the Engenho da Ponte in Bahia. Mawe has given us a eulogy of the garimpeiro and in a page full of enthusiasm—of the Anglo-Saxon variety—has shown the extent to which the garimpeiros contributed to the discovery of new mines and the increase of trade within the colony. [The author is referring to John Mawe's *Travels in the Interior of Brazil, particularly in the Gold and Diamond Districts of that Country* (London, 1812).—Translator.]

[41] *Voyage aux Sources du Rio de São Francisco II*, p. 140.

Stock Rearing
(pp. 213–241)

[1] *Descrição do Território dos Pastos Bons*, p. 51.

[2] *Roteiro*, p. 124.

[3] This estimate is based on the figures for the income from meat (500 reis for each animal slaughtered) for the years 1795–1798, given by Vilhena in *Recopilação*, p. 69.

⁴ *Memória*, by Francisco Xavier Machado (1810), p. 66.

⁵ P. Le Cointe, *L'Amazonie Brésilienne*, II, p. 70.

⁶ As for the proper selection of fodder to be grown, what we know is that, at the beginning of the last century, certain varieties of grass were imported from Africa, which came to be known under the generic name of "Angola grass." In Bahia, this grass was cultivated by a Swiss immigrant, a certain Senhor Tschfelli, whose acquaintance Martius made, recording the fact that he sold his produce in the city. *Viagem*, II, p. 303. Luccock noted that Angola grass was cultivated in Rio de Janeiro to supply urban requirements. *Notes*, p. 295. Apart from these special cases and other similar attempts probably made, there appears to have been no great concern for the cultivation of selected cattle fodder. We must note, however, that around 1810, Councillor Veloso de Oliveira recommended the cultivation of artificial pasturage in São Paulo using Angola grass. *Memória sôbre o Melhoramento da Provincia de São Paulo*, p. 42.

⁷ *Idéia da População*, p. 30.

⁸ *Cartas Económico-Políticas*, p. 30.

⁹ The following details should be added to what has already been said: the agricultural zone of the northeastern coastlands extended, properly speaking, from Paraíba to the Bay of All Saints. To the north, the semiarid Sertão stretched as far as the sea, and conditions were so unfavorable that even cattle raising failed to develop in the area. South of the Recôncavo there was an agricultural region of secondary importance, where only a poor subsistence agriculture had made any progress. Cattle raising in this region was unfeasible because of the dense forest covering that extended almost as far as the coastline and proved an insurmountable obstacle in view of the slender resources available to the colonists. Apart from this, since it was far from any of the worthwhile markets, to all of which access was difficult, there was nothing to stimulate the development of a grazing industry.

¹⁰ The ranches of the backlands of Bahia were at first the mining centers' sole source of fresh meat. The authorities had prohibited this traffic in the early days of the gold rush in an effort to prevent gold smuggling, but the ban was soon lifted as there was no other possible source of supply. [The author is here referring to the closure of the São Francisco route, the route from Bahia to the mining camps, decreed in February, 1701. As this was the route used for sending most of the mining camps' essential supplies, the prohibition was ignored and the authorities were forced to reopen the route in 1703, but rigorously maintained the prohibition on all other forms of transit, trade, and traffic.—Tr.] The mining code promulgated in 1703 allowed cattle droves from Bahia to enter the mining region, but the permission was hedged about with all sorts of precautions. In this period cattle from Bahia were even driven all the way to São Paulo.

¹¹ *Viagem*, II, p. 401 et seq.

¹² *Roteiro do Maranhão*, p. 88. Another contemporary account observes: ". . . it being so easy to start cattle establishments in these sertões, the expense involved in preliminary preparations being but small,

and the number of workers being so few . . ." Francisco de Paula Ribeiro, *Descrição do Território dos Pastos Bons,* p. 84.

[13] *Roteiro do Maranhão,* p. 88. I have already referred to the way in which the backlands of the northeast were occupied, and this accounts for the presence of the mestizo elements referred to by the author of the *Roteiro,* who also stresses the attraction of the profession of vaqueiro for these people, so averse to an orderly and sedentary life. "Their greatest happiness was to earn the name of vaqueiro," he writes.

[14] Paula Ribeiro, *Descrição dos Pastos Bons,* p. 77.

[15] In Antonil's time, the concentration of estates in the hands of absentee latifundian owners was considerable. According to his account, in a much-quoted passage, nearly all the Sertão of Bahia belonged to two families: the Garcia de Ávila family, collectively known as the *Casa da Torre* (House of the Tower), and the heirs of Camp-Master Antônio Guedes de Brito. The first family owned 340 leagues of land and the second, 160 (*Cultura e Opulência,* p. 264). In Piauí, Domingos Afonso, variously surnamed "Sertão" and "Mafrense" [native of Mafra in Portugal], owned 40 estates, which were bequeathed to the Jesuits as sole heirs. These estates, later confiscated with the order's other possessions, were still in the hands of the crown at the beginning of the last century. Francisco Xavier Machado gives us an account of them in his *Memória,* p. 58. [The d'Avila family was known as the "Casa da Torre" because it owned a castellated stone mansion some thirty miles north of Salvador. Pedro Calmon has written a history of this family: *História da casa da Torre; Uma dinastia de pioneiros.* Rio de Janeiro, 1939 and 1958.— Translator.]

[16] Hence the generic name, *ribeira* (stream), which is found in various regions of the northeastern Sertão. The name comes from the settlements which spread out from the fazendas thus established.

[17] *Memória sôbre as Sesmarias da Bahia,* p. 379.

[18] On the crown fazendas of Piauí the vaqueiro was assigned a "comrade" who supervised the vaqueiro but was not held responsible for the work carried out. The fourth was divided equally between the two. Xavier Machado, *Memória,* p. 58.

[19] Paula Ribeiro, *Descrição dos Pastos Bons,* p. 83. In the fazendas of the Sertão, as in the colony's other cattle-raising regions, bulls were not customarily slaughtered for consumption on the ranch. The bulls were sold and only the cows were killed for meat to supply the ranch's own requirements. This was a fatal practice, which largely contributed to the reduction of the herds and the declining prosperity of the ranches as Ribeiro rightly observes in the work cited (p. 74) and in his *Roteiro,* p. 67.

[20] On the crown estates of Piauí referred to in note 18, of which there were 35 in 1810, these figures were seldom reached. Only two of these estates managed to rear 1,000 calves or more, the figure for the majority being less than 500. A complete account of these fazendas and their herds is given in Xavier Machado's *Memória.* The total number of calves raised annually on these 35 fazendas was 13,325.

21 For the role played by the horse in the northeast, see Freyre's interesting observations in *Nordeste*, the chapter entitled: "O Homem e o Animal" (Man and Beast).

22 *Roteiro do Maranhão*, p. 79.

23 *Viagem*, II, p. 299.

24 On their way to Bahia, for instance, the droves from Piauí had to cross the forbidding wastes extending over the upper sertões of Pernambuco and large areas of the hinterland of Bahia for most of their journey.

25 "When they arrive . . . they are herded into the municipal corrals, from which they are dispatched in fours to the abattoir. . . ." Vilhena, *Recopilação*, p. 161. Only one figure is available to indicate the weight of a slaughtered animal; this is the figure of eight arrobas (about 120 kg.) given for Maranhão by Xavier Machado in *Memória*, p. 66. It was certainly less for Bahia.

26 *Idéia da População*. A circumstance contributing, at least in part, to the vast extents of unused or abandoned lands in the northeastern Sertão was the initial error made in distributing lands, the original sesmarias covering huge areas which, despite the stipulations laid down in the title deeds of the grant, were never properly stocked or else were completely neglected. This explains the decrees reducing the maximum area of sesmarias. The frequent repetition of such legislation indicates that it was either not observed or else was circumvented in some other way. The problem of land grants in the northeast sertões gave rise to interminable disputes, often resolved by the ferocious armed battles which took place throughout the colonial period between the different landowners or between the landowners and persons who had not been given grants of land and who wanted to make use of neglected allotments. The subject, of the greatest interest to the country's social and economic history, still awaits research.

27 Castro Carreira notes the following "great" droughts for the eighteenth century: 1710, 1725–1727, 1736, 1744, 1777 and 1778, 1791–1793. *Descrição Geográfica do Ceará*, p. 111.

28 For details of this part of Minas Gerais, see St. Hilaire's description in chap. XII of his *Voyage aux Provinces de Rio de Janeiro et Minas Gerais*.

29 The Paulistas also contributed to the opening up of the region. Their excursions sometimes led to the establishing of fixed settlements, which extended as far to the north as Paraíba (Domingos Jorge Velho). [The author is here referring to the settlement founded by the Paulista pioneer, D. J. Velho, who had first penetrated the region between the Gurgueia and Parnaíba rivers with a view to settlement in 1671. He then spent many years (1687–1697) fighting against the rebellious tribes of Açu and the runaway Negro settlement of Palmares, and afterwards settled with his immediate followers in the region of Palmares.—Tr.] But these Paulista establishments were completely cut off from their point of departure. Unlike the currents which penetrated the area from the north, progressively settling and colonizing the territories along which they advanced, there was no continuity of settlement in the expansion provoked

by the adventures of the Paulista *bandeiras*. We must also point out that the district of Minas Novas belonged to Bahia up to 1757, when it was incorporated in Minas Gerais by virtue of the decree of May 10 of that year. Ecclesiastical jurisdiction, however, continued to be exercised over the area by the archbishop of Bahia until the nineteenth century.

[30] As the forests were cleared by burning, the cleared patches were planted with Guinea grass, which provides excellent pasturage.

[31] *Roteiro do Maranhão*, p. 93.

[32] If we exclude the Campos Gerais (Paraná), then still within the São Paulo area, this region accounted for the largest cattle herds in the province when the 1835 census was taken. Müller, *Ensaio de Um Quadro Estatístico* (Outline of a Statistical Survey).

[33] For details of this organization, see St. Hilaire, *Voyage aux Sources du Rio de São Francisco*, I, ch. vi, which is the source I have used here.

[34] In the region between Lavras and São João del-Rei, where the terrain is very rocky, these stone walls can still be seen, stretching for miles and miles as far as the eye can see.

[35] St. Hilaire makes this observation, and being a true Frenchman, he was a good judge of cattle. *Voyage aux sources du Rio de São Francisco*, I, p. 67.

[36] The milk of Auvergne is inferior to that of France's northern regions, Normandy and Brittany, famous for their dairy produce. But for Brazil, the comparison was an honorable one. The French traveler also notes that a good cow in Minas produced an average of four bottles of milk a day. Unfortunately he does not state the capacity of these "bottles." *Voyage aux sources*, I, p. 171.

[37] St. Hilaire gives an impersonal and uncritical description of cheese-making in Minas. Mawe, on the other hand, is severely critical of the primitive methods used, particularly the lack of hygienic precautions. *Travels in the Interior of Brazil*.

[38] There were several wealthy fazendeiros in Southern Minas; among others, St. Hilaire cites one who sold to Rio, either from his own herds or from animals bought for resale, between 5,000–6,000 head of cattle every year! *Voyage aux Sources*, I, p. 81.

[39] The anonymous author of *Roteiro do Maranhão* protests against the wide consumption of pork, which he hoped would be replaced by beef. In spite of this antipathy to pork, however, we cannot suspect him of being a "new Christian," since he gives economic arguments in favor of this preference, which in terms of the criteria he advances and in accord with the general spirit of his admirable work are absolutely valid. Indeed his arguments do honor to the acuteness of his observation and his quality as an economist. According to these arguments, the raising of pigs, which calls for a parallel agricultural activity to grow the maize used for feeding them, deflects attention from mining, which is the only activity really valuable to the mother country and engages a large number of people who would otherwise have been more usefully employed in this activity, providing gold for the kingdom's trade and royal fifths for its sovereign. As we can see, the pig was thus on a modest scale a tiny factor in the great

work of achieving the colony's independence! *Roteiro,* p. 99. [The "new" Christians were Jewish converts to the Catholic faith and were suspected of being crypto-Jews.—Tr.]

[40] There are, however, some exceptions to the universal use of pork fat. In the north, particularly in Bahia, palm oil and other vegetable oils are used. In the extreme north, in addition to vegetable oils, "turtle butter" is widely used, a feature to which I shall have occasion to return in a later chapter. [*Manteiga de Tartaruga,* or turtle butter, is an oily paste made from the yolks of turtle eggs.—Tr.]

[41] St. Hilaire, *Voyage aux Sources,* I, p. 73. These hats were made by specialized craftsmen, who were supplied with the raw materials and paid only for their work. Sheep were rarely used for meat. Luccock (*Notes on Brazil,* p. 44) observes that in Rio de Janeiro it was only the English colony who ate mutton, a fact which provoked a certain expansion of sheep raising in the rural outskirts of Rio de Janeiro after the ports were opened, with the consequent influx of foreigners. Luccock explains the Brazilian aversion to mutton as being due to their religious feelings, the idea of eating the flesh of an animal symbolic of Christ being repugnant to a religious people. I am not sure how far Luccock's explanation can be taken seriously, since he was obviously merely repeating the information he had been given, and his informants may have been having a jest at his expense. But it is true that mutton has never been widely consumed in Brazil. From personal observation I know that sheep are used in Minas to transport small burdens, such as firewood, but I cannot say when this practice started.

[42] "Campos Gerais" is the collective name for these plains, but it was particularly applied to the plains which today constitute the Paraná plateau and has now become the proper name of this particular region.

[43] Although connected to each other along the coast (via Laguna) and linked by the settlements established by the gradual infiltration of Paulistas into this area, these two parts remained virtually cut off from each other, and there was no appreciable contact between them until the middle of the eighteenth century, when they were linked by the first proper route established across the plateau.

[44] The Luso-Spanish War, 1801, which had profound repercussions in America, gave back to Brazil the territory of the Seven Peoples, which had been restored to Spain by the Treaty of San Ildefonso.

[45] Alcides Lima, *História Popular do Rio Grande do Sul,* p. 106. An observer still close to the events wrote in 1808, "The man who could count on the protection of the government applied for one sesmaria in his own name, another in the name of his eldest son, and still others in the name of sons and daughters still in the cradle: and in this way, there were households that acquired four or more sesmarias." Manuel Antônio Guimarães, *Almanaque da Vila de Pôrto Alegre,* p. 53.

[46] Alcides Lima, *História Popular,* p. 108.

[47] Dreys, *Notícia Descritiva,* p. 154.

[48] The figures for exports from Rio Grande in the period 1790–1793 are taken from a letter written by Governor Pinto Bandeira, dated Janu-

ary 14, 1794, and included in the "Collection of Letters Written by Various Authorities" previously cited. (*Correspondência de Várias Autoridades,* p. 266). For the period 1805–1819, see St. Hilaire, *Viagem ao Rio Grande do Sul,* p. 132 et seq, where official figures furnished by various authorities are transcribed. In this period, Rio Grande exported large quantitites of charque to Havana, Cuba.

⁴⁹ The only competitor with which the charque of Rio Grande had to contend was the *xarque* of the Plata region. In Rio Grande, an arroba of charque cost 440–480 reis to produce; freight charges and the duty levied at Rio de Janeiro amounted to 280 reis. In contrast to this, an arroba of xarque from the Plata region was sold for 410 reis in Rio de Janeiro. The difference is due to the superior quality of the Plata region's cattle, which yielded 16–20 arrobas of meat per head, whereas the native breed yielded only 8–10. Manuel Antônio de Magalhães, *Almanaque da Vila de Pôrto Alegre,* p. 48. As to quality, contemporary opinions vary; St. Hilaire preferred the Plata product (*Viagem,* p. 114); Dreys held the Brazilian charque to be the superior (*Notícia,* p. 116).

⁵⁰ Manuel Antônio de Magalhães, *Almanaque,* p. 46. The problem of domesticating the wild cattle incorporated into the estancias, automatically, as it were, when the estate was formed, by simply demarcating an area that would include any stray cattle it happened to contain, was one of the captaincy's chief economic problems in the last years of the eighteenth century and for some time thereafter. All the captaincy's governors were concerned with this problem, starting with the first governor appointed in the period we are dealing with, Veiga Cabral, who took office in 1780.

⁵¹ Luccock, *Notes,* p. 116.

⁵² Dreys, *Notícia Descritiva,* p. 135. Luccock confirms this; he gives the figure of 4,000–5,000 head for every three leagues. *Notes,* p. 216.

⁵³ Dreys in *Notícia Descritiva,* p. 133, mentions *gauchos,* which was the term then used to designate these mixed breeds, whom he considered to be a most unruly and badly behaved lot.

⁵⁴ *Notes,* p. 215. St. Hilaire cites the estate owned by Marshal Chagas on the Butuí River, where he spent some days, as having an overseer and ten peões to manage 6,000 head of cattle. The peões earned 8 *patacas* (2½ cruzeiros) per month.

⁵⁵ *Notícias,* p. 136. In 1816, only 95,747 *alqueires* of salt were imported into Rio Grande do Sul, which produced no salt of its own. [An *alqueire* = 13 liters.—Tr.]

⁵⁶ *Documentos Relativos à História da Capitania do Rio Grande do Sul* (Documents relating to the History of Rio Grande do Sul), p. 301.

⁵⁷ Dreys, *Notícia Descritiva,* p. 154.

⁵⁸ St. Hilaire, *Viagem,* p. 90.

⁵⁹ *Voyage aux Provinces de St. Paul,* II, p. 10 et seq.

⁶⁰ Production for 1835, in the absence of any earlier figures, was 17,859 head of cattle and 4,992 horses. Müller, *Ensaio de Um Quadro Estatístico.*

⁶¹ St. Hilaire supplies the following comparative figures: In the

Campos Gerais, salt was distributed every two or even only every three months. In Minas there was a monthly distribution of salt rations. In one of the Campos Gerais fazendas he visited, one alqueire of salt was used for every 100 animals.

[62] Veloso de Oliveira, *Memória para o Melhoramento de São Paulo* (Memoir for the Improvement of São Paulo), p. 39.

[63] This was the first name of the island of Marajó. The latter name applied only to the island's eastern part, where there was grassy vegetation suited to stock rearing. This half of the island was completely different from the western half, which was covered with the semiaquatic *selva* (rain forest) of Amazonia.

[64] This was the fazenda owned by Francisco Rodrigues Perreira situated on the left bank of the Ararí River. P. Le Cointe, *L'Amazonie Brésilienne*, II, p. 62.

[65] The largest fazenda on the island was that of the Mercedarians (Order of Our Lady of Mercy); in 1794 it was taken over by the crown with all the other properties of the order, which was then suppressed. This fazenda, located on the banks of the Ararí River in the main part of the island, had 150 slaves and close to 30,000 head of cattle as well as a large number of horses. Friar Franc. de N. Sra. dos Prazeres, *Poranduba Maranhense*, p. 116 n.

[66] Lieutenant Colonel José Simões de Carvalho, *Notícia sôbre a Ilha de Joanes* (An account of the Island of Joanes), p. 362.

[67] P. le Cointe, *L'Amazonie Brésilienne*, II, p. 70.

[68] The *Roteiro do Maranhão* was written chiefly to stress the need for opening up direct communication by land between Maranhão and Pará to allow cattle to be brought down to Maranhão from the Sertão. As we know, this was never done, and even today overland routes are lacking. This is no doubt partly explained by the fact that improved navigation techniques and other factors dispensed with the need for cattle to undertake long overland journeys and made it possible to transport them by sea. This interesting topic will be dealt with at greater length in a later chapter.

[69] Comandante André Fernandes de Sousa, *Notícias geográficas da capitania do Rio Negro*, p. 455.

Extractive Products
(pp. 242–255)

[1] This does not, of course, include gold and diamond mining, which has been discussed in a separate chapter.

[2] The wages to be paid to Indians were fixed by the Proclamation of May 30, 1773, issued by the governor of Pará. Alexandre Rodrigues Ferreira, *Diário da Viagem Filosófica*, p. 29.

[3] Martius, *Viagem*, III, p. 262.

[4] Martius, *Viagem*, III, p. 262.

[5] Martius gives a detailed description of this interesting industry in *Viagem*, III, p. 241, et seq.

[6] Artur Reis, *A Política de Portugal no Vale Amazônico* (Portugal's Policy in the Amazon Valley), p. 98.

[7] Table of products shipped from this captaincy; Martius, *Viagem*, III, p. 158.

Crafts and Industries
(pp. 256–264)

[1] In the case of the iron and steel industry, it is known that many of the African peoples had mastered the art of working iron in their own continent. They brought with them their knowledge, and their native ability as metalworkers was of great help to the colonists.

[2] *Notes*, p. 395.

[3] We can get some idea of the mechanical trades practiced in the colony's towns and cities from the reports published in the Rio de Janeiro *Almanaques* for 1792 and 1794. An interesting study by Salomão de Vasconcelos, entitled *Ofícios mecânicos em Vila-Rica durante o sec. XVIII* (Mechanical trades practiced in Vila Rica in the 18th century), has recently been published.

[4] *Travels*, I, p. 197.

[5] The corporations were semipublic bodies whose activities were controlled by the municipal councils of their respective towns. Frequent references to these corporations are therefore made in the minutes of the town councils, and they can be studied from these sources. Thus in the published records and minutes of the São Paulo town council, *Registo* and *Atas da Câmara de São Paulo*, we find among numerous other references the following: "Examination for skilled tailor: Letter of confirmation and municipal licence." *Registo*, XII, p. 117. Ditto for skilled blacksmith— *Registo*, XII, p. 409; "Elections for judges and clerks," *Atas*, XX, pp. 230, 232 (1800) and p. 307 (1801).

[6] There are numerous interesting references to the colony's mechanical trades in the diaries of the early nineteenth century travelers. Luccock should be especially mentioned (*Notes*, p. 106), since he displays great interest in the subject and is particularly perceptive.

[7] For the techniques used in Brazil's old buildings, see the practical manual by Rainville, *O Vinhola Brasileiro* (The Brazilian Builder). Although published in 1880, it gives details of many building techniques already in use in the colony.

[8] Luccock, *Notes*, p. 241; and St. Hilaire, *Voyage aux provinces de St. Paul*, II, p. 331.

[9] St. Hilaire, *Segunda Viagem ao Espírito Santo*, p. 159.

[10] Luccock, *Notes*, pp. 344, 364.

[11] Southey, *History*, III, p. 805.

[12] *Voyage aux provinces de St. Paul*, II, p. 355.

[13] Martius, *Viagem*, II, p. 469.

[14] *Ibid.*, p. 471.

[15] *Ibid.*, III, p. 103. [Andiroba oil is obtained from the seeds of the *Carapa guianensis*, or crab tree, native to South America. The oil is known in England as crab oil, a corruption of carap oil.—Translator.]

[16] Luccock, *Notes*, p. 223.

[17] Martius, *Travels*, II, p. 18.

[18] *Ibid.*, I, p. 311. St. Hilaire, *Voyage aux provinces de St. Paul*, II, p. 407.

[19] Martius, *Viagem*, II, p. 329. Prince Maximilian gives details of this craft in his *Voyages*, II, p. 335.

[20] Martius, *Viagem*, II, p. 353.

[21] Martius, *Viagem*, III, p. 242. Rope-making was a crown concern, and was one of the domestic industries founded in the captaincy by Governor Lobo de Almada at the end of the eighteenth century. He also founded a textile industry, ceramics, indigo-processing, etc. For the work of this great administrator of the captaincy of São José do Rio Negro, see Artur Reis, *Lobo de Almada, um estadista colonial* (L. de Almada, a Colonial Statesman).

[22] *Relatório*, p. 459.

[23] An interesting collection of documents relating to the *Alvará* of January 5 and its execution is found in *Documentos oficiais inéditos*, p. 213.

[24] *Notes*, p. 535.

[25] The problem of transporting pig iron was an extremely serious one. Mules could transport a maximum of eight arrobas, and this weight had to be evenly distributed, half on each side of the animal. Iron was imported in ingots, as it was supplied by the manufacturers, weighing more than this maximum. They had therefore to be divided before being despatched to the interior, a delicate operation calling for extreme accuracy and which added greatly to the price of the merchandise, although in point of fact this operation was generally very badly performed. As for the import duties, like the various other onerous tolls and taxes levied on merchandise traveling through the colony and collected at the numerous *registos* (customs posts) and river crossings, these were calculated on a basis of weight, bulk, or the number of animals used to transport the load. This system, which bore less heavily on articles of great unitary value, as was the case with manufactured goods in general, was particularly burdensome when it came to pig iron, imported in bulk.

[26] See, among other testimonies, Bittencourt Câmara's remarks on the subject, in *Memória mineralógica*, addressed to José Bonifácio, then already a Minister [i.e., José Bonifácio de Andrada e Silva, one of the outstanding figures in Brazil's history, who was the great architect of independence.—Translator].

[27] *Ofício do Secretário de Estado Luís Pinto de Sousa* (Official Letter of the Secretary of State, L. P. de Sousa).

[28] *Voyage aux provinces de Rio de Janeiro*, II, p. 285.

[29] St. Hilaire, *Voyage aux provinces de St. Paul*, I, p. 267. Martius, *Travels*, II, p. 18. Sousa Chichorro, *Memória*, p. 239.

[30] St. Hilaire, *Voyage aux provinces de Rio de Janeiro*, I, p. 287.

[31] Fernandes Pinheiro, *Os Últimos Vice-Reis do Brasil* (The Last Viceroys of Brazil), p. 227. For a summary of the laws enacted against goldsmiths and related material, see Eduardo Marques Peixoto, *Os descaminhos do ouro* (Gold Smuggling).

Commerce
(pp. 265–275)

[1] In the 1770's, the anonymous author of *Roteiro do Maranhão* (pp. 126 ff.) had already suggested that imported mules should be heavily taxed. Before this, the governor of Piauí had complained that the captaincy's trade had been ruined by the introduction of mules into the mining districts (*Provisão de 7 de julho de 1763, Publicação do Arquivo Nacional*, I, p. 694). Importation of mules was later expressly prohibited, but the prohibition had no effect.

[2] Nogueira Coelho, *Memória cronológica de Mato Grosso*, p. 185.

[3] Martius gives some details of this trade in *Viagem*, III, p. 275, n. v.

[4] The chartered companies created by Pombal were the Companhia Geral do Comércio do Maranhão e Grão Pará and the Companhia Geral do Comércio de Pernambuco e Paraíba.

[5] The 1654 treaty stipulated that English ships had to join the Brazil fleets, and abolition of the convoy system may have been interpreted as a cancellation of the British privilege.

[6] *Correspondência de várias autoridades*, p. 264.

[7] *Ibid.*, p. 271.

[8] *Correspondência de várias autoridades*, p. 295.

[9] Gayozo, *Compêndio*, p. 245.

[10] Mortality on the slave ships became even higher after English cruisers began to harry the slavers, forcing them to crowd their human cargo into the smallest possible space in the holds below decks to try to keep them out of sight.

[11] In other parts of the colony, where there does not appear to have been the speculative trade which Gayozo so deplored, slaves fetched 130–150 mil-reis a head. According to information supplied by Governor Francisco de Sousa Coutinho in 1797 this was the price of a slave in Pará, *Informação sôbre o Modo por que se efetua a navegação do Pará para Mato Grosso* (Report on the manner in which navigation is effected between Pará and Mato Grosso), p. 48. For Bahia, Martius gives a figure of 140–150 mil-reis. *Viagem*, II, p. 296. Vilhena, in *Recopilação*, also mentions 150 mil-reis as the price of a slave in Bahia (p. 933).

[12] Balbi, *Essai statistique*.

[13] The only reliable statistics for the domestic trade would have been furnished by the documents of the *registos* (customhouses) or inland posts for collecting duties on the merchandise circulating in the colony, known as *alfândegas secas* (dry customs, i.e., not situated in a port), and the tolls established at river crossings and other strategic points. But these documents have probably been irretrievably lost. We have only the stray references given in the official and private documents of the period, and although these give no figures they are nevertheless invaluable. The most important references to the period with which we are here concerned are those which occur in the diaries of the foreign travelers who visited Brazil and were generally interested in the subject. Luccock, in his *Notes on Brazil*, published an appendix listing the items involved in

Rio de Janeiro's maritime trade for April, 1813, to April, 1818. This table does not, however, give the value of these items, but only the overall tonnage by destination for each three-month period. Martius, in his *Viagem* (II, p. 241), gives an interesting table for the port of Malhada, on the São Francisco River, the hub of interregional trade between the captaincies of Minas Gerais, Goiás, and Bahia, for the period April, 1816, to March, 1817. The value of goods shipped from Bahia to Minas and Goiás in this period amounted to 103,090:920 reis, of which 86,718 reis was indisputably accounted for by imported goods, the remainder being nearly all represented by salt (16,145:920 reis). The origin of the salt is not specified; it could have come either from the saltworks of the São Francisco or from abroad. Martius also gives details concerning the flow of goods from the captaincy of Rio Negro to Pará, registered at Gurupá, the port of passage from one to the other. All the items indicated were clearly destined for the foreign market. *Viagem*, III, p. 157 et seq. Eschwege gives a table of imports and exports for Minas Gerais for the period 1818–1819. *Notícias e Reflexões estatísticas.*

14 Portugal's dependence on Brazil did not in fact come to an end with Brazil's independence. An appreciable proportion of her wealth continued to derive, directly or indirectly, from her former colony, whether from the money that Portuguese nationals resident in Brazil continued to remit to the motherland or from the return of many of her natives, who had managed to get rich in Brazil. Apart from this, Brazil was still to represent what it had always represented for the Portuguese, a "career." Brazil figures prominently among the opportunities facing the Portuguese when choosing his future livelihood. He could then, if he so wished, call himself a "Brazilian," just as he would have called himself a "salesman" if he had gone in for selling or a "grocer" if he had gone into the grocery business. [The author's choice of "salesman" and "grocer" is not as arbitrary as it seems in English. The Portuguese words "vend*eiro*" and "merce*eiro*" have the same ending as "Brasil*eiro*," *eiro* being, like the English *ier*, a suffix forming nouns designating employment or profession. Hence, "Brasileiro" becomes, in the specific sense he gives the word by italicizing the suffix in analogy with the two other callings selected, the "profession" represented by being Brazilian.—Translator.] The idea of "business" always associated with the ex-colony, with its profound historical roots—which is why it concerns us here—was never to be entirely abandoned by the Portuguese. We must add that this intromission of Portuguese interests in Brazil was also to play a part in the political evolution of the empire.

Communications and Transport
(pp. 276–309)

1 Later, in the course of the nineteenth century, similar features were displayed by routes in the far south. A current of penetration ascended by way of the Paraguay valley to Mato Grosso, where it joined up with this captaincy's routes to the coast which ran northward and eastward, and

ended up reaching the coast at points extremely distant from the Paraguay outlet on the Plata River. The difference is that in this case the current of penetration and occupation was composed both of Brazilians and of the neighboring Spanish-Americans.

[2] The situation is still the same today. For the motor road link between Rio de Janeiro and Bahia the route chosen runs through the interior, since the coastal highway would have been impractical, at least for the time being.

[3] Martius, *Viagem*, II, p. 408. This figure of 20,000 was given as the number of cattle consumed in Bahia in the chapter on cattle raising. The losses incurred on the trail from Juàzeiro to Bahia were made up for by cattle supplied from regions other than Piauí.

[4] Martius makes this observation, noting that whereas the number of cattle passing through the Juàzeiro registo on their way from Piauí to the markets of Bahia had decreased—the reason for this decrease, which Martius does not specify, being as we have seen the general decadence of cattle raising in the northeast and the competition of charque from Rio Grande—the number of slaves entering along this route had risen. *Viagem*, II, p. 408. The treaty between Portugal and England signed on January 22, 1815, abolished the slave trade in ports north of the Equator and thus cut off the main source of supply, the Gulf of Guinea. The full text of the treaty is transcribed in Pereira Pinto, *Apontamentos*, I, p. 128.

[5] This is the route described in detail by the author of the *Roteiro do Maranhão a Goiás*, so often previously cited in connection with more general matters of much greater importance.

[6] *Derrota dos correios da vila da Fortaleza à cidade da Bahia* (Postal route from the town of Fortaleza to the city of Bahia), marked out by the Governor of Ceará, Francisco Alberto Rubim.

[7] Paula Ribeiro, *Roteiro*, p. 55.

[8] Capistrano de Abreu, citing Gentil Moura, enumerates these passes of the colonial period in *Caminhos antigos* (Old Trails), p. 69, fn.

[9] *Cultura e opulência*, p. 239.

[10] The decree of October 27, 1733, had forbidden the opening up of any new trails to the mines. By the end of the eighteenth century this prohibition was no longer strictly observed. Vieira Fazenda, *Legislação portuguêsa relativa ao Brasil.*

[11] Martius, *Viagem*, II, p. 146.

[12] *Descobrimento de Minas Gerais*, p. 98.

[13] Carneiro da Silva, *Memórias dos Campos dos Goitacases*, p. 44. The *Correio Brasiliense* (April 1820, XXIV, p. 395) also refers to this trail, which ran from the registo on the Rio da Pomba to Salvador.

[14] The official report on the demarcation of this border is transcribed in *Notas, Apontamentos e Notícias para a história do Espírito Santo*, p. 193.

[15] A detailed account of these efforts is given in the *Informação* (Report) of Governor Manuel Vieira de Albuquerque Tovar and in that of Francisco Manuel da Cunha.

[16] See the official *Medição, Direção e Observação da Nova Estrada . . .*

(Survey of the New Road . . .), carried out in 1818. A detailed account is given in Brás da Costa Rubim, *Memória histórica do Espírito Santo*, p. 283.

[17] This road was opened up by Captain Bento Lourenço Vaz de Abreu Lima, who was the first to travel along it from Minas to the coast. Prince Maximilian, *Voyage*, I, p. 362. A map showing this road is published as an Appendix to Vol. II of this work.

[18] A detailed description of this road is given by Prince Maximilian, who traveled along it. *Voyage*, II, pp. 360, 364.

[19] The two routes still compete today. Whereas the Mojiana, prolonged by the São Paulo-Goiás railways, both of Paulista origin, follows the first route, the *Rêde Mineira de Viação* (Minas Railway Network) links Minas to Goiás. But with the building of railroads, natural obstacles became even more formidable than in the past and the political and fiscal factors which influenced the preference for the Minas route disappeared. The Paulista route is therefore destined to emerge triumphant: Goiás will then be brought within the São Paulo orbit as it was originally, and not within that of Minas or Rio de Janeiro.

[20] The route by way of the Tocantins was more direct and afforded easier going, since settlements were established along much of its length; but the Araguaia offered the advantage of leading, by way of its navigable tributary, the Vermelho, right into the heart of the captaincy and its capital, Vila Boa.

[21] A report of this river journey was given in a letter written by Governor Sousa Coutinho, *Viagem de Tomás de Sousa Vila Real pelos rios Tocantins, Araguaia e Vermelho*. [Tomás de Sousa Vila Real was in charge of the expedition.—Translator.]

[22] The diary of his journey is published in *Subsídios para a história da capitania de Goiás*, p. 171.

[23] This was reported in the *Patriota*, Sept., 1813, p. 61, and in *Anais da Provincia da Goiás*, p. 82, by J. M. P. de Alencastre.

[24] The suggestion was made not only in the issue of the *Patriota* cited above, but also by Paula Ribeiro in his *Descrição do território dos Pastos Bons*, p. 71.

[25] Martius, *Travels*, II, p. 67.

[26] A detailed description of a voyage undertaken in 1792 is given by Francisco de Oliveira Barbosa in *Notícias da capitania de São Paulo*, p. 22. Hércules Florence in *Esboço da Viagem de Langsdorff* gives an account of his voyage in 1826.

[27] Martius, *Viagem*, III, p. 421.

[28] *Informação sôbre o módo por que se efetua a navegação do Pará ao Mato-Grosso*.

[29] The inclusion of Ceará and Piauí in the list reveals a complete ignorance of geography on the part of the Portuguese administration, or at least of whoever dictated the royal letters, since the courses followed by the Amazon's tributaries were known well enough by this time.

[30] Martius, *Viagem*, III, p. 421, fn. 1. Baron Duarte da Ponte Ribeiro,

Resenha histórica da navegação e reconhecimento dos rios Guaporé e Mamoré (Historical survey of the navigation and reconnaissance of the Guaporé and Mamoré rivers).

[31] Joaquim da Costa Siqueira, *Compêndio histórico de Cuiabá*, p. 53.

[32] Report of both outward and return voyages is given in *Diário da viagem . . . pelo Arinos.*

[33] *Memória da nova navegação do rio Arinos* (Memoir on the newly opened-up navigation on the Arinos), p. 112.

[34] *Viagem*, III, p. 165.

[35] For the course followed by this road, with a record of distances and descriptions of each of the places passed through, see *Itinerário feito desde os confins setentrionais da capitania do Rio Grande até São Paulo* (Itinerary from the northern border of the captaincy of Rio Grande to São Paulo).

[36] *Voyage aux provinces de St. Paul*, II, p. 161.

[37] An account of the building of this road is given in *Ofício do Vice-Rei Luís de Vasconcelos ao seu sucessor* (1789), p. 136.

[38] The settler's name was Silvestre José Passos, and his letter appeared in the issue for March, 1813, No. 3, p. 23. See also a plan for the new course to be followed by this road put forward in 1816 by Paulo José Miguel de Brito and published in his *Memória política sôbre Santa Catarina*, p. 115. Sousa Chichorro (*Memória sôbre S. Paulo em 1814*, p. 228) refers to another road from Lajes, this one leading to Laguna and known as the "Mata road," which had been abandoned at the time he wrote. This can only be the road described above, which continued, after reaching the coast, as far as Laguna. There was, however, no direct road between Lajes and Laguna. Vasconcelos de Drummond, in commission in Santa Catarina, began rebuilding the Lajes road in 1819, but the work was interrupted by the events of 1821 [the proclamation of Brazil's independence—Tr.]. *Anotações de A.M.V. de Drummond à sua biografia*, p. 10.

[39] "In São Paulo and Santos," wrote Father Antonio Vieira, "the gangs of carriers are burdened not only like human beings but overburdened like pack animals, marching almost completely naked or covered by a miserable loincloth, and given an ear of corn as their ration for the day." [Padre Antonio Vieira, S. J. (1608–1697), was the celebrated Jesuit missionary who spent many years of his life in Brazil. In Portugal he was one of King John IV's most influential advisers and consistently upheld the freedom of the Amerindian. Gifted with remarkable oratorical powers, he became the most popular preacher in Portugal and Brazil, and his sermons and letters are among the great classics of Portuguese literature.—Translator.]

[40] A description of the Sorocaba fairs, somewhat literary but of great interest, is given in Abreu Medeiros, *Curiosidades brasileiras.*

[41] *Viagem*, II, p. 361. The trade in mules coming from the south continued for a long time. Right up to the introduction of railroads, mules were the chief means of transporting goods, and although they were later bred in other regions, the south continued to be the main source of supply. In

the middle of the last century, 40,000–50,000 mules changed hands annually to a value of 3,000–4,000 contos, i.e. 3–4 million reis, a considerable sum for the time.

Further information on the mule trade can be found in St. Hilaire, *Voyage aux provinces de St. Paul*, I, p. 373, and II, p. 104, and in a recent, mainly geographical work by Pierre Deffontaines, *As feiras de burro de Sorocaba* (The mule fairs of Sorocaba).

[42] The only references to paved roads I have been able to trace are the following: the road leading up the mountain on the Pôrto da Estrela (Rio de Janeiro)-Minas route; the ascent between Santos and São Paulo, perhaps Brazil's greatest achievement in roadbuilding up to the beginning of the nineteenth century, built during the governorship of Bernardo José de Lorena; a few hundred feet before Moji das Cruzes on the Jacareí road, surfaced to counter the sponginess of the Tietê floodbank; another small stretch, just beyond Meia Ponte in Goiás, on the road to the capital, Vila Boa. A few may have escaped my attention, but they cannot have been many or very important.

[43] Further on, Eschwege writes: "As an example [of the errors made in plotting courses] I can cite the sinuous route followed by the road linking Rio to Vila Rica, which still preserves its original character. Like man, it runs along in a haphazard way, now across steep scarps, now—which is even worse—through deep valleys; and the 86 leagues it covers could be considerably shortened if a proper course was followed." *Pluto Brasiliensis*, I, p. 41.

[44] In the northeast an ingenious ruse was devised for leading the cattle across a ford, which, according to Capistrano de Abreu, must have been the invention of "an anonymous genius." One of the drovers donned a false bull's head and played the part of leader, so that the cattle followed him across. This system was unknown in the south, and St. Hilaire saw many animals washed away by the current at the Paraíba crossing.

[45] J. C. Fernandes Pinheiro, *Paulo Fernandes e a polícia de seu tempo* (Paulo Fernandes and the Police Force of his time), published in *Gazeta do Rio*, 17th September, 1817, p. 69.

[46] See, among others, the work of engineer Eduardo José de Morais, *Navegação interior do Brasil*.

[47] The only work on the subject is the interesting nineteenth century study by Antônio Alves Câmara, *Ensaio sôbre as construções navais indígenas do Brasil* (Essay on Native Boatbuilding in Brazil), which has recently been republished.

[48] Luccock, *Notes*, p. 585.

[49] Bishop Dom José Joaquim da Cunha Azeredo Coutinho suggested that Indians should be used as sailors for coastal shipping in 1816. An attempt was made to carry out his suggestion, but it failed to produce any results, *Ensaio econômico*. Martius makes sarcastic reference to these attempts but appears to be ignorant of their origin. *Viagem*, II, p. 269.

[50] Sousa Chichorro, *Memória* (1814), p. 241.

[51] Carts, carriages, and chaises were rare, even in the large cities. Only in Rio de Janeiro were they used to any extent and even then only in

modest proportions, until the arrival of the Court. What was perhaps the first long journey on wheels undertaken in Brazil was made by D. Frei Manuel da Cruz, when he was transferred from the Bishopric of Maranhão to the recently created Bishopric of Mariana in 1745. He traveled in a carriage still preserved in the small historical collection attached to the Palace of the Archbishop in Mariana. Had it not been for this evidence, the traditional account of this journey would be open to serious doubt.

[52] On the subject of pack animals, I must mention a suggestion made in 1810 by Councillor Veloso de Oliveira. He advocated the introduction of camels, dromedaries, and buffalo into Brazil. *Memória sôbre a capitania de S. Paulo,* pp. 40, 43. I once found a reference to the successful use of a domesticated tapir as a beast of burden. Oliveira Lima affirms, without quoting his sources, that an attempt to introduce Arabian camels was made in Dom João's time. *D. João, VI no Brasil,* I, p. 240. It is known that a number of years later, one of Ceará's presidents (*sic*) imported camels and attempted to popularize their use in the province. The idea did not catch on, and the animals ended their days in idleness, exhibited in one of the public squares of the provincial capital. Lieut.-Col. Borges de Sampaio revived the notion in his work, *A aclimatação de dromedários nos sertões do Norte do Brasil* (1890) (The Acclimatization of Dromedaries in the Backlands of Northern Brazil).

[53] In these captaincies the roads carried heavy traffic. Thus, between Rio de Janeiro and Vila Rica, particularly on the outskirts of Rio, St. Hilaire found the traffic comparable to that carried by the great European routes. João Severiano da Costa, future Marquis of Queirós, states that in 1821 no fewer than 2,000 pack animals were engaged in transporting merchandise from Rio de Janeiro to the interior (Minas). *Memória,* p. 46, fn.

[54] *Malerische Reise in Brasilien.*

[55] References to the organization, journeys, and so forth, of the pack trains are scattered through the diaries of the early nineteenth century travelers. For the cost of the service and rates charged, see in particular, St. Hilaire, *Voyage aux provinces de St. Paul,* I, p. 199.

[56] *Viagem,* II, p. 361.

[57] On the occasion of his stay in Jundiaí, St. Hilaire was the guest of the town's captain-major, who was engaged in the transportation business. During the season he bought around 1,000 mules in Sorocaba and kept them on the winter pastures of his fazenda to sell to the tropeiros, whom he also supplied with muleteers, providing them with board and lodging until the time came for the mule train to leave. The goods to be transported were brought to his fazenda, where animals were saddled, loaded, and prepared for the journey. *Voyage aux provinces de St. Paul,* I, p. 218.

[58] *Informação de Manuel Vieira de Albuquerque Tovar sôbre a navegação do Rio Doce,* p. 138.

[59] *Viagem,* III, p. 429.

[60] His report appears in a work previously cited, *Itinerário da viagem por terra da Bahia ao Rio de Janeiro.*

[61] A detailed description of this route, with the itinerary and distances involved, is given in J. M. P. de Alencastre's *Anais da Provincia de Goiás,* n. 62.

Social Organization
(pp. 313–346)

[1] John Kellis Ingram, *Slavery.*

[2] England also played a prominent role in the resuscitation of slavery. It is well known that for centuries English merchants had a virtual monopoly of the slave trade, and England even went to war in its interests. But England was never profoundly affected by the harmful consequences of slavery, because her role was always that of intermediary. Slave labor never took hold in the country itself.

[3] This observation would not have been wholly accurate in relation to certain of America's native peoples, such as those of Mexico and the Andean highlands, had not the Conquistadores, with almost unprecedented ferocity, wiped out all their cultural values.

[4] *A escravidão no Brasil,* Part 3, p. 126.

[5] This is particularly evident in the religious syncretism that resulted from the blending of Catholicism and paganism in different measures that became the basic religious background of most of Brazil. It is more a neo-African religion than anything else, and if it has lost the grandeur and spiritual elevation of Christianity, it has also lost the spontaneity and colorful richness of Negro beliefs in their native state.

[6] *Notes,* p. 203.

[7] *A escravidão no Brasil,* Part 3, p. 116.

[8] The classic work on this subject is Perdigão Malheiro, *A escravidão no Brasil,* which has yet to be equaled.

[9] See in particular Vilhena's comments in *Recopilação, passim.*

[10] Koster said of the Brazilian slaveowner: "His easygoing habits and his indolence make him a mild but indifferent master." *Voyages,* II, p. 312. St. Hilaire said more or less the same thing.

[11] Vilhena tells us that in Bahia some households had as many as 60 or 70 indoor slaves. Obviously most of these were kept for display of the master's wealth and power.

[12] Although in *Casa Grande e Senzala* (The Masters and the Slaves), Gilberto Freyre does not expressly make this distinction between the two different sectors of slave labor, he refers mainly and almost exclusively to the domestic sector. The subtitle of his work, *Formação da familia Brasileira* (The Formation of the Brazilian Family), and the main objective he has in view throughout the work clearly indicate this.

[13] *Recopilação,* p. 140.

[14] *Ibid.,* p. 933.

[15] In the pastoral industry, particularly in the backlands of the northeast, free labor was, as we have seen, more common, but this was a sector in which available occupations were few and labor scarce. Besides, owing to the particular conditions in which it developed, it was more or less reserved exclusively to the local population.

[16] *Relatório*, p. 452.

[17] In 1794 there were 33 advocates and 22 solicitors. See the *Almanaques* for 1792 and 1794, published in the *Anais da Biblioteca Nacional*, No. 59.

[18] *Travels*, Book I, p. 53. In 1794 there were nine doctors and 29 surgeons in Rio de Janeiro. *Almanaque, op. cit.*

[19] It was to overcome this shortage of professional men in the colony that the mother country decided in 1799 to instruct the municipal councils to award scholarships for studying at the University of Coimbra or the Academy of Lisbon to individuals who had shown promise. Each council was to pay for the studies of at least two topographers, two hydraulic engineers, one accountant, one doctor, and one surgeon. See the "Circular to the Municipal Council of the Captaincy of São Paulo" sent by the governor and published in *Registo Geral da Câmara Municipal de São Paulo*, XII, p. 381.

[20] Persons received into the Carmelite Order had to affirm that they would "throw out any postulant who was proved to be of Moorish, mulatto, or Jewish stock, or of any other abhorrent race." Frei Caneca, *Obras*, p. 283.

[21] J. M. P. de Alencastre, *Biografia do Cônego Luís Antônio da Silva e Sousa*, p. 241.

[22] Ecclesiastics took second place in parliamentary affairs only in the Second Empire.

[23] *Correspondência de várias autoridades*, p. 291.

[24] *L'esclavage au Brésil*, p. 87.

[25] *Recopilação*, p. 519.

[26] José Veríssimo described these people, although at a later period, but in conditions that must have been the same as three quarters of a century before, in his magnificent work: *As populações indígenas da Amazônia*.

[27] It should be noted that only by analogy can the *quilombos* in many cases be placed in the same category as the other useless or vegetative elements of the population, since their situation in relation to the established order was similar. The quilombos were often far from useless and became extraordinarily active and vigorous organizations of great constructive capacity. Palmares is the most famous example of a large quilombo, but certainly not the only one. These Negro communities of runaway slaves were constantly being formed and dissolved throughout Brazilian history in every part of the colony; and in many instances they clearly demonstrated what they would have been capable of achieving given the opportunity. [The Republic of Palmares, which lasted 67 years (1630–1697), was heroically defended at the last under the leadership of Zumbi, who has been called Brazil's Negro Spartacus.—Translator.]

[28] During the so-called "Praieira" disturbances which culminated in the 1848 revolt. A pamphlet entitled *A eleição para senadores* (Election for Senators) was published at the time and is cited by Joaquim Nabuco, *Um estadista do Império* (A Statesman of the Empire), I, p. 88, in which the whole question is dealt with. [The Praieira Revolution was a bid for power by the Praieira or Liberal Party of Pernambuco against the

Conservative (*Guabiru* or *Miguelista*) Party who held most of the posts in Pedro II's government at the time.—Translator.]

²⁹ *Ofício*, p. 34.

³⁰ *Recopilação*, p. 939.

³¹ *Corografia histórica*, p. 290.

³² Letter dated April 28, 1797, in *Correspondência de várias autoridades*, p. 279.

³³ See, among other passages, St. Hilaire's *Voyage aux sources*, I, p. 127, and Martius's *Viagem*, II, p. 254.

³⁴ The governor made an official visit to the Feitosa estate, and called up the *ordenanças* (military companies) commanded by the head of the Feitosa household on the pretext that he wished to review them. The members of the ordenanças were dismissed at the end of the day after having been forced to perform a series of exhausting military exercises. He then caught Feitosa off guard in his own house and arrested him when he was least expecting it, the prisoner being bundled off as quickly as possible before a hue and cry could be raised. Koster (*Voyages*, I, p. 222) recounts this incident, which had taken place shortly before his stay in Ceará.

³⁵ There is yet another factor which must also have contributed to the impoverishment of the colonial population, although more limited in scope: the entailed estate system, whether in the form of a mortmain entailment or, more commonly, entailment on behalf of a number of *morgados* (heirs). The morgado system attracted the attention of Vilhena, who had a number of interesting comments to make in the last letter included in the *Recopilação*. There were a fair number of entailed estates in Brazil, the most notable being that of the viscounts of Asseca in the Campos dos Goitacases. Entailed estates were abolished under the provisions of Law No. 56 of October 5, 1835.

³⁶ It was also found in the Spanish-American colonies and even in the Southern states of the North American Union. The Brazilian form has been studied by Oliveira Viana, who coined the term "patriarchal clan" (*Populações meridionais do Brasil* (Southern Populations of Brazil), *Evolução do Povo Brasileiro* (Evolution of the Brazilian People), and *Pequenos estudos de psicologia social* (Brief Studies in Social Psychology).) Gilberto Freyre, who develops this theme, accentuated the social and anthropological aspects (*Casa Grande e Senzala* [The Masters and the Slaves], and *Sobrados e Mucambos* [Town House and Slums]).

³⁷ "In Brazil, the cathedral or church, more powerful than the King himself, was replaced by the Big House . . . ; the Church that played so important a role in the formation of Brazil, cementing our unity, was not the cathedral with its bishop . . . nor the isolated church, the monastery or the abbey . . . It was the plantation chapel. . . ." Gilberto Freyre, *Casa Grande e Senzala*, p. 205.

³⁸ *Discurso preliminar*, p. 290. The country and the continent referred to by this author are not Brazil and America, as one might assume from modern geographical terminology, but regions and "Portuguese possessions in America," which were then referred to in this way.

³⁹ Pride of lineage was not, however, very old. Borges da Fonseca, only half a century before the period we are considering, had encountered the greatest difficulty in writing his *Nobiliarquia* of Pernambuco, the oldest center of aristocratic tradition in Brazil, because, in his own words, there were "among the most noble families of the land persons who hardly knew the nationality of their grandparents." *Nobiliarquia Pernambucana* (Pernambucan Peerage), Introduction.

⁴⁰ *Recopilação*, p. 44.

⁴¹ The northeastern cattle estate depicted by José de Alencar in *O Sertanejo,* although largely fictitious, is by and large a reconstruction providing an adequate picture. [José de Alencar is a nineteenth century novelist.—Translator.]

⁴² *Voyage aux sources*, I, p. 77.

⁴³ St. Hilaire described the way of life in this region in great detail. *Voyage aux provinces de St. Paul*, II. It is worth noting his observations on the relative social position of men and women as compared to the colony's great slavocratic centers. Here, woman occupied the dominant position, the exact opposite of the situation in the rest of the country where the inferior position of the woman was one of the most characteristic and prominent traits of patriarchalism. There is clearly a direct relationship between this fact and the particular circumstances in which the region's social evolution took place.

⁴⁴ In many parts of the Brazilian interior, towns are still known locally as *o comércio* (the trading center) even when they are large towns which happen to be official administrative centers of a *município* (county) or district. [Brazilian states are divided into municípios, corresponding roughly to a county, each of which has a county seat called a *cidade* (city) even although it may have only a few hundred inhabitants. Each município is further divided into districts whose headquarters are called a *vila* (village).—Translator.]

⁴⁵ *Memória sôbre a agricultura*, p. 93.

⁴⁶ Report of April 28, 1798, in *Correspondência de várias autoridades*, p. 277.

⁴⁷ The colonial advocate was more than the professional advocate today; his category was that of a high-ranking judicial officer, and he was an integral part of public justice. We find traces of this bygone rank in the formal language still used by contemporary advocates in their official speeches.

⁴⁸ *Recopilação*, p. 50.

⁴⁹ *Relatório*, p. 453. Cf. "In Brazil, there are wealthy merchants who do not even know how to read." *Correio Brasiliense,* January, 1813, X, p. 89.

⁵⁰ "Only toward the end of the Empire period," writes Oliveira Lima, "did even the highest commercial connections cease to be regarded as mésalliances" (*O império brasileiro*, p. 247). The trials and tribulations of a man like Mauá, misunderstood and generally disliked, doubtless had their origin in this attitude; for the lawyers and landowners who governed the empire he was a mere "merchant," a businessman, and in his heart of hearts the emperor shared this opinion. [Irenêo Evangelista de Sousa,

Baron and Viscount of Mauá (1813–1889) was the great pioneer of Brazilian industrialization. He opened a number of ports, a bank, the first Brazilian railway, etc., encountering constant opposition to all his plans. —Translator.]

[51] Vilhena, *Recopilação*, p. 49.

[52] In this respect, and on the ill-feeling between the senhores d'engenho and the sharecroppers on the one hand—chronically in debt and generally hard pressed—and their exigent creditors, the merchants, on the other, see the interesting observations made by the anonymous author of *Discurso Preliminar*, p. 27, applicable to Bahia in the second half of the eighteenth century. The author is openly sympathetic to the planters and bitterly accuses the merchants of "battening on the sap, milk and blood of agriculture . . ." (as we can see, the complaint is an age-old one). He does, however, recognize the "indiscretion and well-known irregularity" in the spending habits of the planters and sharecroppers.

[53] Gayozo tells us that merchants were once more excluded from holding municipal office in São Luís do Maranhão after 1792. (*Compêndio histórico*, p. 132). J. F. Lisboa has doubted the accuracy of this statement (Obras, II, p. 52). In fact, the legal provisions in this respect had fallen into disuse, the last ban having been enacted in 1747. (Lisboa summarizes all the legislation passed in *Obras*, II, p. 169.) It is true that in the nearby town of Alcântara less than three leagues from São Luís there were municipal councillors who were merchants by profession. But J. F. Lisboa gives no basis for his doubts, and it is probable that Gayozo—who was, after all, writing of contemporary events—was telling the truth. In any case, the position of São Luís would have been a unique one in the period we are considering. Gayozo's affirmation may be confirmed by a provision passed by the *Mesa do Desembargo* (Board of Replevin), dated July 17, 1813, which stipulated that municipal councillors for the São Luís municipal council could be drawn from any of the city's residents, even nonnatives.

[54] The role of this rivalry in Brazilian history as a whole is discussed, although only briefly, in my work, *Evolução política do Brasil*, São Paulo, 1933. I shall return to the political aspects of the conflict between merchants, landowners, and the other classes of the population in the last chapter.

Administration
(pp. 347–398)

[1] *A Igreja e o Estado* (Church and State), p. 29. Lacerda de Almeida, as a good Catholic, is naturally opposed to such a distinction on theoretical grounds. I am not, however, considering the question on the theoretical level, which does not concern us here. I quoted this statement merely to emphasize the two different concepts, of equal validity, since they are historical facts rather than given absolutes and should be noted here because current ideas make it difficult to understand many aspects of the colonial administration unless this distinction is borne in mind.

[2] Only Pombal's administration attempted to create something new for

the colony—or, at any rate, this was his intention. If many of his attempts failed, this was because he could count only on the routine procedure and inefficiency of Portuguese bureaucracy, against which he found himself powerless.

³ This happened particularly in the case of the former Indian villages elevated to the status of townships under the provisions of the law promulgated on June 6, 1755. The organization and proper functioning of the câmara and other administrative bodies proved to be possible in only a very few of these "towns."

⁴ As time passed, the military orders became purely honorific, and their "habits," i.e., the insignia of membership, were openly sold. Thus, the father of Viscount Nogueira da Gama, future Steward to the Emperor, acquired a habit for his six-year-old son in 1806 for 10,000 cruzados. *Elogio histórico do Visconde* (Historical Eulogy of the Viscount) pronounced in one of the Instituto Histórico's sessions in 1897. In the *Gazeta do Rio,* July 25, 1810, there was an advertisement offering for sale a "habit of Christ."

⁵ *Obras,* II, p. 75. In Vol. I of the *Publicações do Arquivo Nacional,* there is a catalogue of letters royal, provisions, edicts, instructions, orders, and so forth, despatched to the governors and later viceroys of Rio de Janeiro from 1662–1821. It is worth glancing through this catalogue just to see the trivial matters with which the home government concerned itself.

⁶ In the controversy that arose between the Viceroy of Rio de Janeiro and the Captain-General of São Paulo, Bernardo José de Lorena, over the limits of their respective captaincies—in which the latter finally emerged triumphant—the two were treated as equals. Cf. the terms in which the Viceroy concerned, Luís de Vasconcelos e Sousa, refers to the dispute in his *Ofício,* p. 38. The Viceroy of Rio de Janeiro did exercise a certain jurisdiction over Minas Gerais, although the latter was a "principal" captaincy.

⁷ Minas Gerais, 4; Bahia, 4 (one of which was Sergipe); São Paulo, 3 (including Paraná, which formed the comarca of Paranaguá and Curitiba; in 1811, a further comarca—Itu—was created); Pernambuco, 3 (Alagoas being one); Goiás, 2 (after the division into northern and southern comarcas in 1809). The other captaincies contained only one comarca each.

⁸ The title of "city" was purely honorific and entailed no privileges. In the early years of the nineteenth century the following cities were in existence: São Paulo, Mariana, Rio de Janeiro, Cabo Frio, Salvador, Olinda, Paraíba, Natal, São Luís do Maranhão, and Belém do Pará. Cities which were also sees were known as "episcopal cities" (*episcopais*). Bahia was an archiepiscopal city. Mariana, although an episcopal city, was not even the seat of a comarca, and belonged to the comarca of Vila Rica (Ouro Preto). Cabo Frio was a city because it had adopted the title for some unspecified reason at the time it was founded. The others had been elevated to the status from townships.

⁹ The attempt by some commanders to take the lead in military matters

and challenge the governor's authority, or take parallel action in this respect, was irregular. When such commanders came up against an energetic governor fully aware of his powers, the proper hierarchy was immediately established. See the remarks on this subject by the Marquis of Lavradio in his *Relatório,* p. 413. The governor's functions as commander in chief were sometimes combined with those of commander of a military division. Governors of Bahia, for instance, were also commanders of the 1st Regiment or 3rd Auxiliary of Bahia.

[10] Councillor Veloso de Oliveira, writing in 1822 about the need to reform the Brazilian administration, strongly criticized the military character of colonial administration. *Memória sôbre o melhoramento da capitania de São Paulo,* p. 103.

[11] The governor's powers and limitations are enumerated in Pereira da Silva, *Fundação do Império Brasileiro,* I, p. 173.

[12] The correspondence of the governors with the home government makes the system that operated amply clear. The governors expounded the aims of the administration and asked for instructions. Humble and hesitant suggestions were made, and very occasionally the more energetic and forceful governors tendered advice.

[13] During public ceremonies and when homage to the throne was paid on the occasion of notable events in the life of the reigning monarch— births, marriages, birthdays, etc.—subjects were supposed to kiss the hand of the governor as if he were the sovereign himself. (*Atas da Câmara de São Paulo,* XX, p. 210). In many cases the governor published orders in the name of the sovereign, headed with the ceremonial form "D—King or Queen, etc. . . ." (*Registo da Câmara de São Paulo,* XII, 588). It should be noted that for these and other references to the *Atas da Câmara de São Paulo* (henceforth abbreviated as *Act.*) and to the *Registo da Câmara de São Paulo* (*Reg.*), unless otherwise stated, I have selected only one of numerous similar references for the sake of brevity, the reference chosen being generally one typical of the period we are concerned with here.

[14] It was estimated that a period of two years should be the minimum time allowed for a matter to be finally dealt with. *Consulta do Conselho Ultramarino* (Recommendations of the Overseas Council), 1732. Routine business, at the beginning of the nineteenth century, continued to take a long time to transact at the Portuguese Court since there had been no improvement in the means of communication and the Portuguese administration had not become any more expeditious.

[15] For instances of autonomous and arbitrary actions by certain governors, see St. Hilaire's comments on what he personally witnessed during his travels, especially *Voyage aux provinces de Rio de Janeiro,* I, p. 356.

[16] *Almanaques do Rio de Janeiro.*

[17] In the instructions for recruitment in Rio dated August 16, 1816, specific permission is given for the enlistment of "mulattoes whose color is not too dusky."

[18] Vilhena, *Recopilação,* p. 287. As Regius professor, Vilhena was present at many such scenes.

[19] Vilhena, *Recopilação*, p. 256.

[20] This regiment was also known as the *Henriques*, a name used for many of the colony's Negro corps, and deriving from the companies of freed slaves organized by Henrique Dias during the Dutch Wars [during the revolts against the Dutch, who had installed themselves in Pernambuco and the northern parts of Bahia in 1630 and remained there until their final expulsion in 1654; Henrique Dias was the Negro leader of the abortive Pernambuco Revolt of 1645.—Translator].

[21] For details of military organization, see for Bahia, Letters VI and VII of Vilhena's *Recopilação;* for Rio de Janeiro, the *Almanaques* for 1792 and 1794 and the Marquis of Lavradio's *Relatório.*

[22] Ordenanças were created in Portugal by a law promulgated in December, 1569. Their organization was established by the law of December 10, 1570. After a number of modifications and additions, the relevant laws were embodied in the *Regimento das Ordenanças* (the code governing territorial forces) of April 30, 1758, which included various special provisions for Brazil.

[23] "Senado" (senate) was the special honorific title arrogated to themselves by the colony's municipal councils, although they were not entitled to do so. In only a few instances was their right to use this style legally confirmed.

[24] Lists of electors drawn up for the newly installed municipal councils of São Carlos (Campinas) and Pôrto Feliz in São Paulo are published in *Documentos Interessantes*, III, pp. 3, 32. In towns where there was a juiz-de-fora, councillors were nominated by the central authorities and there were no elections. This was not a general rule, however, and no statutory provisions had been made in this respect—with a few odd exceptions which were not universally applicable (as in the Standing Orders for the High Court of Rio de Janeiro, published on Oct. 13, 1751). It was in any case one of the central authority's most significant invasions of local and municipal powers, the elected municipal councils of seventeenth-century Portugal having been one of its most characteristic features.

[25] I say "in principle" because this was the general practice. But in the case of the reference quoted above (*Documentos Interessantes*) the first elections for the newly installed municipal councils were direct.

[26] J. F. Lisboa has made a detailed study of the great power once exercised by the câmaras. *Obras*, II, p. 46.

[27] See the *autos* (deeds) of creation for the new townships of São Carlos and Pôrto Feliz in São Paulo (*Documentos Interessantes*, III, pp. 3, 32), and the town of Montemor-o-Novo, in Pará (*Autos de criação* . . .).

[28] The question of the câmara's right to dispose of its patrimony was always hotly disputed, an attempt being made to determine the extent of its powers in this respect. See, among others, Lima Pereira, *Da propriedade no Brasil.*

[29] Local taxes were levied by the câmaras on all animals slaughtered in the public abattoirs; on scales used for weighing all basic commodities; and on the public market. Income was also derived from inspecting

weights and measures, from fines arising out of infringements of local by-laws, and finally from the hire of casinhas (huts), known in Bahia and other places as *cabanas* (shacks), to traders dealing in staple items.

30 The Marquis of Lavradio refers to their functions in the following words: "To seek and promote the progress and happiness of the population, not only to keep the peace but also to supervise the trade in animals and watch over agriculture, to see that the people do not fall into lazy ways or erroneous conceptions." *Relatório,* p. 442.

31 Under the provisions of the royal letter of July 22, 1766, the ouvidor was also charged with the functions of intendant of police.

32 Among its administrative functions, to cite only one of many, the relação was empowered to decide on impediments to the holding of offices in the senados da câmara, which in the first instance were determined by the ouvidor (*Reg.,* XII, p. 11).

33 Unlike the câmaras, the captaincies did not have their own treasuries. Their funds were part of the Royal Exchequer. Nor had they any individual patrimonies or sources of revenue; everything belonged to the crown.

34 The name varies: *Tribunal da Junta da Real Fazenda* in Rio de Janeiro; *Junta da Real Fazenda* in São Paulo; *Real Junta da Arrecadação da Real Fazenda* in Bahia; *Junta de Arrecadação e Administração da Real Fazenda* in Maranhão; and so forth.

35 A special subsidy was instituted for a period of ten years in 1756 to defray the expenses involved in rebuilding Lisbon after its destruction by the Great Earthquake of 1755; it continued after the ten-year period stipulated despite the protests of the "voluntary" contributors and was still being collected during the empire period. Theoretically, the subsidy was still being used to rebuild Lisbon. The point is worth emphasizing as an instance of the state of finances in the colony and the empire.

36 In Rio de Janeiro, for instance, the crown purveyor also issued waybills for the payment of certain duties, such as those on goods entering Minas Gerais.

37 At the beginning of the last century, apart from the subsidy for rebuilding Lisbon already referred to, the royal letter of April 6, 1804, provided for the raising of a subsidy "in view of the grievous state in which the kingdom finds itself as a result of the troubles in Europe."

38 In the instructions issued to the Governor of Minas Gerais, the Marquis of Barbacena, there are several observations and reports of incidents revealing the abuses practiced by contractors and the consequent losses to the Treasury. See, in particular, Cls. 109 et seq. of these instructions. Among the crown officials accused of neglecting their duties in this respect and of being in league with the defaulting contractors was the Ouvidor of Vila Rica, Tomás Antônio Gonzaga, Marilia's sensitive *Dirceu.* [T. A. Gonzaga (1744–1810) was also a poet, author of the pastoral "Lyrics to Marilia," written in the guise of an amorous swain, Dirceu.— Translator.]

39 *Voyage aux sources,* I, p. 343.

40 *Relatório,* p. 424.

[41] This does not exclude the use of the militia for the same purposes, although their use was not so widespread. Unlike the ordenanças, the militia units were always primarily military.

[42] If we go through a list of the names of persons nominated to the commanding posts in the ordenança units, we find the cream of the colonial population, the economically and socially powerful representatives. This invariably holds true in all parts of the country. [The "colonel" who never served in the army is a familiar figure in the Brazil of today—the descendants of the former captains-major of the ordenanças.—Translator.]

[43] Koster, *Voyages*, I, p. 210.

[44] Irreligiousness is a modern phenomenon. In the age-old dispute between Church and State, there was no question of excluding religion altogether, as has been done in our times, but of reducing the interference of the Roman Catholic Church in matters which were then of supreme political importance but with which the state no longer concerns itself: the provision of priests, questions of religious dogma, and so on.

[45] Cases involving "sworn contracts" came under ecclesiastical jurisdiction because perjury was considered a sin. The Philippine Code banned sworn contracts for this reason, since violation of contracts made on oath would have come under ecclesiastical jurisdiction (*Ordenações*, Liv. 4, Tit. 73). The ecclesiastical authorities were also empowered to open all testaments because they might contain legacies and bequests to the Church. For general ecclesiastical jurisdiction exercised in the colony, see Lacerda de Almeida, *A Igreja e o Estado*.

[46] The council's dispositions were confirmed in Brazil after independence by the decree of November 3, 1827.

[47] On the subject of ecclesiastical powers, apart from what is generally known on the theory of canon law, it is worth consulting the decrees concerning ecclesiastical offices, published in the colonial documents already in print, the *Registo da Câmara de São Paulo*. Most of these decrees— and the most interesting to the historian, since they refer to the period in question—specify certain ecclesiastical contributions. See, inter alia, *Reg.*, XII, p. 361. It is a pity that ecclesiastical archives are not yet accessible to the public, since they would certainly throw much light upon the intimate life of colonial society.

[48] It should be pointed out that the Church still plays an important role in all these spheres today. But there is an essential difference between present and past: Today it acts as a private body and is distinguished from similar institutions only in quantitative terms; in the colony it acted as a public authority.

[49] See, for instance, the conflict on the respective competence of the two which arose in São Paulo in the last years of the eighteenth century, a case of particular interest since the governor dealt with it in a long *Ofício* (Report) to the bishop, in which he attempts to draw a clear distinction between the ecclesiastical and civil spheres. *Reg.*, XII, p. 473.

[50] For the crown *padroado* see *Alegação jurídica* by D. José Joaquim de Azeredo Coutinho.

[51] See especially the long and minute report written to the secretary of state in 1783 by Viceroy Luís de Vasconcelos, *Negócios eclesiásticos*. See also *Correspondência de várias autoridades,* which includes many letters relating to ecclesiastical jurisdiction, written by the colony's religious authorities to the home government.

[52] St. Hilaire gives an admirable summary of justice and public security in the colony, *Voyage aux provinces de Rio de Janeiro*, I, p. 364 et seq.

[53] Vilhena gives an account of education in Bahia, *Recopilação*, Letter VIII, written with all the authority of a professional teacher. For education in Rio de Janeiro, see the interesting observations contained in representations made to the authorities by Regius professors [i.e., teachers appointed by royal mandate] in 1787 in *Correspondência de várias autoridades*, p. 215. A brief, but well-written summary of colonial education is Moreira de Azevedo's *Instrução nos tempos coloniais*.

[54] For Bahia, see Vilhena, *Recopilação*. For Rio de Janeiro, see Oliveira Lima, *D. João VI no Brasil*. The administration introduced vaccination in the early years of the nineteenth century.

[55] This hospital is described in Pedro Cúrio de Carvalho, *Histórico da hospitalização militar no Brasil*.

[56] We could add a few public buildings, apart from the churches. The claims made for the colonial churches have been greatly exaggerated. Some are of undoubted artistic value, but none has the grandeur or sumptuousness attributed to them by their admirers. Compared to the religious monuments of the Spanish-American colonies, particularly Mexico and Peru, they cut a mediocre figure.

[57] The administration of the Marquis of Lavradio in Rio de Janeiro was unique in this respect. That of Lôbo de Almada in the captaincy of Rio Negro was also remarkable.

[58] *Roteiro*, p. 102; and Rodrigues Barata, *Memória da Capitania de Goiás*, p. 337.

[59] *Documentos relativos à história da capitania de São Pedro do Rio Grande do Sul*, p. 285.

[60] *Voyage aux sources*, I, p. 347.

[61] José Mariano da Conceição Veloso in the natural sciences; José Joaquim da Cunha Azeredo Coutinho in economics; José de Sousa Azevedo Pizarro and Gaspar da Madre de Deus in historiography; and José Maurício Nunes Garcia in music. And these are names chosen only from the period we are considering. It should also be pointed out that the only literary form in which the colony distinguished itself was religious oratory. Our poetry cannot be regarded as of more than domestic interest, nor can it hope to find a place outside the pages of literary scholarship.

[62] Frei Antônio da Vitória, Father Superior of the Rio de Janeiro Capuchins, *Correspondência de várias autoridades*, p. 291.

[63] Letter of October 20, 1787, *Correspondência de várias autoridades*, p. 226.

[64] *Loc. cit.*, p. 228.

[65] *Negócios eclesiásticos* and *Ofício*, p. 33.

[66] *Correspondência de várias autoridades,* pp. 168, 285.

[67] *Correspondência do bispo do Rio de Janeiro* (1754–1800), p. 42. The italics are mine.

[68] *Voyage aux provinces de Rio de Janeiro,* I, Ch. VIII. Although his assertions amount to a vigorous denunciation, St. Hilaire adds that in this matter he may be accused of reticence, but never of exaggeration. In many other pages of his diaries, the French naturalist makes observations on the priests and their conduct in Brazil. As an ardent Catholic, the matter naturally attracted his attention. The greatest and only praise he offers is for the priests of Minas Novas as a body, where he found that "the clergy seem to be less simoniacal than in the rest of the captaincy." *Ibid.,* II, p. 256.

[69] St. Hilaire, *Voyage aux sources,* I, p. 132.

Social and Political Life
(pp. 399–439)

[1] "Slavery was one of the few things approaching organization that this country has ever had. . . . Socially and economically, slavery provided us, for many years, with all the effort and all the order we possess, and laid the foundations for all our material production." *O Problema Nacional,* p. 11.

[2] "Le miracle de l'amour humain, c'est que, sur un instinct très simple, le désir, il construit les édifices de sentiments les plus complexes et les plus délicats" (André Maurois). It was this miracle that the "love" of the slave huts failed to bring about.

[3] There were, however, exceptions, in which more perfected social forms evolved in this sector. But they were rare. The most interesting and well known of these exceptions was the *mutirão*—a work party for clearing, planting, or harvesting fields—a communal practice still extant in some parts of Brazil. St. Hilaire saw a mutirão at work in the region of what is now the Triângulo Mineiro. *Voyage aux sources,* II, p. 269. It would seem, however, that this was a survival of native custom, and the region referred to by St. Hilaire contained a high percentage of mixed bloods. If this is so, the community spirit expressed through the mutirão would not be the expression of new social forms but a cultural vestige of Indian tribal life.

[4] This was not due solely to the perpetuation of the institution of monarchy in the Brazilian national state, invested as it was in the same dynasty—in itself a proof of the artificial nature of the Constitution adopted—since there was no basis other than past custom for Brazil to continue to be governed from the throne. But it was not only this that indicated the persistence of the previous political regime in its new national dress. It was the prolongation of the political situation, and the framework of institutions as a whole, which were changed only at a much later stage of the country's national evolution, so much so that the revolutions and uprisings that broke out in the initial phases of the empire were felt to be reactions against the "Rio de Janeiro government," just as ear-

lier they would have been directed against the "Lisbon government."
Brazilian federalism had its roots in this.

The poverty of Brazilian social life is strikingly confirmed by the political constitution of the independent country. It was the cause of the difficulties and problems of organization and administration with which she
had to cope, and which culminated in the creation of that whimsical and
artificial "constitutional empire" with which she was saddled. To illustrate my point, we need only compare what happened when the English
North American colonies broke away from the mother country: a system
of government not only original but epoch-making, a landmark in the
political evolution of mankind.

[5] *Notes*, p. 17.

[6] *Idéias gerais sôbre a revolução do Brasil*, p. 55. This difference was
so much a result of the environment that, Brazilian by birth and upbringing, the sons of Portuguese who had made money did not, according to
Mariscal, "follow in their father's footsteps" but "fell into the general pattern, which is to say, sank into poverty."

[7] Even a man like José Veríssimo, with his profound knowledge of the
races of his native province, Pará, and his great sympathy for them, did
not entirely grasp the paradoxical situation of Indians brought into contact with European civilization. The indolence and lack of ambition observed in the Indian are simply the result of his complete indifference, or
even hostility, toward the civilization imposed on him, whose values,
despite all the importance attached to them by us, mean nothing to him.
To discern in the Brazilian native, or in any other race whose culture
differs from our own, a lack of character where there is nothing but a lack
of adaptation or a sense of revolt, is a habit to which Anglo-Americans
are particularly addicted. But we cannot help wondering what the reaction of these same energetic Anglo-Saxons would be if they were asked to
do a full day's work in exchange for a plate of *pirão de açaí* [a mash made
from the fruit of the açaí palm—Tr.] or *mandioca puba* (manioc mash)?
Mutatis mutandis, this was what happened in the case of the Indian. The
only incentive provided by civilization which meant anything to him was
cane spirits, and this is why the colonists used it so freely.

[8] José Veríssimo, *Populações indígenas da Amazônia*, p. 308.

[9] *Informação*, p. 66.

[10] *Voyage aux provinces de St. Paul*, I, p. 378.

[11] It would be very interesting to study Brazilian folklore from this
point of view and compare it to that of other countries. From what we
can see for ourselves, we are left in no doubt as to the conclusions that
would be reached. If we compare a popular Brazilian festival with that of
any European country, we will find that the apathy and melancholy of
the former contrasts sharply with the enthusiasm and gaiety of the latter.
Even Brazil's Carnival, if carefully observed, is no exception to the rule.
Apart from manifestations clearly of an orgiastic nature or the opportunity it provides to indulge in ancestral cults and beliefs, which on ordinary days would land the reveler in prison, there is not much to it. Fur-

thermore, the most active Brazilian element in the Carnival is the Negro, with his long tradition of slave labor.

12 Paulo Prado, *Retrato do Brasil* (Portrait of Brazil). The Brazilian melancholy was also noted by St. Hilaire, who contrasted it with the gaiety of the French peasant (*Voyage aux sources*, I, p. 124), referring to it in other pages of his diaries. He was especially struck by the sadness of the children, and deplored their lack of spontaneity and their unhappiness. *Ibid.*, I, p. 374. Rio Grande do Sul, whose formation was in fact so different from that of the rest of the country, can perhaps be excluded from this generality.

13 *Recopilação*, pp. 926, 927. The colony's poverty is attested not only by all the eyewitness reports of contemporary observers but by the scanty and miserable legacy it bequeathed. Where are the buildings, the objets d'art, the monuments, all those memorials that even the mediocre society leaves behind? The traces left by a society that "flourished" less than 150 years ago are paltry and mean; we have little or nothing to remember it by.

14 This is still the case today. We are constantly encountering immigrants who have married in Europe but cohabit in Brazil.

15 This is perhaps why Brazilians are so conscious of family origins. His family distinguished and elevated an individual because it automatically placed him in the limited "upper class." To "belong to a family" was an indication of superiority, almost of nobility.

16 Vilhena provides an admirable summary of these deleterious influences, to which nothing need be added. *Recopilação*, p. 138 et seq. We should recall that he was a teacher and educationist, writing with authority and experience backed by an acute critical intelligence.

17 See in this respect Sierra y Mariscal, *Idéias gerais sôbre a revolução do Brasil*.

18 To cite only one of the many testimonies, I refer the reader to what is said in this respect by one of the most enlightened contemporary observers, Councillor Veloso de Oliveira (*Memória sôbre a agricultura*, p. 123). Not only were the fees which the clergy demanded for officiating at marriages far beyond the means of most people, but there were also frequent abuses. *Provisões*, or marriage licenses, which had been abolished by a decision of the *Junta da Coroa* (Crown Council) dated March 28, 1791, continued to be demanded regardless of protests. On this matter, see the lengthy controversy between the municipal council and the bishop of São Paulo, recorded in the *Registo*, XII, pp. 289, 317, 424, and other pages. The problem of marriage fees and the obstacles to the legalization of irregular unions that these presented played a fairly important role in Brazil, and after the Republic had been installed, the 1891 Constitution included a provision for marriages to be celebrated free. (*Art.* 72, Cl. 4). This provision proved to be useless; the evil was too deeply rooted to be so easily eradicated.

19 St. Hilaire, who had met Governor Delgado de Castilho when in Goiás, relates the tragic event, which had taken place in 1820. *Voyage aux sources*, II, p. 83. Cunha Matos mentions a number of cases in Goiás

where prejudice had been an obstacle to marriage (*Corografia histórica,* p. 298). One of the strongest pressures against marriage with a woman of an inferior class was exerted by the religious lay brotherhoods, whose rules included express provisions in this respect, condemning to expulsion any members who contracted such marriages.

[20] St. Hilaire, *Voyage aux provinces de Rio de Janeiro,* II, p. 28. Governor Delgado Castilho lived publicly with his mistress and children in the governor's palace. No one found this strange. It was marriage outside one's social class and not cohabitation with a person of one's choice that aroused disapproval.

[21] *Esboço da viagem de Langsdorff,* pp. 361, 448.

[22] Letter of January 12, 1778, cited by Fernandes Pinheiro, *Os últimos Vice-Reis do Brasil,* p. 244. A little further on the Marquis adds: "It is so easy for men to find women that very few seek wedlock."

[23] *Voyage aux sources,* I, p. 127. St. Hilaire is sober in his comments on the subject, with the reserve proper to his profoundly religious temperament. His diaries are thus reticent on matters of this nature, and the reader is aware of the distaste he felt in writing of them. But, as the faithful observer he was, he could not help recording what was so scandalously in evidence, hence our interest in his observations, wrung from him in the teeth of his considerable scruples. Other travelers were more outspoken.

[24] *Voyage aux sources,* I, p. 102.

[25] "Les pasteurs semblent considérer comme un jeu l'offense et le pardon," *loc. cit.*

[26] *Voyage aux sources,* II, p. 238.

[27] The distortions of crude superstition also affected the Catholicism of the colony; they were the result of ignorance and the contaminating influence of beliefs and cults alien to Christianity, brought to Brazil from Africa and corrupted by slavery. The contribution of native culture was much smaller, since the religious expressions of this culture were rudimentary. As far as religious instruction is concerned, only the Jesuits made a serious attempt to provide religious education in the colony. Their influence in this sphere was considerable, and it was undoubtedly this influence that led to the "mechanization" of worship, which is one of the most striking characteristics of Brazilian Catholicism. We need only imagine the effect of their educational system, inspired by the famous "Spiritual Exercises," on Brazil's ignorant and primitive colonial society!

[28] See especially Letter 24, the last in his *Compendium,* of particular interest here.

[29] Special mention must be made here of D. Rodrigo de Sousa Coutinho, later Count of Linhares, who became Secretary for Overseas Affairs in 1796, and whose long term of office—which was concluded only in Brazil, whither he had accompanied the Prince Regent in 1808—was distinguished by a constant and intelligent preoccupation with Brazilian affairs. The presence of his brother, D. Francisco, as Governor of Pará, shows the bonds that linked him to the colony. Similar in this respect were those that bound the Marquis of Pombal, whose

brother, Francisco Xavier de Mendonça Furtado, was also a governor of Pará and author of the *Diretório dos Índios.*

[30] The influence of the landed nobility in Portugal was minimal and certainly subordinate to that of the bureaucracy. The size of the kingdom in relation to its vast empire sufficiently accounts for this.

[31] There was only one notable exception to this rule: the *Donatário* system, adopted for the Atlantic islands and repeated in Brazil, which attempted to replace by private initiative the king's (royal) initiative in developing the colonies. In Brazil the system failed completely, or served merely in a few respects as a tentative experiment. Soon after these modest beginnings the intervention of the Donatários practically disappeared, surviving only in the profits they managed to reap in their captaincies without making any contribution to the tasks of colonization, which were to be undertaken solely on the initiative of the crown. After the colony's early days, the Donatários figured in Brazilian history only when their rights and privileges reverted to the crown in the eighteenth century.

[32] The first generations of Brazilian doctors, who qualified in the last quarter of the eighteenth century, were mostly graduates of this university, then Europe's leading center for medical studies.

[33] Martius observed that in Bahia, which he visited in 1819, the upper classes were all completely loyal to Portugal, obeying her laws and following her customs. It was the "rabble" who launched attacks on the Portuguese. *Viagem*, II, p. 291. It should be noted, however, that this hostility was directed toward *individual* Portuguese and not the *regime*, an abstract concept that the masses were as yet unable to grasp.

[34] Since this "harmonization" in all the cases we considered only took place in the period after the one with which we are concerned, it would be out of place to follow the process. But from the analysis of the fundamental contradictions undermining the colonial system undertaken in this chapter, the trend taken by this process clearly emerges.

[35] The subject belongs properly to the colony's economic history and I shall therefore not go into detail. For further information about the financial situation of colonial production and trade at the end of the eighteenth century, see the oft-cited contemporary work, *Descrição econômica.*

[36] "The Portuguese are active and hardworking," wrote Martius, "the Brazilians, born to wealth and brought up among uneducated domestic slaves, prefer pleasure to work and leave commerce to the outsiders, preferring to enjoy the comforts of their estates." *Viagem*, II, p. 479. The social and political crisis that hit Brazil in the early nineteenth century can be largely explained on the basis of this observation.

[37] *Recopilação*, p. 46.

[38] *Inconfidência da Bahia, em 1798. Devassas e sequestros* (The Bahian Conspiracy of 1798: Official Report of Inquiry and Documents Seized). The texts of the seditious documents were published by Brás do Amaral as an appendix to his study, *A conspiração republicana da Bahia de 1798.*

[39] The only person to have studied these revolts up to now is Nina Rodrigues. See his *Os Africanos no Brasil*, p. 166.

40 It should be pointed out that the material claims were sometimes bound up with religious issues, as evident in the 1835 revolt in Bahia. [The rising of Mohammedan Negroes known as *Malês,* the revolt being known historically as the "Malê Uprising." For an account in English of this important revolt, see Donald Pierson, *Negroes in Brazil—a Study of Race Contact at Bahia* (Univ. of Chicago Press, 1942), pp. 43–45.—Translator.]

41 The perfectly justifiable fear in which the colony lived is revealed by the alarm created whenever opinions concerning the legitimacy of slavery were expressed. We learn of one such public outcry, which occurred in 1794, from a letter written by the governor of Bahia, D. Fernando José de Portugal. A Franciscan friar, José de Bolonha, was spreading unorthodox ideas on slavery even by means of the confessional. As soon as this was brought to the attention of the authorities, the fríar was severely punished by the archbishop, forbidden to hear confessions and hastily bundled out of the colony on the first available boat. *Carta do governador,* June 18, 1794. Slave labor also gave rise to many other contradictions inherent in the colonial system, which were only resolved much later, with the abolition of slavery (1888). I have dealt with the subject elsewhere (*Evolução política do Brasil*), and shall therefore not go into further detail here, because although the other contradictions were present in the period we are considering, they belong rather in the later period. I referred in the text only to the general and immediate contradictions resulting from slavery, namely, the antagonism between slaves and masters, for this was what played the most important role in the period concerned, contributing toward the widespread restlessness that was to prove a fertile breeding ground for the imminent changes in the colonial system.

42 The method of levying the royal fifths in Minas Gerais—the ostensible reason for the *Inconfidência*—is one instance of a movement triggered off by an administrative measure.

43 The "Apostolate" was not really Masonic; it was inspired by Masonic patterns and had the same character, although it represented the opposite political trends.

44 *Manifesto maçônico de José Bonifácio.*

45 The observation, although an obvious one, is pertinent, since it counters the fantasies of certain hastily written pseudo-historical works of a pamphleteering type which, with the sole aim of spreading political propaganda or inspired by current political doctrines, have recently become commonplace in Brazil.

46 The *Manifesto maçônico* cited above reveals some of these internal tensions and conflicts.

47 Letter of November 17, 1809, published in Brás do Amaral's *Esclarecimentos sôbre o modo pelo qual se preparou a Independência* (Background to Independence), which contains other documents relating to the subject.

48 See Oliveira Lima's annotations to *História da Revolução de 1817* by Muniz Tavares, p. 73.

[49] Freemasonry's contribution to the spread of Encyclopaedist ideas must also be noted, since it propagated in Brazil what can be described as its official ideology. Another contributory factor to the spread of French influence in Brazil through the Freemasons is the fact that most of the colony's Masonic lodges were affiliated to that of the Orient of the Île de France with its headquarters in Paris. Finally, we must bear in mind the prestige France enjoyed in America after her support for the American War of Independence. All these factors combined explain Brazil's intellectual vassalage to France at this period.

[50] See *Autos da Devassa da Inconfidência Mineira* (Report of Official Inquiry into the Minas Conspiracy) and *Inconfidência da Bahia de 1798, Devassas e Sequestros.*

[51] *Viagem,* II, p. 293.

[52] To give one of many instances, an official inquiry was instituted into the case of a certain merchant in Bahia who was accused of giving a "meat banquet" on Good Friday; the scapegoat found by the officials was "those abominable French principles." *Vigilância do governo português.* See also, Brás do Amaral, *Esclarecimentos,* p. 380.

[53] Councillor Joaquim Caetano Fernandes Pinheiro, *Apontamentos biográficos.*

[54] French ideology was in certain circles so closely related to revolutionary ideas that "Frenchman" became synonymous with "reformer" and "revolutionary." This is clear from the evidence of witnesses at the official inquiry into the 1798 Bahian Conspiracy, who used such expressions as, "He looks like a *Frenchman*"; "It was meet that we should become *Frenchmen* to ensure a life of plenty"; and so forth.

Bibliography

Abbreviations

ABN:	*Anais da Biblioteca Nacional do Rio de Janeiro* (Rio de Janeiro, 1876 to date)
RIHB:	*Revista do Instituto Histórico, Geográfico e Etnográfico Brasileiro* (Rio de Janeiro, 1839 to date)
Rev. do Arq. Pub. Min.:	*Revista do Arquivo Público Mineiro* (25 vols., Belo Horizonte, 1896–1938)

Abrantes, Visconde de. "Origem da cultura e comércio do anil entre nós e quais as causas do seu progresso e decadência," *RIHB,* 15, 42.

Abreu, J. Capistrano de. *Caminhos antigos e povoamento do Brasil.* Pub. by the Sociedade Capistrano de Abreu, 1930.

———. *Capítulos de História Colonial (1500–1800).* Pub. by the Sociedade Capistrano de Abreu, 1928.

Accioli, de Cerqueira e Silva, Inácio. "Dados e informações estatísticas da Vila da Barra en 1828," *Rev. do Arq. Pub. Min.,* IX, 701.

———. "Dissertação histórica, etnográfica e política," *RIHB,* 12, 143.

————. *Memórias Históricas e políticas da Província da Bahia do Coronel Inácio Accioli de Cerqueira e Silva*. Ed. and annotated by Dr. Brás do Amaral, 6 vols., Bahia, 1919–40.

Albuquerque Tovar, Manuel Vieira de. "Informação de Manuel Vieira de Albuquerque Tovar sôbre a navegação importantissima do Rio Doce (1810)," *RIHB*, I, 134.

Alemão, Francisco Freire. "Memória sôbre quais as principais plantas que hoje se acham aclimatadas no Brasil," *RIHB*, 19, 539.

Alencastre, J. M. P. de. "Anais da Província de Goiás," *RIHB*, 27, II and 28, II.

————. "Biografia do Cônego Luís Antônio da Silva e Sousa," *RIHB*, 30, II, 241.

Alincourt, Luís D'. "Resultado dos trabalhos e indagações estatísticas da Província de Mato Grosso (Cuiabá, 1828)," *ABN*, 3, 68.

Almanaque da Cidade do Rio de Janeiro para 1792 (also for 1794), *ABN*, LIX.

Almeida, Lacerda de. *A Igreja e o Estado*. Rio de Janeiro, 1924.

Almeida e Sá, Luís de França. "Armações da Pesca da Baleia," *RIHB*, 62, II, 186.

Almeida Serra, Ricardo Franco de. "Descrição geográfica da província de Mato Grosso feita em 1797," *RIHB*, 6, 156.

Amaral, Brás do. "A Conspiração Republicana da Bahia de 1798," *RIHB*, 99, 344.

————. "Esclarecimentos sôbre o modo pelo qual se preparou a Independência do Brasil," *RIHB*, 101, 357.

Andrada e Silva, José Bonifácio de. "Memória sôbre a pesca das baleias e extração do seu azeite; com algumas reflexões a respeito das nossas pescarias," *Memórias Econômicas da Academia de Sciencias de Lisboa*, 1790, II, 388.

Antonil, André João (pseudonym of Giovanni Antonio Andreoni, S.J.). *Cultura e Opulência do Brasil*. Companhia Melhoramentos de São Paulo, 1923.

Antonina, Barão de. "Ofício do Barão de Antonina ao Instituto Histórico, de 18 de Abril, 1848, sôbre explorações por êle mandadas para a descoberta de um caminho para Mato Grosso pelos Sertões do Paraná," *RIHB*, 10, 259.

Arquivo Nacional do Rio de Janeiro. Catálogo das cartas régias, provisões, alvarás, avisos, portarias, etc. expedidas ao governador e mais tarde Vice-Rei do Rio de Janeiro, 1662–1821.

Arquivo Publico do Estado de São Paulo. *Documentos interessantes para a história e costumes de São Paulo*. Many volumes have been published in this series.

Arruda Câmara, Manuel de. *Memória sôbre a cultura dos algodoeiros*. Lisbon, 1789.

Atas da Camara da Vila de São Paulo. Publicação oficial do Arquivo Publico Municipal de São Paulo, 1914–   ; 38 vols. have been published.

"Autos da Criação da vila de Montemor-o-Novo do Grão-Pará," *RIHB, 35, I, 133.*

Autos da devassa da Inconfidência Mineira. 7 vols., published by the Ministry of Education, Rio de Janeiro, Biblioteca Nacional, 1936–38.

Azeredo Coutinho, José Joaquim da Cunha de. *Alegação jurídica, na qual se mostra que são do padroado da Coroa, e não da Ordem Militar de Cristo, as Igrejas, Dignidades e Benefícios dos Bispados do Cabo de Bojador para o Sul, em que se compreendem os Bispados do Cabo Verde, São Tomé, Angola, Índia, até a China.* Lisbon, 1804.

––––––. *Ensaio econômico sôbre o comércio de Portugal e suas colónias, pelo Bispo D. José Joaquim da Cunha Azeredo Coutinho.* Lisbon, 1816.

Azevedo, João Lucio de. *Novas Epanáforas.* Lisbon, 1932.

Azevedo, M. D. Moreira de. "Instrução pública nos tempos coloniais do Brasil," *RIHB,* 55, II, 141.

Balbi, Adrien. *Essai statistique sur le royaume de Portugal.* . . . Paris, Rey et Gravier, 1822.

Barata, Francisco José. "Memória en que se mostram algumas providências tendentes ao melhoramento da agricultura e comércio da Capitania do Goiás, escrita e dedicada ao Conde de Linhares por Francisco José Barata, Sgto.-mór da capitania do Pará," *RIHB,* 11, 336.

Barata, Manuel de Melo Cardoso. "Efemérides paraenses," *RIHB,* 90.

Barbacena, Visconde de. *See* Mendonça, Luís Antônio Furtado de.

Barbosa, Francisco de Oliveira. *See* Oliveira Barbosa.

Borges da Fonseca, Antônio José Vitorino. "Nobiliarquia Pernambucana," *ABN,* 47 and 48.

Brito, João Rodrigues de. *Cartas econômico-políticas sôbre a agricultura e comércio da Bahia, pelo Desembargador João Rodrigues de Brito.* Lisbon, 1821. Also published by the govt. of the State of Bahia, 1924.

Brito, Paulo José Miguel de. *Memória política sôbre a capitania de Santa Catharina.* . . . Lisbon, Academia real das sciencias, 1829.

Calógeras, João Pandía. *As minas do Brasil e a sua legislação.* 3 vols., Rio de Janeiro, 1904–1905.

––––––. "Política exterior do Império," *RIHB,* special series on Dom Pedro II, Vols. 2 and 3 (1927–1928).

Camara, Antônio Alves. *Ensaio sôbre as construções navais in-*

dígenas do Brasil. Rio de Janeiro, 1888. 2d ed., Brasiliana series, Estado Nacional, São Paulo, 1937.

Camara, José de Sá Bittencourt. "Memória mineralógica do terreno mineiro da Comarca de Sabará," *Rev. do Arq. Pub. Min.,* II (1897), 599.

Camara, Manuel de Arruda. See Arruda Camara.

Caneca, Frei Joaquim do Amor Divino. *Obras políticas e literárias de Frei Joaquim do Amor Divino Caneca.* Ed. by Antônio Joaquim de Melo. Recife, 2 vols., 1875.

Cardoso, João Pedro, *jt. author. See* Morais Filho, Prudente de.

"Carta Regia de 12 de Maio de 1798, estimulando explorações e utilização dos rios que levam ao Amazonas," *RIHB,* 5, 81.

"Carta Regia de 12 de Maio de 1798, sôbre navegação do Rio Madeira," *RIHB,* 4, 232.

"Carta Regia de 12 de Maio de 1798, sôbre os Indios do Pará e abolindo o Diretório de 3 de Maio de 1757," *RIHB,* 19, 314.

"Carta Regia de 13 de março de 1797, sôbre cortes de madeiras," *RIHB,* 6, 497.

Carvalho, João Antônio Rodrigues de. "Projeto de uma estrada da cidade do Destêrro às Missões do Uruguai e outras províncias que deve servir de ensaio ao melhoramento da província de Santa Catarina (1824)," *RIHB,* 7, 508 (3d ed.).

Carvalho, José Simões de. "Noticia sôbre a ilha de Joanes (1800)," *RIHB,* 12, 362.

Carvalho, Pedro Cúrio de. "Histórico da hospitalização militar no Brasil," *RIHB,* special series published for the First Congress of National History, V, 501.

Castro, Miguel João de and Antônio Tomé de França. "Diário da viagem que por ordem do Ilmo. e Exmo. Snr. João Carlos Augusto de Oeynhausen Grevenburg fizeram os capitães Miguel João de Castro e Antônio Tomé de França pelo rio Arinos em 1812," *RIHB,* 31, I, 107.

Coelho, Felipe José Nogueira. "Memórias cronológicas da capitania de Mato Grosso." *RIHB,* 13, 137.

Coleção da Legislação Portuguesa desde a última compilação das Ordenações. Ed. by Antônio Delgado da Silva. Lisbon, 1825–30 (includes legislation passed between 1750 and 1820).

Coman, Katharine. *Industrial History of the United States.* New York, The Macmillan Company, 1917.

"Considerações sôbre as duas classes de povoadores mais importantes da capitania de Minas Gerais" (attributed to J. Vieira Couto), *RIHB,* 25, 421.

Corografia Brasilica ou Relação Histórico-Geográfica do Reino do Brasil composta e dedicada a Sua Majestade Fidelíssima por

um presbítero secular do Gran-Priorado do Crato (Aires de Casal).
2 vols., Rio de Janeiro, 1817.

Corrêa, Mendes. *Os Povos Primitivos da Lusitânia.* Oporto, 1924.

Correio Brasiliense ou Armazém Literário. Published in London by
Hipólito José da Costa Pereira from 1808 to 1822.

"Correspondência do Bispo do Rio de Janeiro com o govêrno metro-
politano nos anos de 1754 a 1800," *RIHB,* 63, I, 39.

"Correspondência de várias autoridades e avulsos; Capitania do Rio
de Janeiro, 1797–99," *RIHB,* 65, I, 71.

Costa, Antônio Rodrigues da. "Consulta do Conselho Ultramarino
a S.M. no ano de 1732, feita pelo Conselheiro Antônio Rodrigues
da Costa," *RIHB,* 7, 475 (3d ed.).

Costa, João Severiano Maciel da. *Memória sôbre a necessidade de
abolir a introdução de escravos africanos no Brasil.* Coimbra,
1821.

Costa Rubim, Brás da. "Memórias históricas e documentadas da
província do Espírito Santo," *RIHB,* 24, 171.

Costa Siqueira, Joaquim da. "Compêndio histórico cronológico das
notícias de Cuiabá, repartição de Mato Grosso, desde 1778 até
1817," *RIHB,* 13, 5.

Coutinho, Francisco de Sousa. *See* Sousa Coutinho.

Coutinho, José da Cunha de Azeredo. *See* Azeredo Coutinho.

Couto, José Vieira. "Memória sôbre a capitania de Minas Gerais,
seu território, clima, etc. (1799)," *RIHB,* 2, 289.

Couty, Louis. *L'Esclavage au Brésil.* Paris, 1881.

Cunha, Francisco Manuel da. "Informação que Francisco Manuel
da Cunha deu sôbre a Província então capitania do Espírito
Santo ao Ministro de Estado Antônio de Araújo e Azevedo
(1811)," *RIHB,* 4, 240.

Cunha Matos, Raimundo José da. "Corografia histórica da província
de Goiás," *RIHB,* 37, I, 213 and 38, I, 5.

Deffontaines, Pierre. "As Feiras de burro de Sorocaba." *Geografia,*
São Paulo, vol. 1, no. 3, 1935.

"Derrota dos correios da Vila da Fortaleza à Cidade da Bahia,
marcada pelo governador do Ceará, Francisco Alberto Rubim,"
RIHB, 5, 480.

"Descobrimento de Minas Gerais" (detailed description of this
captaincy written by an anonymous author in 1807), *RIHB,* 29, I,
5.

"Discurso preliminar, histórico e introdutivo com natureza de
descrição econômica da Comarca e Cidade da Bahia," *ABN,* 27,
281.

Divisas de São Paulo e Minas Gerais. Introduction by Orville Derby. *Documentos Interessantes,* Vol. XI, 1896.

Documentos Interessantes, series. *See* Arquivo Público do Estado de São Paulo.

"Documentos oficiais; Vários assuntos," *RIHB,* 6, 455.

"Documentos relativos à história da capitania, depois província de São Pedro do Rio Grande do Sul. Copiados na Secretaria do Governo de Pôrto Alegre por ordem do Cons. Barão Homem de Melo, ex-presidente da mesma província," *RIHB,* Vols. 40, 41 and 42.

Documentos sôbre o tratado de 1750, com introdução de Rodolfo Garcia. *ABN,* vols. 52 and 53.

Drummond, A. M. V. de. "Anotações à sua biografia publicada em 1836," *ABN,* XIII, 2, 1.

"Edital que S. M. mandou imprimir para os moradores das Ilhas dos Açores e casais e todos os mais que se quisessem alistar para povoadores deste estabelecimento de Santa Catarina," *RIHB,* 40, I, 213.

Eschwege, Baron W. L. von. "Noticias e Reflexões Estadísticas da Província de Minas Gerais por Guilherme, Barão de Eschwege," *Rev. do Arq. Pub. Min.,* IV, 737.

———. *Pluto Brasiliensis.* Tradução de Domício de Figueiredo Murta. 2 vols., Brasiliana series. São Paulo, n.d.

"Estabelecimento de Mazagão do Grão-Pará (O); Histórico e relação das pessoas transferidas, segundo documento do Arquivo Público do Pará," *RIHB,* 84, 609.

Fazenda, Vieira. *See* Vieira Fazenda.

Fernandes Pinheiro, Joaquim Caetano. "Apontamentos biográficos do Visconde de S. Leopoldo pelo seu sobrinho o Cônego Joaquim Caetano Fernandes Pinheiro," *RIHB,* 19, 132.

———. "Paulo Fernandes e a polícia de seu tempo," *RIHB,* 39, II, 65.

———. "Os Ultimos Vice-Reis do Brasil," *RIHB,* 28, II, 225.

Fernandes Pinheiro, José Feliciano, Visconde de São Leopoldo. "Memórias," *RIHB,* 37, II, 5

Ferreira, Alexandre Rodrigues. "Diário da Viagem Filosófica pela capitania de S. José do Rio Negro, com informação do estado presente (1787)," *RIHB,* Vols. 48, 49, 50, and 51.

Florence, Hércules. "Esboço da viagem de Langsdorff no interior do Brasil desde setembro de 1825 até março de 1829," *RIHB,* 38.

Fonseca, Antônio José Vitorino Borges da. *See* Borges da Fonseca.

França, Antônio Tomé de, *jt. author. See* Castro, Miguel João de.

Freire, Felisbelo. *História Territorial do Brasil (Bahia, Sergipe, Espírito Santo).* Rio de Janeiro, 1906.

Freitas, José Joaquim da Silva, *jt. author. See* Moreira, J. M. M.

Freyre, Gilberto. *Casa Grande e Senzala.* Rio de Janeiro, 1933.

————. *Nordeste.* Documentos Brasileiros series, Rio de Janeiro, 1937.

————. *Sobrados e Mucambos.* Brasiliana series, São Paulo, 1936.

Gayozo, Raimundo José de Sousa. *Compêndio histórico-político dos princípios da lavoura do Maranhão.* Paris, 1818.

Gonçalves Ledo. "Manifesto maçônico de José Bonifácio," *ABN,* 43/44, p. V.

Handelmann, Henrique. "História do Brasil." Brazilian translation by the Instituto Histórico e Geográfico Brasileiro, 1931. *RIHB,* 108.

Hansen, Marcus Lee. *The Atlantic Migration: 1607–1860.* Cambridge, Massachusetts, 1941.

————. *The Immigrant in American History,* Cambridge, Massachusetts, 1940.

História da Colonização portuguesa do Brasil. Ed. by C. Malheiro Dias. 3 vols., Oporto, 1921–1924.

"Idéia da população da capitania de Pernambuco e das suas anexas . . . desde o ano 1774," *ABN,* 40, 1.

"Inconfidência da Bahia em 1798 (A); Devassas e Sequestros," *ABN,* 43, 44, and 45.

"Informacões sôbre os índios barbaros dos sertões de Pernambuco. Ofício do bispo de Olinda accompanhado de várias cartas," *RIHB,* 46, I, 103.

Ingram, John Kellis. "Slavery," *Encyclopaedia Britannica,* 13th ed., 1926.

Jacob, Rodolfo, ed. *Coletânea de Cientistas Estrangeiros.* Published for the centenary celebrations of Minas Gerais, Belo Horizonte, 1922. Vol. I contains Mawe's "Travels in the Interior of Brazil," trans. by Dermeval Lima, and Eschwege's "Pluto Brasiliensis," trans. by Rodolfo Jacob.

Jones, Clarence Fielden. *Economic Geography.* New York, 1941.

Koster, Henri. *Voyages pittoresques, scientifiques et historiques en Amérique; Brésil.* Traduits par M. A. Jay, 2 vols., Paris, 1846.

Lago, Antônio Bernardino Pereira do. *See* Pereira do Lago.

Lavradio, Marquês do. "Relatório do Marquês do Lavradio, Vice-Rei do Rio de Janeiro, entrogando o govêrno a Luís de Vasconcelos e Sousa que o sucedeu no Vice-Reinado," *RIHB,* 4, 409.

————. "Relações que accompanham êste Relatório," *RIHB,* 76, I, 285.

Le Cointe, Paul. *L'Amazonie Brésilienne.* 2 vols. Paris, 1922. The third vol. of this work has been published in Portuguese: *A Amazônia Brasileira,* vol. III, "Arvores e plantas úteis," Belém, Pará, 1934.

Ledo, Gonçalves. *See* Gonçalves Ledo.

Leroy-Beaulieu, Paul. *De la colonisation chez les peuples moderne.* Paris, 1886.

Lima, Alcides. *História popular do Rio Grande do Sul.* Rio de Janeiro, 1882.

Lima, Augusto de. "Um Município de Ouro," *RIHB*, 65, II, 141.

———. *Resumo histórico sôbre os limites entre Minas e São Paulo.*

Lima, Francisco das Chagas. "Memória sôbre o descobrimento e colónia de Guarapuava (1809)," *RIHB*, 4, 43.

Lima Pereira, J. O. de. *Da Propriedade no Brasil.* São Paulo, 1932.

"Limites entre S. Paulo e Minas Gerais." Memória organizada pelos delegados de S. Paulo, Prudente de Morais Filho e João Pedro Cardoso.

Lisboa, Alfredo. "Vias de Communicação, Portos do Brasil," *Dicionário Histórico, Geográfico e Etnográfico do Brasil,* Instituto Histórico Brasileiro, Rio de Janeiro, 1922.

Lisboa, Baltasar da Silva. *See* Silva Lisboa.

Lisboa, João Francisco. *Obras.* Ed. and rev. by Luís Carlos Pereira de Castro and A. Henriques Leal, 2 vols. Lisbon, 1901.

Luccock, John. *Notes on Rio de Janeiro and the Southern Parts of Brazil, Taken from 1808 to 1819.* London, 1820.

Machado, Francisco Xavier. "Memória relativa às capitanias do Piauí e Maranhão (1810)," *RIHB*, 17, 56.

Magalhães, Manuel Antônio de. "Almanaque da Vila de Pôrto Alegre, com reflexões sôbre o estado da Capitania do Rio Grande do Sul (1808)," *RIHB*, 30, I, 43.

Malheiro, Perdigão. *A Escravidão no Brasil.* 3 vols., Rio de Janeiro, 1867.

Martius, C. F. P. von, *jt. author. See* Spix, J. B. von.

Matos, Raimundo José da Cunha. *See* Cunha Matos.

Maximilian, Prince. *Voyage au Brésil dans les années 1815, 1816, 1817, par S. A. S. Maximilien, Prince de Wied-Neuwied.* Traduit de l'allemand par J. B. B. Eyriès, 3 vols., Paris, 1821.

Medeiros, Abreu. *Curiosidades Brasileiras.* Rio de Janeiro, 1864.

"Medição, direção e observação da nova estrada que da cachoeira do rio Santa Maria, têrmo da Vila de Vitória, segue pelo sertão intermédio à Vila Rica (1818)," *RIHB*, 6, 471.

Mémoire présenté par les États Unis du Brésil au gouvernement de la Confédération Suisse, arbitre entre la France et le Brésil. 3 vols., 1899.

"Memória da nova navegação do rio Arinos até a vila de Santarém, no Estado do Grão Pará," *RIHB*, 19, 99.

"Memória histórica da Cidade de Cabo Frio e de todo o seu distrito no ano de 1797," *RIHB*, 46, I, 205.

Memória sôbre as sesmarias da Bahia (fragmento)," *RIHB*, 3, 373.
"Memórias públicas e econômicas da cidade de S. Sebastião do Rio de Janeiro para uso do Vice-Rei, Luís de Vasconcelos, por observação curiosa dos anos de 1779 até o de 1789," *RIHB*, 47, I, 25.
Mendonça, Luís Antônio Furtado de, Visconde de Barbacena. "Instrução para o Visconde de Barbacena, gov. e Cap. gen. da cap. de Minas Gerais," *RIHB*, 6, 3.
Montenegro, Caetano Pinto de Miranda. "População da capitania de Mato Grasso em 1800. Carta do gov. Caetano Pinto de Miranda Montenegro de 17 de abril de 1802," *RIHB*, 28, I, 123.
Morais, Eduardo José de. *Navegação interior do Brasil*. Rio de Janeiro, 1869.
Morais Filho, Prudente de and João Pedro Cardoso. *Limites entre São Paulo e Minas Gerais*.
Moreira, José Mendonça Matos and José Joaquim da Silva Freitas. "Relação das matas das Alagoas (1809)," *RIHB*, 7, 483 (3rd ed.).
Müller, Daniel Pedro. *Ensaio de um quadro estatístico da província de S. Paulo*. São Paulo, 1838, 2nd impression, 1923.
Nabuco, Joaquim. *Um Estadista do Império*. 3 vols., Paris and Rio de Janeiro (1898–1900).
Nascimento, Alfredo. "Elogio histórico do Visconde Nogueira da Gama, feito pelo Dr. Alfredo Nascimento em sessão magna do Instituto Histórico Brasileiro de 15 de dezembro de 1897," *RIHB*, 60, II, 466.
Navarro, Luís Tomás de. "Itinerário da Viagem que fêz por terra da Bahia ao Rio de Janeiro en 1808 o Desembargador Luís Tomás de Navarro." *RIHB*, 7, 417 (3d ed.).
Nery, F. J. de Santa Anna, ed. *Le Brésil en 1889*. Publié sous la direction de F. J. de Santa Anna Nery, Paris, 1889.
Nina Rodrigues. *Os Africanos no Brasil*. Revision and preface by Homero Pires, Brasiliana series, São Paulo, 1931.
"Nota de todas as marinhas em que se faz sal na costa do Brasil," *RIHB*, 46, I, 173.
"Notícias e reflexões sôbre as minas de Cantagalo, escritas no fim do ano de 1805 por ***," *RIHB*, 12, 518.
Nunes, Antônio Duarte. "Almanaque histórico da cidade de S. Sebastião do Rio de Janeiro, composto por D. Antônio Duarte Nunes para o ano de 1799," *RIHB*, 21, 5 (2d ed.).
Oliveira, Antônio Rodrigues Veloso de. "A Igreja no Brasil," *RIHB*, 29, I, 159.
———. "Memória sôbre a agricultura no Brasil," *RIHB*, 36, I, 91.
———. "Memória sôbre o melhoramento da província de São Paulo, aplicável em grande parte às províncias do Brasil," *RIHB*, 31, I, 5.
Oliveira, Joaquim Machado de. "Notas, apontamentos e notícias

para a história da província do Espírito Santo," *RIHB*, 19, 161.

Oliveira Barbosa, Francisco de. "Notícias da capitania de São Paulo, da América Meridional escritas no ano de 1792," *RIHB*, 5, 22.

Oliveira Lima, Manuel de. *D. João VI no Brasil: 1808–1821*. Rio de Janeiro, 1908.

———. *O Império Brasileiro, 1822–1889*. Comp. Melhoramentos de São Paulo [1927?].

Oliveira Viana, F. J. de. *Pequenos estudos de psicologia social*. 2d ed., São Paulo, 1923.

———. *Populações meridionais do Brasil*. 2d ed., São Paulo, 1922.

"Ordem de S. M. para o situado dos casais neste estabelecimento de Santa Catarina," *RIHB*, 40, I, 215.

Patriota (*O*). Jornal literário, político, mercantil, etc. Rio de Janeiro, 1813–14. Pub. monthly in 1813 and bimonthly in 1814. 3 vols.

Paula Ribeiro, Francisco de. "Descrição do território dos Pastos Bons nos sertões do Maranhão," *RIHB*, 12, 41.

Paulet, A. J. da Silva. "Descrição geográfica abreviada da Capitania do Ceará, pelo coronel de engenheiros A. J. da Silva Paulet," ed. by Dr. Liberato de Castro Carreira, *RIHB*, 60, II, 109.

Peixoto, Eduardo Marques. "Os Descaminhos do ouro," *RIHB*, 72, II, 167.

Pereira, José da Costa. See Correio Brasiliense.

Pereira, J. O. de Lima. See Lima Pereira.

Pereira da Silva, João Manuel. *História da Fundação do Império Brasileiro*. 7 vols., Rio de Janeiro, 1864–68.

Pereira do Lago, Antônio Bernardino. "Itinerário da província do Maranhão (1820)," *RIHB*, 35, I, 385.

Pinheiro, Joaquim Caetano Fernandes. See Fernandes Pinheiro.

Pinto, Antônio Pereira. *Apontamentos para o Direito Internacional ou Coleção completa dos tratados celebrados pelo Brasil com diferentes nações estrangeiras*. 4 vols., Rio de Janeiro, 1864.

Pinto, Joaquim Almeida. *Dicionário de Botânica Brasileira*. Rio de Janeiro, 1873.

Pizarro e Araújo, José de Sousa Azevedo. *Memórias históricas do Rio de Janeiro e das províncias anexas à jurisdição do Vice-Rei do Estado do Brasil*. 9 vols., Rio de Janeiro, 1820–22 (2d ed., Rio de Janeiro, 1945).

Pohl, Johann Emmanuel. *Reise im innern von Brasilien in den Jahren 1817–1821*. Vienna, 1832.

Portugal, Fernando José de. "Carta do gov. da Bahia, D. Fernando José de Portugal de 18 de Junho de 1794, sôbre opinião de um frade capuchinho relativamente à escravidão no Brasil," *RIHB*, 60, II, 155.

————. "Carta de 21 de outubro de 1795, sôbre os embaixadores do Rei de Dagomé," *RIHB*, 59, I, 413.

Prado, Paulo. *Retrato do Brasil.* São Paulo, 1931.

Prado Júnior, Caio. *Evolução Política do Brasil; Ensaio de interpretação materialista da história brasileira.* São Paulo, 1933.

Prazeres, Frei Francisco de Nossa Senhora dos. "Poranduba Maranhense ou Relação histórica da província do Maranhão," *RIHB*, 54, I, 9.

Rainville, César de. *O Vinhola Brasileiro; Novo manual prático do engenheiro, arquiteto pedreiro, carpinteiro, marceneiro e serralheiro.* Rio de Janeiro, 1880.

Ramos, Artur. *Culturas negras no novo mundo.* Biblioteca de Divulgação Científica, Rio de Janeiro, 1937.

Registo Geral da Câmara Municipal de S. Paulo. Publicação oficial do Arquivo Municipal de São Paulo. São Paulo 1917– , 28 vols. published.

Reis, Artur. *Lobo de Almada, um estadista colonial.* 2d ed., Manaus, 1940.

————. *Política de Portugal no vale amazônico.* Belem, 1940.

Rendon, José Arouche Toledo. "Memória sôbre as aldeias de índios da província de S. Paulo, segundo observações feitas no ano de 1798," *RIHB*, 4, 295.

Resende, Conde de. "Produtos exportados da cidade do Rio de Janeiro em 1796; Mapas remetidos pelo Vice-Rei Conde de Resende," *RIHB*, 46, I, 195.

Ribeiro, Barão Duarte da Ponte. *Resenha histórica da navegação e reconhecimentos dos rios Guaporé e Mamoré.* Rio de Janeiro, 1876.

Ribeiro, Francisco de Paula. *See* Paula Ribeiro.

Rodrigues, José Honório. "A Literatura brasileira sôbre o açucar no século XIX," *Brasil Açucareiro*, May, 1942.

Rodrigues, Nina. *See* Nina Rodrigues.

Roscio, Francisco João. "Breve notícia da extensão de terreno que ocupam os Sete Povos das Missões Guaranis (1801)," *RIHB*, 21, 271 (2d ed.).

"Roteiro do Maranhão a Goiás pela capitania do Piauí," *RIHB*, 62, I, 60

Rubim, Brás da Costa. *See* Costa Rubim.

Rubim, Francisco Alberto. "Derrota dos correios da Vila da Fortaleza à Cidade da Bahia marcada pelo governador do Ceará, Francisco Alberto Rubim," *RIHB*, 5, 480.

Rugendas, Moritz. *Malerische Reise in Brasilien.* Mühlhausen, 1835.

Saint Adolphe, R. Milliet de. *Dicionário geográfico, histórico e descritivo do Império do Brasil.* Paris, 1845.

Sainte-Hilaire, Auguste de. *Segunda viagem ao interior do Brasil;*

Espírito Santo. Trans. by Carlos Madeira, Brasiliana series, São Paulo, 1938.

Sainte-Hilaire, Auguste de. *Segunda viagem do Rio de Janeiro a Minas Gerais e a São Paulo (1822).* Trans. by Afonso de Taunay, Brasiliana series, São Paulo, 1938.

————. *Viagem ao Rio Grande do Sul, 1820–21.* Trans. by Leonam de Azevedo Pena, Brasiliana series, São Paulo, 1939.

————. *Voyage dans les provinces de Rio de Janeiro et de Minas Gerais.* 2 vols., Paris, 1830.

————. *Voyage dans les provinces de St. Paul et de Sainte Catherine.* 2 vols., Paris, 1851.

————. *Voyage aux sources du rio de São Francisco et dans la province de Goyaz.* 2 vols. Paris, 1847.

Salvador, Frei Vicente do. *História do Brasil, 1500–1627.* Ed. by Capistrano de Abreu and Rodolfo Garcia, São Paulo, 1931.

São Leopoldo, Visconde de. *See* Fernandes Pinheiro, José Feliciano.

São Paulo, Câmara Municipal. *See* Atas da Câmara da Vila de São Paulo *and* Registo geral da câmara municipal de São Paulo.

Santos, Joaquim Felício dos. *Memórias do Distrito Diamantino na Comarca do Serro Frio.* New ed. with a biographical study of the author by Nazaré Meneses, Rio de Janeiro, 1924.

Serra, Ricardo Franco de Almeida. *See* Almeida Serra.

Sierra y Mariscal, Francisco de. "Idéias gerais sôbre a revolução do Brasil," *ABN,* 43/44.

Silva, Antônio Delgado da. *See* Coleção da legislação Portuguesa.

Silva, J. Carneiro da. *Memória topográfica e histórica sôbre os campos dos Goitacases.* Rio de Janeiro, 1819.

Silva, Joaquim Caetano da. *L'Oyapoc et l'Amazone; Question brésilienne et française.* 3rd ed., 2 vols., Paris, 1859.

Silva e Sousa, Luís Antônio da. "Memória sôbre o descobrimento, govêrno, população e cousas mais notáveis da capitania de Goiás (1812)," *RIHB,* 12, 429.

Silva Lisboa, Baltasar da. *Anais do Rio de Janeiro.* 8 vols., Rio de Janeiro, 1834.

Siqueira, Joaquim da Costa. *See* Costa Siqueira.

Sousa, André Fernandes de. "Notícias geográficas da capitania do Rio Negro no grande rio Amazonas," *RIHB,* 10, 411.

Sousa, Luís Pinto de. "Ofício do Secretário do Estado sôbre a remoção dos impostos sôbre o sal e o ferro, datado de Queluz em 27 de maio de 1795." *Documentos Interessantes,* XXV, 133.

Sousa Chichorro, Manuel da Cunha de Azevedo Coutinho de. "Memória em que se mostra o estado econômico, militar e político da capitania de S. Paulo em 1814," *RIHB,* 36, I, 197.

Sousa Coutinho, Francisco de. "Informação sôbre o modo por que se efetua a navegação do Pará para Mato Grosso (1797), pelo governador da capitania, D. Francisco de Sousa Coutinho," *RIHB*, 28, I, 38.

Southey, Robert. *History of Brazil*. 3 vols., London, 1810–1819.

Spix, J. B. von and C. F. P. von Martius. *Travels in Brazil, in the years 1817–20*. London, 1824. Brazilian translation by Lucia Furquim Lahmeyer, *Viagem pelo Brasil*. 4 vols., Rio de Janeiro, 1938.

Tavares, Francisco Muniz. *História da revolução de Pernambuco em 1817*. 3rd ed., revised and annotated by Oliveira Lima, Recife, 1917.

Tôrres, Alberto. *O Problema Nacional*. Rio de Janeiro, 1914.

Tovar, Manuel Vieira de Albuquerque. *See* Albuquerque Tovar.

Varnhagen, Francisco Adolfo de, Visconde de Pôrto Seguro. *História Geral do Brasil*. 3rd ed., annotated by Rodolfo Garcia, 5 vols., São Paulo, n.d.

Vasconcelos, Diogo de. *História média de Minas Gerais*. Belo Horizonte, 1918.

Vasconcelos, Salomão de. "Ofícios mecânicos em Vila Rica durante o século XVIII," *Revista do Patrimônio Histórico*, IV, 331.

Vasconcelos e Sousa, Luís de. "Carta do Vice-Rei Luís de Vasconcelos e Sousa, de 15 de julho de 1781, sôbre a fazenda publica no Rio de Janeiro," *RIHB*, 51, II, 183.

———. "Negócios eclesiásticos no Brasil Colonial. Informação do Vice-Rei Luís de Vasconcelos e Sousa em 1783," *RIHB*, 51, II, 97.

———. "Ofício para ser entregue ao seu sucessor (1789)," *RIHB*, 4, 3.

———. *See also* "Memórias públicas e econômicas da cidade de São Sebastião do Rio de Janeiro. . . ."

Veríssimo, José. "Populações indígenas e mestiças da Amazônia; sua linguagem, suas crenças e seus costumes," *RIHB*, 50, I, 295.

Viana, F. J. Oliveira. *See* Oliveira Viana.

Vieira Fazenda. "Legislação Portuguesa relativa ao Brasil," *RIHB*, 105, 201.

"Vigilância do govêrno português contra os princípios jacobinos no Brasil," *RIHB*, 59, I, 406.

Vila Real, Tomás de Sousa. "Viagem pelos rios Tocantins, Araguaia e Vermelho (1793)," *RIHB*, 11, 401.

Vilhena, Luís dos Santos. *Recopilação de Notícias Soteropolitanas e Brasílicas contidas em XX cartas*. Ed. by Brás do Amaral. Bahia, 1927.

Wätjen, Hermann. *Das holländische Kolonialreich in Brasilien*. Gotha, 1921.

Index

515